# The

# Tabletalk

## of

# Martin Luther

*Translated and edited by*
*William Hazlitt, Esq.*

*Along with*
## The Life of Martin Luther
*By Alexander Chalmers*

*With Additions from*
*Michelet and Audin*

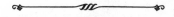

*Also*

## Luther's Catechisms

# THE

# TABLETALK

## of

# MARTIN LUTHER

*Luther's comments on
life, the church and the Bible*

Copyright © Christian Focus Publications 2003

ISBN 1 85792 415 0
ISBN 978 1 85792 415 2

Republished in 2003, reprinted in 2009
In the
Christian Heritage Imprint
by
Christian Focus Publications, Geanies House,
Fearn, Ross-shire, IV20 1TW, Scotland

www.christianfocus.com

Cover design by Owen Daily

Printed and bound by Bercker, Germany

# Contents

# Introduction

~~~

THE history of this remarkable volume, almost as extraordinary as its contents, is thus given by Captain Bell:

## CAPTAIN HENRY BELL'S NARRATIVE:

*Or, Relation of the miraculous preserving of Dr. Martin Luther's Book, entitled, Colloquia Mensalia, or, his Divine Discourses at his Table, held with divers learned Mesa and pious Divines; such as Philip Melancthon, Caspar Cruciger, Justus Jonas,Vitus Dietrich, John Bugenhagen, John Forster, etc.: containing Divers Discourses touching Religion, and other main Points of Doctrine; as also many notable Histories, and all sorts of Learning, Comforts, Advices, Prophecies, Admonitions, Directions, and Instructions.*

I, Captain Henry Bell, do hereby declare, both to the present age, and also to posterity, that being employed beyond the seas in state affairs divers years together, both by king James, and also by the late king Charles, in Germany, I did hear and understand, in all places, great bewailing and lamentation made, by reason of the destroying and burning of above fourscore thousand of Martin Luther's books, entitled, 'His Last Divine Discourses'.

For after such time as God stirred up the spirit of Martin Luther to detect the corruptions and abuses of popery, and to preach Christ, and clearly to set forth the simplicity of the gospel, many kings, princes, and states, imperial cities, and Hans-towns, fell from the popish religion, and became protestants, as their posterities still are, and remain to this very day.

And for the further advancement of the great work of reformation then begun, the aforesaid princes, and the rest did then order, that the said Divine Discourses of Luther should forthwith be printed; and that every parish should have and receive one of the aforesaid printed books into every church throughout all their principalities and dominions, to be chained up, for the common people to read therein.

Upon which divine work, or Discourses, the Reformation, began before in Germany, was wonderfully promoted and increased, and spread both here in England, and other countries besides.

But afterwards it so fell out, that the pope then living, viz., Gregory XIII, understanding what great hurt and prejudice he and his popish religion had already received, by reason of the said Luther's Divine Discourses, and also fearing that the same might bring further contempt and mischief upon himself, and upon the popish church, he therefore, to prevent the same, did fiercely stir up and instigate the emperor then in being, viz., Rudolphus II to make an edict throughout the whole empire, that all the aforesaid printed books should be burnt; and also, that it should be death for any person to have or keep a copy thereof, but also to burn the same; which edict was speedily put in execution accordingly; insomuch that not one of all the said printed books, nor so much as any one copy of the same, could be found out nor heard of in any place.

Yet it pleased God, that, anno 1626, a German gentleman, named Casparus Van Sparr, with whom, in the time of my staying in Germany about King James's business, I became very familiarly known and acquainted, having occasion to build upon the old foundation of a house, wherein his grandfather dwelt at that time, when the said edict was published in Germany for the burning of the aforesaid books ; and digging deep into the ground, under the said old foundation, one of the said original books was there happily found, lying in a deep obscure hole, being wrapped in a strong linen cloth, which was waxed all over with bees-wax, within and without; whereby the book was preserved fair, without any blemish.

And at the same time Ferdinandus II being emperor in Germany, who was a severe enemy and persecutor of the protestant religion, the aforesaid gentleman, and grandchild to him that had hidden the said books in that obscure hole, fearing that if the said emperor should get knowledge that one of the said books was yet forthcoming, and in his custody, whereby not only himself might be brought into trouble, but also the book in danger to be destroyed, as all the rest were so long before; and also calling me to mind, and knowing that I had the high Dutch tongue very perfect, did send the said original book over hither into England unto me; and therewith did write unto me a letter, wherein he related the passages of the preserving and finding out the said book.

And also he earnestly moved me in his letter, that for the advancement of God's glory, and of Christ's church, I would take the pains to translate the said book, to the end, that *that* most excellent divine work of Luther might be brought again to light.

Whereupon I took the said book before me, and many times began to translate the same, but always I was hindered therein, being called upon about other business: insomuch, that by no possible means I could remain by that work. Then, about six weeks after I had received the said book, it fell out, that I being in bed with my wife one night, between twelve and one of the clock, she being asleep, but myself yet awake, there appeared unto me an ancient man, standing at my bedside, arrayed all in white, having a long and broad white beard hanging down to his girdle steed, who taking me by my right ear, spake these words following unto me: 'Sirrah! will not you take time to translate that book which is sent unto you out of Germany? I will shortly provide for you both place and time to do it;' and then he vanished away out of my sight.

Whereupon being much thereby affrighted, I fell into an extreme sweat: insomuch, that my wife awaking, and finding me all over wet, she asked me what I ailed? I told her what I had seen and heard; but I never did heed nor regard visions nor dreams. And so the same fell soon out of my mind.

Then about a fortnight after I had seen that vision, on a Sunday, I went to Whitehall to hear the sermon; after which ended, I returned to my lodging, which was then at King Street; at Westminster, and sitting down to dinner with my wife, two messengers were sent from the whole council-board, with a warrant to carry me to the keeper of the Gatehouse, Westminster, there to be safely kept, until further order from the lords of the council; which was done without showing me any cause[1] at all wherefore I was committed. Upon which said warrant 1 was kept ten whole years close prisoner, where I spent five years thereof about the translating of the said book; insomuch as I found the words very true which the old man, in the aforesaid vision, did say unto me – 'I will shortly provide for you both place and time to translate it.'

Then after I had finished the said translation in the prison, the late archbishop of Canterbury, Dr. Laud, understanding that I had translated such

1. The cause of the captain's commitment was his pressing the Lord Treasurer for arrears of pay.

a book, called 'Martin Luther's Divine Discourses,' sent unto me his chaplain, Dr. Bray, into the prison, with this message following:

'Captain Bell,

'My lord grace of Canterbury, hath sent me unto you, to tell you, that his grace hath understood that you have translated a book of Luther's; touching which book his grace, many years before, did hear of the burning of so many thousands in Germany, by the then emperor. His grace therefore doth desire you, that you would send unto him the said original book in Dutch, and also your translation; which, after his grace hath perused, shall be returned safely unto you:

'Whereupon I told Doctor Bray, that I had taken a great deal of pains in translating the said book, and was very loath to part with it out of my hands; and, therefore, I desired him to excuse me to his grace, that I could not part from it; with which answer he at that time returned again to his master.

'But the next day after be sent him unto me again, and bid him tell me that, upon his honour, the book should be as safe in his custody, if not safer, than in mine own; for he would lock it up in his own cabinet, to the end no man might come unto it, but only himself. Thereupon, I knowing it would be a thing bootless for me to refuse the sending of them, by reason he was then of such great power, that he would have them, *nolens volens,* I sent them both unto him. Then after he had kept them in his custody two months, and had daily read therein, he sent the said doctor unto me, to tell me that I had performed a work worthy of eternal memory, and that he had never read a more excellent divine work; yet saying that some things therein were fitting to be left out, and desired me not to think long, that he did not return them unto me so soon again. The reason was, because that the more he did read therein, the more desire he had to go on therewith; and so presenting me with ten livres in gold, he returned back again.

'After which, when he had them in his custody one whole year, and that I understood he had perused it all over, then I sent unto his grace, and humbly desired, that his grace would be pleased to return me my books again. Whereupon he sent me word by the said Dr. Bray, that he had not as yet perused them so thoroughly over as he desired to do; then I stayed yet a year longer before I sent to him again.

'In which time I heard for certain, that it .was concluded by the king and council, that a parliament should forthwith be called; at which news I did much rejoice. And then I sent unto his grace an humble petition, and therein desired the returning of my book again; otherwise I told him I should be enforced to make it known, and to complain of him to the parliament, which was then coming on. Whereupon he sent unto me again safely both the said original book, and my translation, and caused his chaplain, the said doctor, to tell me, that he would make it known unto his majesty what an excellent piece of work I had translated, and that he would procure an order from his majesty to have the said translation printed, and to be dispersed throughout the whole kingdom, as it was in Germany, as he had heard thereof; and thereupon he presented me again with forty livres in gold.

'And presently after I was set at liberty by warrant from the whole House of Lords, according to his majesty's direction in that behalf: but shortly afterwards the archbishop fell into his troubles, and was by the parliament sent unto the Tower, and afterwards beheaded. Insomuch that I could never since hear anything touching the printing of my book.

'The House of Commons having then notice that I had translated the aforesaid book, they sent for me, and did appoint a committee to see it, and the translation, and diligently to make enquiry whether the translation did agree with the original or no; whereupon they desired me to bring the same before them, sitting then in the Treasury Chamber. And Sir Edward Dearing being chairman, said unto me, that he was acquainted with a learned minister beneficed in Essex, who had lived long in England, but was born in High Germany, in the Palatinate, named Mr. Paul Amiraut, whom the committee sending for, desired him to take both the original and my translation into his custody, and diligently to compare them together, and to make report unto the said committee whether he found that I had rightly and truly translated it according to the original: which report he made accordingly, and they being satisfied therein, referred it to two of the assembly, Mr. Charles Herle, and Mr. Edward Corbet, desiring them diligently to peruse the same, and to make report unto them if they thought it fitting to be printed and published.

'Whereupon they made report, dated the 10th of November, 1646, that they found it to be an excellent divine work, worthy the light and publishing, especially in regard that Luther, in the said Discourses, did revoke his opinion, which he formerly held, touching Consubstantiation in the Sacrament. Whereupon the House of Commons, the 24th of February, 1646, did give order for the printing thereof.

'Thus having been lately desired to set down in writing the relation of the passages above said concerning the said book, as well for the satisfaction of judicious and godly Christians, as for the conservation of the perpetual memory of God's extraordinary providence in the miraculous preservation of the aforesaid Divine Discourses, and now bringing them again to light, I have done the same according to the plain truth thereof, not doubting but they will prove a notable advantage of God's glory, and the good and edification of the whole church, and an unspeakable consolation of every particular member of the same.

'Given under my hand the third day of July, 1650.

HENRY BELL'[2]

The contents of the book themselves were gathered from the mouth of Luther, by his friends and disciples, and chiefly by Antony Lauterbach and John Aurifaber (Goldschmidt), who were very much with the great Reformer towards the close of his life. They consist of notes of his discourses, of his opinions, his cursory observations, in the freedom of private friendship, in his walks, during the performance of his clerical duties, and at table, The reporters were brim-full of zeal: whatever 'the man of God' uttered was forthwith entered upon their tablets. They were with him at his uprising and his down-lying; they looked over his shoulder as he read or wrote his letters; did he utter an exclamation of pain or of pleasure, of joy or of sorrow, down it went: did he aspirate a thought above breath, it was caught by the intent ear of one or other of the listeners, and committed to paper. An anecdote, told by Luther himself to Dr. Zincgreff, amusingly illustrates the assiduity of these German Boswells. During a colloquy, in which Dominus Martinus was exhibiting his wonted energetic vivacity, he observed a disciple hard at work

---

2. *A Copy of the Order from the House of Commons*
24th February, 1646
Whereas Captain Henry Bell has strangely discovered and found a book of Martin Luther's, called his Divine Discourses, which was for a long time very marvellously preserved in Germany: the which book, the said Henry Bell at his great costs and pains, hath translated into the English out of the German tongue which translation and substance thereof is approved by Reverend Divines of the Assembly, as appears by a certificate under their hands:

It is ordered and ordained by the Lords and Commons assembled in parliament, that the said Henry Bell shall have the sole disposal and benefit of printing the said book, translated into English by him as aforesaid, for the space of fourteen years, to commence from the date hereof. And that none do print or reprint the same, but such as shall be licensed by the said captain by authority under his hand.

(Vera Copia)     HENRY ELSYNG

with pencil and paper. The doctor, slily filling his huge wooden spoon with the gruel he was discussing by way of supper, rose, and going up to the absorbed note-taker, threw the gruel in his face, and said, laughing lustily: 'Put that down too.' There can be as little doubt of the completeness as of the authenticity of their notes. Filled with the most profound respect for 'the venerable man of God', they would have deemed it sacrilege to omit, or alter, or modify, aught that fell from his lips. The oracle had spoken; it was their pride and glory to repeat his words with the most scrupulous fidelity. We will describe the result., in the words of an eloquent letter to the translator, prefixed to the folio edition of 1652:

Herein is a full character of the free and zealous spirit of Martin Luther, who was a man of God raised in his generation with invincible courage to beat down the strongest holds of Satan, wherein for manic generations he had captivated the spirits of our forefathers under poperie. The depth and soliditie of his judgment may be discovered in the writings which he himself did publish in his life-time: but in this collection of his extemporary discourses published since his death, the fullness of his affection, and genuine readiness of his spirit, may be seen, which did incline him to advance the truth of the gospel, and manifest the testimonie of Jesus upon all occasions. And truly, I have met (in that which I have looked upon) with many excellent and fundamental truths, necessarie to be minded in this age, as well as in that wherein he spake them ; and the gracefulness which they have in their familiar and careless dress, doth make them the more commendable to all men of ingenuitie, not only of popular capacities, but even of more raised thoughts. Whence I do probably conjecture that the plainness and great variety of matters contained in these discourses, did in the first reformation ingratiate the delivery and insinuate the consideration of most eminent truths with acceptance into all men's apprehensions, so far as to cause the enemies of those truths to endeavour the suppressing of this book, which they found to be so much taking with everybody, and so full of deadly blows given to their superstition and hierarchic, to their profaneness, hypocrisie, and impietie.

We should, indeed, seek in vain elsewhere for more striking and interesting specimens of the talents, the disposition, and the manners of the great Reformer, than in this volume of his '*Table-Talk*'. And certainly if the personal character of any individual deserves to be dwelt upon, it is that of Luther. In no other instance have such great events depended upon the courage, sagacity, and energy of a single man, nor can there be found a more profitable study than the temper and peculiarities of one, who, by his sole and unassisted efforts, made his solitary cell the heart and centre of the most wonderful and important commotion the world ever witnessed; who, by the native force and vigour of his genius, attacked and successfully resisted, and at length overthrew the most awful and sacred authority that ever imposed its commands on mankind.

In perusing the work itself, we may here observe, it must always be recollected that they show the Reformer in his undress, and are not to be taken as specimens of what he wrote or preached when girded up for great occasions; – though it maybe observed that, like most men of genius, there was less difference in the language and manner of Luther in private and public, than is the case with those who cannot afford to be free, homely, and familiar: – a great peculiarity of both his preaching and writing was, that, despising all form and authority, he went straight to the hearts of his hearers and readers, and never hesitated to use an image or impression, however coarse or homely, provided it conveyed his meaning with liveliness and force.

The first German edition of the Tischreden, or Table-Talk, of Martin Luther, a folio volume, was published at Eisleben, in 1566, under the editorial care of John Aurifaber. This edition was reprinted twice in 1567, and a fourth time in 1568. The last reprint is prefaced by some new pages from the pen of the editor, who complains of one Dr. Kugling, as having, in a rival edition, made material alterations of the text. This rival edition, however, would appear never to have got beyond the manuscript form; at all events, it is unknown to bibliographers. The four editions already specified are exact reproductions, the one of the thero, infinite typographical blunders included. In 1569 appeared a new edition (Frankfurt, folio), with an appendix 'of prophecies which the venerable man of God, just before his holy death, delivered unto divers learned theologians and ecclesiastics, with many consolatory letters, opinions, narratives, replies, etc., never before made public.' The dedication 'to the Council of Rauschemberg,' dated 24th March, 1568, intimates that the editor, John Fink, had derived his new materials from various books and writings of Martin Luther. The Prophecies, it is added, were due to the research of George Walther, preacher at Hallé.

Fabricius (Centifolium Lutheranum, p. 301) mentions two other editions in folio, Eisleben, 1569 and 1577, but no copies of these editions are at present known.

The next editor of the Tischreden was Andrew Stangwald, a Prussian, the continuator of the *Centuries of Magdeburg,* who, in his preface, complains of the previous editions as very defective in their matter, and full of flagrant errors of typography. He states that his own corrected and enlarged edition had been prepared from various manuscript conversations in his possession, aided by ample marginal notes to a copy of the original edition, formerly belonging to one of Luther's intimate associates, Dr. Joachim Merlinus. Stangwald's compilation, which appeared in 1571 (Frankfurt), was reprinted in 1590, with a dedication to the council of Mulhausen, and a preface, wherein the editor announces a supplementary volume of colloquies and sayings, which, however, was never produced. The same text, but with Aurifaber's preface in lieu of Stangwald's, was reprinted in 1603 (Jena), and again in 1621 (Leipzig), and once more, after an interval of 80 years, in 1700 (Leipzig), when Stangwald's preface was given as well as Aurifaber's, and Walther's collection of Prophecies appended. This arrangement was re-produced in 1723 (Dresden and Leipzig).

Another contemporary with Luther, Nicholas Selneuer, had also applied himself to the task of arranging his master's Table-Talk, and the result of his labours, prefaced by a Life of the great Reformer, appeared in 1577, and again in 1580, folio. This edition, however, does not materially depart from the text of Stangwald.

The Tischreden, which had been hitherto excluded from the various collective editions of Luther's German works, were incorporated by Walch in the ponderous edition of 1743 (Hallé), but they were never inserted in the folio editions of the Reformer's Latin works. A selection from them, indeed, appeared in Latin, immediately after their first publication in German. This selection (Frankfurt, 1566, 8vo.) is entitled *'Silvula Sententiaram, exemplarum, Historiarurn, allegoriarum, similitudinum, facetiarum, parting ex reverendi Viri D. Martini Lutheri ac Philippi Melancthonis cum privatis tum publicis relationibus, partim ex aliorum veterum atque recentium dectorum monumentis observata.'* The translator, Dr. Ericius, however, while making extracts only from Aurifaber, gives a number of articles omitted by the German editor. Next, in 1558–1571, Dr. Henry Peter Rebenstok, pastor of Eschersheim, sent forth in two volumes (Frankfurt-on-the-Maine, 8vo.): 'Colloquia, *Meditationes, Consolationes, Consilia, judicia, sententiae, narrationes, responsa, facetiae, D. Martini Lutheri, piae et sanctae memorise in mens prandiiâ et caenae et in peregrenationibus observata et fideliter transcripta.'* Dr. Rebenstok informs us that his version was rendered not from Aurifaber, but from later editors. It was from this translation, couched in the most barbarous Latin, and replete with blunders of every description, that

Bayle criticised the 'Colloquia *Xensalia*'. The edition itself, now excessively rare, is described by the Marquis du Roure, in his '*Analecta-biblion*' (Techener, 1840).

Of the English translation, by Captain Bell, an account has already been given.

In preparing that translation, the captain appears to have been animated by the same closely scrupulous and somewhat indiscriminating fidelity which characterized the labours of those who compiled the original work. Some of the more impossible *facetiae,* indeed, which escaped the plain-spoken German in the elasticity of post-prandial converse, the translator has omitted or modified, but the infinite repetitions of 'Meditationes, Consolationes, consilia, judicia, narrationes, responsa', in the same or closely similar words, he has reproduced with the most provoking pertinacity.

It is by the omission – carefully considered – of these repetitions, that I have been enabled in the present version, and its companion volume of the 'EUROPEAN LIBRARY', the Life of Luther, to give, not merely the contents of Aurifaber's collection, but large additions from the various other editors above specified. The chapters, in particular, of Antichrist, of the Devil and his Works, and of the Turks (which Michelet specifies as peculiarly interesting) have all been materially enlarged in this way. The ample index now given is an entirely new feature.

W. HAZLITT
Middle Temple

# ĐR. JOHN ᾺURIFABER'S ĐREFACE

*To the Honourable and Right Worshipful the Head Governors, the Mayors and*
*Aldermen of the Imperial Cities, Strasburg, Augsburg, Ulm, Nuremberg, Lubeck,*
*Hamburg, Brunswick, Frankfurt on the Maine, etc.*
Grace and peace from God the Father, through Christ Jesus our Lord.

THE holy and royal prophet David, in the 78th Psalm, says: "God made a covenant with Jacob, and gave Israel a law, which he commanded our fathers to teach their children, that their posterity might know it, and the children which were yet unborn; to the intent, that when they came up, they might show their children the same. That they might put their trust in God, and not forget the works of God, but to keep his commandments.'

In these words the great benefits of God are set forth and praised, in that he reveals to mankind his Holy Word, his covenants and laws, makes himself known, instructs us of sin and righteousness, of death and life, of condemnation and salvation, of hell and heaven, and in such wise gathers a Christian church to live with him everlastingly; and the prophet wills also, that we should learn God's Word with diligence, and should teach others therein, and should make it known to all people, and in nowise forget the wonderful works of God, but render thanks to him for them.

Therefore, when God had suffered the children of Israel a long time to be plagued with severe servitude in Egypt, and thereby to fall into idolatry and false serving of God; to suffer great persecutions, and many other miseries, then he sent unto them Moses and Aaron, who kindled the light of God's Word again, and, drew them from the abominable idolatry of the heathens, and opened unto them the knowledge of the true God.

Then he led them also with a powerful hand out of the bondage of Egypt, brought them through the Red Sea, and before their eyes overthrew and drowned the tyrant Pharaoh, with all the Egyptians. He showed unto them great goodness also in the Wilderness; namely, he gave his commandments unto them on Mount Sinai; he fed them with manna, or bread from heaven, and with quails, and gave them water to drink out of the rock; and moreover, he gave manifold victories unto them, as against the Amalekites, and other enemies.

Then he gave unto them strict charge that they should always remember those unspeakable benefits, that they should speak thereof unto their children, and should be thankful for the same.

For this cause they were yearly to observe and keep the feasts of Easter, of Whitsuntide, and of the Tabernacles, to the end they might always be mindful of God's goodnesses towards them; as is written in Exodus 13:11: 'Thou shalt show thy son in that day, saying, This is done because of that which the Lord did unto me when I came out of the land of Egypt. And it shall be for a sign unto thee upon thine hand, and for a memorial between thine eyes, that the Lord's law may be in thy mouth; for with a strong hand hath the Lord brought thee out of Egypt.' But the children of Israel, after their wonderful deliverance, gave no great thanks to God for so many and great benefits; for, not long after they erected the golden calf, and danced about it. As also at the waters of strife they murmured against God, angered him, and drew his punishments upon them.

We should also place before our eyes this admonition of the 78th Psalm, and should thoroughly consider the example of the children of Israel, who so soon forgot their deliverance out of Egypt. For we may also well rejoice, that now, in our days, we have restored to us again God's Word gloriously bright and clear: so that we should show this inestimable treasure to our children's children, and how we are delivered and freed from the kingdom of antichrist, the pope of Rome, and from the traditions of men, which was a right Egyptian captivity, yea, a Babylonian imprisonment; in which our forefathers were worse tormented and plagued than the children of Israel were in Egypt. For God hath given also unto us in Germany a Moses, to be our captain and leader, namely, the much enlightened and famous man, Martin Luther, who, through God's special providence, has brought us out of Egyptian slavery, and has unveiled and cleared all the chief articles of the Christian religion; God so powerfully protecting and defending his doctrine, that it has remained and stood fast against the gates of hell.

For although many learned men, universities, popes, cardinals, bishops, friars, and priests, and after them emperors, kings, and princes, raised their strong battery against this one man, Luther, and his doctrine, intending quite to suppress it, yet, notwithstanding, all their labour was in vain. And this doctrine, which is the true and ancient doctrine of Christ, and of his apostles, remains and stands fast to this present day.

And we should look back, and consider, how, and in what a lamentable manner it stood with us fifty years past, concerning the religion and government of the church, and in what miserable bondage we have been in Popedom; for this is unknown to our children; yea, we that are old have almost forgotten it.

And, first, in the temple of God sat the man of sin, and the child of perdition, namely, the Romish antichrist, of whom St. Paul prophesied, 2 Thessalonians 2: 'Who exalteth himself above all that is called God,' or that is worshipped; he altered and perverted God's Word, laws, and statutes; and, in their place, instituted all manner of divine services, ceremonies, and ordinances, after his own will and pleasure, and in manifold ways and meanings, yea, oftentimes the one contrary to the other; so that in Popedom no man could know what was certain or uncertain, what was true or false, what was commanded or forbidden.

He sold all things for money; he forced all people under his yoke, so that emperors were constrained to kiss his feet, and from him to receive their crowns; no king or prince dared to oppose him, nor once to frown at his commands or prohibitions.

Hence he boasted, in his decrees and bulls, that he was God's general vicar on earth; that he was head of the church, supreme bishop, and lord of all bishops and learned men in the universal world; that he was a natural heir and an inheritor of the empire, and of all kingdoms when they fell void. His crown at Rome was named *regnum mundi*, every man must bow to him as to the most holy father and god on earth. And his hypocritical canonists maintained that he was not, only a man, but that he was both god and man together; who could not sin, and who had all divine and human wisdom in the cabinet of his heart; from whose stool or chair even the Holy Scriptures must have and receive their power, virtue, and authority.

He was the master of faith; and he only was able to expound the Sacred Writ, and to understand it; yea, he was so sanctified, and so far from reproach, that although he should lead the third part of all the souls of mankind into the pit of hell, yet no man must dare to question or reprove him, or to demand why he did it. For every one ought to believe, that his sacred *celsitude*, and sanctified power, neither would, should, nor could err. He had authority to make void and to annihilate both the New and Old Testaments. The church was built upon him, he could neither err nor fail, whence it followed of necessity that he was higher and more eminent than all the apostles.

He had also power and authority to erect new articles of faith, which must be equal in value to the Holy Scripture, and which ought to be believed if people intended to be saved.

He was likewise far above all councils and fathers, and to be judged by no terrestrial jurisdiction, but all must be subject only and alone to his judgments and decrees.

He made his Romish church the mother of all other churches, whence it came that all the world appealed thither. He was only and alone the governor of the church, as being far more abler and fitter to govern than the apostles themselves if they had been living.

He had power to command all people on earth, the angels in heaven, and the devils in hell. To conclude, the chair of Rome was so holy of itself, that although a wicked villain had been elected to be pope, yet so soon as he was set upon that chair, then instantly he was altogether holy.

These boastings the pope gave out himself; and his dissembling trencher-chaplains, the recorders of his decrees, decretals, Clementines and extravagants, propagated the same of him in writing; so that his gorged paunch was puffed up, and he became so full of pride (as by his acts he showed) that, as a contra-Christ, he brought all into confusion. For it is apparent in what manner he raged in and about the doctrine of the law, or ten commandments, and how these were demolished and taken away by him.

He utterly threw down the first three precepts; for he made a god of man's free-will, in that he taught, with his school-divines, that the natural strength of man, after the fall, remained sound and unspoiled; and that a man by his own human strength (if he did but that which only lay in his own power to do) was able to observe and fulfil all the commandments, and thereby should stand justified before God. He taught also, that it was not grounded in the Scriptures, that the assistance of the Holy Ghost, with his grace, was needful to accomplish good works; but that every man, by his own natural strength and ability, has a free-will, in divine duties, to do well, good, and right.

The other seven commandments the pope quite beats down, and exalted himself above parents and magistrates, and above the obedience due unto them, and instigated and stirred up children against their parents, and subjects against their rulers (as plainly appears by the imperial histories); great and fearful sins and transgressions against the fifth commandment.

He also usurped and drew to himself the temporal sword, and taught, that it is right and lawful to resist and drive away power with power: and that it is not an absolute command (but only an advice) to love our enemies, to suffer wrong, etc. Such doctrine is quite opposite to the sixth commandment.

Then, contrary to the seventh precept, he forbad his friars, priests, and nuns, to marry; and made way for them to live in licentiousness, without reproof; yea, and moreover received a yearly income and rent of such wretches.

Contrary to the eighth commandment, he usurped to himself kingdoms, principalities, countries, people, cities, towns, and villages, and took possession of the most delightful places and dwellings in the world, sucked poor people, and filled his thievish purse in such manner, that his spiritual shavelings are richer than temporal princes.

He tore also in pieces, and made void all manner of solemn vows, promises, and covenants of peace, which were made without his popish consent and authority, directly against the ninth commandment.

Lastly, and against the tenth commandment, he taught, that the wicked lusts of mankind were no sins, but proceed only out of human weakness.

In such a manner, and out of a diabolical instinct, did the pope throw down all God's commandments, and instead thereof erected human laws and precepts.

The like course he took also touching the preaching of the gospel. He preached nothing at all of Christ, of his person, works, precious merits, and benefits; nor in any way comforted distressed sorrowful consciences. And people were altogether ignorant how or where they might obtain true remission of their sins, eternal life, and salvation.

The papists declared also to the people, in their sermons, that the only Mediator between God and man, our Lord and Saviour Jesus Christ, was a severe and an angry judge, who would not be reconciled with us, except we had other advocates and intercessors besides himself.

By this doctrine, people were seduced, and carried away to heathenish idolatry, and took their refuge in dead saints to help and deliver them, and made them their gods, in whom they put more trust and confidence than in our blessed Saviour Christ Jesus; and especially, they placed the Virgin Mary, instead of her son Christ, for a mediatrix on the throne of grace.

Hence proceeded the pilgrimages to saints, where they sought for pardon and remission of sins. They also sought for pardons of the pope, of the fraternities of friars, and of other orders. And people were taught, that they must purchase heaven by their own good works, austerities, fastings, and so on.

And whereas prayer is the highest comfort of a Christian, yea, his asylum, his shield and buckler against all adversities; therefore the pope out of prayer made a naked work, a tedious babbling without spirit and truth. People prayed in Latin psalters, and books which they understood not; they observed in praying, *Horae Canonicae*, or the seven times, with garlands of roses, with so many Bridget prayers, and other collects to the dead saints; and thereby wrought terror of consciences, so that people received no hope or true comfort at all. Yet, notwithstanding, they were made to believe that such praying should merit pardons and remissions of sins for the space of many thousand years.

Baptism, in Popedom, likewise had almost lost its lustre, for it was not only stained with human toys and additions, as with holy water, lights, oil, etc., but also it was celebrated in the Latin tongue, so that the laity, standing by, could not understand it; and in its place they constituted monkery as a second baptism, of equal value and operation, through which they were to be as pure and clean as those that received Christ's baptism, taking therein new names, (as the pope at his election,) contemning their first names, that they received in Christ's baptism.

The Lord's Supper, in Popedom, also was dishonoured, corrupted, turned into idolatry, and wickedly abused; for they used the same not in remembrance of Christ, but as the offering of some wicked priest, and a self-merit of some despairing wretch that daily devoured it without faith, and afterwards sold it to others for money, to be imparted to the souls in purgatory, thereby to redeem them; so that out of the Lords Supper they made a mere market.

Moreover, the pope treacherously stole away from the laity the one part of the sacrament, namely, the wine; while the other part, which was left, was closely shut up and preserved, and yearly, *in die Corporis Christi*, with great solemnity, was carried about and worshipped, and therewith they wrought fearful idolatry.

With confession, the pope likewise brought into confusion the consciences of the whole world, and the souls of many into despair; giving people absolution, by reason of their own good works and merits; and thereby, instead of solace and comfort, he brought fear, disquiet, and discouragement, into the consciences of distressed and sorrowful people; and, instead of true keys, made false, thievish picklocks, which he used in all his wicked proceedings.

Now, when he had darkened and falsified God's Word, and the doctrine of the law and gospel; had frustrated the sweet and comfortable prayers and true devotion towards God; had dishonoured baptism, the Lord's supper; then, at last, he proceeded to tread under foot the divine state and orders in the world; and of the pulpit and church government, made a temporal rule, wherein he sat as head and monarch, and under him, in order, the cardinals, archbishops, bishops, prelates, abbots, friars, nuns, priests, and innumerable other orders ; the poor laity being altogether made a scorned tool of.

By this short relation a man may easily collect in what state and condition the Christian church stood in Popedom. Such fearful darkness did God suffer to go over tire wicked unthankful world as a just judgment.

But God, who is abundant in grace and mercy, caused the light of the gospel again to rise in our time, and dispersed the gloomy clouds of human traditions, in awakening that most famous man of God, Luther, who, with his preaching and doctrine, joined battle with Popedom, and, through God's Word, threw it to the ground, and thereby delivered us from the captivity of Popedom, led us again into the land of promise, and placed us in a paradise where God's Word is cleared, and, God be praised, the church cleansed from the cobwebs of men's traditions, purified and gloriously reformed, for which we never render sufficient thanks to Almighty God.

For God, through Luther, brought forth the Bible, or the Holy Scripture, which formerly lay, as it were, under the table; translated by Luther *ex ipsis fontibus,* out of the Hebrew into the German tongue, it may easily be read and understood by young and old, rich and poor, clergy and laity, so that now, a father or master may daily read the Holy Scriptures to his wife, to his children, and servants, and may instruct them in the doctrines of grace, and direct them in the truth and in the true service of God. Whereas, before, in Popedom the Bible was known to none: nay, the doctors in divinity themselves read not therein; for Luther often affirmed in my hearing, that Dr. Andrew Carlstadt was a doctor in divinity eight years before he began to read in the Bible; that if we Germans were not blind like the moles, we should acknowledge these unspeakable graces and benefits of God; with bended knees daily render hearty thanks, therefore, to God; with the 34th Psalm, say: 'I will always praise the Lord, his praise shall be ever in my mouth: my soul shall ever make her boast in the Lord.' And, with the 103rd Psalm: 'Praise the Lord, O my soul, and all that is within me praise his holy name: Praise the Lord, O my soul, and forget not the good that he hath done for thee.'

We should also pray heartily to God, that he would not extinguish this light of the Gospel, but suffer it long to shine, that our children's children and posterity may walk also in this saving light, rejoice therein and with us eternally be saved.

The devil is a great enemy to this treasure of God's Word and his holy sacraments; he assaults it fiercely to quench this light, as plainly appeared after the death of this holy man of God, Luther. For first, strong attempt was made by the *Interim,* by what means the doctrine of justification by faith, of good works and a Christian kind of living, of the sacraments and well ordered ceremonies in our Christian church, might utterly be overthrown.

Afterwards approached the conciliators, or the qualifiers, who sought to mediate between us and the pope, and to arrange them. They taught, that the nearer one kept himself to the pope, the better; and therefore they proposed to restore the jurisdiction of the church to the popish bishops, and to raise up the fallen ceremonies; and whoso refused to follow them, fell into great danger.

The Autinomians, Swenckfelders, Enthusians, co-agents, were also very diligent to eclipse again the true doctrines which Luther had cleared up, and brought again to light.

All that professed to be Christians and upright teachers and preachers should have resisted these false and wicked errors. But many of them were dumb dogs, that would not bark or set themselves against the ravening wolves to drive them from Christ's sheepfold, to feed the poor sheep, and to provide for them sweet and wholesome pasture. Neither were they any way careful of Joseph's miseries, as the prophet says.

But others, who, like true and constant teachers, fought against those enemies of God, were reviled and held as rebels, boisterous and stiff-necked, that would raise needless strifes and divisions, and were accordingly persecuted and plagued.

In like manner the schools and universities began to fall again, and the pure doctrine of God's Word to be by them not much regarded, school divinity being held again in great repute, and many new phrases and other eloquent arts coming into the church, which gave occasion to falsities and errors.

Thereupon the politicians, the lawyers, and courtiers essayed to rule the church and pulpits, to put in and put out ministers and churchwardens, to try causes of religion, according to their own fancies, as in temporal affairs; so that we see the falsifying of the doctrine, the devastation of the well-disciplined orders of the church in Germany, and the captivity and tyranny of the pope again nigh the door – a result that Luther, in his lifetime, often foretold.

Let us, therefore, make good use of Luther's light, and seriously exercise ourselves in the doctrine of God's Word, as Christ commanded: 'Walk in the light while ye have the light, that ye may be children of the light.' The holy Psalmist prayed: 'That the divine Word may be a lanthorn to his feet and a light to his paths,' that thereby he might direct his ways, and be preserved from darkness and stumbling. And St. Peter charges us: 'That we should take good heed to God's Word, as unto a light that shineth in darkness.'

God Almighty, the Father of our loving Lord and Saviour Jesus Christ, grant his holy spirit, that Christian kings and princes, cities and towns, may acknowledge these unspeakable benefits of the revealing again of the gospel, and the deliverance out of the Egyptian bondage, the kingdom of antichrist; and be heartily thankful to God for the same, and live thereafter in holiness, and not drive away God's Word by contemning thereof, and through sinful and wicked actions bereave ourselves and our posterity of the glorious liberty of the gospel, nor plunge ourselves into the distress and miserable captivity of popish tyranny, under which our forefathers and predecessors suffered; but that this treasure and Depositum of God's Word may remain in Germany, and that this begun work may be sent forward, and proceed to God's glory, honour and praise, and to the preservation and salvation of the Christian church, throughout all the world. God of his infinite mercy grant this for Jesus Christ's sake, Amen.

JOHN AURIFABER, D.D.
Anno 1569

# Memoir

〰

MARTIN LUTHER, the illustrious German divine and reformer of the church, was the son of John Lotter, or Lauther, (which name 'our reformer' changed to Luther,) and of Margaret Lindeman, and was born at Eisleben, a town of Saxony, in the county of Mansfeldt, November 10th, 1483. His father's extraction and condition were originally but mean, and his occupation that of a miner[1]; it is probable, however, that by his application and industry he improved the circumstances of his family, for we find him afterwards raised to the magistracy of a considerable rank and dignity in his province. Luther was initiated very early into letters; and, having learned the rudiments of grammar while he continued at home with his parents, was, at the age of thirteen, sent to a school at Magdeburg. Here he remained only one year, for the circumstances of his parents were at that time so very low, and so insufficient to maintain him, that he was forced, as Melchior Adam relates,

---

1. I am a peasant's son, and my father, grandfather, and great grandfather were all common peasants. My father went to Mansfeldt, where he got employment in the mines ; and there I was born. That I should ever become bachelor of arts, doctor of divinity, and what not, seemed not to be written in the stars. How I must have surprised folks by turning monk; and then, again, by changing the brown cap for another! By so doing I occasioned real grief and trouble to my father. Afterwards I went to loggers with the pope, married a runaway nun, and had children by her. Who foresaw these things in the stars ? Who could have foretold that they were to come to pass?

'Mendicato vivere pane,' to beg his bread for support.[2] From Magdeburg he was removed to a school at Eisenach, a city of Thuringia, for the sake of being among his mother's relations; his mother being descended from an ancient and reputable family in that town.[3] Here he applied himself diligently to study for four years; and began to discover all that force and strength of parts, that acuteness and penetration, that warm and rapid eloquence, which afterwards produced such wonderful effects.

In 1501 he was sent to the university of Erfurt, where he went through the usual courses of logic and philosophy. But Luther did not find his account in these studies; did not feel that use and satisfaction arising from such verbose and thorny sciences as logic and philosophy then were, which he wanted and wished to feel. He therefore applied himself to read the best ancient writers, such as Cicero, Virgil, Livy, etc., and from them laid in such a fund of good sense as enabled him to see through the defects in the systems of the schools, as well as the superstitions and errors of the church. He took a master's degree in the university when he was twenty; and then read lectures upon Aristotle's physics, ethics, and other parts of philosophy. Afterwards, at the instigation of his parents, he studied the civil law, with a view of advancing himself to the bar; but was diverted from this pursuit by an event which he considered as admonitory, and which, by wonderful gradations, led to his future eminence. Walking out into the fields one day, he was struck by lightning, so as to fall to the ground, while a companion was killed by his side; and this affected him so sensibly, that, without communicating his purpose to any of his friends, he withdrew himself from the world, and retired into the order of the hermits of St. Augustine.

Here he employed himself in reading St. Augustine and the schoolmen; but, in turning over the books of the library, he found a copy of the Latin Bible, which he had never seen before.[4] This raised his curiosity to a high degree; he read it over with great avidity, and was amazed to find what a

---

2. We are told this by himself: 'Let no one speak contemptuously before me of the poor "companions", who go about singing and crying at every door, *Panem propter Deum!* (bread for God's sake!) You know that the Psalm says – "Princes and kings have sung." I, myself, was once a poor mendicant, begging my bread from door to door, particularly in Eisenach, my own dear Eisenach!'

3. He obtained an asylum in the house of Dame Ursula, wife or widow of Hans Schweickardt, who took pity on the poor wandering boy; and he was enabled by this charitable woman to study four years at Eisenach. In one of his works, Luther mentions his benefactress in terms of the tenderest emotion.

small portion of the Scriptures was allowed to reach the ears of the people. He made his profession in the monastery of Erfurt, after he had been a novice one year; and took priest's orders, and celebrated his first mass in 1507.[5] The year after he was removed from the convent of Erfurt to the university of

---

4. 'I was twenty years old,' says Luther, 'before I had ever seen the Bible. I had no notion that there existed any other gospels or epistles than those in the service. At last I came across a Bible in the library at Erfurt, and used often to read it to Dr. Staupitz, with still increasing wonder.' 'At that time (says Audin) every monastery in Germany had a library, partly composed of manuscripts, with beautiful illuminations heightened with gold and silver; laborious works, in which were reduced the treasures of pagan antiquity, that but for the monks would have been for ever lost. Luther's most pleasant hours were spent in the library of the Augustineians of Erfurt. Thanks to Guttemberg, an humble mechanic, the industry of the conventual brethren was no longer necessary; printing had been discovered. At Mentz and Cologne, the sacred books were published in every form and size. The monastery had purchased at a large price some Latin bibles, which were reluctantly shown to visitors. Luther opened one, and his eyes rested with inexpressible ecstasy on the story of Hannah and her son Samuel. "My God!" he said, "I woud seek no other wealth than a copy of this book. A mighty change was then wrought in his mind. Human language attired in poetry seemed to him contemptible in comparison with the inspired word; he became disgusted with the study of the law, to which Hans, his father, had wished him to devote himself. How small in his sight became Jodocus Truttvetter, his master, who enjoyed a deserved reputation as a canonist, when compared with Moses, or still more with St. Paul, He was then twenty years old, and study had exhausted his strength; he became ill. An aged priest came to confess him; the youth was pale, wasted, and given up to thoughts which aggravated his complaint. "Courage, my friend," said the good priest to him, "you will not die of this malady; God preserves you for a great end; he will make you a distinguished man, and you in your turn will comfort others, for God loves you, since he chastises you. Doubtless, this confessor was no soothsayer, and little suspected the designs of Providence in regard to his patient.' — *Audin*.

5. Let us hear his own confession of the feelings with which he entered: 'When I said my first mass at Erfurt, I was well nigh dead, for I was without faith. My only notion of myself was, that I was a very worthy person. I had no idea that I was a sinner. The first mass was an event always much looked to, and a considerable sum of money used to be collected. The *horse canoniece* were borne in with large torches. *The dear young lord,* as the peasants used to call their new pastor, had then to dance with his mother, if she happened to be alive, whilst the bystanders wept tears of joy; if she were dead, he put her, as the phrase ran, under the communion-cup, and saved her from purgatory.'

Wittenberg; which being just founded, nothing was thought more likely to bring it into immediate credit than the authority and presence of a man so celebrated for his great parts and learning as Luther. Here he read public lectures in philosophy for three years, not in that servile, dull, mechanical way in which lectures were usually read, but with so much active spirit and force of genius, as to make it presaged that a revolution might one day happen in the schools under his direction and management.

In 1512, seven convents of his order having a quarrel with their vicar-general, Luther was chosen to go to Rome to maintain their cause. He was indeed a proper person for such employments; for he was a man of a most firm and steady temper, with a share of natural courage which nothing could subdue. At Rome he saw the pope and the court, and had an opportunity of observing also the manners of the clergy, whose hasty, superficial, and impious way of celebrating mass he has severely noted. 'I performed mass,' says he, 'at Rome; I saw it also performed by others, but in such a manner that I never think of it, without the utmost horror.' He often spoke afterwards with great pleasure of his journey to Rome; and used to say that he 'would not but have made it for a thousand florins.' As soon as he had adjusted the dispute which was the business of his journey, he returned to Wittenberg, and was created doctor of divinity, at the expense of Frederic, elector of Saxony, who had often heard him preach, was perfectly acquainted with his merit, and reverenced him highly. Luther, it appears, at first declined the honour of this degree on account of his being, in his own opinion, too young, for he was only in his thirtieth year; but he was told that 'he must suffer himself to be dignified, for that God intended to bring about great things in the church by his means'; which, though it was certainly said in jest, proved at length a very serious truth.

He continued in the university of Wittenberg, where, as professor of divinity, he employed himself in the business of his calling. The university, as we have observed, had been lately founded by Frederic, elector of Saxony, who was one of the richest and most powerful princes at that time in Germany, as well as one of the most magnificent and bountiful; and who brought a great many learned men thither, by large pensions and other encouragements, and amongst the rest Luther. Here then he began in the most earnest manner to read lectures upon the sacred books: he explained the epistle to the Romans, and the Psalms, which he cleared up and illustrated in a manner so entirely new, and so different from what had been pursued by former commentators, that 'there seemed, after a long and dark night, a new day to arise, in the judgment of all pious and prudent men'. He settled the precise difference between the law and gospel, which before had been confounded; refuted many errors, commonly received both in the church and the schools; and brought many necessary truths to light, which might have been vainly sought in Scotus and Aquinas. The better to qualify himself for the task he had undertaken, he applied himself attentively to the Greek and Hebrew languages; to which, we are told, he was particularly excited by the writings of Erasmus; who, though he always remained in appearance a Papist, or at least, had nothing decided in his character, yet contributed much to the dispelling of monkish ignorance, and overthrowing the kingdom of darkness. In the mean time, Luther, while he was active in propagating truth and instruction by his lectures and sermons, maintained an exemplary severity in his life and conversation, and was a most rigid observer of that discipline which he enjoined to others. This gained him vast credit and authority, and made all he delivered, however new or unusual, more readily accepted by those who heard him.

In this manner was he employed when the general Indulgences were published in 1517. Leo X, who succeeded Julius II in March, 1513, formed a design of building the magnificent church of St. Peter's at Rome, which was, indeed, begun by Julius II., but still required very large sums to be finished. The treasure of the apostolic chamber was much exhausted, and the pope himself, though of a rich and powerful family, was far from being able to do it at his own proper charge, on account of the excessive debts he had contracted before his advancement to the popedom.[6] There was nothing new in the method of raising money by indulgences. This had been formerly on several occasions practised by the court of Rome; and none had been found more effectual. Leo, therefore, in 1517, published general indulgences throughout all Europe, in favour of those who would contribute any sum to the building of St. Peter's; and appointed persons in different countries to preach up

---

6. Leo X had begun his pontificate by selling to Francis I, what did not belong to him, the rights of the Church of France; and at a later period, as a means of raising money, he created thirty cardinals at once; but these were trifling resources. He was not owner of the mines of Mexico; his mines were the ancient faith of the people, their easy credulity; and he had sold the right of working them in Germany to the Dominicans. The Dominican, Tetzel, an impudent mountebank, went about with great bustle, display, and expense, hawking his ware in the churches, public streets, and taverns. He paid over to his employers as little as possible, pocketing the balance, as the pope's legate proved against him some time after.

these indulgences, and to receive money for them. Albert of Brandenburg, archbishop of Mentz and Magdeburg, who was soon after made a cardinal, had a commission for Germany; and Luther assures us that he was to have half the money that was to be raised, which does not seem improbable, for Albert's court was at that time very luxurious and splendid; and he had borrowed 30,000 florins of that opulent family the Fuggers of Augsburg, to pay the pope for the bulls of his archbishopric, which sum he was bound to repay. Be this however as it will, Albert gave out this commission to John Tetzel, or Tecelius, a Dominican friar, and others of his order. These indulgences were immediately exposed to sale; and Tetzel boasted of 'having so large a commission from the pope, that though a man should have deflowered the Virgin Mary, yet for money he might be pardoned'. He added further, that 'he did not only give pardon for sins past, but for sins to come'. A book came out also at the same time, under the sanction of the archbishop, in which orders were given to the commissioners and collectors to enforce and press the power of indulgences. These persons performed their offices with great zeal indeed, but not with sufficient judgment and policy. They over-acted their parts, so that the people, to whom they were become very troublesome, saw through the cheat; being at length convinced, that under a pretence of indulgences they only meant to plunder the Germans; and that, far from being solicitous about saving the souls of others, their only view was to enrich themselves.

These strange proceedings gave great offence at Wittenberg, and particularly inflamed the pious zeal of Luther, who, being naturally warm and active, and in the present case unable to repress his indignation, was determined to declare against them, whatever might be the consequence.[7] Upon the eve of All Saints, therefore, in 1517, he publicly fixed up, at the

---

7. It has been said by Father Paul, in his *History of the Council of Trent,* and after him by Hume, in his *History of England,* as well as by others, that the Austin friars had been usually employed in preaching indulgences in Saxony; and that Luther was prompted at first to oppose Tetzel and his associates, and to deny indulgences, by a desire of taking revenge for this injury offered to his order. Such was the representation of Bossuet; and other writers, misled by his authority, have circulated a similar opinion. It is proper, therefore, to observe, that the publication of indulgences in Germany was not usually committed to the Augustines: from 1229 that lucrative commission was principally entrusted to the Dominicans, and they had been employed in the same office a short time before the present period: the promulgation of them at three different periods under Julius II. was granted to the Franciscans, and the guardian

church near to the castle of that town, a thesis upon indulgences; in the beginning of which he challenged anyone to oppose it, either by writing or disputation. This thesis contained ninety-five propositions in which, however, he did not directly oppose indulgences in themselves, nor the power of the church to grant them, but only maintained, 'That the pope could release no punishments but what he inflicted, and indulgences could be nothing but a relaxation of ecclesiastical penalties; that they affected only the living; that the dead were not subject to canonical penances, and so could receive no benefit by indulgences; and that such as were in purgatory could not by them be delivered from the punishment of their sins; that indeed the pope did not grant indulgences to the souls of the dead, by virtue of the power of the keys, but by way of suffrage; that indulgences seldom remit all punishment; that those who believe they shall be saved by indulgences only shall be damned with their masters; that contrition can procure remission of the fault and punishment without indulgences, but that indulgences can do nothing without contrition; that the pope's indulgence is not to be condemned, because it is the declaration of a pardon obtained of God, but only to be preached up with caution, lest the people should think it preferable to good works; that Christians should be instructed, how much better it is to abound in works of mercy and charity to the poor, than to purchase a pardon; and that it is a matter of indifference either to buy, or not to buy, an indulgence; that indulgences are not to be trusted; that it is hard to say what that treasure of the church is, which is said to be the foundation of indulgences; that it is not

---

of the Franciscans was joined in the trust with Albert on this occasion, though he refused to accept it ; and it is remarkable that, for half a century before Luther – viz., from 1450 to 1517 – the name of an Austin friar employed in this service occurs but once. To these facts it may be added, that it is far from being probable that Luther would have been solicitous about obtaining for himself or his order, a commission of this kind, at a time when the preaching of indulgences was become very unpopular; when all the princes of Europe, and many bishops, as well as other learned men, abhorred the traffic; and even the Franciscans and Dominicans, towards the conclusion of the fifteenth century, opposed it publicly, both in their discourses and writings: nor was this commission given to the Dominicans in general, but solely to Tetzel. Finally, Luther was never accused of opposing the publication of indulgences from resentment or envy, either in the edicts of the pontiffs of his time, or in the reproaches of his contemporary writers, who defended the cause of Rome from 1517 to 1546, and who were far from being sparing of their invectives and calumnies. *See on this subject Mosheim and Robertson.*

the merits of Christ or his saints, because they produce grace in the inner man, and crucify the outward man, without the pope's interposing; that this treasure can be nothing but the power of the keys, or the gospel of the glory and grace of God; that indulgences cannot remit the most venial sin in respect of the guilt; that they remit nothing to them who by a sincere contrition have a right to a perfect remission; and that Christians are to be exhorted to seek pardon of their sins by the pains and labour of penance, rather than to get them discharged without reason.'

This is the doctrine of Luther's thesis; in which, if he does not attack indulgences directly, he certainly represents them as useless and ineffectual. He also condemns in it several propositions which he attributes to his adversaries, and inveighs against several abuses of which he affirms them guilty, as for example, 'The reserving ecclesiastical penances for purgatory, or commuting them into the pains of purgatory; teaching that indulgences free men from all the guilt and punishment of sin; preaching that the soul, which they please to release out of purgatory, flies immediately to heaven when the money is cast into the chest; maintaining, that these indulgences are an inestimable gift, by which man is reconciled to God; exacting from the poor, contrary to the pope's intentions; causing the preaching of the word of God to cease in other churches that they may have a greater concourse of people in those where indulgences are preached; advancing this scandalous assertion, that the pope's indulgences have such a virtue as to be able to absolve a man though he has ravished the mother of God, which is a thing impossible; publishing that the cross with the arms of the pope is equal to the cross of Christ, etc. 'Such positions as these,' says he, 'have made people ask, and justly, why the pope, out of charity, does not deliver all souls out of purgatory, since he can deliver so great a number for a little money, given for the building of a church? Why he suffers prayers and anniversaries for the dead, which are certainly delivered out of purgatory by indulgences? Why the pope, who is richer than several Croesuses, cannot build the church of St. Peter with his own money, but at the expense of the poor?' etc. In thus attacking indulgences, and the commissioners appointed to publish them, Luther seemed to attack Albert, the archbishop of Mentz, under whose name and authority they were published. Of this he was himself aware; and, therefore, the very eve on which he fixed up his thesis, he wrote a letter to him,[8] in which, after humbly representing to him the grievances just recited, he besought him to remedy and correct them: and concluded with imploring pardon for the freedom he had taken, protesting that what he did was out of duty, and with a faithful and submissive temper of mind.

Luther's propositions concerning indulgences were no sooner published, than Tetzel, the Dominican friar and commissioner for selling them, maintained and published at Frankfurt, a thesis containing a set of propositions directly contrary to them. He also stirred up the clergy of his order against Luther; anathematized him from the pulpit as a most damnable heretic; and burnt his thesis publicly at Frankfurt. Eight hundred copies of Tetzel's thesis were also burnt in return by some persons at Wittenberg; but Luther himself disowned having had any hand in that procedure, and in a letter to Jodocus, a professor at Eisenach, who had formerly been his master, asked him, 'If he thought Luther so void of common sense as to do a thing of that kind in a place where he had not any jurisdiction, and against a divine of so great authority as Tetzel?' Luther, indeed, although he perceived that his propositions were very well liked, and entertained as perfectly sound and orthodox, yet behaved himself at first with great calmness and submission. He proposed them to be discussed only in the way of disputation, till the church should determine what was to be thought of indulgences. He wrote to Jerome of Brandenburg, under whose jurisdiction he was, and submitted what he had written to that bishop's judgment. He entreated him either to scratch out with his pen, or commit to the flames, whatever should seem to him unsound; to which, however, the bishop replied, that he only begged him to defer the

---

8. The following are extracts from the letter:

'Venerable father in Christ, most illustrious prince, vouchsafe to cast a favourable eye on me, who am but dust and ashes, and to receive my request with pastoral kindness. Persons are now hawking throughout the country, under the name and august title of your highness, papal indulgences for the erection of the cathedral of St. Peter's at Rome. I say nothing about the vapourings which I have not myself heard, but I complain bitterly of the preachers, the fatal errors in which they are influencing the poor, simple, and unlearned, who are everywhere openly avowing their fond imaginations on the subject. This pains and sickens me.... They believe that souls will be delivered from purgatory as soon as their money clinks in the preacher's bag. They believe the indulgence to be powerful enough to save the greatest sinner, even one (such is their blasphemy) who might have violated the holy mother of our Saviour! ... Great God! these poor souls, then, are to be led, under your authority, to death and not to life. You will incur a fearful and heavily-increasing responsibility.... Be pleased, noble and venerable father, to read and take into consideration my Propositions, showing the vanity of the indulgences which the preachers proclaim as a certainty.'

publication of his propositions; and added, that he wished no discourse had been started about indulgences. Luther complied with the bishop's request; and declared that 'it gave him more pleasure to be obedient, than it would to work miracles, if he was ever so able'. And so much justice must be done to Luther, even by those who are not of his party, as to acknowledge that he was willing to be silent, and to say nothing more of indulgences, provided the same conditions might be imposed upon his adversaries.

But the spirit of peace deserted the church for a season; and a quarrel begun by two private monks, ended as we shall see, in a mighty revolution. Luther was now attacked by adversaries innumerable from all sides; three of the principal of whom were, John Eckius, divinity-professor and vice-chancellor of the university of Ingolstadt, who wrote notes upon his thesis, which Luther answered by other notes; Sylvester Prierius, or Prierio, a Dominican, and master of the holy palace; and one Jacob Hogostratus, a friar-preacher, who singled out some of his propositions, and advised the pope to condemn and burn him, if he would not immediately retract them. Luther contented himself with publishing a kind of manifesto against Hogostratus, in which he reproaches him with cruelty and ignorance; but as Prierius had drawn up his animadversions in the form of a dialogue, to which was prefixed a dedication to the pope, and built all he had advanced against Luther upon the principles of Thomas Aquinas, Luther in an epistle to the reader, opposed Holy Scripture to the authority of this saint; and declared among other things, that 'if the pope and the cardinals were, like this Dominican, to set up any authority against that of Scripture, it could no longer be doubted that Rome was itself the very seat of antichrist; and then happy would Bohemia and all other countries be, who should separate themselves from it as soon as possible'.

In 1518, Luther, though dissuaded from it by his friends, yet, to show his obedience to authority, went to the monastery of St. Augustine at Heidelberg, while the chapter was held; and here maintained, April 26th, a dispute concerning 'justification by faith', which Bucer, who was present, took down in writing, and afterwards communicated to Beatus Rhenanus, not without the highest commendations. Luther has given an account of this dispute, and says, that 'the doctors there opposed him with such moderation and good manners, that he could not but think the better of them for it. And although the doctrine he maintained was perfectly new to them, yet they all acquitted themselves very acutely, except one of the juniors, who created much mirth and laughter by observing, that if the country people were to hear what strange positions were admitted, they would certainly stone the whole assembly.'

In the mean time, the zeal of his adversaries grew everyday more active against him; and he was at length accused to Leo X as an heretic. As soon as he returned therefore from Heidelberg, he wrote a letter to that pope, in the most submissive terms; and sent him at the same time an explication of his propositions about indulgences. He tells his holiness in this letter, that 'he was greatly troubled at being represented to him as a person who opposed the authority and power of the keys and pope; that this accusation amazed him, but that he trusted to his own innocence'. Then he sets forth the matter of fact, and says, that the 'preachers of the jubilee thought all things lawful for them under the pope's name, and taught heretical and impious propositions, to the scandal and contempt of the ecclesiastical power, and as if the decretals against the abuses of collectors did not concern them; that they had published books, in which they taught the same impieties and heresies, not to mention their avarice and exactions; that they had found out no other way to quiet the offence their ill conduct had given, than by terrifying men with the name of pope, and by threatening with fire, as heretics, all those who did not approve and submit to their exorbitances; that being animated with a zeal for Jesus Christ, and pushed on by the heat of youth, he had given notice of these abuses to the superior powers; whose not regarding it had induced him to oppose them with lenity, by publishing a position which he invited the most learned to dispute with him. This,' says he, 'is the flame which they say has set the whole world on fire. Is it that I have not a right, as a doctor of divinity, to dispute in the public schools upon these matters? These theses were made only for my own country; and I am surprised to see them spread into all parts of the world. They were rather disputable points than decisions; some of them obscure, and in need of being cleared. What shall I do? I cannot withdraw them, and yet I see I am made odious. It is a trouble to me to appear in public, yet I am constrained to do it. It is to appease my adversaries, and give satisfaction to several persons, that I have published explications of the disputes I have engaged in; which I now do under the protection of your holiness, that it may be known how sincerely I honour the power of the keys, and with what injustice my adversaries have represented me. If I were such a one as they give out, the elector of Saxony would not have tolerated me in his university thus long.' He concludes in the following words: 'I cast myself, holy father, at your feet, with all I am and have. Give me life, or put me to death; confirm or revoke, approve or disapprove, as you please. I own your voice as that of Jesus Christ, who rules and speaks by you; and if I have deserved death I refuse not to die.' This letter is dated Trinity Sunday, 1518, and was accompanied with a protestation, in which he declared, that 'he did not pretend to advance or defend anything contrary to the Holy Scripture, or to the doctrine of the fathers, received and observed by the church of Rome, or to the canons and decretals of the popes; nevertheless, he thought he had the liberty, either to approve or disapprove the opinions of St. Thomas, Bonaventure, and other schoolmen and canonists, which are not grounded upon any text.'

The Emperor Maximilian was equally solicitous with the pope about putting a stop to the propagation of Luther's opinions in Saxony; since the great number of his followers, and the resolution with which he defended them, made it evident beyond dispute, that if he were not immediately checked, he would become troublesome both to the church and empire. Maximilian therefore applied to Leo in a letter dated August 5th, 1518, and begged him to forbid by his authority, these useless, rash, and dangerous disputes; assuring him also that he would strictly execute in the empire whatever his holiness should enjoin.[9] The pope on his part ordered Jerome de Genutiis, bishop of Ascula, or Aacoli, auditor of the apostolic chamber, to cite Luther to appear at Rome within sixty days, that he might give an account of his doctrine to the auditor and master of the palace, to whom he had committed the judgment of that cause. He wrote at the same time to Frederic, the elector of Saxony, to pray him not to protect Luther; and let him know that he had cited him, and had given Cardinal Cajetan, his legate in Germany,

---

9. At the same time, however, he recommended the papal court not to precipitate matters, but in vain, as the zeal of Maximilian was somewhat mistrusted at Rome; for certain sayings of his had travelled thither, which sounded ill in the pope's ear. 'What your monk is doing, is not to be regarded with contempt,' the emperor had said to Pfeffinger, the elector of Saxony's minister; 'the game is about to begin with the priests. Make much of him; it may be that we may want him.' More than once he had indulged in bitter complaints against the priests and clergy. 'This pope,' said he, speaking of Leo X, 'has acted towards me like a knave. I can truly say that I have never met with sincerity or good faith in any pope; but, with God's blessing, I trust this will be the last.' This was threatening language; and it was recollected moreover that Maximilian, by way of definitively settling the dispute between the empire and the holy see, had entertained the idea of making himself pope. Leo X, therefore, took good care not to make him umpire in this dispute, which was daily assuming fresh importance.

the necessary instructions upon that occasion. He exhorts the elector to put Luther into the hands of this legate, that he might be carried to Rome; assuring him that, if he were innocent, he would send him back absolved, and if he were guilty, would pardon him upon his repentance. This letter to Frederic was dated August 23rd, 1518, and it was by no means unnecessary; for though Luther had nothing to trust to at first but his own personal qualities, his parts, his learning, and his courage, yet he was afterwards countenanced and supported by this elector, a prince of great personal worth.[10] At the same time, also, the pope sent a brief to Cardinal Cajetan, in which he ordered him to bring Luther before him as soon as possible; and to hinder the princes from being any impediment to the execution of this order, he denounced the punishments of excommunication, interdiction, and privation of goods against all who should receive Luther and give him protection; and promised a plenary indulgence to those who should assist in delivering him up.

In the mean time, Luther, as soon as he understood what was transacting about him at Rome, used all imaginable means to prevent his being carried thither, and to obtain a hearing of his cause in Germany. The university of Wittenberg interceded for him, and wrote a letter to the pope to excuse him from going to Rome, because his health would not permit it; and assured his holiness that be had asserted nothing contrary to the doctrine of the church, and that all they could charge him with was his laying down some propositions

---

10. Luther's hopes lay in the elector's protection. Either out of regard for his new university or personal attachment to Luther, this prince had always shown him peculiar favour. He had undertaken to defray the expenses of his doctor's degree; and in 1517, Luther thanks him by letter for a present of cloth to make a gown for the winter. Luther felt pretty sure, too, that the elector would not be offended with him for getting up an excitement, which laid all the blame upon the archbishop of Mentz and Magdeburg, a prince of the house of Brandenburg, and, consequently, an enemy to that of Saxony. Finally (and this was a powerful motive to inspire him with confidence), the elector had announced that he recognised no other rule of faith than the actual words of Scripture. Luther reminded him of this in the following passage (March 27th, 1519): 'Dr. Staupitz, my true father in Christ, told me that, talking one day with your electoral highness respecting those preachers who, instead of declaring the pure word of God, preach to the people nothing but wretched quibbles or human traditions, you said to him that the Holy Scripture speaks with such majesty and fullness of evidence as to need no adventitious aid of polemics, compelling one to admit, "never man spoke like this man. He does not teach like the Scribes and Pharisees, but as one having authority."'

in disputation too freely, though without any view of deciding upon them. The elector also was against Luther's going to Rome, and desired of Cardinal Cajetan, that he might be heard before him, as his legate in Germany. Upon these addresses, the pope consented that the cause should be tried before Cardinal Cajetan, to whom he had given power to decide it. Luther, therefore, set off immediately for Augsburg, poor, and on foot, as he says in his narrative, and carried with him letters from the elector.[11] He arrived here in October, 1518, and upon an assurance of his safety, was admitted into the cardinal's presence. The legate told him, that he did not intend to enter into any dispute with him, but should only propound three things to him, on the pope's behalf; and he did admonish him, 'First, to become a sound member of the church, and to recant his errors; secondly, to promise that he would not teach such pernicious doctrines for the future; and thirdly, to take care that the peace of the church was not broken by his means.' Luther beseeched the legate to acquaint him what his errors were, who alleged to him a decretal of Clement VI in which 'the merits of Jesus Christ are affirmed to be a treasure of indulgences', which he the said Luther denied; and objected to him also his teaching that 'faith was necessary for all who should receive the sacrament, so as to obtain any benefit by it'. Luther replied, that 'he had read the decretal of Clement, which the legate alleged; but did humbly conceive that it was not of sufficient authority to retract any opinion which he believed to be

---

11. On the eve of his departure on this expedition, so hazardous to himself and so important in its consequences to the world, he wrote a short letter to his intimate friend, Melancthon, which strongly marks the intrepidity of his character: 'I know nothing new or extraordinary here,' says he, 'except that I am become the subject of conversation throughout the whole city, and that every one wishes to see the man who is to be the victim of such a conflagration. You will act your part properly, as you have always done; and teach the youth intrusted to your care. I go, for you, and or them, to be sacrificed if it should so please God. I rather choose to perish, and, what is more afflicting, to be for ever deprived even of your society, than to retract what I have already justly asserted, or to be the means of affording the stupid adversaries of all liberal studies an opportunity of accomplishing their purpose.' – *Roscoe s Leo X.* (Bohn's edit., ii. 98.)

Luther set out at daybreak from Wittenberg, on foot, without a penny in his pocket, and dressed in a threadbare gown. Great and small, clergy and laymen, were waiting to take leave of him at the gates. When he appeared, they cried – 'Luther for ever!' 'Christ for ever, and his word!' replied Martin. Some of the crowd quitted the crowd, and did homage to the pilgrim. 'Courage, master,' said they, 'and God help you!' 'Amen!' replied Luther, *Audin.*

conformable to Holy Scripture.' The legate then had recourse to the authority of the pope, who, he said, 'could only decide upon the sense of Scripture'; upon which Luther desired time to deliberate upon what the legate had proposed to him, and so the dispute ended for that day.

The next day, (October 12th) Luther returned to a second conference with the legate, accompanied with four counsellors of the empire and a notary; and brought with him a protestation, in which he declared that 'he honoured and would obey the holy church of Rome in all things: that if he had said or done anything contrary to its decisions, he desired it might be looked upon as never said or done'; and for the three propositions made to him by the legate, he declared, 'That, having sought only the truth, he had committed no fault, and could not retract errors of which he had not been convinced, nor even heard; that he was firmly persuaded of his having advanced nothing contrary to Scripture and the doctrines of the fathers; that nevertheless, being a man and subject to error, he would submit himself to the lawful determination of the church; and that he offered, further, to give reasons in that place and elsewhere of what he had asserted, answer the objections, and hear the opinions of the doctors of the famous universities of Basil, Friburg, Louvain,' etc. The legate only repeated what he had said the day before about the authority of the pope, and exhorted Luther again to retract. Luther answered nothing, but presented a writing to the legate, which, he said, contained all he had to answer. The legate received the writing, but paid no regard to it; he pressed Luther to retract, threatening him with the censures of the church if he did not; and commanded him not to appear any more in his presence unless he brought his recantation with him. Luther was now convinced that he had more to fear from the cardinal's power than from disputations of any kind; and therefore, apprehensive of being seized if he did not submit, withdrew from Augsburg upon the 20th.[12] But, before his departure, he published a formal appeal to the pope, in which he declared, that 'though he had submitted to be tried by Cardinal Cajetan, as his legate, yet he had been so borne down and injured by him that he was constrained at length to appeal to the judgment of his holiness.' He wrote likewise a letter

---

12. Luther quitted Augsburg in haste. Staupitz had provided a horse and a guide who knew the country well. A magistrate of Augsburg, Langemantel led him in the night, through the bystreets, to a small gate which opened on the ramparts, and there took leave of him. Luther had not even taken time to don his breeches or his shoes. Next day a monk by order of the prior of the Carmelites, who had himself made haste to escape, affixed the appeal to the gates of the monastery. — *Audin.*

to the cardinal, and told him that 'he did not think himself bound to continue any longer at Augsburg; that he would retire after he had made his appeal; that he would always submit himself to the judgment of the church; but for his censures, that as he had not deserved, so he did not value them.'

Though Luther was a man of invincible courage, yet he was animated in some measure to these firm and vigorous proceedings by an assurance of protection from Frederic of Saxony; being persuaded, as he says in his letter to the legate, that an appeal would be more agreeable to that elector than a recantation. On this account, the first thing which the legate did, after Luther's departure, was to send an account to the elector of what had passed at Augsburg. He complained that Luther left him without taking leave, and without his knowledge; and although he had given him hopes that he would retract and submit, yet had retired without affording him the least satisfaction. He acquainted the elector that Luther had advanced and maintained several propositions of a most damnable nature, and contrary to the doctrine of the holy see. He prayed him to discharge his conscience, and to keep unspotted the honour of his illustrious house, by either sending him to Rome, or banishing him from his dominions. He assured him that this matter could not continue long as it was at present, but would soon be prosecuted at Rome; and that, to get it out of his own hands, he had written to the pope about it. When this letter (Oct. 25th, 1518) was delivered to the elector, he communicated it to Luther, who immediately drew up a defence of himself against it. In this defence he offered to the elector to leave his country, if his highness thought proper, that he might be more at liberty to defend himself against the papal authority, without bringing any inconveniences upon his highness by that means.[13] But his friends advised him very wisely to remain in Saxony; and the university of Wittenberg presented an address to the elector, praying him to afford Luther so much favour and protection that he might not be obliged to recant his opinions, till it was made appear that they ought to be condemned. But this address was needless; the elector was resolved not to desert Luther, and told the legate in an answer, Dec. 18th, that he 'hoped he would have dealt with Luther in another manner, and not have obliged him to recant before his cause was heard and judged; and that there

---

13. His letter runs thus: 'To avoid involving your highness in any-danger, I will quit your dominions, and go whithersoever God in his mercy shall conduct me, confiding myself in all things to his divine will. I therefore humbly offer my respects to your highness; and among whatsoever people I may take my abode, I shall remember your kindness with unceasing gratitude.'

were several men in his own and in other universities who did not think Luther's doctrine either impious or heretical; that if he had believed it such, there would have been no need of admonishing him not to tolerate it; that Luther not being convicted of heresy, he could not banish him from his states, nor send him to Rome; and that, since Luther offered to submit himself to the judgment of the universities, he thought they ought to hear him, or at least show him the errors which he taught in his writings.' Luther, seeing himself thus supported, continued to teach the same doctrines at Wittenberg, and sent a challenge to all the inquisitors to come and dispute with him; offering them not only a safe conduct from his prince, but assuring them also of good entertainment, and that their charges should be borne so long as they remained in Wittenberg.

While these things passed in Germany, Leo attempted to put an end to these disputes about indulgences, by a decision of his own; and for that purpose, November 9th, published a brief directed to Cardinal Cajetan, in which he declared that 'the pope, the successor of St. Peter, and vicar of Jesus Christ upon earth, hath power to pardon, by virtue of the keys, the guilt and punishment of sin, the guilt by the sacrament of penance, and the temporal punishments due for actual sins by indulgences; that these indulgences are taken from the overplus of the merits of Jesus Christ and his saints, a treasure at the pope's own disposal as well by way of absolution as suffrage; and that the dead and the living, who properly and truly obtain these indulgences, are immediately freed from the punishment due to their actual sins, according to the divine justice, which allows these indulgences to be granted and obtained.' This brief ordains, that 'all the world shall hold and preach this doctrine, under the pain of excommunication reserved to the pope; and enjoins Cardinal Cajetan to send it to all the archbishops and bishops of Germany, and cause it to be put into execution by them.' Luther knew very well that after this judgment made by the pope, he could not possibly escape being proceeded against, and condemned at Rome; and therefore, upon the 28th of the same month, published a new appeal from the pope to a general council, in which he asserts the superior authority of the latter over the former. The pope, foreseeing that he should not easily manage Luther so long as the elector of Saxony continued to support and protect him, sent the elector a golden rose, such an one as he used to bless every year, and send to several princes as marks of his particular favour to them. Miltitius, or Miltitz, his chamberlain, who was a German, was entrusted with this commission; by whom the pope sent also letters in Jan. 1519 to the elector's counsellor and secretary, in which he prayed those ministers to use all possible interest with their master, that he would stop the progress of Luther's errors, and imitate therein piety of his ancestors. It appears by Seckendorf's account of Miltitz's negotiation, that Frederic had long solicited for this bauble from the pope; and that three or four years before, when his electoral highness was a bigot to the court of Rome, it had probably been a most welcome present. But it was now too late: Luther's contests with the see of Rome had opened the elector's eyes, and enlarged his mind; and therefore, when Miltitz delivered his letters, and discharged his commission, he was received but coldly by the elector, who valued not the consecrated rose, nor would receive it publicly and in form, but only privately, and by his proctor; and to the remonstrances of Miltitz respecting Luther, answered that he would not act as a judge, nor oppress a man whom he bad hitherto considered as innocent. It is thought that the death of the emperor Maximilian, who expired on the 12th of this month, greatly altered the face of affairs, and made the elector more able to determine Luther's fate. Miltitz thought it best, therefore, to try what could be done by fair and gentle means, and to that end came to a conference with Luther. He poured forth many commendations upon him, and earnestly entreated him that he would himself appease that tempest which could not but be destructive to the church. He blamed, at the same time, the behaviour and conduct of Tetzel, whom he called before him, and reproved with so much sharpness that he died of melancholy a short time after. Luther, amazed at all this civil treatment, which he had never before experienced, commended Miltitz highly, owned that if they had behaved to him so at first, all the troubles occasioned by these disputes had been avoided; and did not forget to cast the blame upon Albert, Archbishop of Mentz, who had increased these troubles by his severity. Miltitz also made some concessions; as that the people had been seduced by false opinions about indulgences, that Tetzel had given the occasion, that the archbishop had employed Tetzel to get money, that Tetzel had exceeded the bounds of his commission, etc. This mildness and seeming candour on the part of Miltitz gained so wonderfully upon Luther that he wrote a most submissive letter to the pope, on March 13th, 1519. Miltitz, however, taking for granted that they would not be contented at Rome with this letter of Luther's, written, as it was, in general terms only, proposed to refer the matter to some other judgment; and it was agreed between them that the elector of Triers should be the judge, and Coblentz the place of conference; but this came to nothing: for Luther afterwards gave some reasons for not going to Coblentz, and the pope would not refer the matter to the elector of Triers.

During all these treaties, the doctrine of Luther spread and prevailed; and he himself received great encouragement at home and abroad. The Bohemians about this time sent him a book of the celebrated John Huss, who had fallen a martyr in the work of reformation; and also letters, in which they exhorted him to constancy and perseverance, owning that the theology which he taught was pure, sound, and orthodox. Many great and learned men had joined themselves to him: among the rest Philip Melancthon, whom Frederic had invited to the university of Wittenberg in August, 1518, and Andrew Carlstadt, archdeacon of that town, who was a great linguist. They desired, if possible, to draw over Erasmus to their party; and to that end we find Melancthon thus expressing himself in a letter to that great man, dated Leipzig, Jan. 5th, 1519: 'Martin Luther, who has a very great esteem for you, wishes of all things that you would thoroughly approve of him'; and Luther himself wrote to Erasmus in very respectful and even flattering terms. The elector of Saxony was desirous also to know Erasmus's opinion of Luther, and might probably think, that as Erasmus had most of the monks for his enemies, and some of those who were warmest against Luther, he might easily be prevailed on to come over to their party. It would, indeed, have been a considerable object if they could have gained this point; for the reputation of Erasmus was so great, that if he at once declared for Luther, almost all Germany would have declared along with him.

But Erasmus, whatever he might think of Luther's opinions, had neither his impetuosity nor his courage. [14] He contented himself, therefore, with acting and speaking in his usual strain of moderation, and wrote a letter to the

---

14. The following letter, written by Luther to Erasmus five years later (*i.e.,* 1524), brings out in strong colours the opinion the Reformer entertained respecting the character and conduct of the Philosopher of Rotterdam: 'I have remained silent long enough, dear Erasmus; charity commands me to set you the example. I have waited month after month in the expectation that you, as my superior, would be the first to renew our correspondence; as you have not done so, charity commands me to do so. I do not reproach you with having kept aloof from us through fear of embarrassing the cause which you abetted against our enemies, the papists; indeed, the only vexation I feel is your having harassed us with some sharp stings and bites in various passages of the works which you have published to catch their favour or mitigate their anger. We have seen clearly enough that the Lord has not yet granted you sufficient energy and direction of mind to attack these monsters freely and courageously, and we are not the men who would exact from you efforts above your strength. We have respected in you the will of God, who has meted out to you in this respect but limited gifts. On

elector Frederic, in which he declared 'his dislike of the arts which were employed to make Luther odious; that he did not know Luther, and so could neither approve nor condemn his writings, because indeed he had not read them; that however he condemned the railing at him with so much violence, because he had submitted himself to the judgment of those whose office it was to determine, and no man had endeavoured to convince him of his error; that his antagonists seemed rather to seek his death than his salvation; that they mistook the matter in supposing that all error is heresy; that there are errors in all the writings of both ancients and moderns; that divines are of different opinions; that it is more prudent to use moderate than violent means; that the elector ought to protect innocence, and that this was the intent of Leo X.' Erasmus wrote also a friendly letter in answer to Luther's, and told him that 'his books had raised such an uproar at Louvain as it was not possible for him to describe; that he could not have believed divines could have been such madmen if he had not been present and seen them with his eyes; that, by defending him, he had rendered himself suspected; that many abused him as the leader of this faction, so they call it; that there were many in England, and some at Louvain, no inconsiderable persons, who highly approved his opinions; that, for his own part, he endeavoured to carry himself as evenly as he could with all parties, that he might more effectually serve the interests of learning and religion; that, however, he thought more might be done by civil and modest means than by intemperate heat and passion; that it would be better to inveigh against those who abuse the pope's authority, than against

the other hand, there is no one can deny that it is you who have mainly contributed to the flourishing rise of letters we have witnessed, and which give so powerful an assistance to the right understanding of Scripture; the powers which God has given you in this respect are great, admirable, magnificent, and heartily do we thank him for bestowing them upon you. Impressed with these feelings, I have never desired to see you step beyond the limits assigned you by Providence, and come over to our camp. Great, doubtless would be the services you could render us by your talent and eloquence; but since your heart fails, better serve us in your own way. There was a fear that you might suffer yourself to be led away by our adversaries to attack our doctrine publicly, when I should feel bound to oppose you face to face; and I have had great difficulty in persuading some of our friends to lay aside books that had been written with the design of forcing you into the arena: hence, I should have been glad that the Hutten's *Expostulatio* and still more your *Sponge for Hutten,* had not been published. If you will reflect upon the production, you must feel how easy it is to write about moderation, and to accuse Luther of intemperance, but how difficult and impossible to practise these lessons except by a singular gift of grace.'

the popes themselves; that new opinions should rather be promoted in the way of proposing doubts and difficulties, than by affirming and deciding peremptorily; that nothing should be delivered with faction and arrogance; but that the mind, in these cases, should be kept entirely free from anger, hatred, and vainglory. I say not this,' says Erasmus, 'as if you wanted any admonitions of this kind, but only that you may not want them hereafter any more than you do at present.' When this letter was written, Erasmus and Luther had never seen each other: it is dated from Louvain, May 30th, 1519; and it is hardly possible to read it without suspecting that Erasmus was entirely in Luther's sentiments, if he had possessed the courage to declare it. He concludes in these words, which seem to imply as much: 'I have dipped into your commentaries upon the Psalms; they please me prodigiously, and I hope will be read with great advantage. There is a prior of the monastery of Antwerp who says he was formerly your pupil, and loves you most affectionately. He is a truly Christian man, and almost the only one of his society who preaches Christ, the rest being attentive either to the fabulous traditions of men or to their own profit. I have written to Melancthon. The Lord Jesus pour upon you his spirit, that you may abound more and more every day to his glory in the service of the church. Farewell.'

In 1519 Luther had a famous dispute at Leipsig with John Eckius. Eckius, as we have observed, wrote notes upon Luther's thesis, which Luther first, and afterwards Carlstadt, answered. While the dispute was pending, a conference was Proposed at Leipsig, with the consent of George, Duke of Saxony, who was cousin-german to Frederic the elector; and accordingly Luther went thither at the end of June, accompanied by Carlstadt and Melancthon.[15] Melchior Adam relates that Luther could not obtain leave to dispute for some time, but was only a spectator of what passed between Carlstadt and Eckius, till Eckius got at last a protection for him from the duke. It is certain, however, that they disputed upon the most delicate points;

---

15. To enable him to make a decent appearance at Leipsig, Luther was obliged to ask the parsimonious elector, who for the last two or three years had omitted to supply him with clothes, for a gown; his letter is a curiosity: 'I beseech your electoral grace to have the kindness to buy me a white surplice and a black one. I humbly ask for the white one, but your highness owes me the black, having promised it to me two or three years ago. There is so much difficulty in inducing Pfeffinger to untie his purse-strings, that I have been forced to procure one myself. I humbly pray your highness, who considered that the *Psalmster* deserved a black surplice, not to deem *St. Paul* unworthy of a white one.'

upon purgatory, upon indulgences; and especially upon the authority of the pope. Luther objected to this last as being an invidious and unnecessary subject; and that he would not have meddled with it if Eckius had not put it among the propositions which they were to argue. Eckius answered, and it must be owned with some reason, that Luther had first given occasion to that question by touching upon it himself, and teaching several things contrary to the authority of the holy see. In this dispute, after many texts of Scripture and many passages from the fathers had been cited and canvassed by both sides, they came to settle the sense of the famous words, 'Thou art Peter, and upon this rock will I build my church.' Luther asserted, that by rock is to be understood either power or faith: if power, then our Saviour hath added to no purpose, 'and I will give thee the keys, etc.'; if faith, as it ought, then it is also common to all other churches, and not peculiar to that of Rome. Eckius replied, that these words settled a supremacy upon St. Peter; that they ought to be understood of his person according to the explication of the fathers, that the contrary opinion was one of the errors of Wicliff and John Huss, which were condemned; and that he followed the opinion of the Bohemians. Luther was not to be silenced with this, but said, that although all the fathers had understood that passage of St. Peter in the sense of Eckius, yet he would oppose them with the authority of St. Paul and St. Peter himself; who say that Jesus Christ is the only foundation and corner-stone of his church; and as to his following the opinion of the Bohemians, in maintaining a proposition condemned with John Huss, that 'the dignity of the pope was established by the emperor', though he did not, he said, approve of the schism of the Bohemians, yet he should make no scruple to affirm that, among the articles condemned with John Huss, there were some very sound and orthodox. This dispute ended at length, like all others, the parties not the least nearer in opinions, but more at enmity with each other's persons. It seems, however, granted on all sides, that while Eckius made the best possible defence for his party, Luther did not acquire in this dispute that success and applause which he expected; and it is agreed also that he made a concession to Eckius, which he afterwards retracted, that the pope was head of the church by human though not by divine right, which made George Duke of Saxony say, after the dispute was over, 'Sive jure divino, live humane sit papa, est tamen papa' 'Whether he be pope by divine right or human, he is nevertheless pope.'

This same year, 1519, Luther's books concerning indulgences were formally censured by the divines of Louvain and Cologne. The former having consulted with the cardinal of Tortosa, afterwards Adrian VI, passed their censure on the 7th of November; and the censure of the latter, which was made at the request of the divines of Louvain, was dated the 30th of August. Luther wrote immediately against these censures, and declared that he valued them not: that several great and good men, such as Occam, Picus Mirandula, Laurentius Valla, and others, had been condemned in the same unjust manner; nay, he would venture to add to the list Jerome of Prague and John Huss. He charged those universities with rashness in being the first that declared against him, and accused them of want of proper respect and deference to the holy see, in condemning a book presented to the pope on which judgment had not yet been passed. About the end of this year Luther published a book, in which he contended for the communion being celebrated in both kinds. This was condemned by the Bishop of Misnia, Jan. 24th, 1520. Luther, seeing himself so beset with adversaries, wrote a letter to the new emperor, Charles V of Spain, who was not yet come into Germany, and another to the elector of Mentz; in both which he humbly implores protection till he should be able to give an account of himself and his opinions; adding, that he did not desire to be defended if he were convicted of impiety or heresy, but only that he might not be condemned without a hearing. The former of these letters is dated Jan. 15th, 1520; the latter, Feb. 4th. The elector Frederic fell about this time into a dangerous illness, which threw the whole party into great consternation, and occasioned some apprehensions at Wittenberg: but of this he happily recovered.

While Luther was labouring to excuse himself to the emperor and the bishops of Germany, Eckius had gone to Rome to solicit his condemnation, which, it may easily be conceived, was not now very difficult to be obtained, as he and his whole party were had in abhorrence, and the elector Frederic was out of favour on account of the protection which he afforded Luther. The elector excused himself to the pope in a letter dated April 1st, which the pope answered, and sent him at the same time a copy of a bull, in which he was required 'either to oblige Luther to retract his errors, or to imprison him for the disposal of the pope'. This peremptory proceeding alarmed at first the court of the elector, and many German nobles who were of Luther's party, but their final resolution was to protect and defend him. Is the mean time, though Luther's condemnation was determined at Rome, Miltitz did not cease to treat in Germany, and to propose means of accommodation. To this end he applied to the chapter of the Augustine friars these; and prayed them to interpose their authority, and to beg of Luther that he would endeavour to conciliate the pope by a letter full of submission and respect. Luther consented to write, and his letter bears date April 6th;[16] but matters had been carried too far on both sides ever to admit of a reconciliation. The mischief Luther had done, and continued to do, to the papal authority was irreparable, and the rough usage and persecutions he had received from the pope's party had now inflamed his active spirit to that degree that it was not possible to appease it but by measures which the pope and the court of Rome could never be expected to adopt. At all events, the letter he wrote at this juncture could not be attended with any healing consequences; the style and sentiments were too irritating for a less degree of pride than that which presided at Rome. In this epistle Luther says, 'that among the monsters of the age with whom he had been engaged for three years past, he had often called to mind the blessed father Leo: that now he began to triumph over his enemies and to despise them; that, though he had been obliged to appeal from his holiness to a general council, yet he had no aversion to him; that he had always wished and prayed for all sorts of blessings upon his person and see; that his design was only to defend the truth; that he had never spoken dishonourably of his *holiness,* but had called him a Daniel in the midst of Babylon; to denote the innocence and purity he had preserved among so many corrupt men; that the court of Rome was visibly more corrupt than either Babylon or Sodom; and that his holiness was as a lamb among wolves, a Daniel among lions, and an Ezekiel among scorpions; that there were not above three or four cardinals of any learning or piety; that it was against these disorders of the court of Rome he was obliged to appear; that Cardinal Cajetan, who was ordered by his holiness to treat with him, had shown no inclinations to peace: that his nuncio, Miltitz, had indeed come to two conferences with him, and that he had promised Miltitz to be silent, and submit to the decision of the Archbishop of Triers; but that the dispute at Leipzig had hindered the execution of this project, and put things into greater confusion; that Miltitz had applied a third time to the chapter of his order; at whose instigation he had written to his holiness; and that he now threw himself at his feet, praying him to impose silence upon his enemies; but that, as for a recantation on his part, he must not insist upon it unless he would increase

---

16. There has been much controversy respecting the date of this letter. In the edition of Jena, it bears the date 6th April, 1520, which, no doubt, is the correct one, although *Seckendorf* is inclined to place it in October of the same year; that is to say, long, after the publication of Leo's bull. *Roscoe,* in his Leo X, vol. ii. chap. xix., and Appendix (Bohn's edit. p. 468), enters fully into the subject, and unravels it with great clearness.

the troubles; nor prescribe him rules for the interpretation of the word of God; because it ought not to be limited. Then he admonishes the pope not to suffer himself to be seduced by his flatterers into a persuasion that he can command and require all things, that he is above a council and the universal church, that he alone has a right to interpret Scripture; but to believe those rather who debase than those who exalt him.'

The continual importunities of Luther's adversaries with Leo caused him at length to publish a formal condemnation of him in a bull dated June 15th, 1520. In the beginning of this bull the pope directs his speech to Jesus Christ, to St. Peter, St. Paul, and all the saints, invoking their aid, in the most solemn expressions against the new errors and heresies, and for the preservation of the faith, peace and unity of the church. Then he expresses his great grief for the late propagation of these errors in Germany; errors either already condemned by the councils and constitutions of the pope, or new propositions heretical, false, scandalous, apt to offend and seduce the faithful. Then, after enumerating forty-one propositions collected from Luther's writings, he does, by the advice of his cardinals, and after mature deliberation, condemn them as respectively heretical; and forbids all Christians, under the pain of excommunication, and deprivation of all their dignities, which they should incur *ipso facto*, to hold, defend, or preach any of these propositions or to suffer others to preach them. As to Luther, after accusing him of disobedience and obstinacy, because he had appealed from his citation to a council, though he thought he might at that instant condemn him as a notorious heretic, yet he gave him sixty days to consider, assuring him that if in that time he would revoke his errors and return to his duty, and give him real proofs that he did so by public acts and by burning his books, he should find in him a true paternal affection: otherwise he declares, that he should incur the punishment due to heretics.[17]

Luther, now perceiving that all hopes of an accommodation were at an end, no longer observed the least reserve or moderation. Hitherto he had treated his adversaries with some degree of ceremony, paid them some regard; and, not being openly separated from the church, did not quite abandon the discipline of it. But now he kept no measures with them, broke off all his engagements to the church, and publicly declared that he would no longer

---

17. When the bull of condemnation reached Germany, the whole people were in commotion, At Erfurt the students took it out of the booksellers' shops, tore it in pieces, and threw it into the river with this pun, 'A bubble (*bulla*) it is, and as a bubble let it swim.'

communicate in it. The first step he took after the publication of the pope's bull was to write against it, which he did in very severe terms, calling it 'the execrable bull of Antichrist'. He published likewise a book called *The Captivity of Babylon,* in which he begins with a protestation, 'That he became every day more knowing; that he was ashamed and repented of what he had written about indulgences two years before, when he was a slave to the superstitions of Rome; that he did not indeed then reject indulgences, but had since discovered that they are nothing but impostures, fit to raise money, and to destroy the faith; that he was then content with denying the papacy to be *jure divino,* but had lately been convinced that it was the kingdom of Babylon; that he then wished a general council would settle the communion in both kinds, but now plainly saw that it was commanded by Scripture; that he did absolutely deny the seven sacraments, owning no more than three, baptism, penance, and the Lord's supper,' etc. About the same time also he published another treatise in the German language, to make the court of Rome odious to the Germans, in which 'he gives a history of the wars raised by the popes against the emperors, and represents the miseries Germany had suffered by them. He strives to engage the emperor and princes of Germany to espouse his party against the pope by maintaining that they had the same power over the clergy as they had over the laity, and that there was no appeal from their jurisdiction. He advises the whole nation to shake off the pope's power, and proposes a reformation, by which he subjects the pope and bishops to the power of the emperor, etc.' Lastly, that he might not be wanting in anything which should testify his abhorrence of the proceedings in the court of Rome, Luther determined to treat the pope's bull and decretals in the same manner as they had ordered his writings to be treated; and therefore, calling the students at Wittenberg together, he flung them into a fire prepared for that purpose, saying, 'Because thou hast troubled the holy one of God, let eternal fire trouble thee.' This ceremony was performed Dec. 10th, 1520.

The bull of Luther's condemnation was carried into Germany, and published there by Eckius, who had solicited it at Rome; and who, together, with Jerome Aleander, a person eminent for his learning and eloquence, was entrusted by the pope with the execution of it. In the mean time, Charles V of Spain, after he had adjusted the affairs of the Low Countries, went into Germany, and was crowned emperor, October 21st, at Aix-la-Chapelle. The plague preventing his remaining long in that city, he went to Cologne, and appointed a diet at Worms, to meet January 6th, 1521. Frederic, elector of Saxony, could not be present at the coronation, but was left sick at Cologne, where Alexander, who accompanied the emperor, presented him with a brief, which the pope had sent by him, and by which his holiness gave him notice of the decree he had made against the errors of Luther. Alexander told the elector, that the pope had entrusted himself and Eekius with the affair of Luther, which was of the utmost consequence to the whole Christian world, and, if there were not a speedy stop put to it, would undo the empire; that he did not doubt but that the elector would imitate the emperor and other princes of the empire, who had received the pope's judgment respectfully. He informed his highness also, that he had two things to request of him in the name of the pope – 'First, that he would cause all Luther's books to be burnt; and, secondly, that he would either put Luther to death, or imprison him, or send him to the pope.' The pope sent also a brief to the university of Wittenberg, to exhort them to put his bull in execution against Luther; but neither the elector nor the university paid any regard to his briefs. Luther, at the same time, renewed his appeal to a future council, in terms very severe upon the pope, calling him tyrant, heretic, apostate, antichrist and blasphemer; and in it prays the emperor, electors, princes, and lords of the empire, to favour his appeal, nor suffer the execution of the bull, till he should be lawfully summoned, heard and convicted before impartial lines. This appeal is dated November 17th. Erasmus, indeed, and other German divines, were of the opinion that things ought not to be carried to this extremity, foreseeing, that the fire which consumed Luther's books would soon put all Germany into a flame. They proposed, therefore, to agree upon arbitrators, or to refer the whole cause to the first general council. But these pacific proposals came too late; and Eckius and Alexander pressed the matter so vigorously both to the emperor and the other German princes, that Luther's books were burnt in several cities of Germany. Alexander also earnestly importuned the emperor for an edict against Luther; but he found many and great obstacles. Luther's party was very powerful; and Charles V was not willing to give so public an offence to the elector of Saxony, who had lately refused the empire that he might have it.

To overcome these difficulties Alexander gained a new bull from Rome, which declared, that Luther had incurred by obstinacy the penalty denounced in the first. He also wrote to the court of Rome for the assistance of money and friends, to be used at the diet of Worms; and, because the Lutherans insisted that the contest was chiefly about the jurisdiction of the pope and the abuses of the court of Rome, and that they were only persecuted for the sake of delivering up Germany to the tyranny of that court, he undertook to show that Luther had broached many errors relating to the mysteries of religion, and revived the heresies or Wicliff and John Huss. The diet of Worms was held in the beginning of 1521, where Alexander, in the absence of Luther, employed his eloquence and interest so successfully that the emperor and princes of the empire were about to execute the pope's bull against Luther with severity, and without delay. The only way which the elector of Saxony and Luther's friend could invent to ward off the blow was to say, 'That it was not evident that the propositions objected to were his; that his adversaries might attribute them to him falsely; that the books from which they were taken might be forged; and, above all, that it was not just to condemn him without summoning and hearing him.' The emperor, therefore, with the consent of the princes of the diet, sent Sturmius, an officer, from Worms to Wittenberg, to conduct Luther safely to the diet. Sturmius carried with him a 'safe-conduct' to Luther, signed by the emperor and princes of the diet, and also a letter from the emperor, dated March 21st, 1521, and directed 'To the honourable, beloved, devout doctor, Martin Luther, of the order of St. Augustine'; in which he summoned him to appear at the diet, and assured him that he need not fear any violence or ill-treatment.[18] Nevertheless, Luther's friends were much against his going, some telling him that by burning his books he might easily know what censure would be passed on himself; others reminding him of the treatment they had, upon a like occasion, shown to John Huss. But Luther despised all dangers; and, in a strain which is extremely characteristic of him, declared, that 'If he knew there were as many devils at Worms as tiles upon the houses, he would go.'

He arrived accordingly at Worms, April 16th, where a prodigious multitude of people were assembled, for the sake of seeing a man of whom so much had now been heard. When he appeared before the diet, he had two questions put to him by John Eckius: 'First, whether he owned those books that went under his name; and, secondly, whether he intended to retract or defend what was contained in them.' These queries produced an altercation

---

18. The Emperor's mandate was in the following terms: 'Honourable, dear, and devoted Luther, – Ourself and the states of the holy Roman empire, assembled at Worms, having resolved to demand an explanation from you on the subject of your doctrines and your writings, we send you herewith a safe conduct, to ensure your personal security. Wherefore, immediately set out, for such is our will, so that within twenty days of the receipt of our mandate, you may appear before us and the States. You have neither violence nor snares to fear. We wish you to confide in our imperial word, and rely on your obedience to our earnest wishes.'

which lasted some days, but which ended at length in this single and peremptory declaration of Luther, that 'unless he was convinced by texts of Scripture or evident reason (for he did not think himself obliged to submit to the pope or his councils), he neither could nor would retract anything, because it was not lawful for him to act against his conscience.' This being Luther's final resolution, the emperor declared to the diet that he was determined to proceed against him as a notorious heretic, but that he intended, nevertheless, he should return to Wittenberg, according to the conditions laid down in his 'safe-conduct'. Luther left Worms, April 26th, conducted by Sturmius, who had brought him; and being arrived at Friburg, he wrote letters to the emperor and princes of the diet to commend his cause to them, and to excuse himself for not submitting to a recantation. These letters were conveyed by Sturmius, whom he sent back, on pretence that he was then out of danger; but in reality, as it is supposed, that Sturmius might not be present at the execution of a scheme which had been concerted before Luther set out from Worms; for the elector of Saxony, foreseeing that the emperor was going to make a bloody edict against Luther, and finding it impossible to support and protect him any longer without involving himself in difficulties, resolved to have him taken away and concealed. This was proposed to Luther, and accordingly when he went from Eisenach, May 3rd, through a wood, on his way to Wittenberg, he was suddenly set upon by some horsemen in disguise, deputed for that purpose, who pretended to take him by force, and carried him secretly into the castle of Wittenberg.[19] Melchior Adam relates that there were only eight nobles privy to this expedition, which was executed with so much address and fidelity that no man knew what was become of him or where he was. This contrivance produced two advantages to Luther: as first, it caused people to believe that he was taken away by the intrigues of his enemies, which made them odious and exasperated men's minds against them; and secondly, it secured him against the prosecution which the pope and the emperor were making against him.

---

19. The following is his own account: 'I crossed the forest to rejoin my parents, and had just quitted them, intending to go to Walterhausen, when I was made prisoner near the fortress of Altenstein. Amsdorf, no doubt, was aware that it was arranged to seize me, but he does not know where I am kept. My brother, having seen the horsemen coming up, leapt from the carriage without leave-taking, and I have been told that he reached Walterhausen on foot that evening. As for me, they took off my robe, and made me dress myself as a cavalier, with a false beard, and I have since allowed my hair and beard to grow. You would scarcely recognise me indeed, I hardly know myself. However, here I am, living in Christian liberty, freed from all the tyrant's laws.'

Before the diet of Worms was dissolved, Charles V caused an edict to be drawn up, which was dated the 8th of May, and solemnly published on the 26th in the assembly of the electors and princes held in his palace. In this edict, after declaring it to be the duty of an emperor, not only to defend the limits of the empire, but to maintain religion and the true faith, and to extinguish heresies in their origin, he commands, That Martin Luther be, agreeably to the sentence of the pope, henceforward looked upon as a member separated from the church, a schismatic, and an obstinate and notorious heretic. He forbids all persons, under the penalty of high treason, loss of goods, and being put under the ban of the empire, to receive or defend, maintain or protect him, either in conversation or in writing; and he orders, that, after the twenty-one days allowed in his safe-conduct, he should be proceeded against according to the form of the ban of the empire, in what place soever he should be: or, at least, that he should be seized and imprisoned, till his imperial majesty's pleasure should be further known. The same punishments are denounced against all the accomplices, adherents, followers, or favourers of Luther; and also all persons are forbidden to print, sell, buy, or read any of his books: and, because there had been published several books concerning the same doctrines, without his name, and several pictures dispersed that were injurious to the pope, cardinal, and bishops, he commands the magistrates to seize and burn them, and to punish the authors and printers of those pictures and libels. Lastly, it forbids in general the printing of any book concerning matters of faith, which hath not the approbation of the ordinary, and some neighbouring university.

While the bull of Leo X, executed by Charles V, was thundering throughout the empire, Luther was safely shut up in his castle, which he afterwards called his Hermitage and his Patmos. Here he held a constant correspondence with his friends at Wittenberg, and was employed in composing books in favour of his own cause, and against his adversaries. He did not however so closely confine himself, but that he frequently made excursions into the neighbourhood, though always under some disguise or other. One day he assumed the title and appearance of a nobleman: but it may be supposed that he did not act his part very gracefully; for a gentleman who attended him under that character, to an inn upon the road, was, it seems, so fearful of a discovery, that he thought it necessary to caution him against that absence of mind peculiar to literary men; bidding him, 'keep close to his sword, without taking the least notice of books, if by chance any should fall in his way.' He used sometimes even to go out a hunting with those few who were in his secret; which, however, we may imagine, he did more for health than for pleasure, as indeed may be collected from his own curious account of it. 'I was,' says he, 'lately two days a hunting, in which amusement I found both pleasure and pain. We killed a brace of hares, and took some unhappy partridges; a very pretty employment truly for an idle man! However, I could not forbear theologizing amidst dogs and nets; for, thought I to myself, do not we, in hunting innocent animals to death with dogs, very much resemble the devil, who, by crafty wiles and the instruments of wicked priests, is perpetually seeking whom he may devour? Again: We happened to take a leveret alive; which I put into my pocket, with an intent to preserve it; yet we were not gone far before the dogs seized upon it, as it was in my pocket, and worried it. Just so the pope and the devil rage furiously to destroy the souls that I have saved, in spite of all my endeavours to prevent them. In short, I am tired of hunting these little innocent beasts; and had rather be employed, as I have been for some time, in spearing bears, wolves, tigers, and foxes; that is, in opposing and confounding wicked and impious divines, who resemble those savage animals in their qualities.'

Weary at length of his retirement, he appeared publicly again at Wittenberg, March 6th, 1522, after he had been absent about ten months.[20] He appeared indeed without the elector's leave, but immediately wrote him a letter, to prevent his being offended. The diet of Charles V, severe as it was,

---

20. A curious account of his journey to Wittenberg is given by one of the historians of the Reformation:

'John Kessler, a young theologian of Saint-Gall on his way with a friend to Wittenberg to finish his studies there, fell in one evening in an inn near the gates of Jena with Luther, dressed as a cavalier. They did not know him. The cavalier was seated at a table reading a little book, which, as they saw afterwards, was the Psalter in Hebrew. He politely saluted them, and invited them to seat themselves at his table. In the course of conversation, he inquired what was thought of Luther in Switzerland? Kessler replied, that some did not know how to praise him enough, and daily thanked God for having sent him on earth to exalt the truth; whilst others, and especially the priests, denounced him as a heretic who ought to be condignly punished. From something which the innkeeper let drop to the young travellers, they suspected him to be Ulrich von Hutten. Presently after two traders came in. One of them drew from his pocket, and placed on the table, a newly printed pamphlet of Luther's, in sheets, and asked if they had seen it. Luther said a few words about the indifference towards serious matters manifested by the princes at that time assembled at the diet of Nuremberg. He also expressed a fervent hope "that the Gospel truth would bear fuller fruit in succeeding generations, not poisoned as heretofore with papal error."

had given little or no check to Luther's doctrine; for the emperor was no sooner gone into Flanders, than his edict was neglected and despised, and the doctrine seemed to spread even faster than before. Carlstadt, in Luther's absence, had acted with even more vigour than his leader, and had attempted to abolish the use of the mass, to remove images out of the churches, to set aside auricular confession, invocation of saints, the abstaining from meats; had allowed the monks to leave their monasteries, to neglect their vows and to marry, and thus had quite changed the doctrine and discipline of the church at Wittenberg: all which, though not against Luther's sentiments, was yet blamed by him, as being rashly and unseasonably done.[21] The reformation was still confined to Germany; it had not extended to France; and Henry VIII of England made the most vigorous acts to prevent its entering his realm;

---

One of the traders replied, "I am unskilled in these questions; but, to my mind, Luther must either be an angel from heaven or a devil from hell; at all events, he is so remarkable a person, that I will spend the last ten florins I have saved in going to confess to him." This conversation took place during supper. Luther had previously arranged with the host to pay the reckoning of the whole party. When they separated, Luther shook hands with the two Swiss (the traders had been called away by their business), and begged them to bear his remembrances to Doctor Jerome Schurff, their countryman, as soon as they reached Wittenberg. On their asking him whose remembrances they were to bear, he replied, "Simply tell him that he who is to come salutes him; he will not fail to comprehend these words." When the traders returned, and learnt that it was Luther with whom they had been talking, they were inconsolable at not having known it sooner, that they might have paid more respect, ands spared themselves the mortification of having spoken so foolishly in his presence. The following morning they were up betimes on purpose to see him before he left, and to tender him their most humble excuses. Luther only owned to its being himself by implication.'

21. Carlstadt, having thrown down the images, proceeded to preach against image-worship; Staupitz showed him the reformer's letter, but Carlstadt only smiled, replying, 'It is written, It is better to obey God than man.' Staupitz urged the pain which these profanations of the sanctuary had caused to their common leader. The archdeacon replied, 'It is no new thing that the world should be troubled for God's word. Herod, with all his court, was alarmed on hearing of the birth of Jesus; the earth shook and the sun was darkened at the death of Christ. That the multitude and the sages are offended with it is an evidence that my teaching is true.' 'But;' rejoined Staupitz, 'our father condemns, like you, the worship of images, but he does not wish violence to be used.' 'Hold your peace,' replied Carlstadt; 'you forget what Luther has said: The word of the Lord is not a word of peace, but a sword.' Staupitz then menaced him with the rigour of the secular power. Carlstadt smiled: 'My father,' said he, ' the same menace

and to shew his zeal for the Holy See, wrote a treatise 'Of the Seven Sacraments', against Luther's book 'Of the Captivity of Babylon'; which he presented to Leo X in October 1521. The pope received it favourably, and complimented Henry with the title of 'Defender of the Faith'. Luther, however, paid no regard to his dignity, but treated both his person and performance in the most contemptuous manner. Henry complained of this rude usage to the princes of Saxony; and Fisher, bishop of Rochester, replied, in behalf of Henry's treatise: but neither the king's complaint, nor the bishop's reply, were attended with any visible effects.

Luther now made open war with the pope and bishops; and, that he might make the people despise their authority as much as possible, he wrote one book against the pope's bull, and another against the order falsely called 'the order of bishops'. The same year, 1522, he wrote a letter, July 29th, to the assembly of the States of Bohemia, in which he assured them that he was labouring to establish their doctrine in Germany, and exhorted them not to return to the communion of the church of Rome; and he published also this year a translation of the 'New Testament' in the German tongue, which was afterwards corrected by himself and Melancthon. This translation having been printed several times, and in general circulation, Ferdinand, archduke of Austria, the emperor's brother, made a very severe edict, to suppress its publication, and forbade all the subjects of his imperial majesty to have any copies of it, or of Luther's other books. Some other princes followed his example, which provoked Luther to write a treatise 'Of the Secular Power', in which he accuses them of tyranny and impiety. [22] The diet of the empire was held at Nuremberg, at the end of the year; to which Adrian VI sent his brief, dated Nov. 25th; for Leo X died Dec. 2nd, 1521, and Adrian had been

---

was addressed to brother Martin by the messenger of Cardinal Cajetan, and do you not recollect his reply: *I will go whither God pleases, beneath his heaven*. I make the same answer to you.' With these words the interview terminated; Staupitz immediately communicated the particulars to Luther, who from that day forth vowed against his old master in theology a hatred which time neither extinguished nor weakened.

22. In this violent invective Luther says: 'Princes are of the world, and the world is alien from God; so that they live according to the world, and against God's law. Be not astonished, therefore, by their furious warring against the Gospei, for they cannot act contrary to their own nature. From the beginning of the world a wise and prudent prince has been a *rara avis*, and an honest and upright prince still more rare. They are generally great fools, good-for-nothing fellows, and the greatest rascals on earth (*maxime fatui, pessimi nebulones super terrain*). And so the worst is always to be expected

elected pope the 9th of January following. In this brief, among other things, he informs the diet, that he had heard, with grief, that Martin Luther, after the sentence of Leo X, which was ordered to be executed by the edict of Worms, continued to teach the same errors, and daily to publish books full of heresies: that it appeared strange to him, that so large and so religious a nation could be seduced by a wretched apostate friar: that nothing, however, could be more pernicious to Christendom: and that, therefore, he exhorts them to use their utmost endeavours to make Luther, and the authors of these tumults, return to their duty; or, if they refuse and continue obstinate, to proceed against them according to the laws of the empire, and the severity of the last edict.

The resolution of this diet was published in the form of an edict, March 6th, 1523; but it had no effect in checking the Lutherans, who still went on in the same triumphant manner. This year Luther wrote a great many tracts: among the rest, one upon the dignity and office of the supreme magistrate; with which Frederic, elector of Saxony, is said to have been highly pleased. He sent, about the same time, a writing in the German language to the Waldenses, or Picarda, in Bohemia and Moravia, who had applied to him 'about worshipping the body of Christ in the eucharist'. He wrote also another book, which, he dedicated to the senate and people of Prague, 'concerning the institution of ministers of the church'. He drew up a form of saying mass. He wrote a piece entitled 'An Example of Popish Doctrine and Divinity'; which Dupin calls a satire against nuns, and those who profess a monastic life. He wrote also against the vows of virginity, in his preface to his commentary on 1 Corinthians 7: and his exhortations here were, it seems,

---

from them, and scarcely ever any good; especially when the salvation of souls is concerned. They serve God as lictors and executioners when he wishes to punish the wicked. Our God is a great and mighty King, and it is necessary that he have noble, illustrious, rich executioners and lictors, such as they, and it pleases Him that they should have riches and honour in abundance, and be feared of all. It is His divine pleasure that we style his executioners very merciful lords, that we prostrate ourselves at their feet, that we be their most obedient and humble subjects. But these very executioners do not push their artifices so far as to pretend to be good shepherds of their flock. If a prince be wise, upright, a Christian, we regard it as a great miracle, a precious sign of divine favour; for, commonly, it happens as with the Jews, to whom God said, "I will give thee a king in my anger, and take him away in my wrath." *(Dabo tibi regem in furore meo, et auferam in indignatione meâ.)* And look at our Christian princes who protect the faith, forsooth, while they devour the faith. Good people, trust not to them.'

followed with effects; for, soon after, nine nuns eloped from a nunnery, and were brought to Wittenberg. Whatever offence this proceeding might give to the papists, it was highly extolled by Luther; who, in a book written in the German language, compares the deliverance of these nuns from the slavery of a monastic life, to that of the souls which Jesus Christ has delivered by his death.[23] This year he had occasion to lament the death of two of his followers, who were burnt at Brussels, and were the first who suffered martyrdom for his doctrine. He wrote also a consolatory epistle to three noble ladies at Misnia, who were banished from the duke of Saxony's court at Friburg, for reading his books.

In the beginning of 1524, Clement VII sent a legate into Germany to the diet which was to be held at Nuremberg. This pope had succeeded Adrian, who died in October, 1523, and had, a little before his death, canonized Benno, who was bishop of Meissen in the time of Gregory VII, and one of the most zealous defenders of the holy see. Luther, imagining that this was done directly to oppose him, drew up a piece with this title, 'Against the New Idol and Devil set up at Meissen'; in which he treats the memory of Gregory with great freedom, and does not spare even Adrian. Clement VII's legate, therefore, represented to the diet at Nuremberg the necessity of enforcing the execution of the edict of Worms, which had been strangely neglected by the princes of the empire; but, notwithstanding the legate's solicitations, which were very pressing, the decrees of that diet were thought so ineffectual, that they were condemned at Rome, and rejected by the emperor. It was in this year that the dispute between Luther and Erasmus began about free-will.

---

23. We give his own words: 'Nine nuns came to me yesterday, who had escaped from their imprisonment in the convent of Nimptschen; among them were Staupitza, and two other members of Zeschau's family' (April 6th, 1523). 'I greatly commiserate these poor girls, and still more those others who are dying in crowds of this accursed and incestuous chastity. This most feeble sex is united to the male by nature, by God himself; if they are separated, it perishes. O cruel, tyrannical parents! …You ask my intentions with respect to them. In the first place, I shall communicate to their parents my desire that they may be permitted to return home; if they refuse, I shall provide an asylum for them elsewhere. Their names are – Magdalen Staupitza, Elsa von Canitz, Ave Grossin, Ave Schonfeld, and her sister Margaret Schonfeld, Laneta von Golis, Margaret Zeschau, and Catherine von Bora (afterwards his wife). They made their escape in the most surprising manner. Pray beg some money for me of your rich courtiers, to enable me to support these poor girls for a week or a fortnight, until I restore them to their parents, or to those friends who have promised me to take care of them in the event of their being rejected by their parents' (April 10th, 1523).

Erasmus had been much courted by the papists to write against Luther, but had hitherto avoided the task, by saying, 'that Luther was too great a man for him to write against', and that he had learned more from one short page of Luther, than from all the large books of Thomas Aquinas. Besides, Erasmus was all along of opinion, that writing would not be found an effectual way to end the differences, and establish the peace of the church. Tired out, however, at length, with the importunities of the pope and the catholic princes, and desirous at the same time to clear himself from the suspicion of favouring a cause which he would not seem to favour, he resolved to write against Luther, though, as he tells Melancthon, it was with some reluctance; and he chose free-will for the subject. His book was entitled 'A Diatriba, or Conference about Free-will', and was written with much moderation, and without personal reflections. He tells Luther in the preface, 'that he ought not to take his differing from him in opinion ill, because he had allowed himself the liberty of differing from the judgment of popes, councils, universities, and doctors of the church.' Luther was some time before he answered Erasmus's book, but at last published a treatise, 'De servo arbitrio, or, Of the Servitude of Man's Will'; and though Melancthon had promised Erasmus, that Luther should answer him with civility and moderation, yet Luther had so little regard to Melancthon's promise, that he never wrote anything more severe. He accused Erasmus of being careless about religion, and little solicitous what became of it, provided the world continued in peace, and that his notions were rather philosophical than Christian. Erasmus immediately replied to Luther, in a piece called 'Hyperaspistes'; in the first part of which he answers his arguments, and in the second his personal reflections.

In October, 1524, Luther threw off the monastic habit, which, though not premeditated and designed, was yet a very proper Preparative to a step he took the year after; we mean, his marriage with Catherine von Bora. Catherine von Bora was a gentleman's daughter, who had been a nun, and was one of those whom we mentioned as escaping from the nunnery in 1523. Luther married her June 13th, 1525; and for this was blamed, not only by the catholics, but, as Melancthon says, by those of his own party.[24] He was even for some time ashamed of it himself; and owns, 'that his marriage had made him so despicable, that he hoped his humiliation would rejoice the

---

24. It seems that she had been previously attached to a young student at Nuremberg, Jerome Baumgärtner; and we find Luther writing to him, Oct. 12th, 1524: 'If you are anxious to have your Catherine, come here at once, or she will become the

angels, and vex the devils'. Melancthon found him so afflicted with what he had done, that he wrote some letters of consolation to him: he adds, however, that 'this accident may possibly not be without its use, as it tends to humble him a little: for it is dangerous,' says he, 'not only for a priest, but for any man, to be too much elated and puffed up; great success giving occasion to the sin of a high mind, not only, as the orator says, in fools, but sometimes even in wise men.' It was not so much the marriage, as the circumstances of the time, and the precipitation with which it was done, that occasioned the censures passed upon Luther. He married very suddenly, and at a time when Germany was groaning under the miseries of war, which was said at least to be owing to Lutheranism. It was thought also an indecent thing in a man of forty-two years of age, who was then, as he declared, restoring the gospel and reforming mankind, to involve himself in marriage with a woman of six and twenty, upon any pretext. But Luther, as soon as he had recovered himself a little from this abashment, assumed his former air of intrepidity, and boldly supported what he had done with reasons. 'I took a wife,' says he, 'in obedience to my father's commands, and hastened the consummation, in order to prevent impediments, and stop the tongues of slanderers.' It appears from his own confessions, that this reformer was very fond of Catherine von Bora, and used to call her his Kate, which occasioned some slanderous reflections: and therefore, says he, 'I married of a sudden, not only that I might not be obliged to hear the clamours which I knew would be raised against me, but to stop the mouths of those who already reproached me.' Luther also gives us to understand that he did it partly as concurring with his grand scheme of opposing the catholics. 'See,' says he, 'because they are thus mad, I have so prepared myself, that, before I die, I may be found by God in the state in which I was created, and, if possible, retain nothing of my former popish life. Therefore let them rave yet more, and this will be their last farewell; for my mind presages that I shall soon be called by God unto his grace: therefore, at my father's commands, I have taken a wife.' In another letter he speaks thus: 'I hope I shall live a little longer, and I would not deny this last obedience to my father, who required it in hopes of issue, and also to confirm the doctrines I have taught.'

Luther, notwithstanding, was not himself altogether satisfied with these reasons. He did not think the step he had taken could be sufficiently justified

property of another, who has already got her with him in his house. Still, she has not yet overcome her love for you. And, after all, I should perhaps be better pleased that you, having a prior title, should be united to her.'

upon the principles of human prudence; and therefore we find him, in other places, endeavouring to account for it from a supernatural impulse. 'The wise men amongst us are greatly provoked,' says he; 'they are forced to own the thing to be of God; but the disguise of the persons under which it is transacted, namely, of the young woman and myself, makes them think and say everything that is wicked.' And elsewhere: 'The Lord brought me suddenly, when I was thinking of other matters, to a marriage with Catherine von Bora, the nun.' His party seem also to have favoured this supposition. Thus says Melancthon: 'As for the unreasonableness and want of consideration in this marriage, on which account our adversaries will chiefly slander us, we must take heed lest that disturb us: for perhaps there is some secret, or something divine couched under it, concerning which it does not become us to inquire too curiously; nor ought we to regard the scoffs of those who exercise neither piety towards God, nor virtue towards men.' But whether there was anything divine in it or not, Luther found himself extremely happy in his new state, and especially after his wife had brought him a son. 'My rib gate,' says he, in the joy of his heart, 'desires her compliments to you, and thanks you for the favour of your kind letter. She is very well, through God's mercy. She is obedient and complying with me in all things, and more agreeable, I thank God, than I could have expected; so that I would not change my poverty for the wealth of Croesus.' He was heard to say, Seckendorf tells us, 'that he would not exchange his wife for the kingdom of France, nor for the riches of the Venetians, and that for three reasons: first, because she had been given him by God, at the time when he implored the assistance of the Holy Ghost in finding a good wife: secondly, because, though she was not without faults, yet she had fewer than other women: and, thirdly, because she religiously observed the conjugal fidelity she owed him.' There was at first a report that Catherine von Bora was brought to bed soon after her marriage with Luther; but Erasmus, who wrote that news to one of his friends, acknowledged the falsehood of it a little after, in one of his letters, dated the 13th of March, 1526: 'Luther's marriage is certain; the report of his wife's being so speedily brought to bed is false; but I hear she is now with child. If the common story be true, that antichrist shall be born of a monk and a nun, as some pretended, how many thousands of antichrists are there in the world already? I was in hopes that a wife would have made Luther a little tamer: but he, contrary to all expectation, has published, indeed, a most elaborate, but as virulent a book against me, as ever he wrote. What will become of the pacific Erasmus, to be obliged to descend upon the stage at a time of life when gladiators are usually dismissed from the service, and not only to fight, but to fight with beasts!'

In the mean time the disturbances in Germany increased every day; and the war with the Turks, which brought the empire into danger, forced Charles V at length to call a diet at Spires by his letters, May 24th, 1525. After he had given the reasons why the diet was not held the year before, as it was appointed, he said, 'That it was not because he thought that the imperial diets ought not to meddle with matters of religion; for he acknowledged, that, on the contrary, it was his duty to protect the Christian religion, to maintain the rights settled by their ancestors, and to prevent novelties and pernicious doctrines from arising and spreading; but that, being certified that the edict of Worms was not executed in some parts of Germany, that there had been commotions and rebellions in some places, that the princes and members of the empire had many quarrels among themselves, that the Turk was ready to break in upon the territories of the empire, and that there were many disorders which needed a reformation, he had therefore appointed an imperial diet to meet at Augsburg upon the 1st of October.' Few of the princes, however, being able to meet at Augsburg, on account of the popular tumults which prevailed, the diet was prorogued, and fixed again at Spires, where it was held in June, 1526. The emperor was not present in person: but Ferdinand, his brother, and six other deputies, acted in his name. The elector of Saxony, and the landgrave of Hesse, who were of Luther's party, came to it. At the opening of it, upon the 25th, the emperor's deputies proposed such things as were to be the subject of consultation, and said, 'That it was the emperor's design that the members of this diet should prescribe the means of securing the Christian religion, and the ancient discipline of the church derived to us by tradition; the punishments they should suffer who did anything contrary; and how the popish princes might assist each other best in executing the edict of Worms.' The deputies nominated to debate this matter were, among others, the landgrave of Hesse; Sturmius, deputy of Strasburg; and Cressy, deputy of Nuremberg, who embraced Luther's doctrine; so that they could form no resolution conformable to the edict of Worms, but disputes ensued, and things were likely to end in a rupture. The elector of Saxony, landgrave of Hesse, and their party, were ready to withdraw; but Ferdinand, and the emperor's deputies, foreseeing that if the diet broke up with these animosities, and came to no conclusion, all Germany would be in danger of falling into quarrels, took pains to pacify them, and brought them at last to make the following resolution, viz: 'That it being necessary for the welfare of religion and the public peace, to call a national council in Germany, or a general one in Christendom, which should be opened within a year, deputies should be sent to the emperor, to desire him to return to Germany as soon as he could, and to hold a council; and that, in the mean time, the princes and states should so demean themselves concerning the edict of Worms, as to be able to give an account of their carriage to God and the emperor.'

Before this resolution of the diet appeared, the elector of Saxony and landgrave of Hesse proposed to the deputies of Strasburg and Nuremberg to make a league in the defence of those who should follow the new doctrine, and to bring the cities of Frankfurt and Ulm into it; but the deputies could then give no other answer than that they would consult their cities about it. Affairs were now in great confusion in Germany, and they were not less so in Italy; for a quarrel arose between the pope and the emperor, during which Rome was twice taken and the pope imprisoned. While the princes were thus employed in quarrelling with each other, Luther persisted in carrying on the work of the Reformation as well as by opposing the papists, as by combating the anabaptists and other fanatical sects; which, having taken the advantage of his contest with the church of Rome, had sprung up and established themselves in several places. In 1527, Luther was suddenly seized with a coagulation of the blood about the heart, which had like to have put an end to his life; but, recovering from this, he was attacked a second time with a spiritual temptation which he calls 'Colaphus Satanæ – a blow of Satan'. He seemed, as he tells us, to perceive at his left ear a prodigious beating, as it were of the waves of the sea, and this not only within, but also without his head; and so violent withal, that he thought every moment he was going to expire. Afterwards, when he felt it only in the inner part of his head, he grew almost senseless, was all over chilly, and not able to speak; but, recovering himself a little, he applied himself to prayer, made a confession of his faith, and lamented grievously his unworthiness of martyrdom which he had so often and so ardently desired. In this situation he made a will, for he had a son, and his wife was again with child, in which he recommended his family to the care of heaven: 'Lord God,' says he, 'I thank thee that thou wouldst have me poor upon earth, and a beggar. I have neither house, nor land, nor possessions, nor money to leave. Thou hast given me a wife and children; take them, I beseech thee, under thy care, and preserve them as thou hast preserved me.' He was, however, permitted to recover from this terrible condition; bur he often spoke of it afterwards to his friends as one of the severest buffetings he had ever received from Satan. Perhaps our *medical* readers will be disposed to consider it in a very different light.

The troubles of Germany still continuing, the emperor was forced to call a diet at Spires in 1529, to require the assistance of the princes of the empire against the Turks, who had taken Buda, and to find out some means of allaying the contests about religion, which increased daily. In this diet were long and violent debates, after which the decree of the former diet of Spires was again agreed to, in which it was ordered, that concerning the execution of the edict of Worms, the princes of the empire should act in such a manner, as that they might give a good account of their management to God and the emperor. But, because some had taken occasion from these general terms, to maintain all sorts of new doctrines, they made a new decree in this diet, to explain that of the former; by which it was appointed, 'That in those places where the edict of Worms had hitherto been observed, they should still keep to the execution of it, till a council should be called by the emperor; that those who had taken up new opinions, and could not be brought to quit them without the hazard of some sedition, should be quiet for the future, and not admit of any alterations till the meeting of the council; that the new doctrine about the eucharist, which had been started of late, should not be entertained; that the mass should not be left off, nor the celebration of it be hindered, even in those places where the reformed doctrine prevailed; that the anabaptists should be proscribed; that the ministers of the word of God should preach it according to the interpretation of the church, and should abstain from speaking of any other doctrines till the council should meet; that all the provinces of the empire should live in peace, and not commit acts of hostility upon one another, under a pretence of religion; and that one prince should not protect the subjects of another.'

The elector John of Saxony (for Frederic was dead), the elector of Brandenburg, Ernest and Francis, dukes of Brunswick and Lunenburg, the landgrave of Hesse, and the prince of Anhalt, protested against this decree of the diet. Their reasons were, 'That they ought not to do anything to infringe upon the determination of the former diet, which had granted liberty in religion, till the holding of the council; that that resolution having been taken by the unanimous consent of all the members of the empire, could not be repealed but by the like consent; that, in the diet of Nuremberg, the original cause of all the differences in religion was searched into, and that, to allay them, they had offered to the pope eighty articles, to which his holiness had given no answer; that the effect of their consultations had always been, that the best way to end disputes and reform abuses was to hold a council; that they could not suffer opinions to be forced from them, which they judged true and agreeable to the word of God, before the council was held; that their ministers had proved, by invincible arguments taken out of Scripture, that the popish mass was contrary to the institution of Jesus Christ and the practice of the apostles, so that they could not agree to what was ordered in the diet; that they knew the judgment of their churches concerning the presence of the body and blood of Christ in the eucharist; but that they ought not to make a decree against those who were of a contrary opinion, because they were neither summoned nor heard; that they could indeed venture to approve of the clause about preaching the gospel according to the interpretation received in the church, since that did not determine the matter, it being yet in dispute what was the true church; that there was nothing more certain than the word of God itself, which explains itself, and therefore they would take care that nothing else should be taught but the Old and New Testament in their purity; that they are the only infallible rule, and that all human traditions are uncertain; that the decree of the former diet was made for the preservation of peace, but that this last would infallibly beget wars and troubles. For these reasons they could not approve of the decree of the diet, but yet would do nothing that should be blameworthy, till a council, either general or national, should be held.' Fourteen cities, viz., Strasburg, Nuremberg, Ulm, Constance, Retlingen, Windsheim, Memmingen, Lindow, Gempten, Hailbron, Isny, Weissemburg, Nortlingen, St. Gall, joined in this protestation, which was put into writing, and published April 19th, 1529, by an instrument, in which they appealed for all that should be done, to the emperor, a future council, either general or national, or to unsuspected judges; and accordingly they appointed deputies to send to the emperor, to petition that this decree might be revoked. This was the famous protestation, which gave the name of Protestants to the reformers in Germany.

After this, the protestant princes laboured to make a firm league among themselves, and with the free cities, that they might be able to defend each other against the emperor, and the catholic princes. This league had been several times proposed before; but, after the protestation just related, they judged it necessary not to delay it any longer, and so drew up a form of it at Nuremberg. The deputies of the princes and cities having met at Swaback, the affair was there proposed; but the deputies of the elector of Saxony alleging, that since this league was made for the security of the true Christian doctrine, they ought all unanimously to agree about this doctrine; they ordered, therefore, that a summary of their doctrine, contained in several heads, should be read, that it might be received, and approved unanimously by the whole assembly. The deputies of the Protestants, at the diet of Spires, soon after, viz., September 12th, waited upon the emperor at Placentia, where he stayed a little, as he returned from his coronation at Bologna; and assured him, that 'their masters had opposed the decree of that diet for no other reason but because they foresaw it would occasion many troubles; that they implored his imperial majesty not to think ill of them, and to believe, that they would bear their part in the war against the Turks, and other charges of the empire, according to their duty; that they begged his protection, and a favourable answer to the memorial they had presented him'. The emperor, content with their submission, promised them an answer when he had communicated it to his council: and October 13th, sent them word in writing, that 'the decree of the diet seemed to prevent all innovations, and preserve the peace of the empire; that the elector of Saxony and his allies ought to approve of it; that he desired a council as much as they, though that would not have been necessary if the edict of Worms had been duly executed; that what had been once enacted by the major part of the members of the diet could not be disannulled by the opposition of some of them; that he had written to the elector of Saxony and others, to receive and execute the decree of the diet: and hoped they would the sooner submit to his order, because union and peace were necessary at this time, when the Turk was in Germany.'

The deputies having received this answer, drew up an act of appeal, and caused it to be presented to the emperor; which enraged him so extremely, that he confined them to their lodgings, and forbade them to write into Germany upon pain of death. One of the deputies, who happened to be absent when this order was given, wrote immediately to the senate of Nuremberg an account of what had passed; and this was transmitted to the elector of Saxony, the landgrave of Hesse, and other confederates, who met at Smalkald in November. Here it was first of all proposed, to agree upon a confession of faith; which accordingly was prepared, and afterwards offered at the diet of Augsburg, in June, 1530. The emperor would not suffer it to be read in a full diet, but only in a special assembly of the princes and other members of the empire; after which the assembly was dismissed, that they might consult what resolutions should be formed. Some thought that the edict of Worms should be put in execution; others were for referring the matter to the decision of a certain number of honest, learned, and indifferent persons; a third party were for having it confuted by the catholic divines, and the confutation to be read in a full diet before the protestants; and these prevailed. The Protestants afterwards presented an apology for their confession; but the emperor would not receive it; they were, however, both made public. This confession of faith, which was afterwards called 'The confession of Augsburg', was drawn up by Melancthon, the most moderate of all Luther's followers, as was also the apology. He revised and corrected it several times, and, as Dupin tells us, could hardly please Luther at last. Maimbourg says, however, that Luther was exceedingly pleased with it, when Melancthon sent him a copy of it; and Seckendorf allows that Luther was very glad of the opportunity which was offered of letting the world know what he and his followers taught. It was signed by the elector of Saxony, the marquis of Brandenburg, Ernest and Francis, dukes of Brunswick and Lunenburg, the landgrave of Hesse, the princes of Anhalt, and the deputies of the cities of Nuremberg and Retlingen.

Luther had now nothing else to do but to sit down and contemplate the mighty work he had finished; and the remainder of his life was spent in exhorting princes, states, and universities, to confirm the reformation which had been brought about through him, and in publishing from time to time such writings as might encourage, direct, and aid them. The emperor threatened temporal punishments with armies, and the pope eternal with bulls and anathemas; but Luther cared for none of their threats. His friend and coadjutor Melancthon was not so indiferent, owing to the moderation and diffidence of his temper; and hence we find many of Luther's letters written, on purpose to comfort him under his anxieties. 'I am,' says he, in one of these letters, 'much weaker than you in private conflicts, if I may call those conflicts private which I have with the devil; but you are much weaker than me in public. You are all diffidence in the public cause; I, on the contrary, am very sanguine, because I am confident it is a just and a true cause, the cause of God and of Christ, which need not look pale and tremble; whereas the case is very different with me in my private conflicts, who am a very miserable sinner, and therefore have great reason to look pale and tremble. Upon this account it is, that I can be almost an indifferent spectator amidst all the noisy threats and bullyings of the papists; for if we fall, the kingdom of Christ falls with us; and, if it should fall, I had rather fall with Christ than stand with Caesar.' So again, a little further: 'You, Melancthon, cannot bear these disorders, and labour to have things transacted by reason, agreeably to that spirit of calmness and moderation which your philosophy dictates. You might as well attempt to be mad with reason. Do not you see that the matter is entirely out of your power and management, and that even Christ himself forbids your measures to take place?' This letter was written in 1530.

In 1533 Luther wrote a consolatory epistle to the citizens of Oschatz, who had suffered some hardships for adhering to the Augsburg confession of faith; in which, among other things, he says, 'The devil is the host, and the world is his inn, so that wherever you come, you shall be sure to find this ugly host.' He had also about this time a warm controversy with George, duke of Saxony, who had such an aversion to Luther's doctrine, that he obliged his subjects to take an oath that they would never embrace it. Sixty or seventy citizens of Leipzig, however, were found to have deviated a little from the catholic doctrine in some point or other, and they were known previously to have consulted Luther about it; on which George complained to the elector John, that Luther had not only abused his person, but also preached up rebellion among his subjects. The elector ordered Luther to be acquainted with this, and to be told at the same time, that if he did not clear himself of the charge, he could not possibly escape punishment. Luther, however, easily refuted the accusation, by proving that he had been so far front stirring up his subjects against him on the score of religion, that, on the contrary, he had exhorted them rather to undergo the greatest hardships, and even to suffer themselves to be banished.

In 1534, the Bible, translated by him into German, was first printed, as the old privilege, dated at Bibliopolis, under the elector's own hand, shows, and was published the year after. He also published this year a book 'against masses and the consecration of priests', in which he relates a conference he had with the devil upon those points; for it is remarkable in Luther's whole history, that he never had any conflicts of any kind within, which he did not attribute to the personal agency of the devil.[25] In February, 1537, an assembly was held at Smalkald about matters of religion, to which Luther and

---

25. On this subject the following expressions are recorded of Luther: 'When the devil comes to me in the night, I give him these and the like answers – "Devil! I must now sleep, for the command and ordinance of God is, that we should labour by day, and sleep by night." Then, if he goes on with the old story, and accuses me with being a sinner, I say to vex him, *"Holy Satan, pray for me!"* or else, "Physician, *heal thyself!"* 'If you would comfort one who is under temptation, you must kill Moses and stone the law; if, on the contrary, he becomes himself again, and forgets his temptation, you must preach the law to him; "let him who has been afflicted, *be afflicted no more."* The best way to drive out the devil, if he will not go for texts of Scripture, is to jeer and flout him, for he cannot bear scorn.'

Melancthon were called. At this meeting Luther was seized with so dangerous an illness, that there was no hope of his recovery. He was afflicted with the stone, and had a stoppage of urine for eleven days. In this condition he insisted on travelling, notwithstanding all his friends could do to prevent him: his resolution, however, was attended with a good effect, for the night after his departure he began to be better. As he was carried along he made his will, in which he bequeathed his detestation of popery to his friends and brethren; agreeably to what he often used to say, 'Pestis cram vivens, moriens ero morn tua, papa'; that is, 'I was the plague of popery in my life, and shall be its destruction in my death.'

This year the court of Rome, finding it impossible to deal with the protestants by force, began to have recourse to stratagem. They affected, therefore, to think, that though Luther had indeed carried things to a violent extreme, yet what he had pleaded *in* defence of these measures was not entirely without foundation. They talked with a seeming show of moderation; and Pius III, who succeeded Clement VII, proposed a reformation first among themselves, and even went so far as to fix a place for a council to meet at for that purpose. But Luther treated this farce as it deserved to be treated; unmasked and detected it immediately; and, to ridicule it the more strongly, caused a picture to be drawn, in which was represented the pope seated on high upon a throne, some cardinals about him with foxes' tails, and seeming to evacuate upwards and downwards, 'sursum deorsum repurgare', as Melchior Adam expresses it. This was fixed against the title-page to let the readers see at once the scope and design of the book; which was, to expose that cunning and artifice with which those subtle politicians affected to cleanse and purify themselves from their errors and superstitions. Luther published about the same time 'A Confutation of the pretended grant of Constantine to Sylvester bishop of Rome', and also 'Some letters of John Huss', written from his prison at Constance to the Bohemians.

In this manner he was employed till his death, which happened in 1546. That year, accompanied by Melancthon, he paid a visit to his own country, which he had not seen for many years, and returned again in safety: But soon after he was called thither again by the earls of Manafeldt, to compose some differences which had arisen about their boundaries. He had not been used to such matters; but because he was born at Eisleben, a town in the territory of Mansfeldt, he was willing to do his country what service he could, even in this way. Preaching his last sermon, therefore, at Wittenberg, January 17th, he set off on the 23rd; and at Hall in Saxony lodged with Justus Jonas, with whom he stayed three days, because the waters were out. On the 28th he passed over the river with his three sons, and Jonas; and being in some danger, he said to the doctor, 'Do not you think it would rejoice the devil exceedingly, if I and you, and my three sons, should be drowned?' When he entered the territories of the earl of Mansfeldt, he was received by 100 horsemen or more, and conducted in a very honourable manner; but was at the same time so very ill that it was feared he would die. He said that these fits of sickness often came upon him when he had any great business to undertake: of this, however, he did not recover, but died February 18th, in his sixty-third year. A little before he expired, he admonished those that were about him to pray to God for the propagation of the gospel; 'because,' said he, 'the council of Trent, which had sat once or twice, and the pope, will devise strange things against it.' Soon after, his body was put into a leaden coffin, and carried with funeral pomp to the church at Eisleben, when Jonas preached a sermon upon the occasion. The earls of Mansfeldt desired that his body should be interred in their territories; but the elector of Saxony insisted upon his being brought back to Wittenberg, which was accordingly done; and there he was buried with the greatest pomp that perhaps ever happened to any private man. Princes, earls, nobles, and students without number, attended the procession; and Melancthon made his funeral oration.

A thousand falsehoods were invented by the papists about his death. Some said that he died suddenly; others, that he killed himself; others, that the devil strangled him; others, that his corpse stunk so abominably that they were forced to leave it in the way as it was carried to be interred. Similar slanders were even invented about his death, while he was yet alive; for a pamphlet was published at Naples, and in other places of Italy, the year before, wherein was given the following amount: 'Luther, being dangerously sick, desired to communicate, and died as soon as he had received the viaticum. As he was dying, he desired his body might be laid upon the altar, to be adored; but that request being neglected, he was buried. When, lo! at his interment there arose a furious tempest, as if the world was at an end; and the terror was universal. Some, in lifting their hands up to heaven, perceived that the host, which the deceased had presumed to take, was suspended in the air; upon which it was gathered up with great veneration, and laid in a sacred place, and the tempest ceased for the present; but it arose the night following with greater fury, and filled the whole town with consternation; and the next day Luther's sepulchre was found open and empty, and a sulphureous stench proceeded from it, which nobody could bear. The assistants fell sick of it, and many of them repented, and returned to the catholic church.' We have related this as a specimen of the innumerable falsehoods that the papists have invented about Luther; in which, as Bayle observes very truly, they have shewn no regard either to probability, or to the rules of the art of slandering, but have assumed all the confidence of those who fully believe that the public will blindly and implicitly receive their stories, be they ever so absurd and incredible. Luther, however, to give the most effectual refutation of this account of his death, published an advertisement of his being alive; and wrote a book at the same tune to prove that 'Papacy was founded by the devil'. Amidst all this malice of the papists towards Luther, we must not forget a generous action of the emperor Charles V which is an exception to it. While Charles' troops quartered at Wittenberg in 1547, one year after Luther's death, a soldier gave Luther's effigies, in the church of the castle, two stabs with his dagger; and the Spaniards earnestly desired that his tomb might be pulled down, and his bones dug up and burnt: but the emperor wisely answered, 'I have nothing further to do with Luther; he has henceforth another judge, whose jurisdiction it is not lawful for me to usurp. Know, that I make not war with the dead, but with the living, who still make war with me.' He would not therefore suffer his tomb to be demolished; and he forbad any attempt of that nature upon pain of death.

After this long, but we trust, not uninteresting account of the great founder of the Reformation, we shall select only, on the part of the Roman catholics, the opinion of Père Simon respecting his talents as an interpreter of scripture, for this is a part of his character which must appear very important, as he was the first who boldly undertook to reform an overgrown system of idolatry and superstition by the pure word of God. 'Luther,' says this critical author, 'was the first protestant who ventured to translate the Bible into the vulgar tongue from the Hebrew text, although he understood Hebrew but very indifferently. As he was of a free and bold spirit, he accuses St. Jerome of ignorance in the Hebrew tongue; but he had more reason to accuse himself of this fault, and for having so precipitately undertaken a work of this nature, which required more time than he employed about it. Thus we find that he was obliged to review his translation, and make a second edition; but, notwithstanding this review, the most learned protestants of that time could not approve of either the one or the other, and several of them took the liberty to mark the faults, which were very numerous.' In another place he speaks of him not as a translator, but as a commentator, in the following manner: 'Luther, the German Protestants' patriarch, was not satisfied with making a translation of the whole Bible both from the Hebrew and Greek, into his mother tongue, but thought he ought to explain the word of God according to his own method, for the better fixing of their minds whom he had drawn to his party.[26] But this patriarch could succeed no better in his commentaries upon the Bible than in his translation. He made both the one and the other with too little consideration; and he very often consults only his own prejudices. That he might be thought a learned man, he spends time to no purpose in confuting other people's opinions, which he fancies ridiculous. He mixes very improperly theological questions and several other things with his commentaries, so that they may rather be called lectures, and disputes in divinity, than real commentaries. This may be seen in his exposition on Genesis, where there are many idle digressions. He thought, that by reading of morality, and bawling against those who were not of his opinion, he might very much illustrate the word of God; yet one may easily see by his own books, that he was a turbulent and passionate man, who had only a little flashy wit and quickness of invention. There is nothing great or learned in his commentaries upon the Bible; everything low and mean: and as he had studied divinity, he has rather composed a rhapsody of theological questions, than a commentary upon the scripture text: to which we may add, that he wanted understanding, and usually followed his senses instead of his reason.'

This is the language of those in the church of Rome who speak of Luther with any degree of moderation; for the generality allow him neither parts nor learning, nor any attainment intellectual or moral. They tell you that he was not only no divine, but even an outrageous enemy and calumniator of all kinds of science; and that he committed gross, stupid, and abominable errors against the principles of divinity and philosophy. They accuse him of having confessed, that after struggling for ten years together with his conscience, he at last became a perfect master of it, and fell into atheism; and add, that he frequently said he would renounce his portion in heaven, provided God would allow him a pleasant life for one hundred years upon earth. And, lest we should wonder that such monstrous and unheard of impiety should be found

---

26. In speaking of his translations, he says: 'I sweat blood and water in my efforts to render the Prophets into the vulgar tongue. Good God! what a labour to make these Jew writers speak German. They struggle furiously against giving up their beautiful language to our barbarous idiom. 'Tis as though you would force a nightingale to forget her sweet melody, and sing like the cuckoo' (14th June, 1528). He says, elsewhere, that whilst translating the Bible, he sometimes occupied several weeks in hunting out, and meditating upon the signification of a single word.

in a mere human creature, they make no scruple to say that an incubus begat him. These, and many more such scandalous imputations, Bayle has been at the pains to collect, and has treated them with all the contempt and just indignation they deserve.

On the protestant side, the character given of Luther by Dr. Robertson, seems, on the whole, the most just and impartial that has yet appeared. 'As he was raised by Providence,' says this excellent historian, 'to be the author of one of the greatest and most interesting revolutions recorded in history, there is not any person, perhaps, whose character has been drawn with such opposite colours. In his own age, one party, struck with horror and inflamed with rage, when they saw with what a daring hand he overturned everything which they held to be sacred or valued as beneficial, imputed to him not only the defects and vices of a man, but the qualities of a demon. The other, warmed with the admiration and gratitude which they thought he merited, as the restorer of light and liberty to the Christian church, ascribed to him perfections above the condition of humanity, and viewed all his actions with a veneration bordering on that which should be paid only to those who are guided by the immediate inspiration of heaven. It is his own conduct, not the undistinguishing censure or the extravagant praise of his contemporaries that ought to regulate the opinions of the present age concerning him. Zeal for what he regarded as truth; undaunted intrepidity to maintain his own system; abilities, both natural and acquired, to defend his principles; and unwearied industry in propagating them; are virtues which shine so conspicuously in every part of his behaviour, that even his enemies must allow him to have possessed them in an eminent degree. To these may be added, with equal justice, such purity and even austerity of manners, as became one who assumed the character of a reformer; such sanctity of life as suited the doctrine which he delivered; and such perfect disinterestedness, as affords no slight presumption of his sincerity. Superior to all selfish considerations, a stranger to the elegancies of life, and despising its pleasures, he left the honours and emoluments of the church to his disciples, remaining satisfied himself in his original state of professor in the university, and pastor of the town of Wittenberg, with the moderate appointments annexed to these offices. His extraordinary qualities were allayed by no inconsiderable mixture of human frailties and human passions. These, however, were of such a nature, that they cannot be imputed to malevolence or corruption of heart, but seem to have taken their rise from the same source with many of his virtues.[27] His mind, forcible and vehement in all its operations, roused by great objects, or agitated by violent passions, broke out, on many occasions, with an impetuosity which astonishes men of feebler spirits, or such as are placed in a more tranquil situation. By carrying some praiseworthy dispositions to excess, he bordered sometimes on what was culpable, and was often betrayed into actions which exposed him to censure. His confidence that his own opinions were well founded, approached to arrogance; his courage in asserting them, to rashness; his firmness in adhering to them, to obstinacy; and his zeal in confuting his adversaries, to rage and scurrility. Accustomed himself to consider everything as subordinate to truth, he expected the same deference for it from other men; and, without making any allowances for their timidity or prejudices, he poured forth against such as disappointed him in this particular, a torrent of invective mingled with contempt. Regardless of any distinction of rank or character, when his doctrines were attacked he chastised all his adversaries indiscriminately, with the same rough hand: neither the royal dignity of Henry VIII, nor the eminent learning and abilities of Erasmus, screened them from the same gross abuse with which he treated Tetzel or Eckius.

'But these indecencies of which Luther was guilty, must not be imputed wholly to the violence of his temper. They ought to be charged in part on the manners of the age. Among a rude people, unacquainted with those maxims, which, by putting constraint on the passions of individuals, have polished society, and rendered it agreeable, disputes of every kind were managed with heat, and strong emotions were uttered in their natural language without reserve or delicacy. At the same time, the works of learned men were all composed in Latin; and they were not only authorized, by the example of eminent writers in that language, to use their antagonists with the most illiberal scurrility; but, in a dead tongue, indecencies of every kind appear less shocking than in a living language, whose idioms and phrases seem gross, because they are familiar.

'In passing judgment upon the characters of men, we ought to try them by the principles and maxims of their own age, not by those of another. For, although virtue and vice are at all times the same, manners and customs vary continually. Some parts of Luther's behaviour which to us appear most

---

27. To this sketch may be added: Luther was fond of simple enjoyments. He often joined his guests, in their musical entertainments, and played at skittles with them. Melancthon says of him: 'Whoever was familiarly acquainted with Luther, and knew his habits, will allow that he was a most excellent man, agreeable and gentle in society, and in no respect dogmatic, or a lover of disputation, yet with all the gravity becoming his character.'

culpable, gave no disgust to his contemporaries. It was even by some of those qualities which we are now apt to blame, that he was fitted for accomplishing the great work he undertook. To rouse mankind, when sunk in ignorance or superstition, and to encounter the rage of bigotry armed with power, required the utmost vehemence of zeal, as well as a temper daring to excess. A gentle call would neither have reached, nor have etched those to whom it was addressed. A spirit more amiable, but less vigorous than Luther's, would have shrunk back from the dangers which he braved and surmounted. Towards the close of Luther's life, though without any perceptible diminution of his zeal or abilities, the infirmities of his temper increased upon him, so that he grew daily more peevish, more irascible, and more impatient of contradiction. Having lived to be a witness of his own amazing success; to see a great part of Europe embrace his doctrines; and to shake the foundation of the papal throne, before which the mightiest monarchs had trembled, he discovered, on some occasions symptoms of vanity and self-applause. He must have been, indeed, more than man, if, upon contemplating all that he actually accomplished, he had never felt any sentiments of this kind rising in his breast.'

His works ware collected after his death, and printed at Wittenberg in seven volumes folio. Catherine von Bora survived her husband a few years, and continued the first year of her widowhood at Wittenberg, though Luther had advised her to seek another place of residence. She went from thence in 1597, when the town was surrendered to the emperor Charles V. Before her departure, she had received a present of fifty crowns from Christian III, King of Denmark; and the elector of Saxony, and the counts of Mansfeldt, gave her good tokens of their liberality. With these additions to what Luther had left her, she was enabled to maintain herself and her family handsomely. She returned to Wittenberg when the town was restored to the elector, where she lived a very devout and pious life, till the plague obliged her to leave it again in 1552. She sold what she had at Wittenberg, and retired to Torgau, with a resolution to end her life there. An unfortunate mischance befell her in her journey thither, which proved fatal to her. The horses growing unruly, and attempting to run away, she leaped out of the vehicle, and had a fall, of which she died abort a quarter of a year after, at Torgau, Dec. 20th, 1552. She was buried there in the great church, where her tomb and epitaph are still to be seen; and the university of Wittenberg, which was then at Torgau because the plague raged at Wittenberg, made a public programma concerning the funeral pomp.[28]

Lutheranism has undergone some alteration since the time of its founder. Luther rejected the epistle of St. James, as inconsistent with the doctrine of

St. Paul, in relation to justification; he also set aside the Apocalypse; both of which are now received as canonical in the Lutheran church. Luther reduced the number of sacraments to two, viz., baptism, and the eucharist; but he believed the impanation, or consubstantiation: that is, that the matter of the bread and wine remain with the body and blood of Christ; and it is in this article, that the main difference between the Lutheran and English churches consists. Luther maintained the mass to be no sacrifice; he exploded the adoration of the host, auricular confession, meritorious works, indulgences, purgatories, the worship of images, etc. which had been introduced in the corrupt times of the Romish church. He also opposed the doctrine of free-will; maintained predestination; asserted that we are necessitated in all we do; that all our actions done in a state of sin, and even the virtues themselves of heathens, are crimes; that we are justified only by the merits and satisfaction of Christ. He also opposed the fastings in the Roman church, monastical vows, the celibacy of the clergy, etc.

---

28. Audin (the Catholic biographer) gives a somewhat different account of the last days of Luther's widow. He says: 'The Protestant princes soon forgot her. Some years after the death of her husband, she was involved in the deepest distress, and had not bread to give her children. Even king Christian gave her assistance on only one occasion. After wandering about, and begging her bread for some years, she died in 1552, at Torgau, and was buried in the parish church there.' The *Petites Affiches* of Altona, for the 15th of November, 1837, contains the following advertisement, headed 'Luther's Orphans':

'These are the children of Joseph Charles Luther, born at Erfurt, 11th November, 1792, and who returned to the Catholic church. He died in Bohemia.

'M. Reinthaler, administrator of the institution of St. Martin, erected at Erfurt in honour of Luther, has received these poor orphans under his care.

'On May 6th, 1830, Antony, the eldest, born in 1821, came to the ancient convent of the Augustines. Instructed in the principles of the Reformation, he made his first communion at Easter. He has since been apprenticed to a cabinet-maker. Two of his sisters, Mary and Ann, are at service in an inn; the youngest, Theresa, is at school.'

M. Reinthaler made this appeal to his co-religionists (the Protestants) with scarcely any effect. Frankfurt-on-the-Maine and Leipzig sent fifty thalers, and that was all.

# CATECHISM OF DR. MARTIN LUTHER

———

## I. THE FIRST HEAD

THE HOLY TEN COMMANDMENTS OF GOD, OR THE DECALOGUE
God spake these words, and said, I am the Lord thy God.

### THE FIRST COMMANDMENT

Thou shalt have no other Gods but me. Thou shalt not make to thyself any graven image, nor the likeness of any thing that is in heaven above or in the earth beneath, or in the water under the earth. Thou shalt not bow down to them, nor worship them: for I the Lord thy God am a jealous God and visit the sins of the fathers upon the children, unto the third and fourth generation of them that hate me: and shew mercy unto thousands of them that love me, and keep my commandments.

*What doth this Commandment teach?*
That we ought to fear and love God above all things, and to put our trust in him only.

### THE SECOND COMMANDMENT

Thou shalt not take the name of the Lord thy God in vain: for the Lord will not hold him guiltless that taketh his name in vain.
*What doth this Commandment teach?*

That we ought to fear and love God, and to avoid profane cursing, imprecations, conjurations, lies and deceits, by his holy name; and that in all our wants we must call upon that name, worship it, and praise it with thanksgivings.

### THE THIRD COMMANDMENT
Remember that thou keep holy the Sabbath-day. Six days shalt thou labour, and do all that thou hast to do; but the seventh day is the Sabbath of the Lord thy God: in it thou shalt do no manner of work, thou, and thy son, and thy daughter, thy man-servant and thy maid-servant, thy cattle, and the stranger that is within thy gates. For in six days the Lord made heaven and earth, the sea, and all that in them is, and rested the seventh day: wherefore the Lord blessed the seventh day and hallowed it.

*What doth this Commandment teach?*
That we ought to fear and love God, and not despise godly preaching or his Word; but that we account it holy, willingly hear and learn it.

### THE FOURTH COMMANDMENT
Honour thy father and thy mother, that thy days may be long in the land, which the Lord thy God giveth thee.

*What doth this Commandment teach?*
That we ought to fear and love God, and not despise our parents or superiors, neither provoke them to anger, but honour them, serve them, reverence them, love and highly esteem them.

### THE FIFTH COMMANDMENT
Thou shalt do no murder.

*What doth this Commandment teach?*
That we ought to fear and love God, and not to molest or damage the life of our neighbour, but that we assist him and serve him in every want or danger both of soul and body.

### THE SIXTH COMMANDMENT
Thou shalt not commit adultery.

*What doth this Commandment teach?*
That we ought to fear and love God, that we may live modestly and chastely both in word and deed; and that all who are married do love and honour each other.

## THE SEVENTH COMMANDMENT
Thou shalt not steal.

*What doth this Commandment teach?*
That we ought to fear and love God, and not take away from our neighbour his goods or money, or obtain them by fraud or bad wares; but that we labour to preserve his substance, and better his circumstances.

## THE EIGHTH COMMANDMENT
Thou shalt not bear false witness against thy neighbour.

*What doth this Commandment teach?*
That we ought to fear and love God, and not to distress, betray, or traduce our neighbour by any falsehood, nor bring any infamy upon him; but that we excuse for him, think and speak well of him, and that we receive and interpret all things of him in a favourable light.

## THE NINTH COMMANDMENT
Thou shalt not covet thy neighbour's house.

*What doth this Commandment teach?*
That we ought to fear and love God, and not seize by wicked cunning the inheritance or house of our neighbour, and under shadow of right or law annex them to our own; but rather we ought to assist him, that his property may be kept entire.

## THE TENTH COMMANDMENT
Thou shalt not covet thy neighbour's wife, nor his servant, nor his maid, nor his ox, nor his ass, nor any thing that is his.

*What doth this Commandment teach?*
That we ought to fear and love God, so that we do not alienate from our neighbour, or withdraw from him his wife, his man-servants, his maidservants, or his cattle; but that we exhort urge and admonish them severally with all diligence to discharge their duty.

*What saith God generally concerning all these Commandments?*
I, the Lord thy God am a jealous God, visiting the iniquity of the fathers upon the children, unto the third and fourth generation of them that hate me, and showing mercy unto thousands on them that love me, and keep my commandments.

*What do these words mean?*
God threateneth punishment to all that transgress and violate his commands; we ought therefore to tremble at and fear God's wrath, and to do nothing against his commands; again he also promises his grace, and all good things to all who keep his commandments; therefore we ought to love God and trust in him, and to frame earnestly and diligently our lives always according to his commands.

## II. THE SECOND HEAD

THE APOSTLES' CREED

### *THE FIRST ARTICLE – OF CREATION*
I BELIEVE in God the Father Almighty, Maker of heaven and earth.

*What meaneth this Article?*
I believe that God hath created me together with all creatures; that he hath given me a body, a soul, eyes, ears, and all my members, reason, and all my senses, and these he still preserveth. Moreover that he plentifully and daily giveth me food and raiment, an habitation, wife, children, lands, flocks, and all good things, with all the necessaries of life; that he protecteth me against all dangers, freeth and delivereth me from all evils, and he doth all these things out of his mere fatherly and divine goodness and mercy, without any desert of mine, or any worth; for all which things I deservedly ought with all my might to thank, to praise, to worship and obey him. This is most assuredly true.

### *THE SECOND ARTICLE – OF REDEMPTION*
AND in Jesus Christ his only Son our Lord, who was conceived by the Holy Ghost, born of the Virgin Mary, suffered under Pontius Pilate, was crucified, dead and buried; he descended into hell; the third day he rose again from the dead; he ascended into heaven, and sitteth on the right hand of God the Father Almighty; from thence he shall come to judge the quick and the dead.

*What meaneth this Article?*

I believe that Jesus Christ, the true God, and also true man, born of the Virgin Mary, is my Lord, who hath redeemed me a lost and condemned man, and hath delivered me from all sins, from death, and the power of Satan; not with gold and silver, but with his holy and precious blood, and by his innocent sufferings and death, that I might be wholly his, and might live under him in his kingdom, and serve him in everlasting righteousness, innocency, and happiness, in like manner as he himself rose from the dead, and liveth and reigneth for ever and ever. This is most assuredly true.

### THE THIRD ARTICLE – OF SANCTIFICATION

I believe in the Holy Ghost; the holy catholic church; the communion of saints; the forgiveness of sins; the resurrection of the body, and the life everlasting. Amen.

*What meaneth this Article?*

I believe that I, by the strength of my own reason, can by no means believe in Jesus Christ, or approach or come unto him; but the Holy Ghost through the Gospel hath called me and enlightened me with his gifts, sanctified me by a true faith, and has preserved me; even as he is wont to call, to assemble, to enlighten, and to sanctify the whole church throughout the world, and to preserve them by Jesus Christ in the only true faith; in which church he daily doth most mercifully forgive all sins to me, and all Christians, and in the last day will raise us all from the dead, and will give everlasting life to me, and to all that truly believe in Christ. This is most assuredly true.

## III. THE THIRD HEAD

THE LORD'S PRAYER

*PREFACE*

OUR Father, who art in Heaven.

*What meaneth these words?*

God lovingly inviteth us, in this little preface, truly to believe in him, that he is our true Father and that we are truly his children, so that full of confidence we may more boldly call upon his name, even as we see children with a kind of confidence ask anything of their parents.

## THE FIRST PETITION
Hallowed be thy name.

*What meaneth this Petition?*
The name of God truly is of itself holy, but we ask in this petition that it may be hallowed by us.

*How doth that come to pass?*
When the Word of God is taught with purity and sincerity, and we, as becometh children of God, live godly according thereto; which, that it may be the case, vouchsafe us, O my Father, who art in heaven! But whoso teacheth and practiseth it otherwise than God's Word teacheth, he profaneth God's name amongst us; forbid this from coming to pass, O my heavenly Father!

## THE SECOND PETITION
Thy kingdom come.

*What meaneth this Petition?*
The kingdom of God truly cometh of itself without our prayers, but by this petition we pray also, that it may come unto us.

*How cometh that to pass?*
When the heavenly Father giveth us his Holy Spirit, who worketh by his grace so, that we believe his Holy Word, and live a godly life both in time and eternity.

## THE THIRD PETITION
Thy will be done in earth as it is in heaven.

*What meaneth this Petition?*
The good and merciful will of God is done even without our prayers, but we ask in this petition, that it may be done by us.

*How cometh that to pass?*
When God breaketh and hindereth every evil counsel, will, and attempt, so working that we the less sanctify the name of God, and whereby the coming of his kingdom to us is prevented; such is the will of the devil, the world, and our own flesh; but comforteth and preserveth us steadily in his word and faith to the end of our life; this is the good and merciful will of God.

## THE FOURTH PETITION
Give us this day our daily bread.

*What meaneth this Petition?*
God giveth indeed to all daily bread, though we ask it not, and that to wicked men; but we pray in this petition, that we may acknowledge this benefit, and so may receive our daily bread with thanksgiving.

*What do you mean by daily bread?*
I mean by it every thing that belongeth to the want and supply of our life; that is, meat, drink, clothes, dwelling, gardens, lands, flocks, money, wealth, happy marriage, virtuous children, faithful servants, upright and just magistrates, peaceful government, wholesome air, quietness, health, modesty, honour, true friends, faithful neighbours, and other things of the like kind.

## THE FIFTH PETITION
And forgive us our trespasses as we forgive them that trespass against us.

*What meaneth this Petition?*
We ask in this prayer, that our Heavenly Father would not look upon and examine our sins, and reject our prayers upon that account; seeing, we are worthy of none of those things which we ask, neither are we able to deserve anything, but that he would give us all things through his grace and goodness; because every day we sin many times, and deserve only punishment: and on the other hand, that we may heartily forgive whatsoever others have done against us, and freely render good for evil.

## THE SIXTH PETITION
And lead us not into temptation.

*What meaneth this Petition?*
God indeed tempteth no man; but yet we ask, in this petition, that he would keep and preserve us, lest the devil, the world, and our own flesh delude and draw us away from the true faith, and throw us into superstition, distrust, despair, and other grievous sins and wickedness; and that, if we should be tempted therewith even to the highest degree, we still may conquer, and at last triumph over them.

*THE SEVENTH PETITION*
But deliver us from evil.

*What meaneth this Petition?*
We beg in this prayer, as it were the whole, that our heavenly Father would deliver us from all evils and dangers of body and soul, of goods, and of honour; and that, when the hour of death cometh, he would give us a happy departure out of this world and through his gracious goodness would receive us out of this valley of misery unto himself in heaven.

*CONCLUSION*
For thine is the kingdom, and the power, and the glory, for ever and ever, Amen.

*What is the meaning of this word, Amen?*
Amen meaneth assuredly, namely, that I am sure that petitions of this kind are accepted by my Heavenly Father, and heard by him, because he bath commanded us, that we should pray after this manner, and bath promised that he will hear us. Amen, Amen: that is, truly, certainly, so be it.

# LUTHER'S TABLE-TALK

# OF GOD'S WORD

---

## 1

THAT the Bible is God's word and book I prove thus: All things that have been, and are, in the world, and the manner of their being, are described in the first book of Moses on the creation; even as God made and shaped the world, so does it stand to this day. Infinite potentates have raged against this book, and sought to destroy and uproot it-king Alexander the Great, the princes of Egypt and of Babylon, the monarchs of Persia, of Greece, and of Rome, the emperors Julius and Augustus – but they nothing prevailed; they are all gone and vanished, while the book remains, and will remain for ever and ever, perfect and entire, as it was declared at the first. Who has thus helped it-who has thus protected it against such mighty forces? No one, surely, but God himself, who is the master of all things. And 'tis no small miracle how God has so long preserved and protected this book; for the devil and the world are sure foes to it. I believe that the devil has destroyed many good books of the church, as, aforetime, he killed and crushed many holy persons, the memory of whom has now passed away: but the Bible he was fain to leave subsisting. In like manner have baptism, the sacrament of the altar, of the true body and blood of Christ, and the office of preaching remained unto us, despite the infinitude of tyrants and heretic persecutors. God, with singular strength, has upheld these things; let us, then, baptize, administer the sacrament, and preach, fearless of impediment. Homer, Virgil, and other noble, fine, and profitable writers, have left us books of great antiquity; but they are nought to the Bible.

While the Romish church stood, the Bible was never given to the people in such a shape that they could clearly, understandingly, surely, and easily read it, as they now can in the German translation, which, thank God, we have prepared here at Wittenberg.

## 2

The Holy Scriptures are full of divine gifts and virtues. The books of the heathen taught nothing of faith, hope, or charity; they present no idea of these things; they contemplate only the present, and that which man, with the use of his material reason, can grasp and comprehend. Look not therein for aught of hope or trust in God. But see how the Psalms and the Book of Job treat faith, hope, resignation, and prayer; in a word, the Holy Scripture is the highest and best of books, abounding in comfort under all afflictions and trials. It teaches us to see, to feel, to grasp, and to comprehend faith, hope, and charity, far otherwise than mere human reason can; and when evil oppresses us, it teaches how these virtues throw light upon the darkness, and how, after this poor, miserable existence of ours on earth, there is another and an eternal life.

## 3

St. Jerome, after he had revised and corrected the Septuagint, translated the Bible from Hebrew into Latin; his version is still used in our church. Truly, for one man, this was work enough and to spare. *Nulla enim private persona, tantum a efficere potuisset.* 'Twould have been quite as well had he called to his aid one or two learned men, for the Holy Ghost would then have more powerfully manifested itself unto him, according to the words of Christ: 'Where two or three are gathered together in my name, there am I in the midst of them.' Interpreters and translators should not work alone; for good *et propria verbs* do not always occur to one mind.

## 4

We ought not to criticise, explain, or judge the Scriptures by our mere reason, but diligently, with prayer, meditate thereon, and seek their meaning. The devil and temptations also afford us occasion to learn and understand the Scriptures, by experience and practice. Without these we should never understand them, however diligently we read and listened to them. The Holy Ghost must here be our only master and tutor; and let youth have no shame to learn of that preceptor. When I find myself assailed by temptation, I forthwith lay hold of some text of the Bible, which Jesus extends to me; as this: that he died for me, whence I derive infinite hope.

## 5

He who has made himself master of the principles and text of the word, runs little risk of committing errors. A theologian should be thoroughly in possession of the basis and source of faith-that is to say, the Holy Scriptures. Armed with this knowledge it was that I confounded and silenced all my adversaries; for they seek not to fathom and understand the Scriptures; they run them over negligently and drowsily; they speak, they write, they teach, according to the suggestion of their heedless imaginations. My counsel is, that we draw water from the true source and fountain, that is, that we diligently search the Scriptures. He who wholly possesses the text of the Bible, is a consummate divine. One single verse, one sentence of the text, is of far more instruction than a whole host of glosses and commentaries, which are neither strongly penetrating nor armour of proof. As, when I have that text before me of St. Paul: 'All the creatures of God are good, if they be received with thanksgiving,' this text shows, that what God has made is good. Now eating, drinking, marrying, etc., are of God's making, therefore they are good. Yet the glosses of the primitive fathers are against this text: for Bernard, Basil, Jerome, and others, have written to far other purpose. But I prefer the text to them all, though, in popedom, the glosses were deemed of higher value than the right and clear text.

## 6

Let us not lose the Bible, but with diligence, in fear and invocation of God, read and preach it. While that remains and flourishes, all prospers with the state; 'tis head and empress of all arts and faculties. Let but divinity fall, and I would not give a straw for the rest.

## 7

The school divines, with their speculations in holy writ, deal in pure vanities, in mere imaginings derived from human reason. Bonaventura, who is full of them, made me almost deaf. I sought to learn in his book, how God and my soul had become reconciled, but got no information from him. They tally much of the union of the will and understanding, but 'tis all idle fantasy. The right, practical divinity is this: Believe in Christ, and do thy duty in that sate of life to -which God has called thee. In like manner, the *Mystical divinity of*

*Dionysius is* a mere fable and lie. With Plato he chatters: *Omnia sunt non eras, et omnia sunt ens* — (all is something, and all is nothing ) — and so leaves things hanging.

## 8

Dr. Jonas Justus remarked at Luther's table: There is in the Holy Scripture a wisdom so profound, that no man may thoroughly study it or comprehend it. 'Ay,' said Luther, 'we must ever remain scholars here; we cannot sound the depth of one single verse in Scripture; we get hold but of the A B C, and that imperfectly. Who can so exalt himself as to comprehend this one line of St. Peter: "Rejoice, inasmuch as ye are partakers of Christ's sufferings." Here St. Peter would have us rejoice in our deepest misery and trouble, like as a child kisses the rod.'

## 9

The Holy Scriptures surpass in efficaciousness all the arts and all the sciences of the philosophers and jurists; these, though good and necessary to life here below, are vain and of no effect as to what concerns the life eternal. The Bible should be regarded with wholly different eyes from those with which we view other productions. He who wholly renounces himself, and relies not on mere human reason, will make good progress in the Scriptures; but the world comprehends them not, from ignorance of that mortification which is the gift of God's word. Can he who understands not God's word, understand God's works? This is manifest in Adam: he called his first-born son, Cain — that is, possessor, house-lord; this son, Adam and Eve thought, would be the man of God, the blessed seed that would crush the serpent's head. Afterward, when Eve was with child again, they hoped to have a daughter, that their beloved son, Cain, might have a wife; but Eve bearing again a son, called him Abel — that is, vanity and nothingness; as much as to say, my hope is gone and I am deceived. This was an image of the world and of God's church, showing how things have ever gone. The ungodly Cain was a great lord in the world, while Abel, that upright and pious man, was an outcast, subject and oppressed. But before God, the case was quite contrary: Cain was rejected of God, Abel accepted and received as God's beloved child. The like is daily seen here on earth, therefore let us not heed its doings. Ishmael's was also a fair name — *hearer of God* — while Isaac's was naught. Esau's name means *actor*, the man that shall do the work — Jacob's was naught. The name Absalom, signifies *father of peace*. Such fair and glorious colours do the ungodly ever bear in this world, while in truth and deed they are contemners, scoffers, and rebels to the word of God. But by that word, we, God be praised, are able to discern and know all such; therefore let us hold the Bible in precious esteem, and diligently read it.

To world wisdom, there seems no lighter or more easy art than divinity, and the understanding of God's word, so that the children of the world will be reputed fully versed in the Scriptures and catechism, but they shoot far from the mark. I would give all my fingers, save three to write with, could I find divinity so easy and light as they take it to be. The reason why men deem it so is that they become soon wearied, and think they know enough of it. So we found it in the world, and so we must leave it; but *in fine videbitur, cujus toni*.

## 10

I have many times essayed thoroughly to investigate the ten commandments, but at the very outset, 'I am the Lord thy God,' I stuck fast; that very one word, I, put me to a *non plus*. He that has but one word of God before him, and out of that word cannot make a sermon, can never be a preacher. I am well content that I know, however little, of what God's word is, and take good heed not to murmur at my small knowledge.

## 11

I have grounded my preaching upon the literal word; he that pleases may follow me; he that will not may stay. I call upon St. Peter, St. Paul, Moses, and all the Saints, to say whether they ever fundamentally comprehended one single word of God, without studying it over and over and over again. The Psalm says: *His understanding is infinite*. The saints, indeed, know God's word, and can discourse of it, but the practice is another matter; therein we shall ever remain scholars.

The school theologians have a fine similitude hereupon, that it is as with a sphere or globe, which, lying on a table, touches it only with one point, yet it is the whole table which supports the globe. Though I am an old doctor of divinity, to this day I have not got beyond the children's learning – the Ten Commandments, the Belief, and the Lord's Prayer; and these I understand not so well as I should, though I study them daily, praying, with my son John and my daughter Magdalen. If I thoroughly appreciated these first words of the Lord's Prayer, *Our Father, which art in Heaven*, and really believed that God, who made heaven and earth, and all creatures, and has all things in his hand, was my Father, then should I certainly conclude with myself, that I also am a lord of heaven and earth, that Christ is my brother, Gabriel my servant, Raphael my coachman, and all the angels my attendants at need, given unto me by my heavenly Father, to keep me in the path, that unawares I knock not my foot against a stone. But that our faith may be exercised and confirmed, our heavenly Father suffers us to be cast into dungeons, or plunged in water. So we may see how finely we understand these words, and how belief shakes, and how great our weakness is, so that we begin to think – Ah, who knows how far that is true which is set forth in the Scriptures?

## 12

No greater mischief can happen to a Christian people, than to have God's word taken from them, or falsified, so that they no longer have it pure and clear. God grant we and our descendants be not witnesses of such a calamity.

## 13

When we have God's word pure and clear, then we think ourselves all right; we become negligent, and repose in a vain security; we no longer pay due heed, thinking it will always so remain; we do not watch and pray against the devil, who is ready to tear the Divine word out of our hearts. It is with us as with travellers, who, so long as they are on the highway, are tranquil and heedless, but if they go astray into woods or cross paths, uneasily seek which way to take, this or that.

## 14

The great men and the doctors understand not the word of God, but it is revealed to the humble and to children, as is testified by the Saviour in the Gospel according to St. Matthew 11:25: 'O Father, Lord of heaven and earth, because thou hast hid these things from the wise and prudent, and hast revealed them unto babes.' Gregory says, well and rightly, that the Holy Scripture is a stream of running water, where alike the elephant may swim, and the lamb walk without losing its feet.

## 15

The great unthankfulness, contempt of God's word, and wilfulness of the world, make me fear that the divine light will soon cease to shine on man, for God's word has ever had its certain course.

In the time of the kings of Judah, Baal obscured the brightness of God's word, and it became hard labour to destroy his empire over the hearts of men. Even in the time of the apostles, there were heresies, errors, and evil doctrines spread abroad by false brethren. Next came Arius, and the word of God was hidden behind dark clouds, but the holy fathers, Ambrose, Hilary, Augustine, Athanasius, and others, dispersed the obscurity. Greece and many other countries have heard the word of God, but have since abandoned it, and it is to be feared even now it may quit Germany, and go into other lands. I hope the last day will not be long delayed. The darkness grows thicker around us, and godly servants of the Most High become rarer and more rare. Impiety and licentiousness are rampant throughout the world, and we live, like pigs, like wild beasts, devoid of all reason. But a voice will soon be heard thundering forth: *Behold, the bridegroom cometh.* God will not be able to bear this wicked world much longer, but will come, with the dreadful day, and chastise the scorners of his word.

### 16

Kings, princes, lords, any one will needs understand the gospel far better than I, Martin Luther, ay, or even than St. Paul; for they deem themselves wise and full of policy. But herein they scorn and contemn, not us, poor preachers and ministers, but the Lord and Governor of all preachers and ministers, who has sent us to preach and teach, and who will scorn and contemn them in such sort, that they shall smart again; even He that says: 'Whoso heareth you, heareth me; and whoso toucheth you, toucheth the apple of mine eye.' The great ones would govern, but they know not how.

### 17

Dr. Justus Jonas told Dr. Martin Luther of a noble and powerful Misnian, who above all things occupied himself in amassing gold and silver, and was so buried in darkness, that he gave no heed to the five books of Moses, and had even said to Duke John Frederic, who was discoursing with him upon the gospel: 'Sir, the gospel pays no interest.' 'Have you no grains?' interposed Luther; and then told this fable: 'A lion making a great feast, invited all the beasts, and with them some swine. When all manner of dainties were set before the guests, the swine asked: "Have you no grains?" 'Even so,' continued the doctor, 'even so, in these days, it is with our epicureans: we preachers set before them, in our churches, the most dainty and costly dishes, as everlasting salvation, the remission of sins, and God's grace; but they, like swine, turn up their snouts, and ask for guilders: offer a cow nutmeg, and she will reject it for old hay. This reminds me of the answer of certain parishioners to their minister, Ambrose R. He had been earnestly exhorting them to come and listen to the Word of God: "Well," said they, "if you will tap a good barrel of beer for us, we'll come with all our hearts and hear you." The gospel at Wittenberg is like unto the rain which, falling upon a river, produces little effect; but descending upon a dry, thirsty soil, renders it fertile.'

### 18

Some one asked Luther for his Psalter, which was old and ragged, promising to give him a new one in exchange; but the doctor refused, because he was used to his own old copy, adding: 'A local memory is very useful, and I have weakened mine in translating the Bible.'

### 19

Our case will go on, so long as its living advocates, Melancthon, and other pious and learned persons, who apply themselves zealously to the work, shall be alive; but, after their death, 'twill be a sad falling off. We have an example before us, in Judges 2:10: 'And also all that generation were gathered unto their fathers; and there arose another generation after them, which knew not the Lord, nor yet the works which he had done for Israel.' So, after the death of the apostles, there were fearful fallings off ; nay, even while they yet lived, as St. Paul complains, there was falling off among the Galatians, the Corinthians, and in Asia. We shall be occasioned much suffering and loss by the Sacramentarians, the Anabaptists, the Antinomians, and other sectaries.

### 20

Oh! how great and glorious a thing it is to have before one the Word of God! With that we may at all times feel joyous and secure; we need never be in want of consolation, for we see before us, in all its brightness, the pure and right way. He who loses sight of the word of God, falls into despair; the voice of heaven no longer sustains him; he follows only the disorderly tendency of his heart, and of world vanity, which lead him on to his destruction.

### 21

Christ, in Matthew 5, 6, 7, teaches briefly these points: first, as to the eight happinesses or blessings, how every Christian ought particularly to live as it concerns himself; secondly, of the office of teaching, what and how a man ought to teach in the church, how to season with salt and enlighten, reprove, and comfort, and exercise the faith; thirdly, he confutes and opposes the false expounding of the law; fourthly, he condemns the wicked hypocritical kind of living; fifthly, he teaches what are upright and good works; sixthly, he warns men of false doctrine; seventhly, he clears and solves what might be found doubtful and confused; eighthly, he condemns the hypocrites and false saints, who abuse the precious word of grace.

### 22

St. Luke describes Christ's passion better than the rest; John is more complete as to Christ's works; he describes the audience, and how the cause was handled, and how they proceeded before the seat of judgment, and how Christ was questioned, and for what cause he was slain.

When Pilate asked him: 'Art thou the king of the Jews?' 'Yea,' said Christ, 'I am; but not such a king as the emperor is, for then my servants and armies would fight and strive to deliver and defend me; but I am a king sent to preach the gospel, and give record of the truth which I must speak.'

'What!' said Pilate, 'art thou such a king, and hast thou a kingdom that consists in word and truth? then surely thou canst be no prejudice to me.' Doubtless Pilate took our Saviour Christ to be a simple, honest, ignorant man, one perchance come out of a wilderness, a simple fellow, a hermit, who knew or understood nothing of the world, or of government.

### 23

In the writings of St. Paul and St. John is a surpassing certainty, knowledge, and *plerophoria*. They write as if all they narrate had been already done before their eyes.

Christ rightly says of St. Paul, he shall be a chosen instrument and vessel unto me; therefore be was made a doctor, and therefore he spake so certainly of the cause. Whoso reads Paul may, with a safe conscience, build upon his words; for my part, I never read more serious writings.

St. John, in his gospel, describes Christ, that he is a true and natural man, *à priori*, from former time: 'In the beginning was the word;' and 'Whoso honoureth me, the same honoureth also the Father.' But Paul describes Christ, *à posteriori et effectu,* from that which follows, and according to the actions or works, as, 'They tempted Christ in the wilderness;' 'Take heed, therefore, to yourselves,' etc.

## 24

The book of Solomon's Proverbs is a fine book, which rulers and governors should diligently read, for it contains lessons touching God's anger, wherein governors and rulers should exercise themselves.

The author of the book of Ecclesiasticus preaches the law well, but he is no prophet. It is not the work of Solomon, any more than is the book of Solomon's Proverbs. They are both collections made by other people.

The third book of Esdras I throw into the Elbe; there are, in the fourth, pretty knacks enough; as, 'The wine is strong, the king is stronger, women strongest of all; but the truth is stronger than all these.'

The book of Judith is not a history. It accords not with geography. I believe it is a poem, like the legends of the saints, composed by some good man, to the end he might show how Judith, a personification of the Jews, as God-fearing people, by whom God is known and confessed, overcame and vanquished Holofernes – that is, all the kingdoms of the world. 'Tis a figurative work, like that of Homer about Troy, and that of Virgil about Æneas, wherein is shown how a great prince ought to be adorned with surpassing valour, like a brave champion, with wisdom and understanding, great courage and alacrity, fortune, honour, and justice. It is a tragedy, setting forth what the end of tyrants is. I take the book of Tobit to be a comedy concerning women, an example for house-government. I am so great an enemy to the second book of the Maccabees, and to Esther, that I wish they had not come to us at all, for they have too many heathen unnaturalities. The Jews much more esteemed the book of Esther than any of the prophets; though they were forbidden to read it before they had attained the age of thirty, by reason of the mystic matters it contains. They utterly contemn Daniel and Isaiah, those two holy and glorious prophets, of whom the former, in the clearest manner, preaches Christ, while the other describes and portrays the kingdom of Christ, and the monarchies and empires of the world preceding it. Jeremiah comes but after them.

The discourses of the prophets were none of them regularly committed to writing at the time; their disciples and hearers collected them subsequently, one, one piece, another, another, and thus was the complete collection formed.

When Doctor Justus Jonas had translated the book of Tobit, he attended Luther therewith, and said: 'Many ridiculous things are contained in this book, especially about the three nights, and the liver of the broiled fish, wherewith the devil was seared and driven away.' Whereupon Luther said: ''Tis a Jewish conceit; the devil, a fierce and powerful enemy, will not be hunted away in such sort, for he has the spear of Goliath; but God gives him such weapons, that, when he is overcome by the godly, it may be the greater terror and vexation unto him. Daniel and Isaiah are most excellent prophets. I am Isaiah – be it spoken with humility – to the advancement of God's honour, whose work alone it is, and to spite the devil. Philip Melancthon is Jeremiah; that prophet stood always in fear; even so it is with Melancthon.'

## 25

In the book of the Judges, the valiant champions and deliverers are described, who were sent by God, believing and trusting wholly in him, according to the first commandment; they committed themselves, their actions, and enterprises to God, and gave him thanks: they relied only upon the God of heaven, and said: Lord God, thou hast done these things, and not we; to thee only be the glory. The book of the Kings is excellent – a hundred times better than the Chronicles, which constantly pass over the most important facts, without any details whatever.

The book of Job is admirable; it is not written only touching himself, but also for the comfort and consolation of all sorrowful, troubled, and perplexed hearts, who resist the devil. When he conceived that God began to be angry with him, he became impatient, and was much offended; it vexed and grieved him that the ungodly prospered so well. Therefore it should be a comfort to poor Christians that are persecuted and forced to suffer, that in the life to come, God will give unto them exceeding great and glorious benefits, and everlasting wealth and honour.

## 26

We need not wonder that Moses so briefly described the history of the ancient patriarchs, when we see that the Evangelists, in the shortest measure, describe the sermons in the New Testament, running briefly through them, and giving but a touch of the preachings of John the Baptist, which, doubtless, were the most beautiful.

## 27

Saint John the Evangelist speaks majestically, yet with very plain and simple words; as where he says: 'In the beginning was the Word, and the Word was with God, and the Word was God. The same was in the beginning with God. All things were made by him, and without him was not anything made that was made. In him was life, and the life was the light of men. And the light shineth in darkness, and the darkness comprehendeth it not.'

See how he describes God the Creator, and also his creatures, in plain, clear language, as with a sunbeam. If one of our philosophers or high learned men had described them, what wonderful swelling and high-trotting Words would he have paraded, *de ente et essentia, so* that no man could have understood what he meant. 'Tis a great lesson, how mighty divine truth is, which presses through, though she be hemmed in ever so closely; the more she is read, the more she moves and takes possession of the heart.

## 28

The psalms of David are of various kinds – didactic, prophetic, eucharistic, catechetic. Among the prophetic, we should particularly distinguish the 110th, *Dixit Dominus;* and among the didactic, the *Miserere Mei, De profundis,* and *Domine, exaudi orationem.* The 110th is very fine. It describes the kingdom and priesthood of Jesus Christ, and declares him to be the King of all things, and the intercessor for all men; to whom all things have been remitted by his Father, and who has compassion on us all. 'Tis a noble psalm; if I were well, I would endeavour to make a commentary on it.

## 29

Dr. Luther was asked whether the history of the rich man and Lazarus was a parable or an actual fact? He replied: The earlier part of the story is evidently historical; the persons, the circumstances, the existence of the five brothers, all this is given in detail. The reference to Abraham is allegorical, and highly worthy of observation. We learn from it that there are abodes unknown to us, where the souls of. men are; secrets into which we must not inquire. No mention is made of Lazarus' grave; whence we may judge, that in God's eyes, the soul occupies far more place than the body. Abraham's bosom is the promise and assurance of salvation, and the expectation of Jesus Christ; not heaven itself, but the expectation of heaven.

## 30

Before the Gospel came among us, men used to undergo endless labour and cost, and make dangerous journeys to St. James of Compostella, and where not, in order to seek the favour of God. But now that God, in his Word, brings his favour unto us gratis, confirming it with his sacraments, saying, *Unless ye believe, ye shall surely perish,* we will have none of it.

### 31

I have lived to see the greatest plague on earth – the contemning of God's word, a fearful thing, surpassing all other plagues in the world; for thereupon most surely follow all manner of punishments, eternal and corporal. Did I desire for a man all bitter plagues and curses, I would wish him the contemning of God's word, for he would then have them all at once come upon him, both inward and outward misfortunes. The contemning of God's word is the forerunner of God's punishments; as the examples witness in the times of Lot, of Noah, and of our Saviour.

### 32

Whoso acknowledges that the writings of the Evangelists are God's word, with him we are willing to dispute; but whoso denies this, with him we will not exchange a word; we may not converse with those who reject the first principles.

### 33

In all sciences, the ablest professors are they who have thoroughly mastered the texts. A man, to be a good juris-consult should have every test of the law at his fingers' ends; but in our time, the attention is applied rather to glosses and commentaries. When I was young, I read the Bible over and over and over again, and was so perfectly acquainted with it, that I could, in an instant, have pointed to any verse that might have been mentioned. I then read the commentators, but I soon threw them aside, for I found therein many things my conscience could not approve, as being contrary to the sacred text. 'Tis always better to see with one's own eyes than with those of other people.

### 34

The words of the Hebrew tongue have a peculiar energy. It is impossible to convey so much so briefly in any other language. To render them intelligibly, we must not attempt to give word for word, but only aim at the sense and idea. In translating Moses, I made it my effort to avoid Hebraisms; 'twas an arduous business. The wise ones, who affect greater knowledge than myself on the subject, take me to task for a word here and there. Did they attempt the labour I have accomplished, I would find a hundred blunders in them for my one.

Bullinger said to me, he was earnest against the sectaries, as contemners of God's word, and also against those who dwelt too much on the literal word, who, he said, sinned against God and his almighty power, as the Jews did in naming the ark, God. But he who holds a mean between both, apprehends the right use of the word and the sacraments. To which I answered: 'By this error, you separate the word from the spirit; those who preach and teach the word, from God who works it, the ministers who baptize, from God who commands baptism. You hold that the Holy Ghost is given and works without the word, which word, you say, is an eternal sign and mark to find the spirit that already possesses the heart; so that, according to you, if the word find not the spirit, but an ungodly person, then it is not God's word; thus defining and fixing the word, not according to God, who speaks it, but according as people entertain and receive it. You grant that to be God's word, which purifies and brings peace and life; but when it works not in the ungodly, it is not God's word. You teach that the outward word is as an object or picture, signifying and representing something; you measure its use only according to the matter, as a human creature speaks for himself; you will not grant that God's word is an instrument through which the Holy Ghost works and accomplishes his work, and prepares a beginning to righteousness or justification.

'A true Christian must hold for certain that the Word which is delivered and preached to the wicked, the dissemblers, and the ungodly, is as much God's Word as that which is preached to godly, upright Christians, and that the true Christian church is among sinners, where good and bad are mingled together. And that the Word, whether it produce fruit or no, is, nevertheless, God's strength, which saves all that believe therein. Clearly, it will also judge the ungodly, (John 12 v. 48) otherwise, these might plead a good excuse before God, that they ought not to be condemned, since they had net had God's word, and consequently could not have received it. But I teach that the preacher's words, absolutions, and sacraments, are not his words or works, but God's, cleansing, absolving, binding, etc.; we are but the instruments or assistants, by whom God works. You say, it is the man that preaches, reproves, absolves, comforts, etc., though it is God that cleanses the hearts and forgives; but I say, God himself preaches, threatens, reprove, affrights, comforts, absolves, administers the sacraments, etc. As our Saviour Christ says: 'Whoso heareth you, heareth me; and what ye loose on earth, shall be loosed in heaven,' etc. And again: 'It is not you that speak, but the Spirit of your Father which speaketh in you.'

'I am sure and certain, when I go up to the pulpit to preach or read, that it is not my word I speak, but that my tongue is the pen of a ready writer, as the Psalmist has it. God speaks in the prophets and men of God, as St. Peter in his epistle says: "The holy men of God spake as they were moved by the Holy Ghost."Therefore we must not separate or part God and man, according to our natural reason and understanding. In like manner, every hearer must say: I hear not St. Paul, St. Peter, or a man speak, but God himself.

'If I were addicted to God's Word at all times alike, and always had such love and desire thereunto as sometimes I have, then should I account myself the most blessed man on earth. But the loving apostle, St. Paul, failed also herein, as he complains, with sighs, saying: "I see another law in my members warring against the law of my mind." Should the Word be false, because it bears not always fruit?The search after theWord has been, from the beginning of the world, the source of great danger; few people can hit it, unless God, through his Holy Spirit, teach it them in their hearts.'

Bullinger, having attentively listened to this discourse, knelt down, and uttered these words, 'O, happy hour that brought me to hear this man of God, the chosen vessel of the Lord, declaring his truth! I abjure and utterly renounce my former errors, thus beaten down by God's infallible Word.' He then arose and threw his arms around Luther's neck, both shedding joyful tears.

### 36

Forsheim said that the first of the five books of Moses was not written by Moses himself. Dr. Luther replied: What matters it, even though Moses did not write it? It is, nevertheless, Moses's book, wherein is exactly related the creation of the world. Such futile objections as these should not be listened to.

### 37

In cases of religion and that concern God's Word, we must be sure and certain, without wavering, so that in time of trial and temptation their acknowledgment may be distinct, and we may not afterwards say, *Non putarem*; a course which in temporal matters often involves much danger, but ill divinity is doubly mischievous. Thus the canonists, the popish dissemblers, and other heretics, are right chimaeras; in the face resembling a fair virgin, the body being like a lion, and the tail like a snake. Even so is it with their doctrine; it glitters, and has a fair aspect, and what they teach is agreeable to mortal wisdom and appreciation, and acquires repute. Afterwards, lion-like, it breaks through by force, for all false teachers commonly make use of the secular arm; but in the end, it shows itself a slippery doctrine, having, like a snake, a smooth skin, sliding through the hand.

Once sure that the doctrine we teach is God's Word, once certain of this, we may build thereupon, and know that. this cause shall and must remain; the devil shall not be able to overthrow it, much less the world be able to uproot it, how fiercely so ever it rage. I, God be praised, surely know that the doctrine I teach is God's Word, and have now hunted from my heart all other doctrines and faiths, of what name soever, that do not concur with God's Word. Thus have I overcome the heavy temptations that sometimes tormented me, thus: Art thou, asked the devilish thought within, the only man that has God's Word, pure and clear, all others failing therein? For thus does Satan vex and assault us, under the name and title of God's church; what, says he, that doctrine which the Christian church has so many years held, and established as right, wilt thou presume to reject and overthrow it with thy new doctrine, tis though it were false and erroneous, thereby producing trouble, alteration, and confusion, both in spiritual and temporal government?

I find this argument of the devil in all the prophets, whom the rulers, both in church and state, have ever upbraided, saying: We are God's people, placed and ordained by God in an established government; what we settle and acknowledge as right, that must and shall be observed. What fools are ye that presume to teach us, the best and largest part, there being of you but a handful? Truly, in this case, we must not only be well armed with God's Word and versed therein, but must have also certainty of the doctrine, or we shall not endure the combat. A man must be able to affirm, I know for certain, that what I teach is the only Word of the high Majesty of God in heaven, his final conclusion and everlasting, unchangeable truth, and whatsoever concurs and agrees not with this doctrine, is altogether false, and spun by the devil. I have before me God's Word which cannot fail, nor can the gates of hell prevail against it; thereby will I remain, though the whole world be against me. And withal, I have this comfort, that God says: I will give thee people and hearers that shall receive it; cast thy care upon me; I will defend thee, only remain thou stout and steadfast by my Word.

We must not regard what or how the world esteems us, so we have the Word pure, and are certain of our doctrine. Hence Christ, in John 8: 'Which of you convinceth me of sin? And if I say the truth, why do you not believe me?' All the apostles were most certain of their doctrine; and St. Paul, in special manner, insists on the *Plerophoria*, where he says to Timothy: 'It is a dear and precious word, that Jesus Christ is come into the world to save sinners.' The faith towards God in Christ must be sure and steadfast, that it may solace and make glad the conscience, and put it to rest. When a man has this certainty, he has overcome the serpent; but if he be doubtful of the doctrine, it is for him very dangerous to dispute with the devil.

### 38

A fiery shield is God's Word; of more substance and purer than gold, which, tried in the fire, loses nought of its substance, but resists and overcomes all the fury of the fiery heat; even so, he that believes God's Word overcomes all, and remains secure everlastingly, against all misfortunes; for this shield fears nothing, neither hell nor the devil.

### 39

I never thought the world had been so wicked, when the Gospel began, as now I see it is; I rather hoped that everyone would have leaped for joy to have found himself freed from the filth of the pope, from his lamentable molestations of poor troubled consciences, and that through Christ they would by faith obtain the celestial treasure they sought after before with such vast cost and labour, though in vain. And especially I thought the bishops and universities would with joy of heart have received the true doctrines, but I have been lamentably deceived. Moses and Jeremiah, too, complained they had been deceived.

### 40

The thanks the world now gives to the doctrine of the gospel, is the same it gave to Christ, namely, the cross; 'tis what we must expect. This year is the year of man's ingratitude: the next will be the year of God's chastisement; for God must needs chastise, though 'tis against his nature: we will have it so.

### 41

Ah, how impious and ungrateful is the world, thus to contemn and persecute God's ineffable grace! And we – we ourselves – who boast of the gospel, and know it to be God's Word, and recognise it for such, yet hold it in no more esteem and respect than we do Virgil or Terence. Truly, I am less afraid of the pope and his tyrants, than I am of our own ingratitude towards the Word of God: tis this will place the pope in his saddle again. But, first, I hope the day of judgment will come.

## 42

God has his measuring lines and his canons, called the Ten Commandments; they are written in our flesh and blood: the sum of them is: 'What thou wouldest have done to thyself, the same do thou to another.' God presses upon this point, saying: 'Such measure as thou metest, the same shall be measured to thee again.' With this measuring line has God marked the whole world. They that live and do thereafter, well it is with them, for God richly rewards them in this life.

## 43

Is it true that God speaks himself with us in the Holy Scriptures? thou that doubtest this, must needs think in thy heart that God is a liar, one that says a thing, and performs it not; but thou mayest be sure when he opens his mouth, it is as much as three worlds. God, with one sole word, moulded the whole world. In Psalm 33 it is said: 'When he speaketh, it is done; when he commandeth, it standeth fast.'

## 44

We must make a great difference between God's Word and the word of man. A man's word is a little sound, that flies into the air, and soon vanishes; but the Word of God is greater than heaven and earth, yea, greater than death and hell, for it forms part of the power of God, and endures everlastingly; we should, therefore, diligently study God's Word, and know and assuredly believe that God himself speaks unto us. This was what David saw and believed, who said: 'God spake in his holiness, thereof I am glad.' We should also be glad; but this gladness is oftentimes mixed up with sorrow and pain, of which, again, David is an example, who underwent manifold trials and tribulations in connexion with the murder and adultery he had committed. It was no honeymoon for him, when he was hunted from one place to another, to the end he might after remain in God's fear. In the second Psalm he says: 'Serve the Lord with fear, and rejoice with trembling.'

## 45

The student of theology has now far greater advantages than students ever before had; first, he has the Bible, which I have translated from Hebrew into German, so clearly and distinctly, that any one may readily comprehend it; next, he has Melanctlhon's *Common-place Book* (Loci Communes), which he should read over and over again, until he has it by heart. Once master of these two volumes, he may be regarded as a theologian whom neither devil nor heretic can overcome; for he has all divinity at his fingers' ends, and may read, understandingly, whatsoever else he pleases. Afterwards, he may study Melancthon's Commentary on Romans, and mine on Deuteronomy and on the Galatians, and practise eloquence.

We possess no work wherein the whole body of theology, wherein religion, is more completely summed up, than in Melancthon's *Common-place Book;* all the Fathers, all the compilers of sentences, put together, are not to be compared with this book. Tis, after the Scriptures, the most perfect of works. Melancthon is a better logician than myself; he argues better. My superiority lies rather in the rhetorical way. If the printers would take my advice, they would print those of my books which set forth doctrine – as my commentaries on Deuteronomy, on Galatians, and the sermons on the four books of St. John. My other writings scarce serve better purpose than to mark the progress of the revelation of the gospel.

### 46

Christ (Luke 8) says, 'Unto you it is given to know the mysteries of the kingdom of God.' Here a man might ask, What mystery is that? If a mystery, why do ye preach it? Whereunto I answer: A mystery is a thing hidden and secret; the mysteries of the kingdom of God are such things as he hidden in the kingdom of God; but he that knows Christ aright, knows what God's kingdom is, and what therein is to be found. They are mysteries, because secret and hidden from human sense and reason, when the Holy Ghost does not reveal them; for though many hear of them, they neither conceive nor understand them. There are now many among us who preach of Christ, and hear much spoken of him, as that he gave himself to death for us, but this lies only upon the tongue, and not in the heart; for they neither believe it, nor are sensible of it; as St. Paul says: 'The natural man perceiveth not the things of the Spirit of God.'

Those on whom the Spirit of God falls, not only hear and see it, but also receive it within their hearts and believe, and therefore it is no mystery or secret to them.

### 47

'Twas a special gift of God that speech was given to mankind; for through the Word, and not by force, wisdom governs. Through the Word people are taught and comforted, and thereby all sorrow is made light, especially in cases of the conscience. Therefore God gave to his church an eternal Word to hear, and the sacraments to use. But this holy function of preaching the Word is, by Satan, fiercely resisted; he would willingly have it utterly suppressed, for thereby his kingdom is destroyed.

Truly speech has wonderful strength and power, that through a mere word, proceeding out of the mouth of a poor human creature, the devil, that so proud and powerful spirit, should be driven away, shamed and confounded.

The sectaries are so impudent, that they dare to reject the word of the mouth; and to smooth their damnable opinions, say: No external thing makes one to be saved; the word of the mouth and the sacraments are external things: therefore they make us not to be saved. But I answer: We must discriminate wholly between the external things of God and the outward things of man. The external things of God are powerful and saving; it is not so with the outward things of man.

### 48

God alone, through his word, instructs the heart, so that it may come to the serious knowledge how wicked it is, and corrupt and hostile to God. Afterwards God brings man to the knowledge of God, and how he may be feed from sin, and how, after this miserable, evanescent world, he may obtain life everlasting. Human reason, with all its wisdom, can bring it no further than to instruct people how to live honestly and decently in the world, how to keep house, build, etc., things learned from philosophy and heathenish books. But how they should learn to know God and his dear Son, Christ Jesus, and to be saved, this the Holy Ghost alone teaches through God's word; for philosophy understands nought of divine matters. I don't say that men may not teach and learn philosophy; I approve thereof; so that it be within reason and moderation. Let philosophy remain within her bounds, as God has appointed, and let us make use of her as of a character in a comedy; but to mix her up with divinity may not be endured; nor is it tolerable to make faith an *accidens* or quality, happening by chance; for such words are merely philosophical, – used in schools and in temporal affairs, which human sense and reason may comprehend. But faith is a thing in the heart, having its being and substance by itself, given of God as his proper work, not a corporal thing, that may be seen, felt, or touched.

### 49

We must know how to teach God's word aright, discerningly, for there are divers sorts of hearers; some are struck with fear in the conscience, are perplexed, and awed by their sins, and, in apprehension of God's anger, are penitent; these must be comforted with the consolations of the gospel. Others are hardened, obstinate, stiff-necked, rebel-hearted; these must be affrighted by the law, by examples of God's wrath: as the fires of Elijah, the deluge, the destruction of Sodom and Gomorrah, the downfall of Jerusalem. These hard heads need sound knocks.

## 50

The gospel of the remission of sins through faith in Christ, is received of few people; most men little regard the sweet and comfortable tidings of the gospel; some hear it, but only even so as they hear mass in popedom; the majority attend God's word out of custom, and, when they have done that, think all is well. The case is, the sick, needing a physician, welcome him; but he that is well, cares not for him, as we see by the Canaanitish woman in Matthew 15, who felt her own and her daughter's necessities, and therefore ran after Christ, and in nowise would suffer herself to be denied or sent away from him. In like manner, Moses was fain to go before, and learn to feel sins, that so grace might taste the sweeter. Therefore, it is but labour lost (how familiar and loving soever Christ be figured unto us), except we first be humbled through the acknowledgment of our sins, and so yearn after Christ, as the *Magnificat* says: 'He filled the hungry with good things, and the rich he hath sent empty away,' words spoken for the comfort of all, and for instruction of miserable, poor, needful sinners, and contemned people, to the end that in all their deepest sorrows and necessities they may know with whom to take refuge and seek aid and consolation.

But we must take fast hold on God's Word, and believe all true which that says of God, though God and all his creatures should seem unto us other than as the Word speaks, as we see the Canaanitish woman did. The Word is sure, and fails not, though heaven and earth must pass away. Yet, oh! how hard is this to natural sense and reason, that it must strip itself naked, and abandon all it comprehends and feels, depending only upon the bare Word. The Lord of his mercy help us with faith in our necessities, and at our last end, when we strive with death.

## 51

Heaven and earth, all the emperors, kings, and princes of the world, could not raise a fit dwelling-place for God; yet, in a weak human soul, that keeps his Word, he willingly resides. Isaiah calls heaven the Lord's seat, and earth his footstool; he does not call them his dwelling-place; when we seek after God, we shall find him with them that keep his Word. Christ says: 'If a man love me, he will keep my words, and my Father will love him, and we will come unto him, and make our abode with him.' Nothing could be simpler or clearer than these words of the Saviour, and yet he confounds herewith all the wisdom of the worldly-wise. He sought to speak *non in sublimi sed humili genere*. If I had to teach a child, I would teach him in the same way.

## 52

Great is the strength of the divine Word. In the epistle to the Hebrews, it is called 'a two-edged sword'. But we have neglected and contemned the pure and clear Word, and have drunk not of the fresh and cool spring; we are gone from the clear fountain to the foul puddle, and drunk its filthy water; that is, we have sedulously read old writers and teachers, who went about with speculative reasonings, like the monks and friars.

The words of our Saviour Christ are exceeding powerful; they have hands and feet; they outdo the utmost subtleties of the worldly-wise, as we see in the gospel, where Christ confounds the wisdom of the Pharisees with plain and simple words, so that they knew not which way to turn and wind themselves. It was a sharp syllogism of his: 'Give unto Caesar the things which are Caesar's'; wherewith he neither commanded nor prohibited, but snared them in their own casuistry.

## 53

Where God's Word is taught pure and unfalsified, there is also poverty, as Christ says: 'I am sent to preach the Gospel to the poor.' More than enough has been given to unprofitable, lazy, ungodly people in monasteries and cells, who lead us into danger of body and soul; but not one farthing is given, willingly, to a Christian teacher. Superstition, idolatry, and hypocrisy, have ample wages, but truth goes a begging.

## 54

When God preaches his word, then presently follows the cross to godly Christians; as St. Paul testifies: 'All that will live a godly life in Christ Jesus, must suffer persecution.' And our Saviour: 'The disciple is not greater than the master: have they persecuted me? they will persecute you also.' The work rightly expounds and declares the Word, as the prophet Isaiah: Grief and sorrow teach how to mark the Word. No man understands the Scriptures, unless he be acquainted with the cross.

## 55

In the time of Christ and the apostles, God's Word was a word of doctrine, which was preached everywhere in the world; afterwards in popedom it was a word of reading, which they only read, but understood not. In this our time, it is made a word of strife, which fights and strives; it will endure its enemies no longer, but remove them out of the way.

## 56

Like as in the world a child is an heir only because it is born to inherit, even so, faith only makes such to be God's children as are born of the Word, which is the womb wherein we are conceived, born, and nourished, as the prophet Isaiah says. Now, as through such a birth we become God's children, (wrought by God without our help or doing,) even so, we are also heirs, and being heirs, are freed from sin, death, and the devil, and shall inherit everlasting life.

## 57

I admonish every pious Christian that he take not offence at the plain, unvarnished manner of speech of the Bible. Let him reflect that what may seem trivial and vulgar to him, emanates from the high majesty, power, and wisdom of God. The Bible is the book that makes fools of the wise of this world; it is understood only of the plain and simple hearted. Esteem this book as the precious fountain that can never be exhausted. In it thou findest the swaddling-clothes and the manger whither the angels directed the poor, simple shepherds; they seem poor and mean, but dear and precious is the treasure that lies therein.

## 58

The ungodly papists prefer the authority of the church far above God's Word; a blasphemy abominable and not to be endured; wherewith, void of all shame and piety, they spit in God's face. Truly, God's patience is exceeding great, in that they be not destroyed; but so it always has been.

## 59

In times past, as in part of our own, 'twas dangerous work to study, when divinity and all good arts were contemned, and fine, expert, and prompt wits were plagued with sophistry. Aristotle, the heathen, was held in such repute and honour, that whoso undervalued or contradicted him, was held, at Cologne, for an heretic; whereas they themselves understood not Aristotle.

## 60

In the apostles' time, and in our own, the gospel was and is preached more powerfully and spread further than it was in the time of Christ; for Christ had not such repute, nor so many hearers as the apostles had, and as now we have. Christ himself says to his disciples: Ye shall do greater works than I; I am but a little grain of mustard-seed; but ye shall be like the vine-tree, and as the arms and branches wherein the birds shall build their nests.

## 61

All men now presume to criticise the gospel. Almost every old doting fool or prating sophist must, forsooth, be a doctor in divinity. All other arts and sciences have masters, of whom people must learn, and rules and regulations which must be observed and obeyed; the Holy Scripture only, God's word, must be subject to each man's pride and presumption; hence, so many sects, seducers, and offences.

## 62

I did not learn my divinity at once, but was constrained by my temptations to search deeper and deeper; for no man, without trials and temptations, can attain a true understanding of the Holy Scriptures. St. Paul had a devil that beat him with fists, and with temptations drove him diligently to study the Holy Scripture. I had hanging on my neck the pope, the universities, all the deep-learned, and the devil; these hunted me into the Bible, wherein I sedulously read, and thereby, God be praised, at length attained a true understanding of it. Without such a devil, we are but only speculators of divinity, and according to our vain reasoning, dream that so and so it must be, as the monks and friars in monasteries do. The Holy Scripture of itself is certain and true: God grant me grace to catch hold of its just use.

# Of God's Works

---

### 63

ALL the works of God are unsearchable and unspeakable, no human sense can find them out; faith only takes hold of them without human power or aid. No mortal creature can comprehend God in his majesty, and therefore did he come before us in the simplest manner, and was made man, ay, sin, death, and weakness.

In all things, in the least creatures, and in their members, God's almighty power and wonderful works clearly shine. For what man, how powerful, wise, and holy soever, can make out of one fig a fig tree, or another fig? or, out of one cherry-stone, a cherry, or a cherry-tree? or what man can know how God creates and preserves all things, and makes them grow.

Neither can we conceive how the eye sees, or how intelligible words are spoken plainly, when only the tongue moves and stirs in the mouth; all which are natural things, daily seen and acted. How then should we be able to comprehend or understand the secret counsels of God's majesty, or search them out with our human sense, reason, or understanding. Should we then admire our own wisdom? I, for my part, admit myself a fool, and yield myself captive.

### 64

In the beginning, God made Adam out of a piece of clay, and Eve out of Adam's rib: he blessed them, and said: 'Be fruitful and increase' – words that will stand and remain powerful to the world's end. Though many people die daily, yet others are ever being born, as David says in his psalm: 'Thou sufferest men to die and go away like a shadow, and sayest, Come again ye children of men.' These and other things which he daily creates, the ungodly blind world see not, nor acknowledge for God's wonders, but think all is done by chance and haphazard, whereas, the godly, wheresoever they cast their eyes, beholding heaven and earth, the air and water, see and acknowledge all for God's wonders; and, full of astonishment and delight, laud the Creator, knowing that God is well pleased therewith.

## 65

For the blind children of the world the articles of faith are too high. That three persons are one only God; that the true Son of God was made man; that in Christ are two natures, divine and human, etc., all this offends them, as fiction and fable. For just as unlikely as it is to say, a man and a stone are one person, so it is unlikely to human sense and reason that God was made man, or that divine and human natures, united in Christ, are one person. St. Paul showed his understanding of this matter, though he took not hold of all, in Colossians: 'In Christ dwelleth all the fulness of the Godhead bodily.' Also: 'In him lies hid all treasure of wisdom and knowledge.'

## 66

If a man ask, Why God permits that men be hardened, and fall into everlasting perdition? Let him ask again: Why God did not spare his only Son, but gave him for us all, to die the ignominious death of the cross, a more certain sign of his love towards us poor people, than of his wrath against us. Such questions cannot be better solved and answered than by converse questions. True, the malicious devil deceived and seduced Adam; but we ought to consider that, soon after the fall, Adam received the promise of the woman's seed that should crush the serpent's head, and should bless the people on earth. Therefore, we must acknowledge that the goodness and mercy of the Father, who sent his Son to be our Saviour, is immeasurably great towards the wicked ungovernable world. Let, therefore, his good will be acceptable unto thee, oh, man, and speculate not with thy devilish queries, thy whys and thy wherefores, touching God's words and works. For God, who is creator of all creatures, and orders all things according to his unsearchable will and wisdom, is not pleased with such questions.

Why God sometimes, out of his divine counsels, wonderfully wise, unsearchable to human reason and understanding, has mercy on this man, and hardens that, it beseems not us to inquire. We should know, undoubtingly, that he does nothing without certain cause and counsel. Truly, if God were to give an account to every one of his works and actions, he were but a poor, simple God.

Our Saviour said to Peter, 'What I do thou knowest not now, but thou shalt know hereafter.' Hereafter, then, we shall know how graciously our loving God and Father has been affected unto us. In the meantime, though misfortune, misery, and trouble be upon us, we must have this sure confdence in him, that he will not suffer us to be destroyed either in body or soul, but will so deal with us, that all things, be they good or evil, shall redound to our advantage.

### 67

When one asked, where God was before heaven was created? St. Augustine answered: He was in himself. When another asked me the same question, I said: He was building hell for such idle, presumptuous, fluttering and inquisitive spirits as you. After he had created all things, he was everywhere, and yet he was nowhere, for I cannot take hold of him without the Word. But he will be found there where he has engaged to be. The Jews found him at Jerusalem by the throne of grace (Exod. 25). We find him in the Word aid faith, in baptism and the sacraments; but in his majesty, he is nowhere to be found.

It was special grace when God bound himself to a certain place where he would be found, namely, in that place where the tabernacle was, towards which they prayed; as first, in Shilo and Sichem, afterwards at Gibeon, and lastly at Jerusalem, in the temple.

The Greeks and heathens in after times imitated this, and built temples for their idols in certain places, as at Ephesus for Diana, at Delphos for Apollo, etc. For, where God built a church there the devil would also build a chapel. They imitated the Jews also in this, namely, that as the Most Holiest was dark, and had no light, even so and after the same manner, did they make their shrines dark where the devil made answer. Thus is the devil ever God's ape.

### 68

God is upright, faithful, and true, as he has shown, not only in his promises, through Christ, of forgiveness of sins, and deliverance from everlasting death, but also, in that he has laid before us, in the Scriptures, many gracious and comforting examples of great and holy saints, who of God were highly enlightened and favoured, and who, notwithstanding, fell into great and heavy sins.

Adam, by his disobedience, hereditarily conveyed sin and death upon all his posterity. Aaron brought a great sin upon Israel, insomuch that God would have destroyed her. David also fell very heavily. Job and Jeremiah cursed the day wherein they were born. Jonas was – sorely vexed, because Nineveh was not destroyed. Peter denied, Paul persecuted Christ.

These and such like innumerable examples does Holy Writ relate to us; not that we should live securely, and sin, relying upon the mercy of God, but that, when we feel his anger, 'which will surely follow upon the sins,' we should not despair, but remember these comfortable examples, and thence conclude, that, as God was merciful unto them, so likewise he will be gracious unto us, out of his mere goodness and mercy shown in Christ, and will not impute our sins unto us.

We may also see by such examples of great holy men falling so grievously, what a wicked, crafty, and envious spirit the devil is, a very prince and god of the world.

These high, divine people, who committed such heavy sins, fell, through God's counsel and permission, to the end they should not be proud or boast themselves of their gifts and qualities, but should rather fear. For, when David had slain Uriah, had taken from him his wife, and thereby given cause to God's enemies to blaspheme, he could not boast he had governed well, or shown goodness: but he said: 'I have sinned against the Lord,' and with tears prayed for mercy. Job also acknowledgingly says: 'I have spoken foolishly, and therefore do I accuse myself, and repent.'

### 69

When God contemplates some great work, he begins it by the hand of some poor, weak, human creature, to whom he afterwards gives aid, so that the enemies who seek to obstruct it, are overcome. As when he delivered the children of Israel out of the long, wearisome, and heavy captivity in Egypt, and led them into the land of promise, he called Moses, to whom he afterwards gave his brother Aaron as an assistant. And though Pharaoh at first set himself hard against them, and plagued the people worse than before, yet he was forced in the end to let Israel go. And when he hunted after them with all his host, the Lord drowned Pharaoh with all his power in the Red Sea, and so delivered his people.

Again, in the time of Eli the priest, when matters stood very evil in Israel, the Philistines pressing hard upon them, and taking away the Ark of God into their land, and when Eli, in great sorrow of heart, fell backwards from his chair and broke his neck, and it seemed as if Israel were utterly undone, God raised up Samuel the prophet, and through him restored Israel, and the Philistines were overthrown.

Afterwards, when Saul was sore pressed by the Philistines, so that for anguish of heart he despaired and thrust himself through, three of his sons and many people dying with him, every man thought that now there was an end of Israel. But shortly after, when David was chosen king over all Israel, then came the golden time. For David, the chosen of God, not only saved Israel out of the enemies' hand, but also forced to obedience all kings and people that set themselves against him, and helped the kingdom up again in such manner, that in his and Solomon's time it was in full flourish, power, and glory.

Even so, when Judah was carried captive to Babylon, then God selected the prophets Ezekiel, Haggai, and Zachariah, who comforted men in their distress and captivity; making not only promise of their return into the land of Judah, but also that Christ should come in his due time.

Hence we may see that God never forsakes his people, nor even the wicked; though, by reason of their sins, he suffer them a long time to be severely punished and plagued. As also, in this our time, he has graciously delivered us from the long, wearisome, heavy, and horrible captivity of the wicked pope. God of his mercy grant we may thankfully acknowledge this.

## 70

God could be rich readily enough, if he were more provident, and denied us the use of his creatures; let him, for ever so short a while, keep back the sun, so that it shine not, or lock up air, water, or fire, ah! How willingly would we give all our wealth to have the use of these creatures again.

But seeing God so liberally heaps his gifts upon us, we claim them as of right; let him deny them if he dare. The unspeakable multitude of his benefits obscures the faith of believers, and much more so, that of the ungodly.

## 71

When God wills to punish a people or a kingdom, he takes away from it the good and godly teachers and preachers, and bereaves it of wise, godly, and honest rulers and counsellors, and of brave, upright, and experienced soldiers, and of other good men. Then are the common people secure and merry; they go on in all wilfulness, they care no longer for the truth and for the divine doctrine; nay, they despise it, and fall into blindness; they have no fear or honesty; they give way to all manner of shameful sins, whence arises a wild, dissolute, and devilish kind of living, as that we now, alas! see and are too well cognizant of, and which cannot long endure. I fear the axe is laid to the root of the tree, soon to cut it down. God of his infinite mercy take us graciously away, that we may not be present at such calamities.

## 72

God gives us sun and moon and stars, fire and water, air and earth, all creatures, body and soul, all manner of maintenance, fruits, grain, corn, wine, whatever is good for the preservation and comfort of this temporal life; moreover he gives unto us his all-saving Word, yea, himself.

Yet what gets he thereby? Truly, nothing, but that he is wickedly blasphemed, and that his only Son is contemned and crucified, his servants plagued, banished, persecuted, and slain. Such a godly child is the world; woe be to it.

## 73

God very wonderfully entrusts his highest office to preachers that are themselves poor sinners who, while teaching it, very weakly follow it. Thus goes it ever with God's power in our weakness; for when he is weakest in us, then is he strongest.

## 74

How should God deal with us? Good days we cannot bear, evil we cannot endure. Gives he riches unto us? then are we proud, so that no man can live by us in peace; nay, we will be carried upon heads and shoulders, and will be adored as gods. Gives he poverty unto us? then are we dismayed, impatient, and murmur against him. Therefore, nothing were better for us, than forthwith to be covered over with the shovel.

## 75

Since God, said some one, knew that man would not continue in the state of innocence, why did he create him at all? Dr. Luther laughed, and replied: The Lord, all powerful and magnificent, saw that he should need in his house, sewers and cess-pools; be assured he knows quite well what he is about. Let us keep clear of these abstract questions, and consider the will of God such as it has been revealed unto us.

## 76

Dr. Henning asked: 'Is reason to hold no authority at all with Christians, since it is to be set aside in masters of faith?' The Doctor replied: Before faith and the knowledge of God, reason is mere darkness; but in the hands of those who believe, 'tis an excellent instrument. All faculties and gifts are pernicious, exercised by the impious; but most salutary when possessed by godly persons.

## 77

God deals strangely with his saints, contrary to all human wisdom and understanding, to the end, that those who fear God and are good Christians, may learn to depend on invisible things, and through mortification may be made alive again; for God's Word is a light that shines in a dark place, as all examples of faith show. Esau was accursed, yet it went well with him; he was lord in the land, and priest in the church; but Jacob had to fly, and dwell in poverty in another country.

God deals with godly Christians much as with the ungodly, yea, and sometimes far worse. He deals with them even as a house-father with a son and a servant; he whips and beats the son much more and oftener than the servant, yet, nevertheless, he gathers for the son a treasure to inherit, while a stubborn and a disobedient servant he beats not with the rod, but thrusts out of doors, and gives him nothing of the inheritance.

## 78

God is a good and gracious Lord; he will be held for God only and alone, according to the first commandment: 'Thou shall have none other Gods but me.' He desires nothing of us, no taxes, subsidies, money, or goods; he only requires that he may be our God and Father, and therefore he bestows upon us, richly, with an overflowing cup, all manner of spiritual and temporal gifts; but we look not so much as once towards him, nor will have him to be our God.

## 79

God is not an angry God; if he were so we were all utterly lost and undone. God does not willingly strike mankind, except, as a just God, he be constrained thereunto; but, having no pleasure in unrighteousness and ungodliness, he must therefore suffer the punishment to go on. As I sometimes look through the fingers, when the tutor whips my son John, so it is with God; when we are unthankful and disobedient to his word and commandments, he suffers us, through the devil, to be soundly lashed with pestilence, famine, and such like whips; not that he is our enemy, and to destroy us, but that through such scourging, he may call us to repentance and amendment, and so allure us to seek him, run to him, and call upon him for help. Of this we have a fine example in the book of Judges, where the angel, in God's person, speaks thus: 'I have stricken you so often, and ye are nothing the better for it'; and the people of Israel said: 'Save thou us but now; we have sinned and done amiss: punish thou us, O Lord, and do with us what thou wilt, only save us now,' etc. Whereupon he struck not all the people to death. In like manner did David, when he had sinned, (in causing the people to be numbered, for which God punished the people with pestilence, so that, 70,000 died) humbled himself, saying: 'Behold, Lord, I have sinned, I have done this misdeed, and have deserved this punishment: What have these sheep done? Let thy hand be upon me, and upon my father's house,' etc. Then the Lord 'repented him of the evil, and said to the angel that destroyed the people, It is enough, stay thy hand.'

He that can humble himself earnestly before God in Christ, has already won; otherwise, the Lord God would lose his deity, whose own work it is, that he have mercy on the poor and sorrowful, and spare them that humble themselves before him. Were it not so, no human creature would come unto him, or call upon him; no man would be heard, no man saved, nor thank him; 'For in hell no man praiseth thee,' says the Psalm. The devil can affright, murder, and steal; but God revives and comforts.

This little word, God, is, in the Scripture, a word with manifold significations, and is oftentimes understood of a thing after the nature of its operation and essence: as the devil is called a god; namely, a god of sin, of death, of despair, and damnation.

We must make due difference between this god and the upright and true God, who is a God of life, comfort, salvation, justification; and all goodness; for there are many words that bear no certain meanings, and equivocation is always the mother of error.

## 80

The wicked and ungodly enjoy the most part of God's creatures; the tyrants have the greatest power, lands, and people; the usurers the money; the farmers eggs, butter, corn, barley, oats, apples, pears, etc.; while godly Christians must suffer, be persecuted, sit in dungeons, where they can see neither sun nor moon, be thrust out into poverty, be banished, plagued, etc. But things will be better one day; they cannot always remain as now; let us have patience, and steadfastly remain by the pure doctrine, and not fall away from it, notwithstanding all this misery.

### 81

Our Lord God and the devil have two modes of policy which agree not together, but are quite opposite the one to the other. God at the first affrights, and afterwards lifts up and comforts again; so that the flesh and the old man should be killed, and the spirit, or new man, live. Whereas the devil makes, at first, people secure and bold, that they, void of all fear, may commit sin and wickedness, and not only remain in sin, but take delight and pleasure therein, and think they have done all well; but at last, when Mr. Stretch-leg comes, then he affrights and scares them without measure, so that they either die of great grief, or else, in the end, are left without all comfort, and despair of God's grace and mercy.

### 82

God only, and not wealth, maintains the world; riches merely make people proud and lazy. At Venice, where the richest people are, a horrible dearth fell among them in our time, so that they were driven to call upon the Turks for help, who sent twenty-four galleys laden with corn; all which, well nigh in port, sunk before their eyes. Great wealth and money cannot still hunger, but rather occasion more dearth; for where rich people are, there things are always dear. Moreover, money makes no man right merry, but much rather pensive and full of sorrow; for riches, says Christ, are thorns that prick people. Yet is the world so mad that it sets therein all its joy and felicity.

### 83

There is no greater anger than when God is silent, and talks not with us, but suffers us to go on in our sinful works, and to do all things according to our own passions and pleasure; as it has been with the Jews for the last fifteen hundred years.

Ah, God, punish, we pray thee, with pestilence and famine, and with what evil and sickness may be else on earth; but be not silent, Lord, towards us. God said to the Jews: 'I have stretched forth mine hand, and have cried, come hither and hear,' etc. 'But ye said, We will not hear.'

Even so likewise do we now; we are weary of God's word; we will not have upright, good, and godly preachers and teachers that threaten us, and bring God's word pure and unfalsified before us, and condemn false doctrine, and truly warn us. No, such cannot we endure; we will not hear them, nay, we persecute and banish them; therefore will God also punish us. Thus it goes with wicked and lost children, that punish us hearken to their parents, nor be obedient unto them; they, will afterwards be rejected of them again.

### 84

Nothing displeases Almighty God more than when we defend and cloak our sins, and will not acknowledge that we have done wrong, as did Saul; for the sins that be not acknowledged, are against the first table of the Ten Commandments. Saul sinned against the first table, David against the second. Those are sinners against the second table, that look on the sermon of Repentance, suffer themselves to be threatened and reproved, acknowledge their sins, and better themselves. Those that sin against the first table, as idolaters, unbelievers, contemners, and blasphemers of God, falsifiers of God's word, etc. attribute to themselves wisdom and power; they will be wise and mighty, both which qualities God reserves to himself as peculiarly his own.

### 85

'Tis inexpressible how ungodly and wicked the world is. We may easily perceive it from this, that God has not only suffered punishments to increase, but also has appointed so many executioners and hangmen to punish his subjects; as evil spirits, tyrants, disobedient children, knaves, and wicked women, wild beasts, vermin, sickness, etc.; yet all this can neither make us bend nor bow.

Better it were that God should be angry with us, than that we be angry with God, for he can soon be at an union with us again, because he is merciful; but when we are angry with him, then the case is not to be helped.

### 86

God could be exceeding rich in temporal wealth, if he so pleased, but he will not. If he would but come to the pope, the emperor, a king, a prince, a bishop, a rich merchant, a citizen, a farmer, and say: Unless you give me a hundred thousand crowns, you shall die on the spot; every one would say: I will give it, with all my heart, if I may but live. But now we are such unthankful slovens, that we give him not so much as a *Deo gratias*, though we receive of him, to rich overflowing, such great benefits, merely out of his goodness and mercy. Is not this a shame? Yet, notwithstanding such unthankfulness, our Lord God and merciful Father suffers not himself to be scared away, but continually shows us all manner of goodness. If in his gifts and benefits he were more sparing and close-handed, we should learn to be thankful. If he caused every human creature to be born but with one leg or foot, and seven years afterwards gave him the other; or in the fourteenth year gave one hand, and afterwards, in the twentieth year, the other, then we should better acknowledge God's gifts and benefits, and value them at a higher rate, and be thankful. He has given unto us a whole sea-full of his Word, all manner of languages and liberal arts. We buy at this time, cheaply, all manner of good books. He gives us learned people, that teach well and regularly, so that a youth, if he be not altogether a dunce, may learn more in one year now, than formerly in many years. Arts are now so cheap, that almost they go about begging for bread; woe be to us that we are so lazy, improvident, negligent, and unthankful.

## 87

We are nothing worth with all our gifts and qualities, how great soever they be, unless God continually hold his hand over us: if he forsake us, then are our wisdom, art, sense, and understanding futile. If he do not constantly aid us, then our highest knowledge and experience in divinity, or what else we attain unto, will nothing serve; for when the hour of trial and temptation comes, we shall be despatched in a moment, the devil, through his craft and subtilty, tearing away from us even those texts in Holy Scripture wherewith we should comfort ourselves, and setting before our eyes, instead, only sentences of fearful threatening.

Wherefore, let no man proudly boast and brag of his own righteousness, wisdom, or other gifts and qualities, but humble himself, and pray with the holy apostles, and say: Ah, Lord! strengthen and increase the faith in us.

## 88

The greater God's gifts and works, the less are they regarded. The highest and most precious treasure we receive of God is, that we can speak, hear, see, etc.; but how few acknowledge these as God's special gifts, much less give God thanks for them. The world highly esteems riches, honour, power, and other things of less value, which soon vanish away, but a blind man, if in his right wits, would willingly exchange all these for sight. The reason why the corporal gifts of God are so much undervalued is, that they are so common, that God bestows them also upon brute beasts, which as well as we, and better, hear and see. Nay, when Christ made the blind to see, drove out devils, raised the dead, etc., he was upbraided by the ungodly hypocrites, who gave themselves out for God's people, and was told that he was a Samaritan, and had a devil. Ah! the world is the devil's, whether it goes or stands still; how, then, can men acknowledge God's gifts and benefits? It is with us as with young children, who regard not so much their daily bread, as an apple, a pear, or other toys. Look at the cattle going into the fields to pasture, and behold in them our preachers, our milk-bearers, butter-bearers, cheese and wool bearers, which daily preach unto us faith in God, and that we should trust in him, as in our loving Father, who cares for us, and will maintain and nourish us.

## 89

No man can estimate the great charge God is at only in maintaining birds and such creatures, comparatively nothing worth. I am persuaded that it costs him, yearly, more to maintain only the sparrows, than the revenue of the French king amounts to. What, then, shall we say of all the rest of his creatures?

## 90

God delights in our temptations, and yet hates them; he delights in them when they drive us to prayer: he hates them when they drive us to despair. The Psalm says: An humble and contrite heart is an acceptable sacrifice to God, etc. Therefore, when it goes well with you, sing and praise God with a hymn: goes it evil, that is, does temptation come, then pray: 'For the Lord has pleasure in those that fear him'; and that which follows is better: 'and in them that hope in his goodness': for God helps the lowly and humble, seeing he says: 'Thinkest thou my hand is shortened, that I cannot help?' He that feels himself weak in faith, let him always have a desire to be strong therein, for that is a nourishment which God relishes in us.

## 91

God, in this world, has scarce the tenth part of the people; the smallest number only will be saved. The world is exceeding ungodly and wicked; who would believe our people should be so unthankful towards the gospel?

## 92

'Tis wonderful how God has put such excellent physic in mere muck; we know by experience that swine's dung stints the blood; horse's serves for the pleurisy; man's heals wounds and black blotches; asses' is used for the bloody flux, and cow's, with preserved roses, serves for epilepsy, or for convulsions of children.

## 93

God seems as though he had dealt inconsiderately in commanding the world to be governed by the Word of Truth, especially since he has clothed and hooded it with a poor, weak and contemned Word of the Cross. For, the world will not have the truth, but lies; neither willingly do they aught that is upright and good, unless compelled thereto by main force. The world has a loathing of the cross, and will rather follow the pleasures of the devil, and have pleasant days, than carry the cross of our blessed Saviour Christ Jesus. He that best governs the world, as most worthy of it, is Satan, by his lieutenant the pope; he can please the world well, and knows how to make it give ear unto him; for his kingdom has a mighty show and repute, which is acceptable to the world, and befits it. Like unto like.

## 94

Pythagoras, the heathen philosopher, said, that the motion of the stars creates a very sweet harmony and celestial concord; but that people, through continual custom, have become cloyed therewith. Even so it is with us; we have surpassing fair creatures to our use, but by reason they are too common, we regard them not.

## 95

Scarcely a small proportion of the earth bears corn, and yet we are all maintained and nourished. I verily believe that there grow not as many sheaves of corn as there are people in the world, and yet we are all fed; yea, and there remains a good surplus of corn at the year's end. This is a wonderful thing, which should make us see and perceive God's blessing.

## 96

The apparent cause why God passed so sharp a sentence upon Adam, was, that he had eaten of the forbidden tree, and was disobedient unto God, wherefore, for his sake, the earth was cursed, and mankind made subject to all manner of miseries, fears, wants, sicknesses, plagues, and death. The reason of the worldly-wise, regarding only the biting of the apple, holds that for so slight and trivial a thing it was too cruel and hard a proceeding upon poor Adam, and takes snuff in the nose, and says, or at least thinks: O, is it then so heinous a matter and sin for one to eat an apple? As people say of many sins that God expressly in his word has forbidden, such as drunkenness, etc.: What harm for one to be merry, and take a cup of tea with good fellows? – concluding, according to their blindness, that God is too sharp and exacting.

Again, these worldlings are offended that Christ, as they think, rejects good, honest, and holy people; that he will not know them, is harsh to them, sends them away from him, and calls them malefactors, though some in his name have prophesied, cast out devils, done miracles, etc., while, on the other hand, he receives public sinners, as strumpets, knaves, publicans, murderers, whom, if they hear his word, and believe in him, he forgives, be their sins ever so great and many, yea, makes them righteous and holy, God's children, and heirs of everlasting life and salvation, out of mere grace and mercy, without any deserts, good works, and worthiness of theirs. This they conceive to be altogether unjust.

Who can be here an arbitrator, the two things being as contrary to each other as fire and water. Herein man's wisdom, his sense, reason, understanding, is made a fool. The Scripture says: 'Except ye be converted, and became like little children, ye shall not enter into the kingdom of God.' They who would investigate these things with human wit and wisdom, give themselves much futile labour and disquiet; they will never learn how God is inclined towards them. In those, also, whoso vainly trouble themselves, whether they be predestinated or forechosen, there goes up a fire in the heart, which they cannot quench; so that their consciences are never at peace, but in the end they must despair. He, therefore, that will shun this enduring evil must hold fast the Word, where he will find that our gracious God has laid a sure and strong foundation, on which we may with certainty take footing – namely, Jesus Christ our Lord, through whom only we must enter into the kingdom of heaven; for he, and no other, 'is the way, the truth, and the life'.

We can understand the heavy temptations of that everlasting predestination, which terrifies many people, nowhere better than from the wounds of our Saviour, Christ Jesus, of whom the Father commanded, saying: 'Him shall ye hear.' But the wise of the world, the mighty, the high-learned, and the great, by no means heed these things, so that God remains unknown to them, notwithstanding they have much learning, and dispute and talk much of God; for it is a short conclusion: Without Christ, God will not be found, known, or comprehended.

If now thou wilt know why so few are saved, and so infinitely many damned, this is the cause: the world will not hear Christ; they care nothing for him, yea, contemn that which the Father testifies of him: 'This is my well-beloved Son, in whom I am well pleased.'

Whereas all people that seek and labour to come to God, through any other means than only through Christ (as Jews, Turks, Papists, false saints, heretics, etc.), walk in horrible darkness and error; and it helps them nothing that they lead an honest, sober kind of life, affect great devotion, suffer much, love and honour God, as they boast, etc. For seeing they will not hear Christ, or believe in him (without whom no man knows God, no man obtains forgiveness of sins, no man comes to the Father), they remain always in doubt and unbelief, know not how they stand with God, and so at last must die, and be lost in their sins. For, 'He that honoureth not the Son, honoureth not the Father' (1 John 2), 'He that believeth not the Son, shall not see life, but the wrath of God remains upon him' (John 3).

## 97

It is often asked: Why desperate wretches have such good days, and live a long time in jollity and pleasure, to their heart's desire, with health of body, fine children, etc., while God allows the godly to remain in calamity, danger, anguish and want all their lives; yea, and some to die also in misery, as St. John the Baptist did, who was the greatest saint on earth, to say nothing of our only Saviour Jesus Christ.

The prophets have all written much hereof, and shown how the godly should overcome such doubts, and comfort themselves against them. Jeremiah says, 'Why goeth it so well with the ungodly, and wherefore are all they happy that deal very treacherously?' But further on, 'Thou sufferest them to go at liberty like sheep that are to be slain, and thou preparest them for the day of slaughter.' Read also Psalms 37, 49, 73.

God is not therefore angry with his children, though he scourge and punish them; but he is angry with the ungodly that do not acknowledge Christ to be the Son of God, and the Saviour of the world, but blaspheme and contemn the Word; such are to expect no grace and help of him. And, indeed, he does not himself scourge and beat his small and poor flock that depend on Christ; but suffers them to be chastened and beaten, when they become over secure and unthankful unto him for his unspeakable graces and benefits shown unto them in Christ, and are disobedient to his word; then permits he that the devil bruise our heels, and send pestilence and other plagues unto us; and that tyrants persecute us, and this for our good, that thereby we may be moved, and in a manner forced to turn ourselves unto him, to call upon him, to seek help and comfort from him, through Christ.

## 98

'God is a God of the living, and not of the dead.' This text shows the resurrection; for if there were no hope of the resurrection, or of another and better world, after this short and miserable life, wherefore should God offer himself to be our God, and say he will give us all that is necessary and healthful for us, and, in the end, deliver us out of all trouble, both temporal and spiritual? To what purpose should we hear his Word, and believe in him? What were we the better when we cry and sigh to him in our anguish and need, that we wait with patience upon his comfort and salvation, upon his grace and benefits, shown in Christ? Why praise and thank him for them? Why be daily in danger, and suffer ourselves to be persecuted and slain for the sake of Christ's Word?

Forasmuch as the everlasting, merciful God, through his Word and Sacraments, talks and deals with us, all other creatures excluded, not of temporal things which pertain to this vanishing life, and which in the beginning he provided richly for us, but as to where we shall go when we depart hence, and gives unto us his Son for a Saviour, delivering us from sin and death, and purchasing for us everlasting righteousness, life, and salvation, therefore it is most certain, that we do not die away like the beasts that have no understanding; but so many of us as sleep in Christ, shall through him be raised again to life everlasting at the last day, and the ungodly to everlasting destruction (John 5, Dan. 12).

## 99

The most acceptable service we can do and show unto God, and which alone he desires of us, is, that he be praised of us; but he is not praised, unless he be first loved; he is not loved, unless he be first bountiful and does well; he does well when he is gracious; gracious he is when he forgives sins. Now who are those that love him? They are that small flock of the faithful, who acknowledge such graces, and know that through Christ they have forgiveness of their sins. But the children of this world do not trouble themselves herewith; they serve their idol, that wicked and cursed Mammon: in the end he will reward them.

### 100

Our loving Lord God wills that we eat, drink, and be merry, making use of his creatures, for therefore he created them. He wills not that we complain, as if he had not given sufficient, or that he could not maintain our poor carcases; he asks only that we acknowledge him for our God, and thank him for his gifts.

### 101

He that has not God, let him have else what he will, is more miserable than Lazarus, who lay at the rich man's gate, starved to death. It will go with such, as it went with the glutton, that they must everlastingly hunger and want, and shall not have in their power so much as one drop of water.

### 102

Of Abraham came Isaac and Ishmael; of the patriarchs and holy fathers, came the Jews that crucified Christ; of the apostles came Judas the traitor; of the city Alexandria (where a fair, illustrious, and famous school was, and whence proceeded many upright and godly learned men) came Arius and Origen; of the Roman church, that yielded many holy martyrs, came the blasphemous Antichrist, the pope of Rome; of the holy men in Arabia, came Mohammad; of Constantinople, where many excellent emperors were, comes the Turk; of married women come adulteresses; of virgins, strumpets; of brethren, sons, and friends, come the cruellest enemies; of angels come devils; of kings come tyrants; of the gospel and godly truth come horrible lies; of the true church come heretics; of Luther come fanatics, rebels, and enthusiasts. What is it then that evil is among us, comes from us, and goes out of us; they must, indeed, be very evil things that cannot stay by such goodness; and they must also be very good, that can endure such cruel things.

### 103

Though by reason of original sin many wild beasts hurt mankind, as lions, wolves, bears, snakes, adders, etc., yet the merciful God has in such manner mitigated our well-deserved punishments, that there are many more beasts that serve us for our good and profit, than of those which do us hurt: many more sheep than wolves, oxen than lions, cows than bears, deer than foxes, lobsters than scorpions, ducks, geese, and hens, than ravens and kites, etc.: in all creatures more good than evil, more benefits than hurts and hindrances.

## 104

God will have his servants to be repenting sinners, standing in fear of his anger, of the devil, death and hell, and believing in Christ. David says, 'The Lord is nigh unto them that are of a broken heart, and helpeth them that be of an humble spirit.' And Isaiah, 'Where shall my Spirit rest, and where shall I dwell? By them that are of humble spirit, and that stand in fear of my Word.' So with the poor sinner on the cross. So with St. Peter, when he had denied Christ; with Mary Magdalen; with Paul the persecutor, etc. All these were sorrowful for their sins, and such shall have forgiveness of their sins, and be God's servants.

The great prelates, the puffed up saints, the rich usurers, the ox drovers that seek unconscionable gain, etc., these are not God's servants, neither were it good they should be; for then no poor people could have access to God for them; neither were it for God's honour that such should be his servants, for they would ascribe the honour and praise to themselves.

In the Old Testament, all the first-born were consecrated to God, both of mankind and of beasts. The first-born son had an advantage over his brethren; he was their lord, as the chief in offerings and riches, that is; in spiritual and temporal government; for he had a right to the priesthood and dominion, etc. But there are many examples in Holy Scriptures, where God rejected the first-born, and chose the younger brethren, as Cain, Ishmael, Esau, Reuben, etc., who were first-born; from them God took their right, and gave it to their younger brethren, as to Abel, Isaac, Jacob, Judah, David, etc. And for this cause: That they were haughty, proud, and presuming on their first-birth, and despised their brethren, that were more goodly and godly than they; this God could not endure, and therefore they were bereaved of their honours, so that they could not boast themselves of their prior birth, although they were highly esteemed in the world, and were possessed of lands and people.

## 105

The Scriptures show two manners of sacrifices acceptable to God. The first is called a sacrifice of thanks or praise, and is when we teach and preach God's Word purely, when we hear and receive it with faith, when we acknowledge it, and do everything that tends to the spreading of it abroad, and thank God from our hearts for the unspeakable benefits which through it are laid before us, and bestowed upon us in Christ, when we praise and glorify him, etc. 'Offer unto God thanksgiving.' 'He that offereth thanks praiseth me.' 'Thank the Lord, for he is gracious, because his mercy endureth for ever.' 'Praise the Lord, O my soul, and all that is within me praise his holy name. Praise the Lord, O my soul, and forget not all his benefits' – Psalms.

Secondly, when a sorrowful and troubled heart in all manner of temptations has his refuge in God, calls upon him in a true and upright faith, seeks help of him, and waits patiently upon him. Hereof the Psalms, 'In my trouble I called upon the Lord, and he, heard me at large.' 'The Lord is nigh unto them that are of a contrite heart, and will save such as be of an humble spirit.' 'The sacrifice of God is a troubled spirit; a broken and contrite heart, O God, shalt thou not despise.' And again: 'Call upon me in the time of need, so will I deliver thee, and thou shalt praise me.'

## 106

If Adam had remained in his innocence, and had not transgressed God's command, yet had begotten children, he should not have lived and remained continually in that state in Paradise; but would have been taken into the everlasting glory of heaven, not through death, but through being translated into another life.

## 107

God scorns and mocks the devil, in setting under his very nose a poor, weak, human creature, mere dust and ashes, yet endowed with the first-fruits of the Spirit, against whom the devil can do nothing, though he is so proud, subtile, and powerful a spirit. We read in histories that a powerful king of Persia, besieging the city of Edessa, the bishop, seeing that all human aid was ineffectual, and that the city could not of itself hold out, ascended to the ramparts and prayed to God, making, at the same time, the sign of the cross, whereupon there was a wonderful host sent from God of great flies and gnats, which filled the horses' eyes, and dispersed the whole army. Even so God takes pleasure to triumph and overcome, not through power, but by weakness.

## 108

False teachers and sectaries are punishments for evil times, God's greatest anger and displeasure; while godly teachers are glorious witnesses, God's graces and mercies. Hence St. Paul names apostles, evangelists, prophets, shepherds, teachers, etc., gifts and presents of our Saviour Christ, sitting at the right hand of the Father. And the prophet Micah compares teachers of the gospel to a fruitful rain.

## 109

Melancthon asked Luther if this word, hardened, 'hardeneth whom he will', were to be understood directly as it sounded, or in a figurative sense? Luther answered: We must understand it specially and not operatively: for God works no evil. Through his almighty power he works all in all; and as he finds a man, so he works in him, as he did in Pharaoh, who was evil by nature, which was not God's, but his own fault; he continually went on in his wickedness, doing evil; he was hardened, because God with his spirit and grace hindered not his ungodly proceedings, but suffered him to go on, and to have his way. Why God did not hinder of restrain him, we ought not to inquire.

## 110

God styles himself, in all the Holy Scriptures, a God of life, of peace, of comfort, and joy, for the sake of Christ. I hate myself, that I cannot believe it so constantly and surely as I should; but no human creature can rightly know how mercifully God is inclined toward those that steadfastly believe in Christ.

## 111

The second Psalm is one of the best Psalms. I love that Psalm with my heart. It strikes and flashes valiantly amongst kings, princes, counsellors, judges, etc. If what this Psalm says be true, then are the allegations and aims of the papists stark lies and folly. If I were our Lord God, and had committed the government to my son, as he to his Son, and these vile people were as disobedient as they, now be, I would knock the world in pieces.

## 112

If a man serve not God only, then surely he nerves the devil; because no man can serve God, unless he have his Word and command. Therefore, if his Word and command be not in thy heart, thou servest not God, but thine own will; for that is upright serving of God, when a man does that which in his Word God has commanded to be done, every one in his vocation, not that which he thinks good of his own judgment.

## 113

It troubles the hearts of people not a little, that God seems as though he were mutable or fickle-minded; for he gave to Adam the promise and ceremonies, which afterwards he altered with the rainbow and the ark of Noah. He gave to Abraham the circumcision, to Moses he gave miraculous signs, to his people, the law. But to Christ, and through Christ, he gave the Gospel; which amounts to the abolition of all the former. Hence the Turks take advantage of these proceedings of God, saying: The laws of the Christians may be established, and endure for a time, but at last they will be altered.

## 114

I was once sharply reprimanded by a popish priest, because, with such passion and vehemence, I reproved the people. I answered him: Our Lord God must first send a sharp, pouring shower, with thunder and lightning, and afterwards cause it mildly to rain, as then it wets finely through. I can easily cut a willow or a hazel wand with my trencher-knife; but for a hard oak, a man must use the axe; and little enough, to fell and cleave it.

## 115

Plato, the heathen, said of God: God is nothing and yet everything; him followed Eck and the sophists, who understood nothing thereof, as their words show. But we must understand and speak of it in this manner: God is incomprehensible and invisible; that, therefore, which may be seen and comprehended, is not God. And thus, in another manner, God is visible and invisible: visible in his word and works; and where his word and works are not, there a man should not desire to have him; or he will, instead of God, take hold of the devil. Let us not flutter too high, but remain by the manger and the swaddling clothes of Christ, 'in whom dwelleth all the fulness of the Godhead bodily.' There a man cannot fail of God, but finds him most certainly. Human comfort and divine comfort are of different natures: human comfort consists in external, visible help, which a man may see, hold, and feel; divine comfort only in words and promises, where there is neither seeing, hearing, nor feeling.

## 116

When we see no way or means, by advice or aid, through which we may be helped in our miseries, we at once conclude, according to our human reason: now our condition is desperate; but when we believe trustingly in God, our deliverance begins. The physician says: Where philosophy ends, physic begins; so we say: Where human help is at an end, God's help begins, or faith in God's word. Trials and temptations appear before deliverance, after deliverance comes joy. To be suppressed and troubled, is to arise, to brow and to increase.

**117**

The devil, too, has his amusement and pleasure, which consists in suppressing God's work, and tormenting those that love God's word, and hold fast thereby; so the true Christians, being God's kingdom, must be tormented and oppressed.

A true Christian must have evil days, and suffer much; our Adam's flesh and blood must leave good and easy days, and suffer nothing. How may these agree together? Our flesh is given over to death and hell: if our flesh is to be delivered from death, hell, and the devil, it must keep and hold to God's commandments – i.e., must believe in Christ Jesus, that he is the Son of God and our Redeemer, and must cleave fast to his word, believing that he will not suffer us to be plagued everlastingly, but will deliver and remove us out of this life into life eternal; giving us, at the same time, patience under the cross, and to bear with the weakness of another, who is also under the cross, and holds with Christ.

Therefore, he that will boast himself to be Christ's disciple, a true Christian, and saved, must not expect good days; but all his faith, hope, and love must be directed to God, and to his neighbour, that so his whole life be nothing else than the cross, persecution, adversity, and tribulation.

**118**

What is it we poor wretched people aim at? We who cannot, as yet, comprehend with our faith the merest sparks of God's promises, the bare glimmering of his commandments and works, – both of which, notwithstanding he himself has confirmed with words and miracles, – weak, impure, corrupt as we are, – presumptuously seek to understand the incomprehensible majesty of the incomprehensible light of God's wonders.

We must know that he dwells in a light to which human creatures cannot come, and yet we go on, and essay to reach it. We know that his judgments are incomprehensible, and his ways past finding out (Rom. 11), yet we undertake to find them out. We look, with blind eyes like a mole, on the majesty of God, and after that light which is shown neither in words nor miracles, but only signified; out of curiosity and wilfulness we would behold the highest and greatest fight of the celestial sun ere we see the morning star. Let the morning star, as St. Peter says, go first up in our hearts, and we shall then see the sun in his noon-tide splendour.

True, we must teach, as we may, of God's incomprehensible and unsearchable will; but to aim at its perfect comprehension is dangerous work, wherein we stumble, fall, and break our necks. I bridle myself with these words of our Saviour Christ to St. Peter: 'Follow thou me: what is it to thee?' etc., for Peter busied himself also about God's works; namely, how he would do with another, how he would do with John? And as he answered Philip, that said, 'Show us the Father' – 'What,' said Christ; 'believest thou not that the Father is in me, and I in the Father? He that seeth me, seeth the Father also,' etc. For Philip would also willingly have seen the majesty and fellowship of the Father. Solomon, the wise king, says: 'What is too high for thee, thereafter inquire thou not.' And even did we know all the secret judgments of God, what good and profit would it bring unto us, more than God's promises and commandments?

Let us abstain from such cogitations, seeing we know for certain that they are incomprehensible. Let us not permit ourselves to be so plagued by the devil with that which is impossible. A man might as well busy himself how the kingdom of the earth shall endure upon the waters, and go not down beneath them. Above all things, let us exercise the faith of God's promises, and the works of his commandments; when we have done this, we may well consider whether it is expedient to trouble oneself about impossible things, though it is a very difficult thing to expel such thoughts, so fiercely drives the devil. A man must as vehemently strive against such cogitations as against unbelief, despair, heresies, and such like temptations. For most of us are deceived herewith, not believing they proceed from the devil, who yet himself fell through those very cogitations, assuming to be equal with the Most Highest, and to know all that God knows, and scorning to know what he ought to know, and what was needful for him.

## 119

High mysteries in the Scriptures being hard to be understood, confound unlearned and light spirits so as to produce many errors and heresies, to their own and others' condemnation. 'Twas therefore Moses described the creation so briefly, whereas he spends a whole chapter in narrating the purchase of the field and cave over against Hebron, that Abraham bought of Ephron the Hittite, for a sepulchre to bury Sara in. He describes, likewise, through many chapters, divers sorts of sacrifices, and other customs and ceremonies, for he well knew that such like produce no heresies. Many things were written and described ere Moses was born. Doubtless, Adam briefly noted the history of the creation, of his fall, of the promised seed, etc. The other patriarchs afterwards, no doubt, each set down what was done in his time, especially Noah. Afterwards Moses, as I conceive, took and brought all into a right method and order, diminishing therefrom, and adding thereunto, such things as God commanded; as, especially, touching the seed that should crush the serpent's head, the history of the creation, etc.; all which, doubtless, he had out of the sermons of the patriarchs, that always one inherited from another. For I verily believe, that the sermon of the woman's seed, promised to Adam and Eve, after which they had so hearty a longing and yearning, was preached more powerfully before the deluge, than now in these dangerous times the sermons of Christ are preached with us.

## 120

I would give a world to have the acts and legends of the patriarchs who lived before the deluge; for therein a man might see how they lived, preached, and what they suffered. But it pleased our Lord God to overwhelm all their acts and legends in the deluge, because he knew that those which should come after, would not regard, much less understand them; therefore God would keep and preserve them until they met again together in the life to come. But then, I am sure, the loving patriarchs who lived after the deluge, Abraham, Isaac, Jacob, etc.; the prophets, the apostles, their posterity, and other holy people, whom in this life the devil would not leave untempted, will yield unto the patriarchs, that lived before the deluge, and give to them pre-eminence in divine and spiritual honour, saying: Ye loving and most venerable patriarchs! I preached but a few years, spreading God's word abroad, and therefore suffered the cross; but what is that in comparison with the great, tedious, intolerable labour and pains, anguish, torments, and plagues, which ye, holy fathers, endured before the deluge, some of you, seven hundred, some eight hundred years, some longer, of the devil and the wicked world.

## 121

As lately I lay very sick, so sick that I thought I should have left this world, many cogitations and musings had I in my weakness. Ah! thought I, what may eternity be? What joys may it have? However, I know for certain, that this eternity is ours; through Christ it is given and prepared for us, if we can but believe. There it shall be opened and revealed; here we shall not know when a second creation of the world will be, seeing we understand not the first. If I had been with God Almighty before he created the world, I could not have advised him how out of nothing to make this globe, the firmament, and that glorious sun, which in its swift course gives light to the whole earth; how, in such manner, to create man and woman, etc., all which he did for us, without our counsel. Therefore ought we justly to give him the honour, and leave to his divine power and goodness the new creation of the life to come, and not presume to speculate thereon.

## 122

I hold that the name Paradise applies to the whole work Moses describes, more particularly what fell within Adam's sight before his fall – a sweet and pleasant place, watered by four rivers. After he had sinned, he directed, his steps towards Syria, and the earth lost its fertility. Samaria, and Judea were once fruitful lands, worthy to be Paradise, but they are now arid sand, for God has cursed them.

Even so, in our time, has God cursed fruitful lands, and caused them to be barren and unfruitful by reason of our sins; for where God gives not his blessing, there grows nothing that is good and profitable, but where he blesses, there all things grow plentifully, and are fruitful.

## 123

Dr. Jonas, inviting Luther to dinner, caused a bunch of ripe cherries to be hung over the table where they dined, in remembrance of the creation, and as a suggestion to his guests to praise God for creating such fruits. But Luther said: Why not rather remember this in one's children, that are the fruit of one's body? For these are far more excelling creatures of God than all the fruits of trees. In them we see God's power, wisdom, and art, who made them all out of nothing, gave them life and limbs, exquisitely constructed, and will maintain and preserve them. Yet how little do we regard this. When people have children, all the effect is to make them grasping, raking together all they can to leave behind them. They do not know, that before a child comes into the world, it has its lot assigned already, and that it is ordained and determined what and how much it shall have. In the married state we find that the conception of children depends not on our will and pleasure; we never know whether we shall be fruitful or no, or whether God will give us a son or a daughter. All this goes on without our counsel. My father and mother did not imagine they should have brought a spiritual overseer into the world. 'Tis God's work, only, and this we cannot enter into. I believe that, in the life to come, we shall have nothing to do, but to meditate on and marvel at our Creator and his creatures.

## 124

A comet is a star that runs, not being fixed like a planet, but a bastard among planets. It is a haughty and proud star, engrossing the whole element, and carrying itself as if it were there alone. 'Tis of the nature of heretics, who also will be singular and alone, bragging and boasting above others, and thinking they are the only people endued with understanding.

## 125

Whereto serve or profit such superfluity, such show, such ostentation, such extraordinarily luxurious kind of life as is now come upon us. If Adam were to return to earth, and see our mode of living, our food, drink, and dress, how would he marvel. He would say: Surely, this is not the world I was in; it was, doubtless, another Adam than I, who appeared among men heretofore. For Adam drank water, ate fruit from the trees, and, if he had any house at all, 'twas a hut, supported by four wooden forks; he had no knife, or iron; and he wore simply a coat of skin. Now we spend immense sums in eating and drinking; now we raise sumptuous palaces, and decorate them with a luxury beyond all comparison. The ancient Israelites lived in great moderation and quiet; Boaz says: 'Dip thy bread in vinegar, and refresh thyself therewith.' Judaea was full of people, as we read in the book of Joshua; and a great multitude of people gives a lesson to live sparingly.

## 126

Adam, our father, was, doubtless, a most miserable, plagued man. 'Twas a mighty solitariness for him to be alone in so wide and vast a world; but when he, with Eve, his only companion and loving consort, obtained Cain their son, then there was great joy, and so, when Abel was born; but soon after followed great trouble, misery, and sorrow of heart, when one brother slew another, and Adam thereby lost one son, and the other was banished and proscribed from his sight. This surely was a great cross and sorrow, so that the murder caused him more grief than his own fall; but he, with his loving Eve, were reduced again to a solitary kind of life. Afterwards, when he was one hundred and thirty years old, he had Seth. Miserable and lamentable was his fall, for during nine hundred years he saw God's anger in the death of every human creature. Ah! no human creature can conceive his perplexities: our sufferings, in comparison with his, are altogether children's toys; but he was afterwards comforted and refreshed again with the promise, through faith, of the woman's seed.

## 127

All wild beasts are beasts of the law, for they live in fear and quaking; they have all swarthy and black flesh, by reason of their fear, but tame beasts have white flesh, for they are beasts of grace; they live securely with mankind.

## 128

After Adam had lost the righteousness in which God had created him, he was, without doubt, much decayed in bodily strength, by reason of his anguish and sorrow of heart. I believe that before the fall he could have seen objects a hundred miles off better than we can see them at half a mile, and so in proportion with all the other senses. No doubt, after the fall, he said: 'Ah, God! what has befallen me? I am both blind and deaf.' It was a horrible fall; for, before, all creatures were obedient unto him, so that he could play even with the serpent.

## 129

Twenty years is but a short time, yet in that short time the world were empty, if there was no marrying and production of children. God assembles unto himself a Christian church out of little children. For I believe, when a little child dies of one year old, that always one, yea, two thousand die with it, of that age or younger; but; when I, Luther, die, that am sixty-three, I believe that not three-score, or one hundred at the most, will die with me of that age, or older; for people now grow not old; not many people live to my years. Mankind is nothing else but a sheep-shambles, where we are slain and slaughtered by the devil. How many sorts of deaths are in our bodies? Nothing is therein but death.

## 130

It is in the fathers power to disinherit a disobedient child; God commanded, by, Moses, that disobedient children should be stoned the death, so that a father may clearly disinherit a son, yet, with, this proviso, that, upon bettering and amendment, he reinstate him.

## 131

What need had our early ancestors of other food than fruits and herbs, seeing these tasted so well and gave such strength? The pomegranates and oranges, without doubt, yielded such a sweet and pleasant smell, that one might have been satisfied with the scent thereof; and I am sure Adam, before his fall, never wanted to eat a partridge; but the deluge spoiled all. It follows not, that because God created all things, we must eat of all things. Fruits were created chiefly as food for people and for beasts; the latter were created to the end we should laud and praise God. Whereunto serve the stars, but only to praise their Creator? Whereunto serve the raven and crows, but to call upon the Lord who nourishes them.

### 132

There's no doubt that all created things have degenerated by reason of original sin. The serpent was at first a lofty, noble animal; eating without fear from Eve's hand, but after it was cursed, it lost its feet, and was fain to crawl and eat on the ground. It was precisely because the serpent, at that time, was the most beautiful of creatures, that Satan selected it for his work, for the devil likes beauty, knowing that beauty attracts men unto evil. A fool serves not as a provocative to heresy, nor a deformed maid-servant to libertinism, nor water to drunkenness, nor rags to vanity. Consider the bodies of children, how much sweeter and purer and more beautiful they are than those of grown persons; 'tis because childhood approaches nearer to the state of innocence: wherein Adam lived before his fall. In our sad condition, our only consolation is the expectation of another life. Here below all is incomprehensible.

### 133

Dr. Luther, holding a rose in his hand, said: 'Tis a magnificent work of God: could a man make but one such rose as this, he would be thought worthy of all honour, but the gifts of God lose their value in our eyes, from their very, infinity. How wonderful is the resemblance between children and their parents. A man shall have half-a-dozen sons, all like him as so many peas are like another, and these sons again their sons, with equal exactness of resemblance, and so it goes on. The heathen noticed these likenesses. Dido says to Aeneas:

'Si mihi parvulus Aenea; uderet in aula,
　Qui to tantum ore referret.'

'Twas a form of malediction among the Greeks, for a man to wish that his enemy's son might be unlike him in face.

### 134

'Tis wonderful how completely the earth 'is fertilized by currents of water running in all directions and constantly replenished by snow, rain, and dew.

# Of the Nature of the World

—※—

**135**

HE that is now a prince, wants to be a king or an emperor. A man in love with a girl is ever casting about how he may come to marry her, and in his eyes there is none fairer than she; when he has got her, he is soon weary of her, and thinks another more fair, whom easily he might have had. The poor man thinks, had I but twenty pounds I should be rich enough; but when he has got that, he would have more. The heart is inconsistent in all things, as the heathen says: *Virtutem praesentem odimus, sublatant ex oculis quaerimus invidi.*

**136**

One knife cuts better than another; so, likewise, one that has learned languages and arts can better and more distinctly teach than another. But in that many of them, as Erasmus and others, are well versed in languages and arts, and yet err with great hurt, 'tis as with the greater sort of weapons, which are made to kill: we must distinguish the thing from the abuse.

**137**

The wickedness of the enemies of the Word is not human, but altogether devilish. A human creature is wicked according to the planner and nature of mankind, and according as he is spoiled through original sin, but when he is possessed and driven of the devil, then begins the most bitter and cruel combat between him and the woman's seed.

## 138

The world will neither hold God for God, nor the devil for the devil. And if a man were left to himself, to do after his own kind and nature, he would willingly throw our Lord God out at the window; for the world regards God nothing at all, as the psalm says: The wicked man saith in his heart, there is no God.

## 139

The god of the world is riches, pleasure, and pride, wherewith it abuses all the creatures and gifts of God.

## 140

We have the nature and manner of all wild beasts in eating. The wolves eat sheep; we also. The foxes eat hens, geese, etc.; we also. The hawks and kites eat fowl and birds; we also. Pikes eat other fish; we also. With oxen, horse, and kine, we also eat salads, grass, etc.

## 141

I much wonder how the heathen could write such fair and excellent things of death, seeing it is so grisly and fearful? But when I remember the nature of the world, then I wonder nothing at all; for they saw great evil and wickedness flourishing among them, and in their rulers, which sorely grieved them, and they had nothing else to threaten and terrify their rulers with, but death.

Now, if the heathen so little regarded death, nay, so highly and honourably esteemed it, how much more so ought we Christians? For they, poor people, knew less than nothing of the life eternal, while we know and are instructed in it; yet, when we only speak of death, we are all affrighted.

The cause hereof is our sins; we live worse than the heathen, and therefore cannot justly complain, for the greater our sins, the more fearful is death. See those who have rejected God's word: when they are at the point of death and are put in mind of the day of judgment, how fearfully do they tremble and shake.

## 142

Here, today, have I been pestered with the knaveries and lies of a baker, brought before me for using false weights, though such matters concern the magistrate rather than the divine. Yet if no one were to check the thefts of these bakers, we should have a fine state of things.

### 143

There is not a more dangerous evil than a flattering, dissembling counsellor. While he talks, his advice has hands and feet, but when it should be put in practice, it stands like a mule, which will not be spurred forward.

### 144

There are three sorts of people: the first, the common sort, who live secure without remorse of conscience, acknowledging not their corrupt manners and natures, insensible of God's wrath against their sins, and careless thereof: The second, those who through the law are scared, feel God's anger, and strive and wrestle with despair. The third, those that acknowledge their sins and God's merited wrath, feel themselves conceived and born in sin, and therefore deserving of perdition, but, notwithstanding, attentively hearken to the gospel, and believe that God, out of grace, for the sake of Jesus Christ, forgives sins, and so are justified before God, and afterwards show the fruits of their faith by all manner of good works.

### 145

That matrimony is matrimony, that the hand is a hand, that goods are goods, people well understand; but to believe that matrimony is God's creation and ordinance, that the hands, that the goods, as food and raiment, and other creatures we use, are given and presented unto us of God, 'tis God's special work and grace when men believe it.

### 146

The heart of a human creature is like quicksilver, now here, now there; this day so, tomorrow otherwise. Therefore vanity is a poor miserable thing, as Ecclesiasticus says. A man desires and longs after things that are uncertain and of doubtful result, but contemns that which is certain, done, and accomplished. Therefore what God gives us we will not have; for which cause Christ would not govern on earth, but gave it over to the devil, saying, 'Rule thou.' God is of another nature, manner, and mind. I, he says, am God, and therefore change not; I hold fast and keep sure my promises and threatenings.

## 147

He must be of a high and great spirit that undertakes to serve the people in body and soul, for he must suffer the utmost danger and unthankfulness. Therefore Christ said to Simon Peter etc., 'Lovest thou me?' repeating it three times together. Then he said: 'Feed my sheep': as if he would say, 'Wilt thou be an upright minister, and a shepherd? Then love must only do it, thy love to me; for how else could ye endure unthankfulness, and spend wealth and health, meeting only with persecution and ingratitude?'

## 148

The highest wisdom of the world is to busy itself with temporal, earthly, and ephemeral things; and when these go ill, it says, Who would have thought it? But faith is a certain and sure expectation of that which a man hopes for, making no doubt of that which yet he sees not. A true Christian does not say: I had not thought it, but is most certain that the beloved cross is near at hand; and thus is not afraid when it goes ill with him, and he is tormented. But the world, and those who live secure in it, cannot bear misfortune; they go on continually dancing in pleasure and delight, like the rich glutton in the gospel. He could not spare the scraps to poor Lazarus; but Lazarus belongs to Christ, and will take his part with him.

## 149

The world seems to me like a decayed house, David and the prophets being the spars, and Christ the main pillar in the midst, that supports all.

## 150

As all people feel they must die, each seeks immortality here on earth, that he may be had in everlasting remembrance. Some great princes and kings seek it by raising great columns of stone, and high pyramids, great churches, costly and glorious palaces, castles, etc. Soldiers hunt after praise and honour, by obtaining famous victories. The learned seek an everlasting name by writing books. With these, and such like things, people think to be immortal. But as to the true, everlasting, and incorruptible honour and eternity of God, no man thinks or looks after it. Ah! We are poor, silly, miserable people!

## 151

To live openly among the people is best; Christ so lived and walked, openly and publicly, here on earth, amongst the people, and told his disciples to do the like. 'Tis in cells and corners that the wicked wretches, the monks and nuns, lead shameful lives. But openly, and among people, a man must live decently and honestly.

## 152

To comfort a sorrowful conscience is much better than to possess many kingdoms; yet the world regards it not; nay, contemns it, calling us rebels, disturbers of the peace, and blasphemers of God, turning and altering religion. They will be their own prophets, and prophesy to themselves; but this to us is a great grief of heart. The Jews said of Christ, If we suffer him to go on in this manner, the Romans will come and take from us land and people. After they had slain Christ, did the Romans come or not? Yea, they came, and slew a hundred thousand of them, and destroyed their city. Even so the contemners and enemies of the Word will disturb the peace, and turn Germany upside down. We bring evil upon ourselves, for we wilfully oppose the truth.

## 153

If Moses had continued to work his miracles in Egypt but two or three years, the people would have become accustomed thereto, and heedless, as we who are accustomed to the sun and moon, hold them in no esteem.

## 154

Abraham was held in no honour among the Canaanites, for all the wells he had dug the neighbours filled up, or took away by force, and said to him: Wilt thou not suffer it? then pack thee hence and be gone, for thou art with us a stranger and a newcomer. In like manner, Isaac was despised. The faith possessed by the beloved patriarchs, I am not able sufficiently to admire. How firmly and constantly did they believe that God was gracious unto them, though they suffered such exceeding trouble and adversity!

## 155

If the great pains and labour I take sprang not from the love, and for the sake of him that died for me, the world could not give me money enough to write only one book, or to translate the Bible. I desire not to be rewarded and paid of the world for my books; the world is too poor to give me satisfaction; I have not asked the value of one penny of my master the Prince Elector of Saxony, since I have been here. The world is nothing but a reversed Decalogue, or the ten commandments backwards, a mask and picture of the devil, all contemners of God, all blasphemers, all disobedient; harlotry, pride, theft, murder, etc. are now almost ripe for the slaughter.

### 156

Dr. Luther's wife complaining to him of the indocility and untrustworthiness of servants, he said: A faithful and good servant is a real God-send, but, truly, 'tis a *rare bird in the land*. We find every one complaining of the idleness and profligacy of this class of people; we must govern them, Turkish fashion, so much work, so much victuals, as Pharaoh dealt with the Israelites in Egypt.

### 157

The philosophers, and learned among the heathen, had innumerable speculations as to God, the soul, and the life everlasting, all uncertain and doubtful, they being without God's Word; while to us, God has given his most sweet and saving Word, pure and incorrupt; yet we contemn it. It is naught, says the buyer. When we have a thing, how good soever, we are soon weary of it, and regard it not. The world remains the world, which neither loves nor endures righteousness, but is ruled by a certain few, even as a little boy of twelve years old rules, governs, and keeps a hundred great and strong oxen upon a pasture.

### 158

Whoso relies on his money prospers not. The richest monarchs have had ill fortune, have been destroyed and slain in the wars; while men with but small store of money have had great fortune and victory; as the emperor Maximilian overcame the Venetians, and continued warring ten years with them, though they were exceedingly rich and powerful. Therefore we ought not to trust in money or wealth, or depend thereon. I hear that the prince elector, George, begins to be covetous, which is a sign of his death very shortly. When I saw Dr. Gode begin to tell his puddings hanging in the chimney, I told him he would not live long, and so it fell out; and when I begin to trouble myself about brewing, malting, cooking, etc., then shall I soon die.

### 159

We should always be ready when God knocks, prepared to take our leave of this world like Christians. For even as the small beast kills the stag, leaping upon his head, and sitting between his horns, and eating out his brains, or catches him fast by the throat, and gnaws it asunder, even so the devil, when he possesses a human creature, is not soon or easily pulled from him, but leads him into despair, and hurts him both in soul and body; as St. Peter says: 'He goeth about like a roaring lion.'

## 160

Before Noah's flood the world was highly learned, by reason men lived a long time, and so attained great experience and wisdom; now, ere we begin rightly to come to the true knowledge of a thing, we he down and die. God will not have that we should attain a higher knowledge of things.

## 161

Mammon has two properties; it makes us secure, first, when it goes well with us, and then we live without fear of God at all; secondly, when it goes ill with us, then we tempt God, fly from him, and seek after another god.

## 162

I saw a dog, at Lintz in Austria, that was taught to go with a hand-basket to the butchers' shambles for meat; when other dogs came about him, and sought to take the meat out of the basket, he set it down, and fought lustily with them; but when he saw they were too strong for him, he himself would snatch out the first piece of meat, lest he should lose all. Even so does now our emperor Charles; who, after having long protected spiritual benefices, seeing that every prince takes possession of monasteries, himself takes possession of bishoprics, as just now he has seized upon those of Utrecht and Liege.

## 163

A covetous farmer, well known at Erfurt, carried his corn to sell there in the market, but selling it at too dear a rate, no man would buy of him, or give him his price. He being thereby moved to anger, said: 'I will not sell it cheaper, but rather carry it home again, and give it to the mice.' When he had come home with it, an infinity of mice and rats flocked into his house, and devoured up all his corn. And, next day, going out to see his grounds, which were newly sown, he found that all the seed was eaten up, while no hurt at all was done to the grounds of his neighbours. This certainly was a just punishment from God, a merited token of his wrath.

Three rich farmers have lately, God be praised, hanged themselves: these wretches, that rob the whole country, deserve such punishments; for the dearth at this time is a wilful dearth. God has given enough, but the devil has possessed such wicked cormorants to withhold it. They are thieves and murderers of their poor neighbours. Christ will say unto them at the last day: 'I was hungry, and ye have not fed me.' Do not think, thou that sellest thy corn so dear, that thou shalt escape punishment, for thou art an occasion of the deaths and famishing of the poor; the devil will fetch thee away. They that fear God and trust in him, pray for their daily bread, and against such robbers as thou, that either thou mayest be put to shame, or be reformed.

### 164

A plan that depends on the riches and honours of this world, forgetting God and the welfare of his soul, is like a little child that holds a fair apple in the hand, of agreeable exterior, promising goodness, but within 'tis rotten and full of worms.

### 165

Where great wealth is, there are also all manner of sins; for through wealth comes pride, through pride, dissension, through dissension, wars, through wars, poverty, through poverty, great distress and misery. Therefore, they that are rich, must yield a strict and great account; for to whom much is given, of him much will be required.

### 166

Riches, understanding, beauty, are fair gifts of God, but we abuse them shamefully. Yet worldly wisdom and wit are evils, when the cause engaged in is evil, for no man will yield his own particular conceit; every one will be right. Much better is it that one be of a fair and comely complexion in the face, for the hard lesson, sickness, may come and take that away; but the self-conceited mind is not so soon brought to reason.

### 167

Wealth is the smallest thing on earth, the least gift that God has bestowed on mankind. What is it in comparison with God's Word – what, in comparison with corporal gifts, as beauty, health, etc.? – nay, what is it to the gifts of the mind, as understanding, wisdom, etc.? Yet are men so eager after it, that no labour, pains, or risk is regarded in the acquisition of riches. Wealth has in it neither material, formal, efficient, nor final cause, nor anything else that is good; therefore our Lord God commonly gives riches to those from whom he withholds spiritual good.

## 168

St. John says: 'He that hath this world's goods, and seeth his brother have need, and shutteth up his bowels of compassion from him, how dwelleth the love of God in him?' And Christ: 'He that desireth of thee, give to him' – that is, to him that needs and is in want; not to idle, lazy, wasteful fellows, who are commonly the greatest beggars, and who, though we give them much and often, are nothing helped thereby. Yet when one is truly poor, to him I will give with all my heart, according to my ability. And no man should forget the Scripture: 'He that hath two coats, let him part with one'; meaning all manner of apparel that one has need of, according to his state and calling, as well for credit as for necessity. As also, by 'the daily bread', is understood all maintenance necessary for the body.

## 169

Lendest thou aught? So gettest thou it not again. Even if it be restored, it is not so soon as it ought to be restored, nor so well and good, and thou losest a friend thereby.

## 170

Before I translated the New Testament out of the Greek, all longed after it; when it was done, their longing lasted scarce four weeks. Then they desired the Books of Moses; when I had translated these, they had enough thereof in a short time. After that, they would have the Psalms; of these they were soon weary, and desired other books. So will it be with the Book of Ecclesiasticus, which they now long for, and about which I have taken great pains. All is acceptable until our giddy brains be satisfied; afterwards we let things lie, and seek after new.

# Of Idolatry

## 171

IDOLATRY is all manner of seeming holiness and worshipping, let these counterfeit spiritualities shine outwardly as glorious and fair as they may; in a word, all manner of devotion in those that would serve God without Christ the Mediator, his Word and command. In Popedom it was held a work of the greatest sanctity for the monks to sit in their cells and meditate of God, and of his wonderful works; to be kindled with zeal, kneeling on their knees, praying, and having their imaginary contemplations of celestial objects, with such supposed devotion, that they wept for joy. In these their conceits, they banished all desires and thoughts of women, and what else is temporal and evanescent. They seemed to meditate only of God, and of his wonderful works. Yet all these seeming holy actions of devotion, which the wit and wisdom of man holds to be angelical sanctity, are nothing else but works of the flesh. All manner of religion, where people serve God without his Word and command, is simply idolatry, and the more holy and spiritual such a religion seems, the more hurtful and venomous it is; for it leads people away from the faith of Christ, and makes them rely and depend upon their own strength, works, and righteousness.

In like manner, all kinds of orders of monks, fasts, prayers, hairy shirts, the austerities of the Capuchins, who in Popedom are held to be the most holy of all, are mere works of the flesh; for the monks hold they are holy, and shall be saved, not through Christ, whom they view as a severe and angry judge, but through the rules of their order.

No man can make the papists believe that the private mass is the greatest blaspheming of God, and the highest idolatry upon earth, an abomination the like to which has never been in Christendom since the time of the apostles; for they are blinded and hardened therein, so that their understanding and knowledge of God, and of all divine matters, is perverted and erroneous. They hold that to be the most upright and greatest service of God, which, in truth, is the greatest and most abominable idolatry. And again, they hold that for idolatry, which, in truth, is the upright and most acceptable service of God, the acknowledging Christ, and believing in him. But we that truly believe in Christ, and are of his mind, we, God be praised, know and judge all things, but are judged of no human creature.

## 172

Dr. Carlstad asked me: Should a man, out of good intention, erect a pious work without God's word or command, does he herein serve a true or a strange God? Luther answered: A man honours God and calls upon him, to the end he may expect comfort, help, and all good from him. Now if this same honour and calling upon God be done according to God's Word that is, when a man expects from him all graces for the sake of his promises made unto us in Christ, then he honours the true, living, and everlasting God. But if a man take in hand a work or a service, out of his own devotion, as he thinks good, thereby to appease God's anger, or to attain forgiveness of sins, everlasting life, and salvation, as is the manner of all hypocrites and seeming holy workers, then, I say flatly, he honours and worships an idol in his heart: and it helps him nothing at all, that he thinks he does it to the honour of the true God; for that which is not of faith is sin.

## 173

Hypocrites and idolaters are of the same quality with singers, who will scarce sing when asked to do so, but, when not desired, begin, and never leave off. Even so with the false workers of holiness; when God orders them to obey his commands, which are to love one's neighbour, to help him with advice, with lending, giving, admonishing, comforting, etc., no man can bring them to this; but, on the contrary, they stick to that which they themselves make choice of, pretending that this is the best way to honour and serve God – a great delusion of theirs. They plague and torment their bodies with fasting, praying, singing, reading, hard lying, etc.; they affect great humility and holiness, and do all these things with vast zeal, fervency, and incessant devotion. But such as the service and work is, such will also the reward be, as Christ himself says: 'In vain do they worship me, teaching for doctrine the commandments of men.'

## 174

The idolatry of Moloch had, I apprehend, a great show, as though it were a worship more acceptable and pleasing to God than the common service commanded by Moses; hence many people who, in outward show, were of devout holiness, when they intended to perform an acceptable service and honour to God, as they imagined, offered up and sacrificed their sons and daughters, thinking, no doubt, that herein they were following the example of Abraham, and doing an act very acceptable and pleasing to God.

Against this idolatry God's prophets preached with burning zeal, calling it, not offerings to God, but to idols and devils, as the 106th Psalm shows, and Jeremiah, chapters 7 and 23. But they held the prophets to be impostors and accursed heretics.

This worshipping of idols was very frequent in Popedom, in my time and still, though in another manner; the papists in Popedom being esteemed holy people that give one or more of their children to the monasteries, to become either monks or nuns, that so they may serve God, as they say, day and night. Hence the proverb: Blessed the mother of the child that is made a spiritual person! True, these sons and daughters in Popedom are not burned and offered to idols corporally, as were the Jewish children, yet, which is far worse, they are thrust into the throat of the devil spiritually, who, through his disciples, the pope and his shaven crew, lamentably murders their souls with false doctrines.

The Holy Scripture often mentions Moloch, as does Lyra; and the commentaries of the Jews say, it was an idol made of copper and brass, like a man holding his hands before him, wherein they put fiery coals. When the image was made very hot, a father approached, and offering to the idol, took his child, and thrust it into the glittering hands of the idol, whereby the child was consumed and burned to death. Meantime, they made a loud noise with timbrels, and cymbals, and horns, to the end the parents should not hear the pitiful crying of the child. The prophets write that Ahab offered his son in this manner.

## 175

The calves of Jeroboam still remain in the world, and will remain to the last day; not that any man now makes calves like Jeroboam's, but upon whatsoever a man depends or trusts – God set aside – this is the calves of Jeroboam, that is, other and strange gods, honoured and worshipped instead of the only, true, living, and eternal God, who only can and will help and comfort in all need. In like manner also, all such as rely and depend upon their art, wisdom, strength, sanctity, riches, honour, power, or anything else, under what title or name soever, on which the world builds, make and worship the calves of Jeroboam. For they trust in and depend on vanishing creatures, which is worshipping of idols and idolatry. We easily fall into idolatry, for we are inclined thereunto by nature, and coming to us by inheritance, it seems pleasant.

### 176

St. Paul shows in these words: 'When ye, knew not God, ye did service,' etc., that is, when as yet ye knew not God or what God's will was towards you, ye served those who by stature were no gods; ye served the dreams and thoughts of your hearts, wherewith, against God's Word, ye feigned to yourselves a God that suffered himself to be conciliated with such works and worshippings as your devotion and good intention made choice of. For all idolatry in the world arises from this, that people by nature have had the common knowledge, that there is a God, without which idolatry would remain unpractised. With this knowledge engrafted in mankind, they have, without God's Word, fancied all manner of ungodly opinions of God, and held and esteemed these for divine truths, imagining a God otherwise than, by nature, he is.

### 177

He that goes from the gospel to the law, thinking to be saved by good works, falls as uneasily, as he who falls from the true service of God to idolatry; for, without Christ, all is idolatry and fictitious imaginings of God, whether of the Turkish Koran, of the pope's decrees, or Moses' laws; if a man think thereby to be justified and saved before God, he is undone.

When a man will serve God, he must not look upon that which he does; not upon the work, but how it ought to be done, and whether God has commanded it or no; seeing, as Samuel says, that 'God hath more pleasure in obedience, than in burnt sacrifice'.

Whoso hearkens not to God's voice, is an idolater, though he perform the highest and most heavy service of God. 'Tis the very nature of idolatry not to make choice of that which is esteemed easy and light, but of that which is great and heavy, as we see in the friars and monks, who have been constantly devising new worshippings of God; but, forasmuch that God in his Word has not commanded these, they are idolatry, and blasphemy. All these sins; they who are in the function of preaching ought undauntedly and freely to reprove, not regarding men's high dignities and powers. For the prophets, as we see in Hosea, reproved and threatened not only the house of Israel in general, but also, in particular, the priests, ay, the king himself, and the whole court. They cared not for the great danger that might follow from the magistrate being so openly assailed, or that themselves thereby should fall into displeasure and contempt, and their preaching be esteemed rebellious. They were impelled by the far greater danger, lest by such examples of the higher powers, the subjects also should be seduced into sin.

## 178

The papists took the invocation of saints from the heathen, who divided God into numberless images and idols, and ordained to each its particular office and work.

These the papists, void of all shame and Christianity, imitated, thereby denying God's almighty power; every man, out of God's Word, spinning to himself a particular opinion, according to his own fancy; as one of their priests, celebrating mass, when about to consecrate many oblations at the altar at once, thought it would not be congruously spoken, or according to grammar rules, to say, 'This is my body,' so said, 'These are my bodies'; and afterwards highly extolled his device, saying: 'If I had not been so good a grammarian, I had brought in a heresy, and consecrated but one oblation.'

Such like fellows does the world produce; grammarians, logicians, rhetoricians, and philosophers, all falsifying the Holy Writ, and sophisticating it with their arts, whereas, it ought to remain, every point in its own place, whereto God ordered and appointed it. Divinity should be empress, and philosophy and other arts merely her servants, not to govern and master her, as Servetus, Carnpanus, and other seducers would do. God preserve his church, which by him is carried as a child in the mother's womb, and defend her from such philosophical divinity.

The invocation of saints is a most abominable blindness and heresy; yet the papists will not give it up. The pope's greatest profit arises from the dead; for the calling on dead saints brings him infinite sums of money and riches far more than he gets from the living. But thus goes the world; superstition, unbelief, false doctrine, idolatry, obtain more credit and profit than the upright, true, and pure religion.

## 179

God and God's worship are relatives; the one cannot be without the other; for God must always be the God of some people or nation, and is always in *predicamento relationis*. God will have some to call upon him and honour him; for, to have a God and to honour him, go together. Therefore, whoso brings in a divine worship of his own selection, without God's command, is an adulterer, like a married woman who consents to another man, seeking another and not the upright true God, and it avails him nothing that he thinks he does God service herein.

## 180

In all creatures are a declaration and a signification of the Holy Trinity. First, the substance signifies the almighty power of God the Father. Secondly, the form and shape declare the wisdom of God the Son; and, thirdly, the power and strength is a sign of the Holy Ghost. So that God is present in all creatures.

## 181

In the gospel of St. John, chapter 3, is plainly and directly shown the difference of the persons, in the highest and greatest work that God accomplished for us poor human creatures, in justifying and saving us; for there it is plainly written of the Father, that he loved the world, and gave to the world his only begotten Son. These are two several persons – Father, and Son. The Father loves the world; and gives unto it his Son. The Son suffers himself to be given to the world, and 'to be lifted up on the cross, as the serpent was lifted up in the wilderness, that whosoever believed in him shall not perish, but have everlasting life'. To this work comes afterwards the third person, the Holy Ghost, who kindles faith in the heart through the Word, and so regenerates us, and makes us the children of God.

This article, though it be taught most clearly in the New Testament, yet has been always assaulted and opposed in the highest measure, so that the holy evangelist, St. John, for the confirmation of this article, was constrained to write his gospel. Then came presently that heretic, Cerinthus, teaching out of Moses, that there was but one God, and concluding thence that Christ could not be God, or God man.

But let us stick to God's Word in the Holy Scripture, namely, that Christ is true God with God the Father, and that the Holy Ghost is true God, and yet there are not three Gods, nor three substances, as three men, three angels, three sons, three windows, etc. No: God is not separated or divided in such manner in his substance, but there is only and alone one divine essence, and no more.

Therefore, although there be three persons. God the Father, God the Son, and God the Holy Ghost, yet notwithstanding, we must not divide or separate the substance for there is but only one God, in one only undivided substance, as St. Paul clearly speaks of Christ, Colossians 1, that he is the express image of the invisible God, the first-born of all creatures; for through him all things are created that are in heaven and on earth, visible, etc., and all is through and in him created, and he is before all, and all things consist in him.

Now what the third person is, the holy evangelist, St. John, teaches, chapter 15, where he says: 'But when the Comforter is come, which I will send unto you from the Father, the Spirit of truth which proceeds from the Father, he shall testify of me.' Here Christ speaks not only of the office and work of the Holy Ghost, but also of his substance and faith: he goes out or proceeds from the Father, that is, his going out, or his proceeding, is without all beginning, and everlasting. Therefore the holy prophet Joel gives him the name, and calls him, 'the Spirit of the Lord'.

Now, although this article seem strange or foolish, what matters it? 'tis not the question whether it be so or no, but whether it be grounded on God's Word, or no. If it be God's word, as most surely it is, then let us make no doubt thereof; He will not lie; therefore, let us keep close to God's Word, and not dispute how Father, Son, and Holy Ghost can be one God; for we, as poor wretches, cannot know how it is that we laugh; or how with our eyes, we can see a high mountain ten miles off; or how it is, that when we sleep, in body we are dead, and yet live. This small knowledge we cannot attain unto; no, though we took to our help the advice and art of all the wise in the world, we are not able to know the least things which concern ourselves; and yet we would climb up with our human wit and wisdom, and presume to comprehend what God is in his incomprehensible majesty.

# Of Jesus Christ

---

### 182

The chief lesson and study in divinity is, that we learn well and rightly to know Christ, who is therein very graciously pictured forth unto us. We take pains to conciliate the good will and friendship of men, that so they may show us a favourable countenance; how much the more ought we to conciliate our Lord Jesus, that so he may be gracious unto us. St. Peter says: 'Grow up in the knowledge of Jesus Christ', of that compassionate Lord and Master, whom all should cleave unto. Christ himself also teaches, that we should learn to know him only out of the Scriptures, where he says: 'Search the Scriptures; for they do testify of me.' St. John says: 'In the beginning was the Word, and the Word was with God, and the Word was God,' etc. The apostle Thomas also calls Christ, God; where he says: 'My Lord, and my God.' In like manner, St. Paul, Romans 9, speaks of Christ, that he is God; where he says: 'Who is God over all, blessed for ever, Amen.' And Colossians 2, 'In Christ dwelleth all the fulness of the Godhead bodily'; that is, substantially.

Christ must needs be true God, seeing he, through himself, fulfilled and overcame the law; for most certain it is, that no one else could have vanquished the law, angel or human creature, but Christ only, so that it cannot hurt those that believe in him; therefore, most certainly he is the Son of God, and natural God. Now if we comprehend Christ in this manner, as the Holy Scripture displays him before us, then certain it is, that we can neither err nor be put to confusion; and may then easily judge what is right to be held of all manner of divine qualities, religion, and worship, that are used and practised in the universal world. Were this picturing of Christ removed out of our sight, or darkened in us undeniably there must needs follow utter disorder. For human and natural religion, wisdom, and understanding, cannot judge aright or truly of the laws of God; therein has been and still is exhausted the art of all philosophers, of all the learned and worldly-wise among the children of men. For the law rules and governs mankind; therefore the law judges mankind, and not mankind the law.

If Christ be not God, then neither the Father nor the Holy Ghost is God; for our article of faith speaks thus: 'Christ is God, with the Father, and the Holy Ghost.' Many there are, who talk much of the Godhead of Christ, as the pope, and others; but they discourse thereof as a blind man speaks of colours. Therefore, when I hear Christ speak, and say: 'Come to me, all ye that are weary and heavy laden, and I will give you rest,' then do I believe steadfastly that the whole Godhead speaks in an undivided and unseparate substance. Wherefore, he that preaches a God to me that died not for me the death on the cross, that God will I not receive.

He that has this article, has the chief and principal article of faith, though to the world it seem unmeaning and even ridiculous. Christ says: The Comforter which I will send, shall not depart from you, but will remain with you, and will make you able to endure all manner of tribulations and evil. When Christ says: I will pray to the Father, then he speaks as a human creature, or as very man; but when he says: I will do this or that, as before he said, I will send the Comforter, then he speaks as very God. In this manner do I learn my article, 'That Christ is both God and man'.

I, out of my own experience, am able to witness, that Jesus Christ is true God; I know full well and have found what the name of Jesus has done for me. I have often been so near death, that I thought verily now must I die, because I teach his Word to the wicked world, and acknowledge him; but always he mercifully put life into me, refreshed and comforted me. Therefore, let us use diligence only to keep him, and then all is safe, although the devil were ever so wicked and crafty, and the world ever so evil and false. Let whatsoever will or can befall me, I will surely cleave by my sweet Saviour Christ Jesus, for in him am I baptized; I can neither do nor know anything but only what he has taught me.

The Holy Scriptures, especially St. Paul, everywhere ascribe unto Christ that which he gives to the Father, namely, the divine almighty power; so that he can give grace, and peace of conscience, forgiveness of sins, life, victory over sin, and death, and the devil. Now, unless St. Paul would rob God of his honour, and give it to another that is not God, he dared not ascribe such properties and attributes to Christ, if he were not true God; and God himself says, Isaiah 42, 'I will not give my glory to another.' And, indeed, no man can give that to another which he has not himself; but, seeing Christ gives grace and peace, the Holy Ghost also, and redeems from the power of the devil, sin and death, so is it most sure that he has an endless, immeasurable, almighty power, equal with the Father.

Christ brings also peace, but not as the apostles brought it, through preaching; he gives it as a Creator, as his own proper creature. The Father creates and gives life, grace, and peace; and even so gives the Son the same gifts. Now, to give grace, peace, everlasting life, forgiveness of sins, to justify, to save, to deliver from death and hell, surely these are not the works of any creature, but of the sole majesty of God, things which the angels themselves can neither create nor give. Therefore, such works pertain to the high majesty, honour, and glory of God, who is the only and true Creator of all things. We must think of no other God than Christ; that God which speaks not out of Christ's mouth, is not God. God, in the Old Testament, bound himself to the throne of grace; there was the place where he would hear; so long as the policy and government of Moses stood and flourished. In like manner, he will still hear no man or human creature, but only through Christ. As numbers of the Jews ran to and fro burning incense, and offerings here and there, and seeking God in various places, not regarding the tabernacle, so it goes now: we seek God everywhere; but not seeking him in Christ, we find him nowhere.

## 183

The feast we call *Annunciatio Mariæ,* when the angel came to Mary, and brought her the message from God, that she should conceive his Son, may be fitly called the 'Feast of Christ's Humanity'; for then began our deliverance. The mystery of the humanity of Christ, that he sunk himself into our flesh, is beyond all human understanding.

## 184

Christ lived three and thirty years, and went up thrice every year to Jerusalem, making ninety-nine times he went thither. If the pope could show that Christ had been but once at Rome, what a bragging and boasting would he make! Yet Jerusalem was destroyed to the ground.

**185**

St. Paul teaches, that Christ was born, to the end he might restore and bring everything to the state in which it was created at the beginning of the world; that is, to bring us to the knowledge of ourselves and our Creator, that we might learn to know who and what we have been, and who and what we now are; namely, that we were created after God's likeness, and afterwards, according to the likeness of man; that we were the devil's vizard through sin, utterly lost and destroyed; and that now we may be delivered from sin again, and become pure, justified, and saved.

**186**

On the day of the conception of our Saviour Christ, we that are preachers ought diligently to lay before the people, and thoroughly imprint in their hearts, the history of this feast, which is given by St. Luke in plain and simple language. And we should joy and delight in these blessed things, more than in all the treasure on earth, disputing not how it came to pass, that he, who fills heaven and earth, and whom neither heaven nor earth is able to comprehend, was inclosed in the pure body of his mother. Such disputations impede our joys, and give us occasion to doubt.

Bernard occupies a whole sermon upon this feast, in laud of the Virgin Mary, forgetting the great author of comfort, that this day God was made man. True, we cannot but extol and praise Mary, who was so highly favoured of the Lord, but when the Creator himself comes, who delivers us from the devil's power, etc., him, neither we nor angels can sufficiently honour, praise, worship, and adore.

The Turk himself, who believes there is only one God, who has created all things, permits Christ to remain a prophet, though he denies that he is the only begotten, true, and natural Son of God.

But I, God be praised, have learned out of the Holy Scripture, and by experience in my trials, temptations, and fierce combats against the devil, that this article of Christ's humanity is most sure and certain; for nothing has more or better helped me in high spiritual temptations, than my comfort in this, that Christ, the true everlasting Son of God, is our flesh and bone, as St. Paul says to the Ephesians, chapter 5: 'We are members of his body, of his flesh and bone; he sitteth at the right hand of God, and maketh intercession for us.' When I take hold of this shield of faith, then I soon drive away that wicked one, with all his fiery darts.

God, from the beginning, has held fast to this article, and powerfully defended the same against all heretics, the pope, and the Turk; and afterwards confirmed it with many miraculous signs, so that all who have opposed the same at last have been brought to confusion.

## 187

All the wisdom of the world is childish foolishness in comparison with the acknowledgment of Christ. For what is more wonderful than the unspeakable mystery, that the Son of God, the image of the eternal Father, took upon him the nature of man. Doubtless, he helped his supposed father, Joseph, to build houses; for Joseph was a carpenter. What will they of Nazareth think at the day of judgment, when they shall see Christ sitting in his divine majesty; surely they will be astonished, and say: Lord, thou helpest build my house, how comest thou now to this high honour?

When Jesus was born, doubtless, he cried and wept like other children, and his mother tended him as other mothers tend their children. As he grew up, he was submissive to his parents, and waited on them, and carried his supposed father's dinner to him, and when he came back, Mary no doubt, often said: 'My dear little Jesus, where hast thou been?' He that takes not offence at the simple, lowly, and mean course of the life of Christ, is endued with high divine art and wisdom; yea, has a special gift of God in the Holy Ghost. Let us ever bear in mind, that our blessed Saviour thus humbled and abased himself, yielding even to the contumelious death of the cross, for the comfort of us poor, miserable, and damned creatures.

## 188

If the emperor should wash a beggar's feet, as the French king used to do on Maundy Thursday, and the emperor Charles yearly, how would such humility be extolled and praised! But though the Son of God, Lord of all emperors, kings, and princes, in the deepest measure humbled himself; even to the death of the cross, yet no man wonders thereat, except only the small heap of the faithful who acknowledge and worship him as their only Lord and Saviour. He abased himself, indeed, enough, when he was held to be the man most despised, plagued, and smitten of God (Isaiah 53), and for our sakes underwent and suffered shame.

## 189

We cannot vex the devil more than by teaching, preaching, singing, and talking of Jesus. Therefore I like it well, when with sounding voice we sing in the church: *Et homo factus est; et verbum caro factum est.* The devil cannot endure these words, and flies away, for he well feels what is contained therein. Oh, how happy a thing were it, did we find as much joy in these words as the devil is affrighted at them. But the world contemns God's words and works, because they are delivered to them in a plain and simple manner. Well, the good and godly are not offended therewith, for they have regard to the everlasting celestial treasure and wealth which therein lies hid, and which is so precious and glorious, that the angels delight in beholding it. Some there are who take offence, that now and then in the pulpits we say: Christ was a carpenter's son, and as a blasphemer and rebel, he was put on the cross, and hanged between two malefactors.

But seeing we preach continually of this article, and in our children's creed, say: That our Saviour Christ suffered under Pontius Pilate, was crucified, dead, and buried, etc. for our sins, why, then, should we not say Christ was a carpenter's son? Especially seeing that he is clearly so named in the gospel, when the people wondered at his doctrine and wisdom, and said: How cometh this to pass? Is not this the carpenter, the son of Mary? (Mark 6).

## 190

Christ, our High-priest, is ascended into heaven, and sits on the right hand of God the Father, where, without ceasing, he makes intercession for us (see Romans 8), where St. Paul, with very excellent, glorious words, pictures Christ to us; as in his death, he is a sacrifice offered up for sins; in his resurrection, a conqueror: in his ascension, a king; in making mediation and intercession, a high priest. For, in the law of Moses, the high-priest only went into the Most Holiest to pray for the people.

Christ will remain a priest and king, though he was never consecrated by any papist bishop or greased by any of those shavelings; but he was ordained and consecrated by God himself, and by him anointed, where he says: 'Thou art a priest for ever.' Here the word Thou is bigger than the stone in the Revelation of John, which was longer than three hundred leagues. And the second psalm says: 'I have set my King upon my holy hill of Sion.' Therefore he will sure remain sitting, and all that believe in him.

God says: 'Thou art a priest for ever, after the order of Melchizedeck.' Therefore let us depend on this priest, for he is faithful and true, given unto us of God, and loving us more than his own life, as he showed by his bitter passion and death. Ah! how happy and blessed were the man that could believe this from his heart.

'The Lord sware and will not repent, thou art a priest' This is the most glorious sentence in the whole psalms, where God declares unto us, that this Christ shall be our bishop and high-priest, who, without ceasing, shall make intercession for those that are his, and none other besides him. It shall be neither Caiaphas, nor Annas, Peter, Paul, nor the pope, but Christ, only Christ; therefore let us take our refuge in him. The epistle to the Hebrews makes good use of this verse.

It is, indeed, a great and a glorious comfort (which every good and godly Christian would not miss, or be without, for all the honour and wealth in the world) that we know and believe that Christ, our high-priest, sits on the right hand of God, praying and mediating for us without ceasing-the true pastor and bishop of our souls, which the devil cannot tear out of his hands.

But then what a crafty and mighty spirit the devil must be, who can affright, and with his fiery darts draw the hearts of good and godly people from this excelling comfort, and make them entertain other cogitations of Christ; that he is not their high-priest, but complains of them to God; that he is not the bishop of their souls, but a stern and an angry judge. The Lord said to Christ: 'Rule in the midst of thine enemies.' On the other hand, the devil claims to be prince and God of the world. He is, therefore, the sworn enemy of Jesus Christ and of his Word, and of those who follow that Word, sincerely and without guile. 'Tis impossible for Jesus Christ and the devil ever to remain under the same roof. The one must yield to the other – the devil to Christ. The Jews and the Apostles were for awhile under the same roof, and the Jews plagued and persecuted the Apostles and their followers, but after a while were themselves thrust out by the Romans. As little can the Lutherans and the papists hold together. One party must yield, and by the blessing and aid of God, this will be the papists.

### 191

*Sheb limini;* that is, 'Sit thou on my right hand.' This *Sheb limini* has many and great enemies, whom we poor, small heap must endure; but 'tis no matter; many of us must suffer and be slain by their fury and rage, yet let us not be dismayed, but, with a divine resolution and courage, wage and venture ourselves, our bodies and souls, upon this his word and promise: 'I live, and ye shall also live; and where I am, there shall ye be also.'

Christ bears himself as though he took not the part of us his poor, troubled, persecuted members. For the world rewards God's best and truest servants very ill; persecuting, condemning, and killing them as heretics and malefactors, while Christ holds his peace and suffers it to be done, so that sometimes I have this thought: I know not where I am; whether I preach right or no. This was also the temptation and trial of St. Paul, touching which he, however, spake not much, neither could, as I think; for who can tell what those words impart: 'I die daily.'

The Scripture, in many places, calls Christ our priest, bridegroom, love's delight, etc., and us who believe in him, his bride, virgin, daughter, etc.; this is a fair, sweet, loving picture, which we always should have before our eyes. For, first, he has manifested his office of priesthood in this, that he has preached, made known, and revealed his Father's will unto us. Secondly, he has also prayed, and will pray for us true Christians so long as the world endures. Thirdly, he has offered up his body for our sins upon the cross. He is our bridegroom, and we are his bride. What he, the loving Saviour Christ has – yea himself, is ours; for we are members of his body, of his flesh and bone, as St. Paul says. And again, what we have, the same is also his; but the exchange is exceeding unequal; for he has everlasting innocence, righteousness, life, and salvation, which he gives to be our own, while what we have is sin, death, damnation, and hell; these we give unto him, for he has taken our sins upon him, has delivered us from the power of the devil and crushed his head, taken him prisoner, and cast him down to hell; so that now we may, with St. Paul, undauntedly say: 'Death, where is thy sting?' Yet, though our loving Saviour has solemnized this spiritual wedding with us, and endued us with his eternal, celestial treasure, and sworn to be our everlasting priest, yet the majority, in the devil's name, run away from him, and worship strange idols, as the Jews did, and as they in popedom do.

## 192

'There is but one God,' says St. Paul, 'and one mediator between God and man; namely, the man Jesus Christ, who gave himself a ransom for all.' Therefore, let no man think to draw near unto God or obtain grace of him, without this mediator, high-priest, and advocate.

It follows that we cannot through our good works, honesty of life, virtues, deserts, sanctity, or through the works of the law, appease God's wrath, or obtain forgiveness of sins; and that all deserts of saints are quite rejected and condemned, so that through them no human creature can be justified before God. Moreover, we see how fierce God's anger is against sins, seeing that by none other sacrifice or offering could they be appeased and stilled, but by the precious blood of the Son of God.

### 193

All heretics have set themselves against Christ. Manicheus opposed Christ's humanity, for he alleged, Christ was a spirit; 'Even,' says he, 'as the sun shines through a painted glass, and the sunbeams go through on the other side, and yet the sun takes nothing away from the substance of the glass, even so Christ took nothing from the substance and nature of Mary.' Arius assaulted the godhead of Christ. Nestorius held there were two persons. Eutychius taught there was but one person; 'for,' said he, 'the person of the Deity was swallowed up.' Helvidius affirmed, the mother of Christ was not a virgin, so that, according to his wicked allegation, Christ was born in original sin. Macedonius opposed only the article of the Holy Ghost, but he soon fell, and was confounded. If this article of Christ remain, then all blasphemous spirits must vanish and be overthrown. The Turks and Jews acknowledge God the Father; it is the Son they shoot at. About this article much blood has been shed. I verily believe that at Rome more than twenty hundred thousands of martyrs have been put to death. It began with the beginning of the world – with Cain and Abel, Ishmael and Isaac, Esau and Jacob, and I am persuaded that 'twas about it the devil was cast from heaven down to hell; he was a fair creature of God, and, doubtless, strove to be the Son.

Next, after the Holy Scripture, we have no stronger argument for the confirmation of that article, than the sweet and loving cross. For all kingdoms, all the powerful, have striven against Christ and this article, but they could not prevail.

### 194

At Rome was a church called Pantheon, where were collected effigies of all the gods they were able to bring together out of the whole world. All these could well accord one with another, for the devil therewith jeered the world, laughing in his fist; but when Christ came, him they could not endure, but all the devils, idols, and heretics grew stark mad and full of rage; for he, the right and true God and man, threw them altogether on a heap. The pope also sets himself powerfully against Christ, but he must likewise be put to confusion and destroyed.

### 195

The history of the resurrection of Christ, teaching that which human wit and wisdom of itself cannot believe, that 'Christ is risen from the dead', was declared to the weaker and sillier creatures, women, and such as were perplexed and troubled.

Silly, indeed, before God, and before the world: first, before God, in that they 'sought the living among the dead'; second, before the world, for they forgot the 'great stone which lay at the mouth of the sepulchre', and prepared spices to anoint Christ, which was all in vain. But spiritually is hereby signified this: if the 'great stone', namely, the law and human traditions, whereby the consciences are bound and snared, be not rolled away from the heart, then we cannot find Christ, or believe that he is risen from the dead. For through him we are delivered from the power of sin and death, Romans 8, so that the hand-writing of the conscience, can hurt us no more.

### 196

Is it not a wonder beyond all wonders, that the Son of God, whom all angels and the heavenly hosts worship, and at whose presence the whole earth quakes and trembles, should have stood among those wicked wretches, and suffered himself to be so lamentably tormented, scorned, derided, and contemned? They spat in his face, struck him in the mouth with a reed, and said: O, he is a king, he must have a crown and a sceptre. The sweet blessed Saviour complains not in vain in the Psalm, *Diminuerunt omnia ossa mea*: now, if he suffered so much from the rage of men, what must he have felt when God's wrath was poured out upon him without measure? as St. Mark says: 'He began to be sore amazed, and very heavy, and saith unto his disciples, My soul is exceeding sorrowful unto death'; and St. Luke says: 'And being in an agony, he prayed more earnestly, and his sweat was as it were great drops of blood falling down to the ground.' Ah! our suffering is not worthy the name of suffering. When I consider my crosses, tribulations, and temptations, I shame myself almost to death, thinking what are they in comparison of the sufferings of my blessed Saviour Christ Jesus. And yet we must be conformable to the express image of the Son of God.

And what if we were conformable to the same, yet were it nothing. He is the Son of God, we are poor creatures; though we should suffer everlasting death, yet were they of no value.

### 197

The wrath is fierce and devouring which the devil has against the Son of God, and against mankind. I beheld once a wolf tearing sheep. When the wolf comes into a sheepfold, he eats not any until he has killed all, and then he begins to eat, thinking to devour all. Even so it is also with the devil; I have now, thinks he, taken hold of Christ, and in time I will also snap his disciples.

But the devil's folly is that he sees not he has to do with the Son of God; he knows not that in the end it will be his bane. It will come to that pass, that the devil must be afraid of a child in the cradle; for when he but hears the name Jesus, uttered in true faith, then he cannot stay. The devil would rather run through the fire, than stay where Christ is; therefore, it is justly said, the seed of the woman shall crush the serpent's head. I believe, indeed, he has so crushed his head, that he can neither abide to hear or see Christ Jesus. I often delight myself with that similitude in Job, of an angle-hook that fishermen cast into the water, putting on the hook a little worm; then comes the fish and snatches at the worm, and gets therewith the hook in his jaws, and the fisher pulls him out of the water. Even so has our Lord God dealt with the devil; God has cast into the world his only Son, as the angler, and upon the hook has put Christ's humanity, as the worm; then comes the devil and snaps at the (man) Christ, and devours him, and therewith he bites the iron hook, that is, the godhead of Christ, which chokes him, and all his power thereby is thrown to the ground. This is called *sapientia divina,* divine wisdom.

### 198

The conversation of Christ with his disciples, when he took his leave of them at his last supper, was most sweet, loving, and friendly, talking with them lovingly, as a father with his children, when he must depart from them. He took their weakness in good part, and bore with them, though now and then their discourse was very full of simplicity; as when Philip said: 'Show us the Father,' etc. And Thomas: 'We know not the way,' etc. And Peter: 'I will go with thee into death.' Each freely showing the thoughts of his heart. Never, since the world began, was a more precious, sweet, and amiable conversation.

### 199

Christ had neither money, nor riches, nor earthly kingdom, for he gave the same to kings and princes. But he reserved one thing peculiarly to himself, which no human creature or angel could do – namely, to conquer sin and death, the devil and hell, and in the midst of death to deliver and save those that through his word believe in him.

### 200

The sweating of blood and other high spiritual sufferings that Christ endured in the garden, no human creature can know or imagine; if one of us should but begin to feel the least of those sufferings, he must die instantly. There are many who die of grief of mind; fair sorrow of heart is death itself. If a man should feel such anguish and pain as Christ had, it were impossible for the soul to remain in the body and endure it – body and soul must part asunder. In Christ only it was possible, and from him issued bloody sweat.

## 201

Nothing is more sure than this: he that does not take hold on Christ by faith, and comfort himself herein, that Christ is made a curse for him, remains under the curse. The more we labour by works to obtain grace, the less we know how to take hold on Christ; for where he is not known and comprehended by faith, there is not to be expected either advice, help, or comfort, though we torment ourselves to death.

## 202

All the prophets well foresaw in the Spirit, that Christ, by imputation, would become the greatest sinner upon the face of the earth, and a sacrifice for the sins of the whole world; would be no more considered an innocent person and without sin, or the Son of God in glory, but a notorious sinner, and so be for a while forsaken (Psalm 8), and have lying upon his neck the sins of all mankind; the sins of St. Paul, who was a blasphemer of God, and a persecutor of his church; St. Peter's sins, that denied Christ; David's sins, who was an adulterer and a murderer, through whom the name of the Lord among the heathen was blasphemed.

Therefore the law, which Moses gave to be executed upon all malefactors and murderers in general, took hold on Christ, finding him with and among sinners and murderers, though in his own person innocent.

This manner of picturing Christ to us, the sophists, robbers of God, obscure and falsify; for they will not that Christ was made a curse for us, to the end he might deliver us from the curse of the law, nor that he has anything to do with sin and poor sinners; though for their sakes alone was he made man and died, but they set before us merely Christ's examples, which they say we ought to imitate and follow; and thus they not only steal from Christ his proper name and title, but also make of him a severe and angry judge, a fearful and horrible tyrant, full of wrath against poor sinners, and bent on condemning them.

## 203

The riding of our blessed Saviour into Jerusalem was a poor, mean kind of procession enough, where was seen Christ, king of heaven and earth, sitting upon a strange ass, his saddle being the clothes of his disciples. This mean equipage, for so powerful a potentate, was, as the prophecy of the prophet Zechariah showed, to the end the scripture might be fulfilled. Yet 'twas an exceeding stately and glorious thing as extolled through the prophecies, though outwardly to the world it seemed poor and mean.

I hold that Christ himself did not mention this prophecy, but that rather the apostles and evangelists used it for a witness. Christ, meantime, preached and wept, but the people honoured him with olive branches and palms, which are signs of peace and victory. Such ceremonies did the heathen receive of the Jews, and not the Jews of the heathen, as some pretend, for the nation of the Jews and Jerusalem was much older than the Greeks and Romans. The Greeks had their beginning about the time of the Babylonish captivity, but Jerusalem was long before the time of the Persians and Assyrians, and therefore much before the Greeks and Romans, so that the heathen received many ceremonies from the Jews, as the elder nation.

## 204

The Jews crucified Christ with words, but the Gentiles have crucified him with words and deeds. His sufferings were prophetical of our wickedness, for Christ suffers still to this day in our church much more than in the synagogue of the Jews; far greater blaspheming of God, contempt, and tyranny, is now among us than heretofore among the Jews. In Italy, when mention is made of the article of faith and of the last day of judgment, then says the pope with his greased crew: O! dost thou believe that? Pluck thou up a good heart, and be merry; let such cogitations alone. These and the like blasphemies are so common in all Italy, that, without fear of punishment, they openly proclaim them everywhere.

## 205

The prophets spoke and preached of the second coming of Christ as we do now; we know that the last day will come, yet we know not what and how it will be after this life, but only in general, that we, who are true Christians, shall have everlasting joy, peace, and salvation. The prophets held likewise, that soon after the coming of Christ, the last day would appear. First, they named the day of the Messiah the last day. Secondly, they set the signs of the first and second coming both together, as if they would happen at one time. Thirdly, in the Epistle to the Corinthians, they demanded of St. Paul, if the last day would appear while they lived. Fourthly, Christ himself related that these signs should come together. O! how willingly would I have been once with our Saviour Christ here on earth, when he rejoiced.

## 206

My opinion is, that Christ descended into hell, to the end he might lay the devil in chains, in order to bring him to the judgment of the great day, as in the 16th Psalm, and Acts 2. Disputatious spirits allege, that the word *Infernus,* Hell, must be taken and understood to be the grave, as in the first book of Moses, but yet here is written not only the Hebrew word *Nabot* – that is, pit, but *Scola* – that is, Ge*henna,* Hell; for the ancients made four different hells.

## 207

The resurrection of our Saviour Christ, in the preaching of the gospel, raises earthquakes in the world now, as when Christ arose out of the sepulchre bodily. To this day the world is moved, and great tumults arise, when we preach and confess the righteousness and holiness of Christ, and that through it only are we justified and saved. But such earthquakes and tumults are wholesome for us, yea, comfortable, pleasant, and delightful to such as live in God's fear, and are true Christians; more to be desired than peace, rest, and quietness, with an evil conscience through *sinning against* God.

The Jews flattered themselves that the kingdom of Christ would have been a temporal kingdom, and the apostles themselves were of this opinion, as is noted, John 14: 'Lord, how is it that thou wilt manifest thyself to us, and not to the world?' As much as to say: We thought the whole world should behold thy glorious state; that thou shouldst be emperor, we twelve kings, among whom the kingdoms should be divided, and to each of us, for disciples, six princes, or dukes, etc., making the number of them seventy-two. In this manner had the loving apostles shared and divided the kingdoms among themselves, according to the Platonic meaning -that is, according to the wit and wisdom of human understanding. But Christ describes his kingdom far otherwise: 'He that loveth me, will keep my word, and my Father will love him, and we will come unto him, and make our abode with him,' etc.

## 208

The communion or fellowship of our blessed Saviour Christ, was doubtless most loving and familiar; for he who thought it no dishonour, being equal with God, to be made man like unto us, yet without sin, served and waited upon his disciples as they sat at table, as my servant waits on me; the good disciples, plain, simple people, were at length so accustomed to it, that they were even content to let him wait. In such wise did Christ fulfil his office; as is written: 'He is come to minister, and not to be ministered unto.' Ah, 'tis a high example, that he so deeply humbled himself and suffered, who created the whole world, heaven and earth, and all that is therein, and who, with one finger, could have turned it upside down and destroyed it.

## 209

How wonderfully does Christ rule and govern his kingdom, so concealing himself that his presence is not seen, yet putting to shame emperors, kings, popes, and all such as think themselves wise, just, and powerful. But hereunto belongs a *Plerophoria* – that is, we are sure and certain of it.

Jesus Christ is the only beginning and end of all my divine cogitations, day and night, yet I find and freely confess that I have attained but only to a small and weak beginning of the height, depth, and breadth of this immeasurable, incomprehensible, and endless wisdom, and have scarce got and brought to light a few fragments out of this most deep and precious profundity.

## 210

Christ's own proper work and office is to combat the law, sin, and death, for the whole world; taking them all upon himself, and bearing them, and after he has laden himself therewith, then only to get the victory, and utterly overcome and destroy them, and so release the desolate, from the law and all evil. That Christ expounds the law, and works miracles, these are but small benefits, in comparison of the true good, for which he chiefly came. For the prophets, and especially the apostles, wrought and did as great miracles as Christ himself.

## 211

That our Saviour, Christ, is come, nothing avails hypocrites, who live confident, not fearing God, nor contemners nor reprobates, who think there is no grace or comfort to be expected, and who by the law are affrighted. But he comes to the profit and comfort of those whom for a time the law has plagued and affrighted; these despair not in their trials and affrights, but with comfortable confidence step to Christ, the throne of grace, who delivers them.

## 212

Is it not a shame that we are always afraid of Christ, whereas there was never in heaven or earth a more loving, familiar, or milder man, in words, works, and demeanour, especially towards poor, sorrowful, and tormented consciences? Hence, the prophet Jeremiah prays, saying: 'O Lord, grant that we be not afraid of thee.'

## 213

It is written in Psalm 51: 'Behold, thou requirest truth in the inward parts, and shalt make me to understand wisdom secretly.' This is that mystery which is hidden from the world, and will remain hidden; it is the truth that lies in the inward parts, and the secret wisdom; not the wisdom of the lawyers, of the physicians, philosophers, and of the crafty ones of the world; no; but thy wisdom, O Lord! which thou hast made me to understand. This is that golden art which Sadoleto had not, though he wrote much of this psalm.

## 214

The preaching of the apostles went forth, and powerfully sounded through the whole world, after Christ's resurrection, when he had sent the Holy Ghost. This master, the Holy Ghost, worked through the apostles, and showed the doctrine of Christ clearly, so that their preaching produced more fruit than when Christ preached, as he himself before had declared, saying: 'He that believeth in me, shall do also the works that I do, and shall do greater than these.'

Christ by force would not break through with his preaching, as he might have done, for he preached so powerfully that the people were astonished at his doctrine, but proceeded softly and mildly in regard to the fathers, to whom he was promised, and of those that much esteemed them, to the end he might take away and abolish the ceremonial law, together with its service and worship.

## 215

Christ preached without wages, yet the godly women, whom he had cleansed and made whole, and delivered from wicked spirits and diseases, ministered unto him of that which they had (Luke 8). They gave him supply, and he also took and received that which others freely and willingly gave him (John 19).

When he sent the apostles forth to preach, he said: Freely ye have received, therefore freely give, etc., wherein he forbids them not to take something for their pains and work, but that they should not take care and sorrow for food and raiment, etc., for whithersoever they went, they should find some people that would not see them want.

## 216

The prophecies that the Son of God should take human nature upon him, are given so obscurely, that I think the devil knew not that Christ should be conceived by the Holy Ghost, and born of the Virgin Mary.

Hence, when he tempted Christ in the wilderness, be said to him: 'If thou art the Son of God?' He calls him the Son of God, not that he held him so to be by descent and nature, but according to the manner of the Scripture, which names human creatures the children of God: 'Ye are all the children of the Most Highest,' etc. It was not desired that these prophecies of Christ's passion, resurrection, and kingdom, should be revealed before the time of his coming, save only to his prophets and other high enlightened people; it was reserved for the coming of Christ, the right and only doctor that should open the understanding.

## 217

The reason why Peter and the other apostles did not expressly call Christ the Son of God, was that they would not give occasion to the godly Jews, who as yet were weak in faith, to shun and persecute their preaching, by appearing to declare a new God, and to reject the God of their fathers. Yet they mention, with express words, the office of Christ and his works; that he is a prince of life; that be raises from the dead, justifies and forgives sins, hears prayers, enlightens and comforts hearts, etc., wherewith they clearly and sufficiently show and acknowledge that he is the true God; for no creature can perform such works but God only.

## 218

The devil assaults the Christian world with highest power and subtlety, vexing true Christians through tyrants, heretics, and false brethren, and instigating the whole world against them.

On the contrary, Christ resists the devil and his kingdom, with a few simple and contemned people, as they seem in the world, weak and foolish, and yet he gets the victory.

Now, it were a very unequal war for one poor sheep to encounter a hundred wolves, as it befell the apostles, when Christ sent them out into the world, when one after another was made away with and slain. Against wolves we should rather send out lions, or more fierce and horrible beasts. But Christ has pleasure therein, to show his highest wisdom and power in our greatest weakness and foolishness, as the world conceives, and so proceeds that all shall eat their own bane, and go to the devil, who set themselves against his servants and disciples.

For he alone, the Lord of Hosts, does wonders; be preserves his sheep in the midst of wolves, and himself so afflicts them, that we plainly see our faith consists not in the power of human wisdom, but in the power of God, for although Christ permit one of his sheep to be devoured, yet he sends ten or more others in his place.

## 219

Many say that Christ having by force driven the buyers and sellers out of the temple, we also may use force against the popish bishops and enemies of God's Word, as Munzer and other seducers. But Christ did many things which we neither may nor can do after him. He walked upon the water, he fasted forty days and forty nights, he raised Lazarus from death, after he had lain four days in the grave, etc.; such and the like we must leave undone. Much less will Christ consent that we by force assail the enemies of the truth; he commands the contrary: 'Love your enemies, pray for them that vex and persecute you'; 'Be merciful, as your Father is merciful'; 'Take my yoke upon you and learn of me, for I am meek and humble in heart'; 'He that will follow me, let him deny himself, take up his cross, and follow me.'

## 220

'Tis a great wonder how the name of Christ has remained in Popedom, where, for hundreds of years, nothing was delivered to the people but the pope's laws and decrees, that is, doctrines and commandments of men, so that it had been no marvel if the name of Christ and his word had been forgotten.

But God wonderfully preserved his gospel in the church, which now from the pulpits is taught to the people, word by word. In like manner, it is a special great work of God, that the Creed, the Lord's Prayer, Baptism, and the Lord's Supper, have remained and cleaved to the hearts of those who were ordained to receive them in the midst of Popedom.

God has also often awakened pious learned men, who revealed his Word, and gave them courage openly to reprove the false doctrines and abuses that were crept into the church, as John Huss, and others.

## 221

The kingdom of Christ is a kingdom of grace, mercy, and of all comfort; Psalm 117: 'His grace and truth is ever more and more towards us.' The kingdom of Antichrist, the pope, is a kingdom of lies and destruction; Psalm 10: 'His mouth is full of cursing, fraud, and deceit; under his tongue is ungodliness and vanity.' The kingdom of Mohammed is a kingdom of revenge, of wrath, and desolation, Ezekiel 38.

### 222

The weak in faith also belong to the kingdom of Christ; otherwise the Lord would not have said to Peter, 'Strengthen thy brethren,' Luke 22; and Romans 14: 'Receive the weak in faith'; also 1 Thessalonians 5: 'Comfort the feeble-minded, support the weak.' If the weak in faith did not belong to Christ, where, then, would the apostles have been, whom the Lord oftentimes, as after his resurrection, Mark 16, reproved because of their unbelief?

### 223

A cup of water, if a man can have no better, is good to quench the thirst. A morsel of bread stills the hunger, and he that needs it seeks it earnestly. Christ is the best, surest, and only physic against the most fearful enemy of mankind, the devil; but men believe it not with their hearts. If they want a physician, living a hundred miles off, who, they think, can drive away temporal death, oh, how diligently is he sent for – no money or cost is spared! But the small and little heap only stick fast to the true physician, and by his art learn that which the holy Simeon well knew by reason of which he joyfully sang: 'Lord, now lettest thou thy servant depart in peace, for mine eyes have seen thy salvation!' Whence came his great joy? Because that with spiritual and corporal eyes he saw the Saviour of the world, the true physician against sin and death. 'Tis a great pain to behold how desirous a thirsty man is of drink, or a hungry man of food, though a cup of water or morsel of bread can still hunger and thirst no longer than two or three hours, while no man, or very few, desires or longs after the most precious of all physicians, though he lovingly calls us to come unto him, saying, 'He that is athirst, let him come to me and drink,' John 7.

### 224

Even as Christ is now invisible and unknown to the world, so are we Christians also invisible and unknown therein. 'Your life,' says St. Paul, Colossians 3, 'is hid with Christ in God.' Therefore the world knows us not, much less does it see Christ in us. But we and the world are easily parted; they care nothing for us, and we nothing for them; Christ the world is crucified unto us, and we to the world. Let them go with their wealth, and leave us to our minds and manners.

When we have our sweet and loving Saviour Christ, we are rich and happy more than enough; we care nothing for their state, honour, and wealth. But we often lose our Saviour Christ, and little think that, he is in us, and we in him; that he is ours, and we are his. Yet although he hide from us, as we think, in the time of need, for a moment, yet are we comforted in his promise, where he says, 'I am daily with you to the world's end'; this is our richest treasure.

## 225

Christ desires nothing more of us than that we speak of him. But thou wilt say: If I speak or preach of him, then the word freezes upon my lips. O, regard not that, but hear what Christ says: 'Ask, and it shall be given unto you,' etc.; and, 'I am with him in trouble', 'I will deliver him, and bring him to honour', etc. Also: 'Call upon me in the time of trouble, so will I hear thee, and thou shalt praise me', etc., Psalm 1. How could we perform a more easy service of God, without all labour or charge? There is no work on earth easier than the true service of God; he loads us with no heavy burthens, but only asks that we believe in him and preach of him. True, thou mayest be sure thou shalt be persecuted for this, but our sweet Saviour gives us a comfortable promise: 'I will be with you in the time of trouble, and will help you out', etc., Luke 12:7. I make no such promise to my servant when I set him to work, either to plough or to cart, as Christ to me, that he will help me in my need. We only fail in belief: if I had faith according as the Scriptures requires of me, I alone would drive the Turk out of Constantinople, and the pope out of Rome; but it comes far short; I must rest satisfied with that which Christ spake to St. Paul: 'My grace is sufficient for thee, for my power is strong in weakness.'

## 226

From these words, John 13, which Christ spake to Peter: 'If I wash thee not, thou hast no part in me,' it is not to be understood that Christ, at the same time, baptized his disciples; for in John 4, it is clearly expressed that he himself baptized none, but that his disciples, at his command, baptized each other. Neither did the Lord speak these words only of water washing, but of spiritual washing, through which he, and none other, washes and cleanses Peter, the other disciples, and all true believers, from their sins, and justifies and saves them; as if he would say: I am the true bather, therefore if I wash thee not, Peter, thou remainest unclean, and dead in thy sins.

The reason that Christ washed not his own, but his disciples' feet, whereas the high-priest in the law washed not others' but his own, was this: the high-priest in the law was unclean, and a sinner like other men, therefore he washed his own feet, and offered not only for the sins of the people, but also for his own. But our everlasting High-priest is holy, innocent, unstained, and separate from sin; therefore it was needless for him to wash his feet, but he washed and cleansed us, through his blood, from all our sins.

Moreover, by this his washing of feet he would show, that his new kingdom which he would establish should be no temporal and outward kingdom, where respect of persons was to be held, as in Moses' kingdom, one higher and greater than the other, but where one should serve another in humility, as he says: 'He that is greatest among you, let him be your servant'; which he himself showed by this example, as he says, John 13: 'If I your Lord and Master have washed your feet, then ought ye to wash one another's feet.'

## 227

So long as Jupiter, Mars, Apollo, Saturn, Juno, Diana, Pallas, and Venus ruled among the heathen – that is, were held and worshipped for gods, the Jews having also very many idols which they served, it was necessary that first Christ, and after him the apostles, should do many miracles, corporal and spiritual, both among the Jews and Gentiles, to confirm this doctrine of faith in Christ, and to take away and root out all worshipping of idols. The visible and bodily wonders flourished until the doctrine of the gospel was planted and received, and baptism and the Lord's Supper established. But the spiritual miracles, which our Saviour Christ holds is for miracles indeed, are daily wrought, and will remain to the world's end, as that of the centurion, in Matthew 8, and that of the Canaanitish woman.

## 228

The greatest wonder ever on earth is, that the Son of God died the shameful death of the cross. It is astonishing, that the Father should say to his only Son, who by nature is God: Go, let them hang thee on the gallows. The love of the everlasting Father was immeasurably greater towards his only begotten Son than the love of Abraham towards Isaac; for the Father testifies from heaven: 'This is my beloved Son, in whom I am well pleased'; yet he was cast away so lamentably, like a worm, a scorn of men, and outcast of the people.

At this the blind understanding of man stumbles, saying, Is this the only begotten Son of the everlasting Father – how, then, deals he so unmercifully with him? He showed himself more kind to Caiphas, Herod, and Pilate, than towards his only beloved Son. But to us true Christians, it is the greatest comfort; for we therein recognise that the merciful Lord God and Father so loved the poor condemned world, that he spared not his only begotten Son, but gave him up for us all, that whosoever believeth in him should not perish, but have everlasting life.

They who are tormented with high spiritual temptations, which every one is not able to endure, should have this example before their eyes, when they are in sorrow and heaviness of spirit, fearing God's wrath, the day of judgment, and everlasting death, and such like fiery darts of the devil. Let them comfort themselves, that although they often feel such intolerable sufferings, yet are they never the more rejected of God, but are of him better beloved, seeing he makes them like unto his only begotten Son; and let them believe, that as they suffer with him, so will he also deliver them out of their sufferings. For such as will live godly in Christ Jesus must suffer persecution; yet one more than another, according to every one's strength or weakness in faith: 'For God is true, who will not suffer us to be tempted above that we are able to bear.'

### 229

It was a wonderful thing when our Saviour Christ ascended up into heaven, in full view of his disciples. Some, no doubt, thought in themselves: We did eat and drink with him, and now he is taken from us, and carried up into heaven; are all these things right? Such reasonings, doubtless, some of them had, for they were not all alike strong in faith, as St. Matthew writes: When the eleven saw the Lord, they worshipped, but some doubted. And during those forty days, from the resurrection until the ascension, the Lord taught them by manifold arguments, and instructed them in all necessary things; he strengthened their faith, and put them in mind of what he had told them before, to the end they should in nowise doubt of his person.

Yet his words made little impression, for when the Lord appeared in the midst of them, on Easter-day, at evening, and said: 'Peace be with you,' they were perplexed and affrighted, supposing they saw a spirit; nor would Thomas believe that the other disciples had seen the Lord, until he saw the print of the nails in his hands. And though for the space of forty days he had communed with them concerning the kingdom of God, and was even ready to ascend, yet, notwithstanding, they asked him, Lord! wilt thou at this time restore again the kingdom to Israel?

But after this, on Whitsunday, when they had received the Holy Ghost, then they were of another mind; they then stood no more in fear of the Jews, but rose up boldly, and with great joyfulness preached Christ to the people. And Peter said to the lame man: Silver and gold have I none, but what I have, that give I thee; in the name of Jesus Christ of Nazareth; rise up and walk. Yet notwithstanding all this, the Lord was fain to show unto him, through a vision, that the Gentiles should be partakers of the promise of life, although, before his ascension, he had heard this command from the Lord himself. 'Go ye into all the world, and preach the gospel to every creature.' And 'Teach all nations.'

The apostles themselves did not know everything, even after they had received the Holy Ghost; yea, and sometimes they were weak in faith. When all Asia turned from St. Paul, and some of his own disciples had departed from him, and many false spirits that were in high esteem set themselves against him, then with sorrow of heart he said: 'I was with you in weakness, fear, and in much trembling.' And 'We were troubled on every side; without were fightings, and within were fears.' Hereby it is evident that he was not always strong in faith: and moreover the Lord was fain to comfort him, saying: 'My grace is sufficient for thee, for my power is strong in weakness.'

This is to me, and to all true Christians, a comfortable doctrine; for I persuade myself also that I have faith, though it is but so so, and might well be better; yet I teach the faith to others, and know, that my teaching is right. Sometimes I commune thus with myself: Thou preachest indeed God's word; this office is committed to thee, and thou art called thereunto without thy seeking, which is not fruitless, for many thereby are reformed; but when I consider and behold my own weakness, that I eat, drink, sometimes am merry, yea, also, now and then am overtaken, being off my guard, then I begin to doubt and say: Ah! that we could but only believe.

Therefore, confident professors are troublesome and dangerous people; who, when they have but only looked on the outside of the Bible, or heard a few sermons, presently think they have the Holy Ghost, and understand and know all. But good and godly hearts are of another mind, and pray daily: 'Lord strengthen our faith.'

### 230

When Jesus Christ utters a word, he opens his mouth so wide that it embraces all heaven and earth, even though that word be but in a whisper. The word of the emperor is powerful, but that of Jesus Christ governs the whole universe.

## 231

I expect more goodness from Kate my wife, from Philip Melancthon, and from other friends, than from my sweet and blessed Saviour Christ Jesus; and yet I know for certain, that neither she nor any other person on earth, will or can suffer that for me which he has suffered; why then should I be afraid of him! This my foolish weakness grieves me very much. We plainly see in the gospel, how mild and gentle he showed himself towards his disciples; how kindly he passed over their weakness, their presumption, yea, their foolishness. He checked their unbelief, and in all gentleness admonished them. Moreover, the Scripture, which is most sure, says: 'Well are all they that put their trust in him.' Fie on our unbelieving hearts, that we should be afraid of this man, who is more loving, friendly, gentle, and compassionate towards us than are our kindred, our brethren and sisters; yea, than parents themselves are towards their own children.

He that has such temptations, let him be assured, it is not Christ, but the envious devil that affrights, wounds, and would destroy him; for Christ comforts, heals, and revives.

Oh! his grace and goodness towards us is so immeasurably great, that without great assaults and trials it cannot be understood. If the tyrants and false brethren had not set themselves so fiercely against me, my writings and proceedings, then should I have vaunted myself too much of my poor gifts and qualities; nor should I with such fervency of heart have directed my prayers to God for, his divine assistance; I should not have ascribed all to God's grace, but to mine own dexterity and power, and so should have flown to the devil. But to the end this might be prevented, my gracious Lord and Saviour Christ caused me to be chastised; he ordained that the devil should plague and torment me with his fiery darts, inwardly and outwardly, through tyrants, as the pope and other heretics, and all this he suffered to be done for my good. 'It is good for me that I have been in trouble, that I may learn thy statutes.'

## 232

I know nothing of Jesus Christ but only his name; I have not heard or seen him corporally, yet I have, God be praised, learned so much out of the Scriptures, that I am well and thoroughly satisfied; therefore I desire neither to see nor to hear him in the body. When left and forsaken of all men, in my highest weakness, in trembling, and in fear of death, when persecuted of the wicked world, then I felt most deeply the divine power which this name, Christ Jesus, communicated unto me.

## 233

It is no wonder that Satan is an enemy to Christ, his people and kingdom, and sets himself against him and his word, with all his power and cunning. 'Tis an old hate and grudge between them, which began in Paradise; for they are, by nature and kind, of contrary minds and dispositions. The devil smells Christ many hundred miles off; he hears at Constantinople and at Rome, what we at Wittenberg teach and preach against his kingdom; he feels also what hurt and damage he sustains thereby; therefore rages and swells he so horribly.

But what is more to be wondered at is, that we, who are of one kind and nature, and, through the bond of love, knit so fast together that each ought to love the other as himself, should have, at times, such envy, hate, wrath, discord and revenge, that one is ready to kill the other. For who is nearer allied to a man than his wife; to the son, than his father; to the daughter, than her mother; to the brother, than his sister, etc.? yet, it is most commonly found that discord and strife are among them.

## 234

It is impossible that the gospel and the law should dwell together in one heart, for of necessity either Christ must yield and give place to the law, or the law to Christ. St. Paul says: 'They which will be justified through the law, are fallen from grace.' Therefore, when thou art of this mind, that Christ and the confidence of the law may dwell together in thy heart, then thou mayst know for certain that it is not Christ, but the devil that dwells in thee, who under the mask and form of Christ terrifies thee. He will have, that thou make thyself righteous through the law, and through thy own good works; for the true Christ calls thee not to an account for thy sins, nor commands thee to trust in thy good works, but says: 'Come unto me all ye that be weary and heavy laden, and I will give you rest,' etc.

## 235

I have set Christ and the pope together by the ears, so trouble myself no further; though I get between the door and the hinges and be squeezed, it is no matter; Christ will go through with it.

## 236

Christ once appeared visible here on earth, and showed his glory, and according to the divine purpose of God finished the work of redemption and the deliverance of mankind. I do not desire he should come once more in the same manner, neither would I he should send an angel unto me. Nay, though an angel should come and appear before mine eyes from heaven, yet it would not add to my belief; for I have of my Saviour Christ Jesus bond and seal; I have his Word, Spirit, and sacrament; thereon I depend, and desire no new revelations. And the more steadfastly to confirm me in this resolution, to hold solely by God's Word, and not to give credit to any visions or revelations, I shall relate the following circumstance: On Good Friday last, I being in my chamber in fervent prayer, contemplating with myself, how Christ my Saviour on the cross suffered and died for our sins, there suddenly appeared upon the wall a bright vision of our Saviour Christ, with the five wounds, steadfastly looking upon me, as if it had been Christ himself corporally. At first sight, I thought it had been some celestial revelation, but I reflected that it must needs be an illusion and juggling of the devil, for Christ appeared to us in his Word, and in a meaner and more humble form; therefore I spake to the vision thus: Avoid thee, confounded devil: I know no other Christ than he who was crucified, and who in his Word is pictured and presented unto me. Whereupon the image vanished, clearly showing of whom it came.

## 237

Alas! what is our wit and wisdom? before we understand anything as we ought, we lie down and die, so that the devil has a good chance with us. When one is thirty years old, he has still *Stultitias carnales*; yea also, *Stultitias spirituales*; and yet 'tis much to be admired at, how in such our imbecility and weakness, we achieve and accomplish much and great matters, but 'tis God does it. God gave to Alexander the Great wisdom and good success; yet he calls him, in the prophet Jeremiah, a youth, where he says, a young boy shall perform it; he shall come and turn the city Tyre upside down. Yet Alexander could not leave off his foolishness, for often he swilled himself drunk, and in his drunkenness stabbed his best and worthiest friends, and afterwards drank himself to death at Babylon. Solomon was not above twenty when he was made king, but he was well instructed by Nathan, and desired wisdom, which was pleasing to God, as the text says: But now, chests full of money are desired. O! say we now, if I had but money, then I would do so and so.

## 238

Christ said to the heathen woman: I am not sent but to the lost sheep of the house of Israel; yet afterwards he helped both her and her daughter; therefore a man might say: Christ here contradicted himself. I reply: True, Christ was not sent to the Gentiles, but when the Gentiles came unto him, he would not reject or put them from him. In person he was sent only to the Jews, and therefore he preached in the land of the Jews. But through the apostles his doctrine went into the whole world. And St. Paul names the Lord Christ, *ministrum circumcisionis,* by reason of the promise which God gave to the fathers. The Jews themselves boast of God's justness in performing what he promised, but we Gentiles boast of God's mercy; God has not forgotten us Gentiles. Indeed, God spake not with us, neither had we king or prophet with whom God spake; but St. Paul, in another place, says: It was necessary that the word should first be preached to you, but seeing you will not receive it, lo! we turn to the Gentiles. At this the Jews are much offended to this day; they flatter themselves: Messiah is only and alone for them and theirs. Indeed, it is a glorious name and title that Moses gives them: Thou art an holy nation: but David, in his psalm, afterwards promises Christ to the Gentiles: 'Praise the Lord all ye nations.'

## 239

We should consider the histories of Christ three manner of ways; first, as a history of acts or legends; secondly, as a gift or a present; thirdly, as an example, which we should believe and follow.

## 240

Christ, our blessed Saviour, forbore to preach and teach until the thirtieth year of his age, neither would he openly be heard; no, though he beheld and heard so many impieties, abominable idolatries, heresies, blasphemings of God, etc. It was a wonderful thing he could abstain, and with patience endure them, until the time came that he was to appear in his office of preaching.

# OF THE HOLY GHOST

## 241

THE Holy Ghost has two offices: first, He is a Spirit of grace, that makes God gracious unto us, and receive us as his acceptable children, for Christ's sake. Secondly, He is a Spirit of prayer, that prays for us, and for the whole world, to the end that all evil may be turned from us, and that all good may happen to us. The spirit of grace teaches people; the spirit of prayer prays. It is a wonder how one thing is accomplished various ways. It is one thing to have the Holy Spirit as a spirit of prophecy, and another to have the revealing of the same; for many have had the Holy Spirit before the birth of Christ, and yet he was not revealed unto them.

We do not separate the Holy Ghost from faith; neither do we teach that he is against faith; for he is the certainty itself in the world, that makes us sure and certain of the Word; so that, without all wavering or doubting, we certainly believe that it is even so and no otherwise than as God's Word says and is delivered unto us. But the Holy Ghost is given to none without the Word.

Mohammad, the pope, papists, Antinomians, and other sectaries, have no certainty at all, neither can they be sure of these things; for they depend not on God's Word, but on their own righteousness. And when they have done many and great works, yet they always stand in doubt, and say: Who knows whether this which we have done be pleasing to God or no; or, whether we have done works enough or no? They must continually think with themselves, We are still unworthy.

But a true and godly Christian, between these two doubts, is sure and certain, and says: I nothing regard these doubtings; I neither look upon my holiness, nor upon my unworthiness, but I believe in Jesus Christ, who is both holy and worthy; and whether I be holy or unholy, yet I am sure and certain, that Christ gives himself, with all his holiness, worthiness, and what he is and has, to be mine own. For my part, I am a poor sinner, and that I am sure of out of God's Word. Therefore, the Holy Ghost only and alone is able to say: Jesus Christ is the Lord; the Holy Ghost teaches, preaches, and declares Christ.

The Holy Ghost goes first and before in what pertains to teaching; but in what concerns hearing, the Word goes first and before, and then the Holy Ghost follows after. For we must first hear the Word, and then afterwards the Holy Ghost works in our hearts; he works in the hearts of whom he will, and how he will, but never without the Word.

## 242

The Holy Ghost began his office and work openly on Whitsunday; for he gave to the apostles and disciples of Christ a true and certain comfort in their hearts, and a secure and joyful courage, insomuch that they regarded not whether the world and the devil were merry or sad, friends or enemies, angry or pleased. They went in all security up and down the streets of the city, and doubtless they had these, or the like thoughts: We regard neither Annas nor Caiaphas, Pilate nor Herod; they are nothing worth, we all in all; they are our subjects and servants, we their lords and rulers.

So went the loving apostles on, in all courage, without seeking leave or licence.

They asked not whether they should preach or no, or whether the priests and people would allow it. O, no! They went on boldly, they opened their mouths freely, and reproved all the people, rulers and subjects, as murderers, wicked wretches, and traitors, who had slain the Prince of Life.

And this spirit, so needful and necessary at that time for the apostles and disciples, is now needful for us; for our adversaries accuse us, like as were the apostles, as rebels and disturbers of the peace of the Church. Whatsoever evil happens, that, say they, have we done or caused. In Popedom, say they, it was not so evil as it is since this doctrine came in; now we have all manner of mischiefs, dearth, wars, and the Turks. Of this they lay all the fault to our preaching, and, if they could, would charge us with being the cause of the devil's falling from heaven; yea, would say we had crucified and slain Christ also.

Therefore the Whitsuntide sermons of the Holy Ghost are very needful for us, that thereby we may be comforted, and with boldness contemn and slight such blaspheming, and that the Holy Ghost may put boldness and courage into our hearts, that we may stoutly thrust ourselves forward, let who will be offended, and let who will reproach us, and, that although sects and heresies arise, we may not regard them. Such a courage there must be that cares for nothing, but boldly and freely acknowledges and preaches Christ, who of wicked hands was crucified and slain.

The preached gospel is offensive in all places of the world, rejected and condemned.

If the gospel did not offend and anger citizen or countryman, prince or bishop, then it would be a fine and an acceptable preaching, and might well be tolerated, and people would willingly hear and receive it. But seeing it is a kind of preaching which makes people angry, especially the great and powerful, and deep-learned ones of the world, great courage is necessary, and the Holy Ghost, to those that intend to preach it.

It was, indeed, undaunted courage in the poor fishers, the apostles, to stand up and preach so that the whole council at Jerusalem were offended, to bring upon themselves the wrath of the whole government, spiritual and temporal – yea, of the Roman emperor himself. Truly, this could not have been done without the Holy Ghost. 'Twas a great wonder that the high-priest, and Pontius Pilate, did not cause these preachers that hour to be put to death, what they said smacking so much of rebellion against the spiritual and temporal government; yet both high-priest and Pilate were struck with fear, to the end that God might show his power in the apostles' weakness.

Thus it is with the church of Christ: it goes on in apparent weakness: and yet in its weakness, there is such mighty strength and power, that all the worldly wise and powerful must stand amazed thereat and fear.

### 243

It is testified by Holy Scripture, and the Nicene creed out of Holy Scripture teaches that the Holy Ghost is he who makes alive, and, together with the Father and the Son, is worshipped and glorified.

Therefore the Holy Ghost, of necessity, must be true and everlasting God with the Father and the Son, in one only essence. For if he were not true and everlasting God, then could not be attributed and given unto him the divine power and honour that he makes alive, and together with the Father and the Son is worshipped and glorified; on this point the Fathers powerfully set themselves against the heretics, upon the strength of Holy Scripture.

The Holy Ghost is not such a comforter as the world is, where neither truth nor constancy is, but he is a true, an everlasting, and a constant comforter, without deceit and lies; he is one whom no man can deceive. He is called a witness, because he bears witness only of Christ and of none other; without his testimony concerning Christ, there is no true or firm comfort. Therefore all rests on this, that we take sure hold of the text, and say: I believe in Jesus Christ, who died for me; and I know that the Holy Ghost, who is called, and is a witness and a comforter, preaches and witnesses in Christendom of none, but only of Christ, therewith to strengthen and comfort all sad and sorrowful hearts. Thereon will I also remain, depending upon none other for comfort. Our blessed Saviour Christ himself preaches that the Holy Ghost is everlasting and Almighty God. Otherwise he would not have directed his commission thus: Go, and teach all nations, and baptize them in the name of the Father, of the Son, and of the Holy Ghost, and teach them to keep and observe all things whatsoever I have commanded of you. It must needs follow, that the Holy Ghost is true, eternal God, equal in power and might with the Father and the Son, without all end. Likewise Christ says: 'And I will pray the Father, and he shall give you another comforter, that he may abide with you for ever; even the Spirit of Truth, whom the world cannot receive, because it seeth him not, neither knoweth him.' Mark well this sentence, for herein we find the difference of the three persons distinctly held out unto us: 'I will pray the Father, and he shall give you another comforter.' Here we have two persons – Christ the Son that prays, and the Father that is prayed unto. Now, if the Father shall give such a comforter, then the Father himself cannot be that comforter; neither can Christ, that prays, be the same; so that very significantly the three persons are here plainly pictured and portrayed unto us. For even as the Father and the Son are two distinct and sundry persons, so the third person of the Holy Ghost is another distinct person, and yet notwithstanding there is but one only everlasting God.

Now, what the same third person is, Christ teaches (John 15): 'But when the Comforter is come, whom I will send unto you from the Father, even the Spirit of Truth, which proceedeth from the Father, he shall testify of me.'

In this place, Christ speaks not only of the office and work of the Holy Ghost, but also of his essence and substance, and says: 'He proceedeth from the Father;' that is, his proceeding is without beginning, and is everlasting. Therefore the holy prophets attribute and give unto him this title, and call him 'The Spirit of the Lord'.

# Of Sins

NONE of the Fathers of the Church made mention of original sin until Augustine came, who made a difference between original and actual sin; namely, that original sin is to covet, lust, and desire, which is the root and cause of actual sin; such lust and desire in the faithful, God forgives, imputing it not unto them, for the sake of Christ, seeing they resist it by the assistance of the Holy Ghost. As St. Paul Romans 8 says. The papists and other sinners oppose the known truth. St. Paul says: 'A man that is an heretic after the first and second admonition, rejects,' knowing that such an one sins, being condemned of himself. And Christ says: 'Let them alone, they are blind leaders of the blind.' If one err through ignorance, he will be instructed; but if he be hardened, and will not yield to the truth, like Pharaoh, who would not acknowledge his sins, or humble himself before God, and therefore was destroyed in the Red Sea, even so will he be destroyed. We are all sinners by nature – conceived and born in sin; sin has poisoned us through and through; we have from Adam a will, – which continually sets itself against God, unless by the Holy Ghost it be renewed and changed. Of this neither the philosophers nor the lawyers know anything; therefore they are justly excluded from the circuit of divinity, not grounding their doctrine upon God's word.

## 245

Sins against the Holy Ghost are, first, presumption; second, despair; third, opposition to and condemnation of the known truth; fourth, not to wish well, but to grudge one's brother or neighbour the grace of God; fifth, to be hardened; sixth, to be impenitent.

## 246

The greatest sins committed against God, are the violations of the first table of the law. No man understands or feels these sins, but he that has the Holy Ghost and the grace of God. Therefore people feeling secure, though they draw God's wrath upon them, yet flatter themselves they still remain in God's favour. Yea, they corrupt the Word of God, and condemn it; yet think they do that which is pleasing and a special service to God. As for example: Paul held the law of God to be the highest and most precious treasure on earth, as we do the gospel. He would venture life and blood to maintain it; and he thought he wanted neither understanding, wisdom, nor power. But before be could rightly look about him, and while he thought his cause most sure, then he heard another lesson, he got another manner of commission, and it was told him plainly, that all his works, actions, diligence and zeal, were quite against God. Yet his doings carried a fair favour with the learned and seeming holy people, who said, Paul dealt herein uprightly, and performed divine and holy works, in showing such zeal for God's honour and for the law.

But God struck him on the ear, that he fell to the ground, and heard, Saul, Saul, why persecutest thou me? As if he should say, Saul, even with that wherein thou thinkest to do me service, thou dost nothing but persecute me, as my greatest enemy. It is true, thou boastest that thou hast my word, that thou understandest the law, and wilt earnestly defend and maintain it; thou receivest testimony and authority from the elders and scribes, and in such thy conceit and blind zeal thou proceedest. But know, that in my law I have commanded, that whoso taketh my name in vain shall die. Thou, Saul, takest my name in vain; therefore thou art justly punished. Whereupon he said: Lord, what wilt thou have me to do? Mark, this man was a master in the law of Moses, and yet he asked what he should do?

## 247

We have within us many sins against our Lord God, and which justly displease him: such as anger, impatience, covetousness, greediness, incontinence, hatred, malice, etc. These are great sins, which everywhere in the world go on with power, and get the upper hand. Yet these are nothing in comparison of contemning of God's word; yea, all these would remain uncommitted, if we did but love and reverence that. But, alas! the whole world is drowned in this sin. No man cares a fillip for the gospel, all snarl at and persecute it, holding it as no sin. I behold with wonder in the church, that among the hearers, one looks this way, another that; and that among so great a multitude, few come to hear the sermon. This sin is so common, that people will not confess it to be like other sins; every one deems it a slight thing to hear a discourse without attention, and not diligently to mark, learn, and inwardly digest it. It is not so about other sins; as murder, adultery, thieving, etc. For, after these sins, in due time follow grief, sorrow of heart, and remorse. But not to hear God's word with diligence, yea, to contemn, to persecute it, of this man makes no account. Yet it is a sin so fearful, that for the committing it both land and people must be destroyed, as it went with Jerusalem, with Rome, Greece, and other kingdoms.

### 248

Christ well knew how to discriminate sins; we see in the, gospel bow harsh he was towards the Pharisees, by reason of their great hatred and envy against him and his Word, while, on the contrary, how mild and friendly he was towards the woman who was a sinner. That same envy will needs rob Christ of his word, for he is a bitter enemy unto it, and in the end will crucify it. But the woman, as the greatest sinner, takes hold on the Word, hears Christ, and believes that he is the only Saviour of the world; she washes his feet, and anoints him with a costly water.

### 249

Let us not think ourselves more just than was the poor sinner and murderer on the cross. I believe if the apostles had not fallen, they would not have believed in the remission of sins. Therefore, when the devil upbraids me, touching my sins, then I say: Good St. Peter, although I am a great sinner, yet I have not denied Christ my Saviour, as you did. In such instances the forgiveness of sins remains confirmed. And although the apostles were sinners, yet our Saviour Christ always excused them, as when they plucked the ears of corn; but, on the contrary, he jeered the Pharisees touching the paying of tribute, and commonly showed his disapprobation of them; but the disciples he always comforted, as Peter, where he says: 'Fear not, thou shalt henceforth catch men.'

### 250

No sinner can escape his punishment, unless he be sorry for his sins. For though one go scot-free for awhile, yet at last he will be snapped, as the Psalm says: 'God indeed is still judge on earth.'

Our Lord God suffers the ungodly to be surprised and taken captive in very slight and small things, when they think not of it, when they are most secure, and live in delight and pleasure, leaping for joy. In such manner was the Pope surprised by me, about his indulgences and pardons, comparatively a slight matter.

### 251

A magistrate, a father or mother, a master or dame, tradesmen and others, must now and then look through the fingers at their citizens, children, and servants, if their faults and offences be not too gross and frequent; for where we will have *summum jus*, there follows often *summa injuria*, so that all must go to wreck. Neither do they which are in office always hit it aright, but err and sin themselves, and must therefore desire the forgiveness of sins.

God forgives sins merely out of grace for Christ's sake; but we must not abuse the grace of God. God has given signs and tokens enough, that our sins shall be forgiven; namely, the preaching of the gospel, baptism, the Lord's Supper, and the Holy Ghost in our heart.

Now it is also needful we testify in our works that we have received the forgiveness of sins, by each forgiving the faults of his brother. There is no comparison between God's remitting of sins and ours. For what are one hundred pence, in comparison of ten thousand pounds? as Christ says, nought. And although we deserve nothing by our forgiving, yet we must forgive, that thereby we may prove and give testimony that we from God have received forgiveness of our sins.

The forgiveness of sins is declared only in God's Word, and there we must seek it; for it is grounded on God's promises. God forgives thee thy sins, not because thou feelest them and art sorry, for this sin itself produces, without deserving, but he forgives thy sins because he is merciful, and because he has promised to forgive for Christ's sake.

### 252

When God said to Cain, through Adam: 'If thou do well, shalt thou not be accepted? And if thou dost not well, sin lieth at the door,' he shows the appearance of sinners, and speaks with Cain as with the most hypocritical and poisonous Capuchin: 'twas as if Adam had said: Thou hast heard how it went with me in Paradise; I also would willingly have hid my offence with fig leaves, lurking behind a tree, but know, good fellow, our Lord God will not be so deceived; the fig leaves would not serve the turn.

Ah! it was, doubtless, to Adam, a heart-breaking and painful task, when he was compelled to banish and proscribe his first-born and only son, to hunt him out of his house, and to say: Depart from me, and come no more in my sight; I still feel what I have already lost in Paradise, I will lose no more for thy sake; I will now, with more diligence, take heed to my God's command. And no doubt Adam afterwards preached with redoubled diligence.

### 253

These two sins, hatred and pride, deck and trim themselves out, as the devil clothed himself, in the Godhead. Hatred will be godlike; pride will be truth. These two are right deadly sins: hatred is killing; pride is lying.

### 254

It can be hurtful to none to acknowledge and confess his sins. Hast thou done this or that sin? – what then? We freely, in God's name, acknowledge the same, and deny it not, but from our hearts say: O Lord God! I have done this sin.

Although thou hast not committed this or that sin, yet, nevertheless, thou art an ungodly creature; and if thou hast not done that sin which another has done, so has he not committed that sin which thou hast done; therefore cry quits one with another. 'Tis as the man said, that had young wolves to sell; he was asked which of them was the best? He answered: If one be good, then they are all good; they are all like one another. If thou hast been a murderer, an adulterer, a drunkard, etc., so have I been a blasphemer of God, who for the space of fifteen years was a friar, and blasphemed God with celebrating that abominable idol, the mass. It had been better for me I had been a partaker of other great wickednesses instead; but what is done cannot be undone; he that has stolen, let him henceforward steal no more.

### 255

The sins of common, untutored people are nothing in comparison with the sins committed by great and high persons, that are in spiritual and temporal offices.

What are the sins done by a poor wretch, that according to law and justice is hanged, or the offences of a poor strumpet, compared with the sins of a false teacher, who daily makes away with many poor people, and kills them both body and soul? The sins committed against the first table of God's ten commandments, are not so much regarded by the world, as those committed against the second table,

### 256

Original sin, after regeneration, is like a wound that begins to heal; though it be a wound, yet it is in course of healing, though it still runs and is sore.

So original sin remains in Christians until they die, yet itself is mortified and continually dying. Its head is crushed in pieces, so that it cannot condemn us.

### 257

All natural inclinations are either without God or against him; therefore none are good. I prove it thus: All affections, desires, and inclinations of mankind are evil, wicked, and spoiled, as the Scripture says.

Experience testifies this; for no man is so virtuous as to marry a wife, only thereby to have children, to love and to bring them up in the fear of God.

No hero undertakes great enterprises for the common good, but out of ambition, for which he is justly condemned: hence it must needs follow, that such original, natural desires and inclinations are wicked. But God bears with them and lets them pass, in those that believe in Christ.

### 258

Schenck proceeds in a most monstrous manner, haranguing, without the least discernment, on the subject of sin. I, myself, have heard him say, in the pulpit at Eisenach, without any qualification whatever, 'Sin, sin is nothing; God will receive sinners; He himself tells us they shall enter the kingdom of heaven.' Schenck makes no distinction between sins committed, sins committing, and sins to be committed, so that when the common people hear him say, 'Sin, for God will receive sinners'; they very readily repeat, 'Well, we'll sin then.' 'Tis a most erroneous doctrine. What is announced as to God's receiving sinners, applies to sinners who have repented; there is all the difference in the world between *agnitum peccatum,* attended by repentance, and *velle peccare* which is an inspiration of the devil.

# Of Free Will

### 259

THE very name, Free-will, was odious to all the Fathers. I, for my part, admit that God gave to mankind a free will, but the question is, whether this same freedom be in our power and strength, or no? We may very fitly call it a subverted, perverse, fickle, and wavering will, for it is only God that works in us, and we must suffer and be subject to his pleasure. Even as a potter out of his clay makes a pot or vessel, as he wills, so it is for our free will, to suffer and not to work. It stands not in our strength; for we are not able to do anything that is good in divine matters.

### 260

I have often been resolved to live uprightly, and to lead a true godly life, and to set everything aside that would hinder this, but it was far from being put in execution; even as it was with Peter, when he swore he would lay down his life for Christ.

I will not lie or dissemble before my God, but will freely confess, I am not able to effect that good which I intend, but await the happy hour when God shall be pleased to meet me with his grace.

The will of mankind is either presumptuous or despairing. No human creature can satisfy the law. For the law of God discourses with me, as it were after this manner: Here is a great, a high, and a steep mountain, and thou must go over it; whereupon my flesh and free-will say, I will go over it; but my conscience says, Thou canst not go over it; then comes despair, and says, If I cannot, then I must forbear. In this sort does the law work in mankind either presumption or despair; yet the law must be preached and taught, for if we preach not the law, then people grow rude and confident, whereas if we preach it, we make them afraid.

## 261

Saint Augustine writes, that free-will, without God's grace and the Holy Ghost, can do nothing but sin; which sentence sorely troubles the school-divines. They say, Augustine spoke *hyperbole* and too much; for they understand that part of Scripture to be spoken only of those people who lived before the deluge, which says: 'And God saw that the wickedness of man was great in the earth, and that every imagination of the thoughts of his heart was only evil continually,' etc.; whereas He speaks in a general way, which these poor school-divines do not see any more than what the Holy Ghost says, soon after the deluge, in almost the same words: 'And the Lord said in his heart, I will not again curse the ground any more for man's sake, for the imagination of man's heart is evil from his youth.'

Hence, we conclude in general, that man, without the Holy Ghost and God's grace, can do nothing but sin; he proceeds therein without intermission, and from one sin falls into another. Now, if man will not suffer wholesome doctrine, but contemns the all-saving Word, and resists the Holy Ghost, then through the effects and strength of his free-will he becomes God's enemy he blasphemes the Holy Ghost, and follows the lusts and desires of his own heart, as examples in all times clearly show.

But we must diligently weigh the words which the Holy Ghost speaks through Moses: 'Every imagination of the thoughts of his heart is evil continually'; so that what a man is able to conceive with his thoughts, with his understanding and free-will, by highest diligence, is evil, and not once or twice, but evil continually; without the Holy Ghost, man's reason, will, and understanding, are without the knowledge of God; and to be without the knowledge of God, is nothing else than to be ungodly, to walk in darkness, and to hold that for best which is direct worst.

I speak only of that which is good in divine things, and according to the holy Scripture; for we must make a difference between that which is temporal, and that which is spiritual, between politics and divinity; for God also allows of the government of the ungodly, and rewards their virtues, yet only so far as belongs to this temporal life; for man's will and understanding conceive that to be good which is external and temporal – nay, take it to be, not only good, but the chief good.

But when we divines speak of free-will, we ask what man's free-will is able to accomplish in divine and spiritual matters, not in outward and temporal affairs: and we conclude that man without the Holy Ghost, is altogether wicked before God, although he were decked up and trimmed with all the virtues of the heathen, and had all their works.

For, indeed, there are fair and glorious examples in heathendom, of many virtues, where men were temperate, chaste, bountiful; loved their country, parents, wives, and children; were men of courage, and behaved themselves magnanimously and generously.

But the ideas of mankind concerning God, the true worship of God, and God's will, are altogether stark blindness and darkness. For the light of human wisdom, reason, and understanding, which alone is given to man, comprehends only what is good and profitable outwardly. And although we see that the heathen philosophers now and then discoursed touching God and his wisdom very pertinently, so that some have made prophets of Socrates, of Xenophon, of Plato, etc., yet, because they knew not that God sent his son Christ to save sinners, such fair, glorious, and wise-seeming speeches and disputations are nothing but mere blindness and ignorance.

### 262

Ah, Lord God! why should we boast of our free-will, as if it were able to do anything ever so small, in divine and spiritual matters? when we consider what horrible miseries the devil has brought upon us through sin, we might shame ourselves to death.

For, first, free-will led us into original sin, and brought death upon us: afterwards, upon sin followed not only death, but all manner of mischiefs, as we daily find in the world, murder, lying, deceiving, stealing, and other evils, so that no man is safe in the twinkling of an eye, in body or goods, but always stands in danger.

And, besides these evils, is afflicted with yet a greater, as is noted in the gospel – namely, that he is possessed of the devil, who makes him mad and raging.

We know not rightly what we became after the fall of our first parents; what from our mothers we have brought with us. For we have altogether a confounded, corrupt, and poisoned nature, both in body and soul; throughout the whole of man is nothing that is good.

This is my absolute opinion: he that will maintain that man's free-will is able to do or work anything in spiritual cases, be they never so small, denies Christ. This I have always maintained in my writings, especially in those against Erasmus, one of the learnedest men in the whole world, and thereby will I remain, for I know it to be the truth, though all the world should be against it; yea, the decree of Divine Majesty must stand fast against the gates of hell.

I confess that mankind has a free-will, but it is to milk kines, to build houses, etc., and no further: for so long as a man is at ease and in safety, and is in no want, so long he thinks he has a free-will, which is able to do something; but when want and need appear, so that there is neither meat, drink nor money, where is then free-will? It is utterly lost, and cannot stand when it comes to the pinch. Faith only stands fast and sure, and seeks Christ. Therefore faith is far another thing than free-will; nay, free-will is nothing at all, but faith is all in all. Art thou bold and stout, and canst thou carry it lustily with thy free-will when plague, wars, and times of dearth and famine are at hand? No: in time of plague, thou knowest not what to do for fear; thou wishest thyself a hundred miles off. In time of dearth thou thinkest: Where shall I find to eat? Thy will cannot so much as give thy heart the smallest comfort in these times of need, but the longer thou strivest, the more it makes thy heart faint and feeble, insomuch that it is affrighted even at the rushing and shaking of a leaf. These are the valiant acts our free-will can achieve.

### 263

Some new divines allege, that the Holy Ghost works not in those that resist him, but only in such as are willing and give consent thereto, whence it would appear that free-will is also a cause and helper of faith and that consequently faith alone justifies not, and that the Holy Ghost does not alone work through the word, but that our will does something therein.

But I say it is not so; the will of mankind works nothing at all in his conversion and justification; *Non est efficiens causa Justificationis sed materialis tantum*. It is the matter on which the Holy Ghost works (as a potter makes a pot out of clay), equally in those that resist and are averse, as in St. Paul. But after the Holy Ghost has wrought in the wills of such resistants, then he also manages that the will be consenting thereunto.

They say and allege further, that the example of St. Paul's conversion is a particular and special work of God, and therefore cannot be brought in for a general rule. I answer: even like as St. Paul was converted, just so are all others converted; for we all resist God, but the Holy Ghost draws the will of mankind, when he pleases, through preaching.

Even as no man may lawfully have children, except in a state of matrimony, though many married people have no children, so the Holy Ghost works not always through the word but when it pleases him, so that free-will does nothing inwardly in our conversion and justification before God, neither does it work with our strength – no, not in the least, unless we be prepared and made fit by the Holy Ghost.

The sentences in Holy Scripture touching predestination, as, 'No man can come to me except the Father draweth him', seem to terrify and affright us; yet they but show that we can do nothing of our own strength and will that is good before God, and put the godly also in mind to pray. When people do this, they may conclude they are predestinated.

Ah! why should we boast that our free-will can do aught in man's conversion? We see the reverse in those poor people, who are corporally possessed of the devil, how he rends, and tears, and spitefully deals with them, and with what difficulty he is driven out. Truly, the Holy Ghost alone must drive him out, as Christ says: 'If I, with the finger of God, do drive out devils, then no doubt the kingdom of God is come upon you.' As much as to say: If the kingdom of God shall come upon you, then the devil must first be driven out, for his kingdom is opposed to God's kingdom, as ye yourselves confess. Now the devil will not be driven out by devils, much less by men, or by man's strength, but only by God's spirit and power. Hence, if the devil be not driven out through God's finger, then the kingdoms of the devil subsists there; and where the devil's kingdom is, there is not God's kingdom.

And again, so long as the Holy Ghost comes not into us, we are not only unable to do anything good, but we are, so long, in the kingdom of the devil, and do what is pleasing unto him.

What could St. Paul have done to be freed from the devil, though all the people on earth had been present to help him? Truly, nothing at all; he was forced to do and suffer that which the devil, his lord and master, pleased until our blessed Saviour Christ came, with divine power.

Now, if he could not be quit of the devil, corporally from his body, how should he be quit of him spiritually from his soul, through his own will, strength, and power? For the soul was the cause why the body was possessed, which also was a punishment for sin. It is a matter more difficult to be delivered from sin than from the punishment; the soul is always heavier possessed than the body; the devil leaves to the body its natural strength and activity; but the soul he bereaves of understanding, reason, and power as we see in possessed people.

Let us mark how Christ pictures forth the devil. He names him a strong giant that keeps a castle; that is, the devil has not only the world in possession, as his own kingdom, but he fortifies it in such a way that no human creature can take it from him, and he keeps it also in such subordination that he does even what he wills to have done. Now, as much as a castle is able to defend itself against the tyrant which is therein, even so much is free-will and human strength able to defend itself against the devil; that is, no way able at all. And even as the castle, must first be overcome by a stronger giant, to be won from the tyrant, even so mankind must be delivered and regained from the devil through Christ. Hereby, we see plainly that our doings and righteousness can help nothing towards our deliverance, but only by God's grace and power.

O! how excellent and comfortable a gospel is that, in which our Saviour Christ shows what a loving heart he bears towards us poor sinners, who are able to do nothing at all for ourselves to our salvation.

For as a silly sheep cannot take heed to itself, that it err not, nor go astray, unless the shepherd always leads it; yea, and when it has erred, gone astray, and is lost, cannot find the right way, nor come to the shepherd, but the shepherd must go after it, and seek until he find it, and when he has found it, must carry it, to the end it be not scared from him again, go astray, or be torn by the wolf: so neither can we help ourselves, nor attain a peaceful conscience, nor outrun the devil, death, and hell, unless Christ himself seek and call us through his Word; and when we are come unto him, and possess the true faith, yet we of ourselves are not able to keep ourselves therein, nor to stand, unless he always hold us up through his Word and spirit, seeing that the devil everywhere lies lurking for us, like a roaring lion, seeking to devour us.

I fain would know how he who knows nothing of God, should know how to govern himself; how he, who is conceived and born in sin, as we all are, and is by nature a child of wrath, and God's enemy, should know how to find the right way and to remain therein, when, as Isaiah says: 'We can do nothing else but go astray.' How is it possible we should defend ourselves against the devil, who is a Prince of this world, and we his prisoners, when, with all our strength, we are not able so much as to hinder a leaf or a fly from doing us hurt? I say, how may we poor miserable wretches presume to boast of comfort, help, and counsel against God's judgment, his wrath and everlasting death, when we cannot tell which way to seek help, or comfort, or counsel, no, not in the least of our corporal necessities, as daily experience teaches us, either for ourselves or others?

Therefore, thou mayest boldly conclude, that as little as a sheep can help itself, but must needs wait for all assistance from the shepherd, so little, yea, much less, can a human creature find comfort, help, and advice of himself, in cases pertaining to salvation, but must expect and wait for these only from God, his shepherd, who is a thousand times more willing to do every good thing for his sheep than any temporal shepherd for his.

Now seeing that human nature, through original sin, is wholly spoiled and perverted, outwardly and inwardly, in body and soul, where is then free-will and human strength? Where human traditions, and the preachers of works, who teach that we must make use of our own abilities, and by our own works obtain God's grace, and so, as they say, be children of salvation? O! foolish, false doctrine! – for we are altogether unprepared with our abilities, with our strength and works, when it comes to the combat, to stand or hold out. How can that man be reconciled to God, whom he cannot endure to hear, but flies from to a human creature, expecting more love and favour from one that is a sinner, than he does from God. Is not this a fine free-will for reconciliation and atonement?

The children of Israel on Mount Sinai, when God gave them the Ten Commandments, showed plainly that human nature and freewill can do nothing, or subsist before God; for they feared that God would suddenly strike among them, holding him merely for a devil, a hangman, and a tormentor, who did nothing but fret and fume.

# OF THE CATECHISM

‒‒‒

### 264

I BELIEVE the words of the apostles' creed to be the work of the Holy Ghost; the Holy Spirit alone could have enunciated things so grand, in terms so precise, so expressive, so powerful. No human creature could have done it, nor all the human creatures of ten thousand worlds. This creed, then, should be the constant object of our most serious attention. For myself, I cannot too highly admire or venerate it.

### 265

The catechism must govern the church, and remain lord and ruler; that is, the ten commandments, the creed, the Lord's prayer, the sacraments, etc. And although there be many that set themselves against it, yet it shall stand fast, and keep the pre-eminence, through him of whom it is written, 'Thou art a priest for ever': for he will be a priest, and will also have priests, despite the devil and all his instruments on earth.

### 266

Sermons very little edify children, who learn little thereby; it is more needful they be taught and well instructed in schools, and at home that they be heard and examined what they have learned; this way profits much; 'tis very wearisome, but very necessary. The papists avoid such pains, so that their children are neglected and forsaken.

### 267

In the catechism, we have a very exact, direct, and short way to the whole Christian religion. For God himself gave the ten commandments, Christ himself penned and taught the Lord's prayer, the Holy Ghost brought together the articles of faith. These three pieces are set down so excellently, that never could anything have been better; but they are slighted and contemned by us as things of small value, because the little children daily say them.

The catechism is the most complete and best doctrine, and therefore should continually be preached; all public sermons should be grounded and built thereupon. I could wish we preached it daily, and distinctly read it out of the book. But our preachers and hearers have it at their fingers' ends; they have already swallowed it all up; they are ashamed of this slight and simple doctrine, as they hold it, and will be thought of higher learning. The parishioners say: Our preachers fiddle always one tune; they preach nothing but the catechism, the ten commandments, the creed, the Lord's prayer, baptism, and the Lord's supper; all which we know well enough already, but the catechism, I insist, is the right Bible of the laity, wherein is contained the whole sum of Christian doctrine necessary to be known by every Christian for salvation.

First, there are the ten commandments of God, *Doctrina Doctrinarum*, the doctrine of all doctrines, by which God's will is known, what God will have of us, and what is wanting in us. Secondly, there is the confession of faith in God and in our Lord Jesus Christ; *Historia Historiarum*, the history of histories, or highest history, wherein are delivered unto us the wonderful works of the divine Majesty from the beginning to all eternity; how we and all creatures are created by God; how we are delivered by the Son of God through his humanity, his passion, death, and resurrection; and also how we are renewed and collected together, the one people of God, and have remission of sins and everlasting life.

Thirdly, there is the Lord's prayer, *Oratio Orationum*, the prayer above all prayers, a prayer which the most high Master taught us, wherein are comprehended all spiritual and temporal blessings, and the strongest comforts in all trials, temptations, and troubles, even in the hour of death.

Fourthly, there are the blessed sacraments, *Cerimoniae Cerimoniarum*, the highest ceremonies, which God himself has instituted and ordained, and therein assured us of his grace. We should esteem and love the catechism, for therein is the ancient, pure, divine doctrine of the Christian church. And whatsoever is contrary thereunto is new and false doctrine, though it have ever so glorious a show and lustre, and we must take good heed how we meddle therewith. In all my youth I never heard any preaching, either of the ten commandments, or of the Lord's prayer.

Future heresies will darken this light, but now we have the catechism, God be praised, purer in the pulpits, than has been for the last thousand years. So much could not be collected out of all the books of the fathers, as, by God's grace, is now taught out of the little catechism. I only read the Bible at Erfurt, in the monastery; and God then wonderfully wrought, contrary to all human expectation, so that I was constrained to depart from Erfurt, and was called to Wittenberg, where, under God, I gave the devil, the pope of Rome, such a blow, as no emperor, king, or potentate could have given him: yet it was not I, but God by me, his poor, weak:, and unworthy instrument.

## 268

The Decalogue – that is, the ten commandments of God, are a looking glass and brief sum of all virtues and doctrines, both how we ought to behave towards God and also towards our neighbour; that is, towards all mankind.

There never was at any time written a more excellent, complete, or compendious book of virtues.

## 269

God says: 'I the Lord thy God am a jealous God.' Now, God is jealous two manner of ways; first, God is angry as one that is jealous of them that fall from him, and become false and treacherous, that prefer the creature before the Creator; that build upon the favours of the great; that depend upon their friends, upon their own power, riches, arts, wisdom, etc.; that forsake the righteousness of faith, and contemn it, and will be justified and saved by and through their own good works. God is also vehemently angry with those that boast and brag of their power and strength; as we see in Sennacherib, king of Assyria, who boasted of his great power, and thought utterly to destroy Jerusalem. Likewise in king Saul, who also thought to defend and keep the kingdom through his strength and power, and to pass it on to his children, when he had suppressed David and rooted him out.

Secondly, God is jealous for them that love him and highly esteem his word; such God loves again, defends, and keeps as the apple of his eye, and resists their adversaries, beating them back, that they are not able to perform what they intended. Therefore, this word jealous comprehends both hatred and love, revenge and protection; for which cause it requires both fear and faith; fear, that we provoke not God to anger, or work his displeasure; faith, that in trouble we believe he will help, nourish, and defend us in this life, and will pardon and forgive us our sins, and for Christ's sake preserve us to life everlasting. For faith must rule and govern, in and over all things, both spiritual and temporal; the heart must believe most certainly that God looks upon us, loves, helps, and will not forsake us, as the Psalm says: 'Call upon me in the time of trouble, so will I deliver thee, and, thou shalt praise me,' etc. Also, 'The Lord is nigh unto all those that call upon him; yea, all that call upon him faithfully.' And, 'He that calleth upon the name of the Lord shall be saved.'

Further, the Lord says: 'And will visit the sins of the fathers upon the children, unto the third and fourth generation,' etc. This is a terrible word of threatening, which justly affrights our hearts, and stirs up fear in us. It is quite contrary to our reason, for we conceive it to be a very unjust proceeding, that the children and posterity should be punished for their fathers and forefathers' offences. But forasmuch as God has so decreed, and is pleased so to proceed, therefore our duty is to know and acknowledge that he is a just God, and that he wrongs none. Seeing that these fearful threatenings are contrary to our understanding, therefore flesh and blood regard them not, but cast them in the wind, as though they signified no more than the hissing of a goose. But we that are true Christians believe the same to be certain, when the Holy Ghost touches our hearts, and that this proceeding is just and right, and thereby we stand in the fear of God. Here again we may see what man's free-will can do, in that it understands and fears nothing. If we did but feel and know how earnest a threatening this is, we should for fear instantly fall down dead; and we have examples, as where God said: that for the sins of Manasseh he will cast the people into miserable captivity.

But some may argue: Then I see well that the posterity have no hope of grace when their parents sin. I answer: Those that repent, from them is the law taken away and abolished, so that their parents' sins do not hurt them: as the prophet Ezekiel says: 'The son shall not bear the iniquity of the father'; yet God permits the external and corporal punishment to go on, yea, sometimes over the penitent children also for examples, to the end that others may fly from sin and lead a godly life.

'But he will do good, and be merciful unto thousands,' etc. This is a great, a glorious, and comfortable promise, far surpassing all human reason and understanding, that, for the sake of one godly person, so many should be partakers of undeserved blessings and mercies. For we find many examples, that a multitude of people have enjoyed mercies and benefits for the sake of one godly man; as for Abraham's sake, many people were preserved and blessed, as also for Isaac's sake; and for the sake of Naaman the whole kingdom of Assyria was blessed of God.

To love God is that we certainly hold and believe that God is gracious unto us, that he helps, assists, and does us good. Therefore, love proceeds from faith, and God requires faith, to believe that he promises all good unto us.

## 270

The first commandment will stand and remain, that God is our God; this will not be accomplished in the present, but in the life everlasting. All the other commandments will cease and end; for, in the life to come, the world will cease and end together with all external worship of God, all world policy and government; only God and the first commandment will remain everlastingly, both here and there.

We ought well to mark with what great diligence and ability Moses handles the first commandment, and explains it. He was doubtless, an excellent doctor. David afterwards was a gate or a door out of Moses. For he had well studied in Moses, and so he became a fine poet and orator; the Psalms are altogether *syllogisms*, or concluding sentences out of the first commandment. *Major*, the first, is God's Word itself; *Minor,* the second, faith. The conclusion is the act, work, and execution, so that it is done, as we believe. As, *Major: Misericors Deus, respicit miseros; Minor Ego sum miser; Conclusio; Ergo Deus me quoque respicit.*

When we believe the first commandment, and so please God, then all our actions are pleasing unto him. If thou hearest his Word, if thou prayest, mortifiest thyself, then says God unto thee; I am well pleased with what thou doest. Moreover, when we observe the first commandment, then that *placet* goes through all the other commandments and works. Art thou a Christian? wilt thou marry a wife? wilt thou buy and sell? wilt thou labour in the works of thy vocation? wilt thou punish and condemn wicked and ungodly wretches? wilt thou eat, drink, sleep? etc. God says continually; *Placet.*

But if thou keepest not the first commandment, then says God to all thy works and actions, *Non placent,* they please me not. Christ takes the first commandment upon himself, where he says: 'He that honoureth me, honoureth the Father; he that honoureth not the Son, honoureth not the Father.'

# Of the Law and the Gospel

---

### 271

WE must reject those who so highly boast of Moses' laws, as to temporal affairs, for we have our written imperial and country laws, under which we live, and unto which we are sworn. Neither Naaman the Assyrian, nor Job, nor Joseph, nor Daniel, nor many other good and godly Jews, observed Moses' laws out of their country, but those of the Gentiles among whom they lived.

Moses's laws bound and obliged only the Jews in that place which God made choice of. Now they are free. If we should keep and observe the laws and rites of Moses, we must also be circumcised, and keep the Mosaical ceremonies; for there is no difference; he that holds one to be necessary, must hold the rest so too. Therefore let us leave Moses to his laws, excepting only the Moralia, which God has planted in nature, as the ten commandments, which concern God's true worshipping and service, and a civil life.

### 272

The particular and only office of the law is, as St. Paul teaches, that transgressions thereby should be acknowledged; for it was added, because of transgressions, till the seed should come, to whom the promise was made. These are the express and plain words of St. Paul; therefore we trouble not ourselves with what the papists allege to the contrary, and spin out of human reason, extolling the maintainers and seeming observers of Moses' law.

### 273

God gives to the emperor the sword, the emperor delivers it to the judge, and causes thieves, murderers, etc., to be punished and executed. Afterwards, when God pleases, he takes the sword from the emperor again; even so does God touching the law; he leaves it to the devil, and permits him therewith to affright sinners.

### 274

The law is used two ways: first, for this worldly life, because God has ordained all temporal laws and statutes to prevent and hinder sin. But here some one may object: If the law hinder sin, then it also justifies. I answer: Oh! no, this does not follow; that I do not murder, commit adultery, steal, etc., is not because I love virtue and righteousness, but because I fear the hangman, who threatens me with the gallows, sword, etc. It is the hangman that hinders me from sinning, as chains, ropes, and strong bands hinder bears, lions, and other wild beasts from tearing and rending in pieces all that come in their way.

Hence we may understand, that the same can be no righteousness that is performed out of fear of the curse, but sin and unrighteousness; for the law binds mankind, who by nature are prone to wickedness, that they do not sin, as willingly they would.

Therefore this is the first point concerning the law, that it must be used to deter the ungodly from their wicked and mischievous intentions. For the devil, who is an abbot and prince of this world, allures people to work all manner of sin and wickedness; wherefore God has ordained magistrates, elders, schoolmasters, laws and statutes, to the end, if they can do no more, that at least they may bind the claws of the devil, and hinder him from raging and swelling so powerfully in those who are his, according to his will and pleasure.

Secondly, we use the law spiritually, as thus: To make transgressions seem greater, as St. Paul says, or to reveal and discover to people their sins, blindness, and ungodly doings, wherein they were conceived and born; namely, that they are ignorant of God, and are his enemies, and therefore have justly deserved death, hell, God's judgments, his everlasting wrath and indignation. But the hypocritical sophists in universities know nothing thereof, neither do those who are of opinion that they are justified by the law and their own works.

But to the end that God might put to silence, smother, suppress, and beat down to the ground these mischievous and furious beasts, he has appointed and ordained a particular Hercules with a club, powerfully to lay hold on such beasts, take them captive, strike them down, and so despatch them out of the way; that is, he gave the law upon the hill of Sinai, with such fearful thundering and lightning, that all people thereat were amazed and affrighted.

It is exceeding necessary for us to know this use of the law. For he that is not an open and a public murderer, an adulterer, or a thief, holds himself to be an upright and godly man; as did the Pharisee, so blinded and possessed spiritually of the devil, that he could neither see nor feel his sins, nor his miserable case, but exalted himself touching his good works and deserts. Such hypocrites and haughty saints can God by no better means humble and soften, than by and through the law; for that is the right club or hammer, the thunder-clap from heaven, the axe of God's wrath, that strikes through, beats down, and batters such stock-blind, hardened hypocrites. For this cause, it is no small matter that we should rightly understand what the law is, whereto it serves, and what is its proper work and office. We do not reject the law and the works thereof, but, on the contrary, confirm them, and teach that we ought to do good works, and that the law is very good and profitable, if we merely give it its right, and keep it to its own proper work and office.

The law opens not nor makes visible God's grace and mercy, or the righteousness whereby we obtain everlasting life and salvation; but our sins, our weakness, death, God's wrath and judgment.

The light of the gospel is a far different manner of light, enlightening affrighted, broken, sorrowful, and contrite hearts, and reviving, comforting, and refreshing them. For it declares that God is merciful to unworthy, condemned sinners, for the sake of Christ, and that a blessing thereby is presented unto them who believe; that is, grace, remission of sins, righteousness, and everlasting life.

When in this way we distinguish the law and the gospel, then we attribute and give to each its right work and office. Therefore, I pray and admonish all lovers of godliness and pure religion, especially those who in time are to be teachers of others, that with highest diligence they study this matter, which I much fear, after our time, will be darkened again, if not altogether extinguished.

### 275

Never was a bolder, harsher sermon preached in the world than that wherein St. Paul abolished Moses and his law, as insufficient for a sinner's salvation.

Hence the continual dissension and strife which this apostle had with the Jews. And if Moses had not cashiered and put himself out of his office, with these words: 'The Lord thy God will raise up unto thee another prophet out of thy brethren, him shalt thou hear;' who then would or could have believed the gospel, and forsaken Moses?

Hence the vehement accusation brought by the worthy Jews, who suborned certain men to accuse the beloved Stephen, saying: 'We have heard him speak blasphemous words against Moses and against God.' Likewise, 'This man ceaseth not to speak blasphemous words against the holy place and the law,' etc. For to preach and teach that the observing of the law was not necessary to salvation, was to the Jews as horrible, as though one should stand up and preach among us Christians: Christ is not the Lamb of God, that taketh away the sins of the world. St. Paul could have been content they had kept and observed the law, had they not asserted it was necessary to salvation. But the Jews would no more endure this, than the papists, with their fopperies, will now endure that we hold and observe the ceremonies, so that every one shall be at liberty either to observe or not observe them, according as occasion serves, and that the conscience therein may not be bound or ensnared, and that God's Word freely be preached and taught. But Jews and papists are ungodly wretches; they are two stockings made of one piece of cloth.

### 276

Moses with his law is most terrible; there never was any equal to him in perplexing, affrighting, tyrannizing, threatening, preaching, and thundering; for he lays sharp hold on the conscience, and fearfully works it, but all by God's express command. When we are affrighted, feeling our sins, God's wrath and judgments, most certainly, in the law is no justification; therein is nothing celestial and divine, but 'tis altogether of the world, which world is the kingdom of the devil. Therefore it is clear and apparent that the law can do nothing that is vivifying, saving, celestial, or divine; what it does is altogether temporal; that is, it gives us to know what evil is in the world, outwardly and inwardly. But, beside this, the Holy Ghost must come over the law, and speak thus in thy heart: God will not have thee affright thyself to death, only that through the law thou shouldest know thy misery, and yet not despair, but believe in Christ, who is the end of the law for righteousness.

### 277

St. Paul now and then speaks scornfully of the law, but he means not that we should contemn the law; he would rather we should esteem and hold it precious. But where he teaches how we become justified before God, it was necessary for him so to speak; for it is far another thing when we talk how we may be justified before God, than when we talk about the law. When we have in hand the righteousness that justifies before God, we cannot too much disdain or undervalue the law.

The conscience must have regard to nothing but Christ; wherefore we must, with all diligence, endeavour to remove Moses with his law far from us out of sight, when we intend to stand justified before God.

### 278

It is impossible for thy human strength, whosoever thou art, without God's assistance, when Moses sets upon thee with his law, accuses and threatens thee with God's wrath and death, to possess such peace as if no law or sin had ever been.

When thou feelest the terror of the law, thou mayest say thus: Madam Law! I have no time to hear you speak; your language is very rough and unfriendly; I would have you know that your reign is over, therefore I am now free, I will endure your bondage no longer. When we thus address the law, we shall find the difference between the law of grace and the law of thundering Moses; and how great a divine and celestial gift it is to hope against hope, when there seems nothing to hope for; and how true the speech of St. Paul is, where he says: 'Through faith in Christ we are justified, and not through the works of the law.' When, indeed, justification is not the matter in hand, we ought highly to esteem the law, extol it, and with St. Paul, call it good, true, spiritual, and divine, as in truth it is.

God will keep his Word through the writing-pen upon earth; the divines are the heads or quills of the pens, the lawyers the stumps. If the world will not keep the heads and quills, that is, if they will not hear the divines, they must keep the stumps, that is, they must hear the lawyers, who will teach them manners.

### 279

I will have none of Moses with his law, for he is an enemy to my Lord and Saviour Christ. If Moses will go to law with me, I will give him his despatch, and say: Here stands Christ.

At the day of judgment Moses will doubtless look upon me, and say: Thou didst understand me rightly, and didst well distinguish between me and the law of faith; therefore we are now friends.

We must reject the law when it seeks to affright the conscience, and when we feel God's anger against our sins, then we must eat, drink, sleep, and be cheerful, to spite the devil. But human wisdom is more inclined to understand the law of Moses, than the law of the gospel. Old Adam will not out.

Together with the law, Satan torments the conscience by picturing Christ before our eyes, as an angry and stern judge, saying: God is an enemy to sinners, for he is a just God; thou art a sinner, therefore God is thy enemy. Hereat is the conscience dejected, beaten down, and taken captive. Now he that can make a true difference in this case, will say: Devil! thou art deceived, it is not so as thou pretendest; for God is not an enemy to all sinners, but only to the ungodly and impenitent sinners and persecutors of his word. For even as sin is two-fold, even so is righteousness two-fold also.

## 280

Two learned men came to me, and asked whether the law of God revealed sin to people without the particular motion of the Holy Ghost? the one affirming that it was so, the other denying it. The first would prove his opinion out of St. Paul, where he says: 'By the law is the knowledge of sin': but the other alleged, that this was the work and office of the Holy Ghost through the law; for many heard the preaching of the law, and yet did not acknowledge their sins.

I answered them: Ye are both in the right if ye well understood one another; your difference consists only in words; for the law must be understood two manner of ways; first, as a law described and heard; when it reveals not the strength or the sting of sin, it goes in at one ear and out at the other; it neither touches nor strikes the heart at all.

Secondly, when the law is taught, and the Holy Ghost comes thereunto, touches the heart, and gives strength to the word, and the heart confesses sin, feels God's wrath, and says: Ah! this concerns me; I have sinned against God, and have offended. Then the law has well and rightly finished its work and office.

After these came a third, and said: 'tis one matter to be simply a law, and another to be God's law; for the law of God must always have its operation and strength, which the law of man has not. To him I made this answer:

The law must be distinguished, understood, and divided three-fold: first, a written law, second, a verbal, third, a spiritual law. The written law, which is written in the book, is like a block, which, without motion, remains lying; that law does nothing except we read therein. The verbal law reveals and shows sin; yea, in the ungodly; for when adulterers hear the seventh commandment, 'Thou shalt not commit adultery', then they understand that this reproves them; but they either contemn it, or else they persecute those by whom they are reproved. But the spiritual law cannot be without the motion of the Holy Ghost, which touches the heart, and moves it, so that a man not only ceases to persecute, but has sorrow for sins committed, and desires to be better.

The same person urged: St. Paul says, that the word works in the hearers; I answered: the word which in that place St. Paul speaks of, must be understood of the gospel; for even that word, whether written or verbal, taught or preached, does nothing without the Holy Ghost, which must kindle it in their hearts, reviving and strengthening them.

## 281

Every law or commandment contains two profitable points; first, a promise; second, a threatening; for every law is, or should be, good, upright, and holy, Romans 7. It commands that which is good, and forbids that which is evil: it rewards and defends the good and godly, but punishes and resists the wicked; as St. Paul says: 'Rulers are not a terror to good works, but to the evil. Wilt thou then not be afraid of the power? do that which is good.' And St. Peter: 'For the punishment of evildoers, and for the praise of them that do well.' And the imperial laws teach the same. Now, seeing there are promises and threatenings in temporal laws, how much more so are they fitting in God's laws, which require upright faith. The emperor's laws, indeed, require faith, true or feigned; for those who do not fear or believe that the emperor will punish or protect, observe not his laws, as we see, but those observe them that fear and believe, whether from the heart or not. Now, where in Scripture there is a promise without the law, there faith only is necessary: as, when Abraham was promised that his seed should multiply as the stars of heaven; he was not commanded at that time to accomplish any work, but he heard of a work which God would accomplish, and which he himself was not able to do. Thus is Christ promised unto us, and is described to have done a work which we cannot do; therefore in this case, faith is needful for us, because by works we cannot take hold thereof.

## 282

The law, with its righteousness, is like a cloud without rain, which promises rain but gives none; even so does the law promise salvation, but gives it not, for the law was not assigned to that end, as St. Paul says, Galatians 3.

## 283

The gospel preaches nothing of the merit of works; he that says the gospel requires works for salvation, I say, flat and plain, is a liar.

Nothing that is properly good proceeds out of the works of the law, unless grace be present; for what we are forced to do, goes not from the heart, nor is acceptable. The people under Moses were always in a murmuring state, would fain have stoned him, and were rather his enemies than his friends.

## 284

He that will dispute with the devil out of the law, will be beaten and taken captive; but he that disputes with him out of the gospel, conquers him. The devil has the written bond against us; therefore, let no man presume to dispute with him of the law or of sin. When the devil says to me: behold, much evil proceeds from thy doctrine, then I say to him: much good and profit come also from it. O! replies the devil, that is nothing to the purpose. The devil is an artful orator; he can make out of a mote a beam, and falsify that which is good; he was never in all his life so angry and vexed as he is now; I feel him well.

If baptism, if the sacrament, if the gospel be false, and if Christ be not in heaven and governs not, then indeed I am in the wrong; but if these are of God's instituting and ordaining, and if Christ is in heaven and rules, then I am sure that the cause I have in hand is good; for what I teach and do openly in the church is altogether of the gospel, of baptism, of the Lords supper, of prayer, etc. Christ and his gospel are here present; therein I must and will continue.

## 285

If we diligently mark the world, we shall find that it is governed merely by its conceited opinions; sophistry, hypocrisy, and tyranny rule it; the upright, pure, and clear divine word must be their handmaid, and by them controlled. Therefore let us beware of sophistry, which consists not only in a double tongue, in twisting words, which may be construed any way, but also blossoms and flourishes in all arts and vocations, and will likewise have room and place in religion, where it has usurped a fine, fictitious colour.

Nothing is more pernicious than sophistry; we are by nature prone to believe lies rather than truth. Few people know what an evil sophistry is; Plato, the heathen writer, made thereof a wonderful definition. For my part, I compare it with a lie, which, like a snowball, the more it is rolled, the greater it becomes.

Therefore, I approve not of such as pervert everything, undervaluing and finding fault with other men's opinions, though they be good and sound. I like not brains that can dispute on both sides, and yet conclude nothing certain. Such sophistications are mere crafty and subtle inventions and contrivances, to cozen and deceive people.

But I love an honest and well-affected mind, that seeks after truth simply and plainly, and goes not about with fantasies and cheating tricks.

## 286

St. Paul says: 'What the law could not do, in that it was weak through the flesh, God sending his own Son in the likeness of sinful flesh, and for sin condemned sin in flesh: that the righteousness of the law might be fulfilled in us,' etc. That is, Christ is the sum of all; he is the right, the pure meaning and contents of the law. Whoso has Christ, has rightly fulfilled the law. But to take away the law altogether, which sticks in nature, and is written in our hearts and born in us, is a thing impossible and against God. And whereas the law of nature is somewhat darker, and speaks only of works, therefore, Moses and the Holy Ghost more clearly declare and expound it, by naming those works which God will have us to do, and to leave undone. Hence Christ also says: 'I am not come to destroy the law.' Worldly people would willingly give him royal entertainment who could bring this to pass, and make out that. Moses, through Christ, is quite taken away. O, then we should quickly see what a fine kind of life there would be in the world! But God forbid, and keep us from such errors, and suffer us not to live to see the same.

## 287

We must preach the law for the sake of the evil and wicked, but for the most part it lights upon the good and godly, who, although they need it not, except so far as may concern the old Adam, flesh and blood, yet accept it. The preaching of the gospel we must have for the sake of the good and godly, yet it falls among the wicked and ungodly, who take it to themselves, whereas it profits them not; for they abuse it, and are thereby made confident. It is even as when it rains in the water or on a desert wilderness, and, meantime, the good pastures and grounds are parched and dried up. The ungodly out of the gospel suck only a carnal freedom, and become worse thereby; therefore, not the gospel, but the law belongs to them. Even as when my little son John offends, if then I should not whip him, but call him to the table to me, and give him sugarplums, thereby I should make him worse, yea, quite spoil him.

The gospel is like a fresh, mild, and cool air in the extreme heat of summer, a solace and comfort in the anguish of the conscience. But as this heat proceeds from the rays of the sun, so likewise the terrifying of the conscience must proceed from the preaching of the law, to the end we may know that we have offended against the laws of God.

Now, when the mind is refreshed and quickened again by the cool air of the gospel, then we must not be idle, lie down and sleep. That is, when our consciences are settled in peace, quieted and comforted through God's Spirit, we must prove our faith by such good works as God has commanded. But so long as we live in this vale of misery, we shall be plagued and vexed with flies, with beetles, and vermin, that is, with the devil, the world, and our own flesh; yet we must press through, and not suffer ourselves to recoil.

### 288

In what darkness, unbelief, traditions, and ordinances of men we have lived, and in how many conflicts of the conscience we have been ensnared, confounded, and captivated under Popedom, is testified by the books of the papists, and by many people now living. From all which snares and horrors we are now delivered and freed by Jesus Christ and his gospel, and are called to the true righteousness of faith; insomuch that with good and peaceable consciences we now believe in God the Father, we trust in him, and have just cause to boast that we have sure and certain remission of our sins through the death of Christ Jesus, dearly bought and purchased. Who can sufficiently extol these treasures of the conscience, which everywhere are spread abroad, offered and presented merely by grace? We are now conquerors of sin, of the law, of death, and of the devil; freed and delivered from all human traditions. If we would but consider the tyranny of auricular confession one of the least things we have escaped from we could not show ourselves sufficiently thankful to God for loosing us out of that one snare. When Popedom stood and flourished among us, then every king would willingly have given ten hundred thousand guilders, a prince one hundred thousand, a nobleman one thousand, a gentleman one hundred, a citizen or countryman twenty or ten, to have been freed from that tyranny. But now seeing such freedom is obtained for nothing, by grace, it is not much regarded, neither give we thanks to God for it.

### 289

The Old Testament is chiefly a law-book, teaching what we should do or not do, and showing examples and acts how such laws are observed and transgressed. But besides the law, there are certain promises and sentences of grace, whereby the holy patriarchs and prophets were preserved then, as we are now. But the New Testament is a book wherein is written the gospel of God's promises, and the acts of those that believed, and those that believed not. And it is an open and public preaching and declaration of Christ, as set down in the sentences of the Old Testament, and accomplished by him. And like as the proper and chief doctrine of the New Testament is grace and peace, through the forgiveness of sins declared in Christ, so the proper and chief doctrine of the Old Testament is, through the law, to discover sin, and to require good works and obedience.

We must take good heed that we make not a Moses out of Christ, nor out of Christ a Moses, as often has been done. But where Christ and his apostles, in the gospel, give out commands and doctrines expounding the law, these are as important as the other works and benefits of Christ. Yet to know only gospel precepts, is not to know the gospel; but when the voice sounds which says, Christ is thine own, with life and works, with death and resurrection, with all what he is, and all he has, by this we see that he forces not, but teaches amicably, saying: 'Blessed are the poor,' etc., 'Come to me all ye that are weary and heavy laden,' etc. And the apostles use the words: 'I admonish,' 'I exhort,' 'I pray,' etc.; so that we see in every place that the gospel is not a lawbook, but a mild preaching of Christ's merits, given to be our own, if we believe.

Hence it follows that no law is given to the faithful, whereby they become justified before God, as St. Paul says, because they are already justified and saved by faith; but they show and prove their faith by their works, they confess and teach the gospel before people freely and undauntedly, and thereupon venture their lives; and whatsoever they take in hand, they direct to the good and profit of their neighbour, and so follow Christ's example. For, where works and love do not break through and appear, there faith is not.

We must make a clear distinction; we must place the gospel in heaven, and leave the law on earth; we must receive of the gospel a heavenly and a divine righteousness; while we value the law as an earthly and human righteousness, and thus directly and diligently separate the righteousness of the gospel from the righteousness of the law, even as God has separated and distinguished heaven from earth, light from darkness, day from night, &c., so that the righteousness of the gospel be the light and the day, but the righteousness of the law, darkness and night. Therefore all Christians should learn rightly to discern the law and grace in their hearts, and know how to keep one from the other, in deed and in truth, not merely in words, as the pope and other heretics do, who mingle them together, and, as it were, make thereout a cake not fit to eat.

### 290

Augustine pictured the strength, office, and operation of the law, by a very fit similitude, to show, that it discovers our sins, and God's wrath against sin, and places them in our sight. 'The law,' says he, 'is not in fault, but our evil and wicked nature; even as a heap of lime is still and quiet, until water be poured thereon, but then it begins to smoke and burn, not from the fault of the water, but from the nature and kind of the lime, which will not endure water; whereas, if oil, instead, be poured upon it, then it lies still, and burns not; even so it is with the law and the gospel.'

### 291

On this matter of the righteousness of the law, St. Paul thoroughly bestirred himself against God's professing people, as in Romans 9, 10, 11, he strives with powerful, well-based arguments; it produced him much sorrow of heart.

The Jews' argument was this: Paul kept the law at Jerusalem, therefore, said they, we must also keep it. Answer: True, Paul for a certain time kept the law, by reason of the weak, to win them; but, in this our time, it is not so, and agrees not in any way therewith; as the ancient father well said: Distinguish times, and we may easily reconcile the Scriptures together.

# Of Justification

⚜

## 292

It is impossible for a papist to understand this article: 'I believe the forgiveness of sins.' For the papists are drowned in their opinions, as I also was when among them, of the cleaving to of inherent righteousness.

The Scripture names the faithful, saints and people of God. It is a sin and shame that we should forget this glorious and comfortable name and title. But the papists are such direct sinners, that they will not be reckoned sinner; and again, they will neither be holy nor held so to be. And in this sort it goes on with them untoward and crosswise, so that they neither believe the gospel which comforts, nor the law which punishes.

But here one may say: the sins which we daily commit, offend and anger God; how then can we be holy? Answer: A mother's love to her child is much stronger than the distaste of the scurf upon the child's head. Even so, God's love towards us is far stronger than our uncleanness. Therefore, though we be sinners, yet we lose not thereby our childhood, neither do we fall from grace by reason of our sins.

Another may say: we sin without ceasing, and where sin is, there the Holy Spirit is not; therefore we are not holy, because the Holy Spirit is not in us, which makes holy. Answer: The text says plainly: 'The Holy Ghost shall glorify me.' Now where Christ is, there is the Holy Spirit. Now Christ is in the faithful, although they have and feel, and confess sins, and with sorrow of heart complain thereof; therefore sins do not separate Christ from those that believe.

The God of the Turks helps no longer or further, as they think, than as they are godly people; in like manner also the God of the Papists. So when Turk and Papist begin to feel their sins and unworthiness, as in time of trial and temptation, or in death, then they tremble and despair.

But a true Christian says: 'I believe in Jesus Christ my Lord and Saviour,' who gave himself for my sins, and is at God's right hand, and intercedes for me; fall I into sin, as, alas! oftentimes I do, I am sorry for it; I rise again, and am an enemy unto sin. So that we plainly see, the true Christian faith is far different from the faith and religion of the pope and Turk. But human strength and nature are not able to accomplish this true Christian faith without the Holy Spirit. It can do no more than take refuge in its own deserts.

But he that can say: 'I am a child of God through Christ, who is my righteousness,' and despairs not, though he be deficient in good works, which always fail us, he believes rightly. But grace is so great that it amazes a human creature, and is very difficult to be believed. Insomuch that faith gives the honour to God, that he can and will perform what he promised, namely, to make sinners righteous, Romans 4, though 'tis an exceeding hard matter to believe that God is merciful unto us for the sake of Christ. O! man's heart is too straight and narrow to entertain or take hold of this.

### 293

All men, indeed, are not alike strong, so that in some, many faults, weaknesses, and offences, are found; but these do not hinder them of sanctification, if they sin not of evil purpose and premeditation, but only out of weakness. For a Christian, indeed, feels the lusts of the flesh, but he resists them, and they have not dominion over him; and although, now and then, he stumbles and falls into sin, yet it is forgiven him, when he rises again, and holds on to Christ, who will not 'That the lost sheep be hunted away, but be sought after'.

### 294

Why do Christians make use of their natural wisdom, and understanding, seeing it must be set aside in matters of faith, as not only not understanding them, but also as striving against them.

Answer: The natural wisdom of a human creature in matters of faith, until he be regenerate and born anew, is altogether darkness, knowing nothing in divine cases. But in a faithful person, regenerate and enlightened by the Holy Spirit, through the Word, it is a fair and glorious instrument, and work of God: for even as all God's gifts, natural instruments, and expert faculties, are hurtful to the ungodly, even so are they wholesome and saving to the good and godly.

The understanding, through faith, receives life from faith; that which was dead, is made alive again; like as our bodies, in light day, when it is clear and bright, are better disposed, rise, move, walk, etc., more readily and safely than they do in the dark night, so it is with human reason, which strives not against faith, when enlightened, but rather furthers and advances it.

So the tongue, which before blasphemed God, now lauds, extols, and praises God and his grace, as my tongue, now it is enlightened, is now another manner of tongue than it was in Popedom; a regeneration done by the Holy Ghost through the Word.

A sanctified and upright Christian says: My wife, my children, my art, my wisdom, my money and wealth, help and avail me nothing in heaven; yet I cast them not away nor reject them when God bestows such benefits upon me, but part and separate, the substance from the vanity and foolery which cleave thereunto. Gold is and remains gold as well when a strumpet carries it about her, as when 'tis with an honest, good, and godly woman. The body of a strumpet is even as well God's creature, as the body of an honest matron. In this manner ought we to part and separate vanity and folly from the thing and substance, or from the creature given and God who created it.

### 295

Upright and faithful Christians ever think they are not faithful, nor believe as they ought; and therefore they constantly strive, wrestle, and are diligent to keep and to increase faith, as good workmen always see that something is wanting in their workmanship. But the botchers think that nothing is wanting in what they do, but that everything is well and complete. Like as the Jews conceive they have the ten commandments at their fingers' end, whereas, in truth, they neither learn nor regard them.

### 296

Truly it is held for presumption in a human creature that he dare boast of his own proper righteousness of faith; 'tis a hard matter for a man to say: I am the child of God, and am comforted and solaced through the immeasurable grace and mercy of my heavenly Father. To do this from the heart, is not in every man's power. Therefore no man is able to teach pure and aright touching faith, nor to reject the righteousness of works, without sound practice and experience. St. Paul was well exercised in this art; he speaks more vilely of the law than any arch heretic can speak of the sacrament of the altar, of baptism, or than the Jews have spoken thereof; for he names the law, the ministration of death, the ministration of sin, and the ministration of condemnation; yea, he holds all the works of the law, and what the law requires, without Christ, dangerous and hurtful, which Moses, if he had then lived, would doubtless have taken very ill at Paul's hands. It was, according to human reason, spoken too scornfully.

### 297

Faith and hope are variously distinguishable. And, first, in regard of the subject, wherein everything subsists: faith consists in a person's understanding, hope in the will; these two cannot be separated; they are like the two cherubim over the mercy-seat.

Secondly, in regard of the office: faith indites, distinguishes, and teaches, and is the knowledge and acknowledgment; hope admonishes, awakens, hears, expects, and suffers.

Thirdly, in regard to the object: faith looks to the word or promise, which is truth; but hope to that which the Word promises, which is the good or benefit.

Fourthly, in regard of order in degree: faith is first, and before all adversities and troubles, and is the beginning of life (Heb. 11). But hope follows after, and springs up in trouble (Rom. 5).

Fifthly, by reason of the contrariety: faith fights against errors and heresies; it proves and judges spirits and doctrines. But hope strives against troubles and vexations, and among the evil it expects good.

Faith, in divinity, is the wisdom and providence, and belongs to the doctrine. But hope is the courage and joyfulness in divinity, and pertains to admonition. Faith is the *dialectica,* for it is altogether prudence and wisdom; hope is the *rhetorica,* an elevation of the heart and mind. As wisdom without courage is futile, even so faith without hope is nothing worth; for hope endures and overcomes misfortune and evil. And as a joyous valour without understanding is but rashness, so hope without faith is spiritual presumption. Faith is the key to the sacred Scriptures, the right *Cabala* or exposition, which one receives of tradition, as the prophets left this doctrine to their disciples. 'Tis said St. Peter wept whenever he thought of the gentleness with which

Jesus taught. Faith is given from one to another, and remains continually in one school. Faith is not a quality, as the schoolmen say, but a gift of God.

### 298

Everything that is done in the world is done by hope. No husbandman would sow one grain of corn, if he hoped not it would grow up and become seed; no bachelor would marry a wife, if he hoped not to have children; no merchant or tradesman would set himself to work, if he did not hope to reap benefit thereby, etc. How much more, then, does hope urge us on to everlasting life and salvation?

### 299

Faith's substance is our will; its manner is, that we take hold on Christ by divine instinct; its final cause and fruit, that it purifies the heart, makes us children of God, and brings with it the remission of sins.

### 300

Adam received the promise of the woman's seed ere he had done any work or sacrifice, to the end God's truth might stand fast – namely, that we are justified before God altogether without works, and obtain forgiveness of sins merely by grace. Whoso is able to believe this well and steadfastly, is a doctor above all the doctors in the world.

### 301

Faith is not only necessary, that thereby the ungodly may become justified and saved before God, and their hearts be settled in peace, but it is necessary in every other respect. St. Paul says: 'Now that we are justified by faith, we have peace with God through our Lord Jesus Christ.'

### 302

Joseph of Arimathea had a faith in Christ, like as the apostles had; he thought Christ would have been a worldly and temporal potentate; therefore he took care of him as of a good friend, and buried him honourably. He believed not that Christ should rise again from death, and become a spiritual and everlasting king.

### 303

When Abraham shall rise again at the last day, then he will chide us for our unbelief, and will say: I had not the hundredth part of the promises which ye have, and yet I believed. That example of Abraham exceeds all human natural reason, who, overcoming the paternal love he bore towards his only son Isaac, was all obedient to God, and, against the law of nature, would have sacrificed that son. What, for the space of three days, he felt in his breast, how his heart yearned and panted, what hesitations and trials he had, cannot be expressed.

### 304

All heretics have continually failed in this one point, that they do not rightly understand or know the article of justification. If we had not this article certain and clear, it were impossible we could criticise the pope's false doctrine of indulgences and other abominable errors, much less be able to overcome greater spiritual errors and vexations. If we only permit Christ to be our Saviour, then we have won, for he is the only girdle which clasps the whole body together, as St. Paul excellently teaches.

If we look to the spiritual birth and substance of a true Christian, we shall soon extinguish all deserts of good works; for they serve us to no use, neither to purchase sanctification, nor to deliver us from sin, death, devil, or hell.

Little children are saved only by faith without any good works; therefore faith alone justifies. If God's power be able to effect that in one, then he is also able to accomplish it in all; for the power of the child effects it not, but the power of faith; neither is it done through the child's weakness or disability; for then that weakness would be merit of itself, or equivalent to merit. It is a mischievous thing that we miserable, sinful wretches will upbraid God, and hit him in the teeth with our works, and think thereby to be justified before him; but God will not allow it.

### 305

This article, how we are saved, is the chief of the whole Christian doctrine, to which all divine disputations must be directed. All the prophets were chiefly engaged upon it, and sometimes much perplexed about it. For when this article is kept fast and sure by a constant faith, then all other articles draw on softly after, as that of the Holy Trinity, etc. God has declared no article so plainly and openly as this, that we are saved only by Christ; though he speaks much of the Holy Trinity, yet he dwells continually upon this article of the salvation of our souls; other articles are of great weight, but this surpasses all.

## 306

A capuchin says: wear a grey coat and a hood, a rope round thy body, and sandals on thy feet. A cordelier says: put on a black hood; an ordinary papist says: do this or that work, hear mass, pray, fast, give alms, etc. But a true Christian says: I am justified and saved only by faith in Christ, without any works or merits of my own; compare these together, and judge which is the true righteousness.

## 307

Christ says: 'The spirit is willing, but the flesh is weak'; St. Paul also says: the spirit willingly would give itself wholly unto God, would trust in him, and be obedient; but natural reason and understanding, flesh and blood, resist and will not go forward. Therefore our Lord God must needs have patience and bear with us. God will not put out the glimmering flax; the faithful have as yet but only the first fruits of the spirit; they have not the fulfilling, but the tenth.

## 308

I well understand that St. Paul was also weak in faith, whence he boasted, and said: 'I am a servant of God, and an apostle of Jesus Christ.' An angel stood by him at sea, and comforted him, and when he came to Rome, he was comforted as he saw the brethren come out to meet him. Hereby we see what the communion and company does of such as fear God. The Lord commanded the disciples to remain together in one place, before they received the Holy Ghost, and to comfort one another; for Christ well knew that adversaries would assault them.

## 309

A Christian must be well armed, grounded, and furnished with sentences out of God's word, that so he may stand and defend religion and himself against the devil, in case he should be asked to embrace another doctrine.

## 310

When at the last day we shall live again, we shall blush for shame, and say to ourselves: 'fie on thee, in that thou hast not been more courageous, bold, and strong to believe in Christ, and to endure all manner of adversities, crosses, and persecutions, seeing his glory is so great. If I were now in the world, I would not stick to suffer ten thousand time more.'

## 311

Although a man knew, and could do as much as the angels in heaven, yet all this would not make him a Christian, unless he knew Christ and believed in him. God says: 'Let not the wise man glory in his wisdom, neither let the mighty man glory in his might; let not the rich man glory in his riches: but let him that glorieth, glory in this, that he understandeth and knoweth me, that I am the Lord, which doth exercise loving-kindness, judgment, and righteousness,' etc.

## 312

The article of our justification before God is as with a son who is born heir to all his father's goods, and comes not thereunto by deserts, but naturally, of ordinary course. But yet, meantime, his father admonishes him to do such and such things, and promises him gifts to make him the more willing. As when he says to him: if thou wilt be good, be obedient, study diligently, then I will buy thee a fine coat; or, come hither to me, and I will give thee an apple. In such sort does he teach his son industry; though the whole inheritance belongs unto him of course, yet will he make him, by promises, pliable and willing to do what he would have done.

Even so God deals with us; he is loving unto us with friendly and sweet words, promises us spiritual and temporal blessings, though everlasting life is presented unto those who believe in Christ, by mere grace and mercy, gratis, without any merits, works, or worthinesses.

And this ought we to teach in the church and in the assembly of God, that God will have upright and good works, which he has commanded, not such as we ourselves take in hand, of our own choice and devotion, or well meaning, as the friars and priest, teach in Popedom, for such works are not pleasing to God, as Christ says: 'In vain do they worship me, teaching for doctrines the commandments of men,' etc. We must teach of good works, yet always so that the article of justification remain pure and unfalsified. For Christ neither can nor will endure any beside himself; he will have the bride alone; he is full of jealousy.

Should we teach: if thou believest, thou shalt be saved, whatsoever thou doest; that were stark naught; for faith is either false and feigned, or, though it be upright, yet is eclipsed, when people wittingly and wilfully sin against God's command. And the Holy Spirit, which is given to the faithful, departs by reason of evil works done against the conscience, as the example of David sufficiently testifies.

### 313

As to ceremonies and ordinances, the kingdom of love must have precedence and government and not tyranny. It must be a willing, not a halter love; it must altogether be directed and construed for the good and profit of the neighbour; and the greater he that governs, the more he ought to serve according to love.

### 314

The love towards our neighbour must be like the pure and chaste love between bride and bridegroom, where all faults are connived at and borne with, and only the virtues regarded.

### 315

Believest thou? then thou wilt speak boldly. Speakest thou boldly? then thou must suffer. Sufferest thou? then thou shalt be comforted. For faith, the confession thereof, and the cross, follow one upon another.

### 316

Give and it shall be given unto you: this is a fine maxim, and makes people poor and rich; it is that which maintains my house. I would not boast, but I well know what I give away in the year. If my gracious lord and master, the prince elector, should give a gentleman two thousand florins, this should hardly answer to the cost of my housekeeping for one year; and yet I have but three hundred florins a year, but God blesses these, and makes them suffice.

There is in Austria a monastery, which, in former times, was very rich, and remained rich so long as it was charitable to the poor; but when it ceased to give, then it became indigent, and is so to this day. Not long since, a poor man went there and solicited alms, which was denied him; he demanded the cause why they refused to give for God's sake? The porter of the monastery answered: We are become poor; whereupon the mendicant said: The cause of your poverty is this: ye had formerly in this monastery two brethren, the one named *Date* (give), and the other *Dabitur* (it shall be given you). The former ye thrust out; the other went away of himself:

We are bound to help one's neighbour three manner of ways — with giving, lending, and selling. But no man gives; every one scrapes and claws all to himself; each would willingly steal, but give nothing, and lend but upon usury. No man sells unless he can over-reach his neighbour; therefore is *Dabitur* gone, and our Lord God will bless us no more so richly. Beloved, he that desires to have anything, must also give: a liberal hand was never in want, or empty.

## 317

Desert is a work nowhere to be found, for Christ gives a reward by reason of the promise. If the prince elector should say to me: Come to the court, and I will give thee one hundred florins, I perform a work in going to the court, yet I receive not the gift by reason of my work in going thither, but by reason of the promise the prince made me.

## 318

I marvel at the madness and bitterness of Wetzell, in undertaking to write so much against the Protestants, assailing us without rhyme or reason, and, as we say, getting a case out of a hedge; as where he rages against this principle of ours, that the works and acts of a farmer, husbandman, or any other good and godly Christian, if done in faith, are far more precious in the sight of God, than all the works of monks, friars, nuns, etc. This poor, ignorant fellow gets very angry against us, regarding not the works which God has commanded and imposed upon each man in his vocation, state, and calling. He heeds only superstitious practices, devised for show and effect, which God neither commands nor approves of.

St. Paul, in his epistles, wrote of good works and virtues more energetically and truthfully than all the philosophers; for he extols highly the works of godly Christians, in their respective vocations and callings. Let Wetzell know that David's wars and battles were more pleasing to God than the fastings and prayings even of the holiest of the old monks, setting aside altogether the works of the monks of our time, which are simply ridiculous.

## 319

I never work better than when I am inspired by anger; when I am angry, I can write, pray, and preach well, for then my whole temperament is quickened, my understanding sharpened, and all mundane vexations and temptations depart.

## 320

Dr. Justus Jonas asked me if the thoughts and words of the prophet Jeremiah were Christianlike, when he cursed the day of his birth. I said: We must now and then wake up our Lord God with such words. Jeremiah had cause to murmur in this way. Did not our Saviour Christ say: 'O faithless and perverse generation! How long shall I be with you, and suffer you?' Moses also took God in hand, where he said: 'Wherefore hast thou afflicted thy servant? Have I conceived all this people? Have I begotten them?'

### 321

A man must needs be plunged in bitter affliction when in his heart he means good, and yet is not regarded. I can never get rid of these cogitations, wishing I had never begun this business with the pope. So, too, I desire myself rather dead than to hear or see God's Word and his servants contemned; but 'tis the frailty of our nature to be thus discouraged.

They who condemn the movement of anger against antagonists, are theologians who deal in mere speculations; they play with words, and occupy themselves with subtleties, but when they are aroused, and take a real interest in the matter, they are touched sensibly.

### 322

'In quietness and in confidence shall be your strength.' This sentence I expounded thus: If thou intendest to vanquish the greatest, the most abominable and wickedest enemy, who is able to do thee mischief both in body and soul, and against whom thou preparest all sorts of weapons, but canst not overcome; then know that there is a sweet and loving physical herb to serve thee, named Patientia.

Thou wilt say: How may I attain this physic? Take unto thee faith, which says: no creature can do me mischief without the will of God. In case thou receivest hurt and mischief by thine enemy, this is done by the sweet and gracious will of God, in such sort that the enemy hurts himself a thousand times more than he does thee. Hence flows unto me, a Christian, the love which says: I will, instead of the evil which mine enemy does unto me, do him all the good I can; I will heap coals of fire upon his head. This is the Christian armour and weapon, wherewith to beat and overcome those enemies that seem to be like huge mountains. In a word, love teaches to suffer and endure all things.

### 323

A certain honest and God-forbearing man at Wittenberg told me, that though he lived peaceably with every one, hurt no man, was ever quiet, yet many people were enemies unto him. I comforted him in this manner: Arm thyself with patience, and be not angry though they hate thee; what offence, I pray, do we give the devil? What ails him to be so great an enemy unto us? only because he has not that which God has; I know no other cause of his vehement hatred towards us. If God give thee to eat, eat; if he cause thee to fast, be resigned thereto; gives he thee honours? take them; hurt or shame? endure it; casts he thee into prison? murmur not; will he make thee a king? obey him; casts he thee down again? heed it not.

### 324

Patience is the most excellent of the virtues, and, in Sacred Writ, highly praised and recommended by the Holy Ghost. The learned heathen philosophers applaud it, but they do not know its genuine basis, being without the assistance of God. Epictetus, the wise and judicious Greek, said very well: 'Suffer and abstain.'

### 325

It was the custom of old, in burying the dead, to lay their heads towards the sun-rising, by reason of a spiritual mystery and signification therein manifested; but this was not an enforced law. So all laws and ceremonies should be free in the church, and not be done on compulsion, being things which neither justify nor condemn in the sight of God, but are observed merely for the sake of orderly discipline.

### 326

The righteousness of works and hypocrisy, are the most mischievous diseases born in us, and not easily expelled, especially when they are confirmed and settled upon us by use and practice; for all mankind will have dealings with Almighty God, and dispute with him, according to their human natural understanding, and will make satisfaction to God for their sins, with their own strength and self-chosen works. For my part, I have so often deceived our Lord God by promising to be upright and good, that I will promise no more, but will only pray for a happy hour, when it shall please God to make me good.

### 327

A popish priest once argued with me in this manner: Evil works are damned, therefore good works justify. I answered: This your argument is nothing worth; it concludes not *ratione contrariorum*; the things are not in connexion; evil works are evil in complete measure, because they proceed from a heart that is altogether spoiled and evil; but good works, yea, even in an upright Christian, are incompletely good; for they proceed out of a weak obedience but little recovered and restored. Whoso can say from his heart: I am a sinner, but God is righteous; and who, at the point of death, from his heart can say;

Lord Jesus Christ, I commit my spirit into thy hands, may assure himself of true righteousness, and that he is not of the number of those that blaspheme God, in relying upon their own works and righteousness.

# OF PRAYER

## 328

NONE can believe how powerful prayer is, and what it is able to effect, but those who have learned it by experience.

It is a great matter when in extreme need, to take hold on prayer. I know, whenever I have earnestly prayed, I have been amply heard, and have obtained more than I prayed for; God, indeed, sometimes delayed, but at last he came.

Ecclesiasticus says: 'The prayer of a good and godly Christian availeth more to health, than the physician's physic.'

O how great a thing, how marvellous, a godly Christian's prayer is! how powerful with God; that a poor human creature should speak with God's high Majesty in heaven, and not be affrighted, but, on the contrary, know that God smiles upon him for Christ's sake, his dearly beloved Son. The heart and conscience, in this act of praying, must not fly and recoil backwards by reason of our sins and unworthiness, or stand in doubt, or be seared away. We must not do as the Bavarian did, who, with great devotion, called upon St. Leonard, an idol set up in a church in Bavaria, behind which idol stood one who answered the Bavarian, and said: Fie on thee, Bavarian; and in that sort often repulsed and would not hear him, till at last, the Bavarian went away, and said: Fie on thee, Leonard.

When we pray, we must not let it come to: Fie upon thee, but certainly hold and believe, that we are already heard in that for which we pray, with faith in Christ. Therefore the ancients ably defined prayer an *Ascensus mentis ad Deum,* a climbing up of the heart unto God.

### 329

Our Saviour Christ as excellently as briefly comprehends in the Lord's prayer all things needful and necessary. Except under troubles, trials, and vexations, prayer cannot rightly be made. God says: 'Call on me in the time of trouble'; without trouble it is only a bald prattling, and not from the heart; 'tis a common saying: 'Need teaches to pray.' And though the papists say that God well understands all the words of those that pray, yet St. Bernard is far of another opinion, who says: God hears not the words of one that prays, unless he that prays first hears them himself. The pope is a mere tormentor of the conscience. The assemblies of his greased crew, in prayer, were altogether like the croaking of frogs, which edified nothing at all; mere sophistry and deceit, fruitless and unprofitable. Prayer is a strong wall and fortress of the church; it is a godly Christian's weapon, which no man knows or finds, but only he who has the spirit of grace and of prayer. .

The three first petitions in our Lord's prayer comprehend such great and celestial things, that no heart is able to search them out. The fourth contains the whole policy and economy of temporal and house government, and all things necessary for this life. The fifth fights against our own evil consciences, and against original and actual sins, which trouble them. Truly that prayer was penned by wisdom itself; none but God could have done it.

### 330

Prayer in Popedom is mere tongue-threshing; not prayer, but a work of obedience. Thence a confused sea of *Horæ Canonicæ,* the howling and babbling in cells and monasteries, where they read and sing the psalms and collects, without any spiritual devotion, understanding neither the words, sentences, nor meaning.

How I tormented myself with those *Horæ Canonicæ* before the gospel came, which by reason of much business I often intermitted, I cannot express. On the Saturdays, I used to lock myself up in my cell, and accomplish what the whole week I had neglected. But at last I was troubled with so many affairs, that I was fain often to omit also my Saturday's devotions. At length, when I saw that Amsdorf and others derided such devotion, then I quite left it off.

From this great torment we are now delivered by the gospel. Though I had done no more but only freed people from that torment, they might well give me thanks for it.

### 331

We cannot pray without faith in Christ the Mediator. Turks, Jews, and papists may repeat the words of prayer, but they cannot pray. And although the Apostles were taught this Lord's prayer by Christ, and prayed often, yet they prayed not as they should have prayed; for Christ says: 'Hitherto ye have not prayed in my name'; whereas, doubtless, they had prayed much, speaking the words. But when the Holy Ghost came, then they prayed aright in the name of Christ. If praying and reading of prayer be but only a bare work, as the papists hold, then the righteousness of the law is nothing worth. The upright prayer of a godly Christian is a strong hedge, as God himself says: 'And I sought for a man among them that should make up the hedge, and stand in the gap before me for the land, that I should not destroy it, but I found none.'

### 332

When Moses, with the children of Israel, came to the Red Sea, then he cried with trembling and quaking; yet he opened not his mouth, neither was his voice heard on earth by the people; doubtless, he cried and sighed in his heart, and said: Ah, Lord God! what course shall I now take? Which way shall I now turn myself? How am I come to this strait? No help or counsel can save us; before us is the sea; behind us are our enemies the Egyptians; on both sides high and huge mountains; I am the cause that all this people shall now be destroyed. Then answered God, and said: 'Wherefore criest thou unto me?' as if God should say: What an alarum dost thou make, that the whole heavens ring! Human reason is not able to search this passage out. The way through the Red Sea is full as broad and wide, if not wider, than Wittenberg lies from Coburg, that so, doubtless, the people were constrained in the night season to rest and to eat therein; for six hundred thousand men, besides women and children, would require a good time to pass through, though they went one hundred and fifty abreast.

### 333

It is impossible that God should not hear the prayers which with faith are made in Christ, though he give not according to the measure, manner, and time we dictate, for he will not be tied. In such sort dealt God with the mother of St. Augustine; she prayed to God that her son might be converted, but as yet it would not be; then she ran to the learned, entreating them to persuade and advise him thereunto. She propounded unto him a marriage with a Christian virgin, that thereby he might be drawn and brought to the

Christian faith, but all would not do as yet. But when our Lord God came thereto, he came to purpose, and made of him such an Augustine, that he became a great light to the church. St. James says: 'Pray one for another, for the prayer of the righteous availeth much.' Prayer is a powerful thing; for God has bound and tied himself thereunto.

### 334

Christ gave the Lord's prayer according to the ideas of the Jews – that is, he directed it only to the Father, whereas they that pray, should pray as though they were to be heard for the Son's sake. This was because Christ would not be praised before his death.

### 335

Justus Jonas asked Luther if these sentences in Scripture did not contradict each other; where God says to Abraham: 'If I find ten in Sodom, I will not destroy it'; and where Ezekiel says: 'Though these three men, Noah, Daniel, and Job, were in it, yet would I not hear,' etc.; and where Jeremiah says: 'Therefore pray not thou for this people.' Luther answered: No, they are not against one another; for in Ezekiel it was forbidden them to pray, but it was not so with Abraham. Therefore we must have regard to the word; when God says: thou shalt not pray, then we may well cease.

### 336

When governors and rulers are enemies to God's Word, then our duty is to depart, to sell and forsake all we have, to fly from one place to another, as Christ commands. We must make for ourselves no tumults, by reason of the gospel, but suffer all things.

### 337

Upright Christians pray without ceasing; though they pray not always with their mouths, yet their hearts pray continually, sleeping and waking; for the sigh of a true Christian is a prayer. As the Psalm saith: 'Because of the deep sighing of the poor, I will up, saith the Lord,' etc. In like manner a true Christian always carries the cross, though he feel it not always.

### 338

The Lord's prayer binds the people together, and knits them one to another, so that one prays for another, and together one with another; and it is so strong and powerful that it even drives away the fear of death.

### 339

Prayer preserves the church, and hitherto has done the best for the church; therefore we must continually pray. Hence Christ says: 'Ask, and ye shall have; seek, and ye shall find; knock, and it shall be opened unto you.'

First, when we are in trouble, he will have us to pray; for God often, as it were, hides himself, and will not hear; yea, will not suffer himself to be found. Then we must seek him; that is, we must continue in prayer. When we seek him, he often locks himself up, as it were, in a private chamber; if we intend to come in unto him, then we must knock, and when we have knocked once or twice, then he begins a little to hear. At last, when we make much knocking, then he opens, and says: What will ye have? Lord, say we, we would have this or that; then, says he, Take it unto you. In such sort must we persist in praying, and waken God up.

# OF BAPTISM

---

### 340

THE ancient teachers ordained three sorts of baptizing; of water, of the Spirit, and of blood; these were observed in the church. The catechumens were baptized in water; others, that could not get such water-bathing, and nevertheless believed, were saved in and through the Holy Spirit, as Cornelius was saved, before he was baptized. The third sort were baptized in blood, that is, in martyrdom.

### 341

Heaven is given unto me freely, for nothing. I have assurance hereof confirmed unto me by sealed covenants, that is, I am baptized, and frequent the sacrament of the Lord's Supper. Therefore I keep the bond safe and sure, lest the devil tear it in pieces; that is, I live and remain in God's fear, and pray daily unto him. God could not have given me better security of my salvation, and of the gospel, than by the death and passion of his only Son: when I believe that he overcame death, and died for me, and therewith behold the promise of the Father, then I have the bond complete. And when I have the seal of baptism and the Lord's Supper prefixed thereto, then I am well provided for.

### 342

I was asked: when there is uncertainty, whether a person has been baptized or not, may he be baptized under a condition, as thus: If thou be not baptized, then I baptize thee? I answered: The church must exclude such baptizing, and not endure it, though there be a doubt of the previous baptizing of any person, yet he shall receive baptism, pure and simple, without any condition.

### 343

The papists, in private confession, only regard the work. There was such a running to confession, they were never satisfied; if one had forgotten to confess anything, however trivial, which afterwards came to his remembrance, off he must be back to his confessor, and confess again. I knew a doctor in law who was so bent upon confessing, that, before he could receive the sacrament, he went three times to his confessor. In my time, while in Popedom, they made our confessors weary, and they again perplexed us with their conditional absolutions; for they absolved in this manner: 'I absolve and loosen thee, by reason of the merits of our Lord Jesus Christ, of the sorrow of thy heart, of thy mouth's confession, and of the satisfaction of thy works,' etc. These conditions, and what pertained thereunto, were the cause of great mischief. All this we did out of fear, that thereby we might be justified and saved before God; we were so troubled and overburdened with traditions of men, that Gerson was constrained to slacken the bridle of the conscience and ease it; he was the first who began to break out of this prison, for he wrote, that it was no mortal sin to neglect the ordinances and commandments of the church, or to act contrary to them, unless it were done out of contempt, wilfully, or from a stubborn mind. These words, although they were but weak and few, yet they raised up and comforted many consciences.

Against such bondage and slavery I wrote a book on Christian liberty, showing that such strict laws and ordinances of human inventions ought not to be observed. There are now, however, certain gross, ignorant, and inexperienced fellows, who never felt such captivity, that presumptuously undertake utterly to contemn and reject all laws and ordinances.

### 344

If a woman that had murdered her child were absolved by me, and the crime were afterwards discovered publicly, and I were examined before the judge, I might not give witness in the matter – we must make a difference between the church and temporal government. She confessed not to me as to a man, but to Christ, and if Christ keep silence thereupon, it is my duty to keep silence also, and to say: I know nothing of the matter thereof; if Christ heard it, then may he speak of it; though, meantime, I would privately say to the woman: Thou wretch, do so no more. For, while I am not the man to speak before the seat of justice, in temporal causes, in matters touching the conscience, I ought to affright sinners with God's wrath against sin, through the law. Such as acknowledge and confess their sins, I must lift up and comfort again, by the preaching of the gospel. We will not be drawn to their seats of justice, and markets of hatred and dissension. We have hitherto protected and maintained the jurisdiction and rights of the church, and still will do so, yielding not in the least to the temporal jurisdiction in causes belonging to doctrine and consciences. Let them mind their charge, wherewith they will find enough to do, and leave ours to us, as Christ has commanded.

### 345

Auricular confession was instituted only that people might give an account of their faith, and from their hearts confess an earnest desire to receive the holy sacrament. We force no man thereunto.

### 346

Christ gave the keys to the church for her comfort, and commanded her servants to deal therewith according to his direction, to bind the impenitent, and to absolve them that, repenting, acknowledge and confess their sins, are heartily sorry for them, and believe that God forgives them for Christ's sake.

### 347

It was asked, did the Hussites well in administering the sacrament to young children, on the allegation that the graces of God apply equally to all human creatures. Dr. Luther replied: they were undoubtedly wrong, since young children need not the communion for their salvation; but still the innovation could not be regarded as a sin of the Hussites, since St. Cyprian, long ago, set them the example.

### 348

Does he to whom the sacrament is administered by a heretic, really receive the sacrament? Yes, replied Dr. Luther: if he be ignorant that the person administering is a heretic. The sacramentarians reject the body of Christ; the anabaptists baptism, and therefore they cannot efficiently baptize; yet if a person apply to a sacramentarian, not knowing him as such, and receive from him the sacrament, himself believing it to be the veritable body of Christ, it is the veritable body of Christ that he actually receives.

### 349

The anabaptists cavil as to how the salvation of man is to be effected by water. The simple answer is, that all things are possible to him who believes in God Almighty. If, indeed, a baker were to say to me: 'This bread is a body, and this wine is blood,' I should laugh at him incredulously. But when Jesus Christ, the Almighty God, taking in his hand bread and wine, tells me: 'This is my body and my blood,' then we must believe, for it is God who speaks — God who with a word created all things.

### 350

It was asked whether, in a case of necessity, the father of a family might administer the Lord's supper to his children or servants. Dr. Luther replied: 'By no means, for he is not called thereto, and they who are not called, may not preach, much less administer the sacrament. 'Twould lead to infinite disorder, for many people would then wholly dispense with the ministers of the church.'

### 351

When Jesus Christ directed his apostles to go and instruct and baptize all nations, he meant not that children should be excluded; the apostles were to baptize all the Gentiles, young or old, great or small. The baptism of children is distinctly enjoined in Mark 10:14: 'The kingdom of God is of little children.' We must not look at this text with the eyes of a calf, or of a cow vaguely gaping at a new gate, but do with it as at court we do with the prince's letters, read it and weigh it, and read it and weigh it again and again, with our most earnest attention.

### 352

The papists say that 'twas Pope Melchiades baptized the emperor Constantine, but this is a fiction. The emperor Constantine was baptized at Nicomedia by Eusebius, bishop of that town, in the sixty-fifth year of his life, and the thirty-third of his reign.

### 353

The anabaptists pretend that children, not as yet having reason, ought not to receive baptism. I answer: That reason in no way contributes to faith. Nay, in that children are destitute of reason, they are all the more fit and proper recipients of baptism. For reason is the greatest enemy that faith has: it never comes to the aid of spiritual things, but – more frequently than not – struggles against the Divine Word, treating with contempt all that emanates from God. If God can communicate the Holy Ghost to grown persons, he can, *a fortiori* communicate it to young children. Faith comes of the Word of God, when this is heard; little children hear that Word when they receive baptism, and therewith they receive also faith.

## 354

When, in a difficult labour, the arm or leg of the child alone presents itself, we must not baptize that limb, under the idea that thereby the infant can receive baptism. Still less can it be pretended that you baptize a child not yet come into the world, by pouring water on the mother. The text of St. John manifestly shows that such practices are prohibited by Scripture: 'Except a man be born again, he cannot see the kingdom of God.' We must not, therefore, baptize a child until it has actually come into the world, whole and entire. When any difficulty occurs, those present must kneel and pray unto Christ, that he will deign to deliver the poor child and its mother from their sufferings, and they must do this in full confidence that the Lord will thereupon listen to the dictates of his merciful nature and wisdom. This prayer, offered up in faith, introduces the child to the Almighty, who himself has said: 'Suffer little children to come unto me, for of such is the kingdom of God.' We may rest assured that, under such circumstances, the child is not excluded from salvation, even though it die without having been regularly baptized. Should an infant, on coming into the world, be so extremely weak and feeble that there is manifest danger of its dying ere it can be carried to the church, then the women present should baptize it themselves, in the usual form. For this purpose, it is always desirable that the mother should have about her at least two or three persons, to attest that baptism has in this way been administered to the child, *ex necessitate*.

## 355

Some one sent to know whether it was permissible to use warm water in baptism? The Doctor replied: 'Tell the blockhead that water, warm or cold, is water.'

## 356

In 1541, Doctor Menius asked Doctor Luther, in what manner a Jew should be baptized? The Doctor replied: You must fill a large tub with water, and, having divested the Jew of his clothes, cover him with a white garment. He must then sit down in the tub, and you must baptize him quite under the water. The ancients, when they were baptized, were attired in white, whence the first Sunday after Easter, which was peculiarly consecrated to this ceremony, was called *dominica in albis*. This garb was rendered the more suitable, from the circumstance that it was, as now, the custom to bury people in a white shroud; and baptism, you know, is an emblem of our death. I have no doubt that when Jesus was baptized in the river Jordan, he was attired in a white robe. If a Jew, not converted at heart, were to ask baptism at my hands, I would take him on to the bridge, tie a stone round his neck, and hurl him into the river; for these wretches are wont to make a jest of our religion. Yet, after all, water and the Divine Word being the essence of baptism, a Jew, or any other, would be none the less validly baptized, that his own feelings and intentions were not the result of faith.

# Of the Sacrament of the
# Lord's Supper

---

### 357

THE blindness of the papists is great and mischievous; for they will neither believe the gospel nor yield thereunto, but boast of the church, and say: She has power to alter, and to do what she pleases; for, say they, Christ gave his body to his disciples in the, evening after supper; but we receive it fasting, therefore we may, according to the church's ordinance, detain the cup from the laity. The ignorant wretches are not able to distinguish between the cup, which pertains to the substance of the sacrament, and fasting, which is an accidental, carnal thing, of no weight at all. The one has God's express word and command, the other consists in our will and choice. We urge the one, because God has commanded it; the other we leave to the election of the will, though we better like it to be received fasting, out of honour and reverence.

### 358

It is a wonder how Satan brought into the church, and ordained, but one kind of the sacrament to be received. I cannot call to mind that ever I read how, whence, or for what cause it was so altered. It was first so ordained in the council of Constance, where nothing, however, is pleaded but only the custom.

### 359

The papists highly boast of their power and authority, which they would willingly confirm with this argument: the apostles altered baptism; therefore, say they, the bishops have power to alter the sacrament of the Lord's supper. I answer: admit that the apostles altered something; yet there is a great difference between an apostle and a bishop; an apostle was called immediately by God with gifts of the Holy Ghost; but a bishop is a person selected by man, to preach God's word, and ordain servants of the church in certain places. So, though the apostles had this power and authority, yet the bishops have not. Although Elijah slew Baal's priests and the false prophets, it is not permitted that every priest shall do the like. Hence St. Paul makes this difference: 'Some hath he given to be apostles, some teachers, some to be pastors and ministers,' etc. Among the apostles was no supremacy or ruling; none was greater or higher in office than another; they were all equal, the one with the other. The definition as to the supremacy and rule of St. Peter above other bishops is false; it reaches further than they define it; they conclude thus: the pope's power and authority is the highest; he may ordain servants, alter kingdoms and governments, depose some emperors and kings, and enthrone others. But we are in nowise to allow of such definitions; for every definition must be direct and proper, set down plain and clear; so that neither more nor less may in the definition be contained, than that which is described and defined.

### 360

They that as yet are not well informed, but stand in doubt, touching the institution of the sacrament, may receive it under one kind; but those that are certain thereof, and yet receive it under one kind, act wrongfully and against their consciences.

### 361

What signifies it to dispute and wrangle about the abominable idolatry of elevating the sacrament on high to show it to the people, which has no approbation of the Fathers, and was introduced only to confirm the errors touching the worship thereof, as though bread and wine lost their substance, and retained only the form, smell, taste. This the papists call transubstantiation, and darken the right use of the sacrament; whereas, even in Popedom, at Milan, from Ambrose's time to the present day, they never held or observed in the mass either canon or elevation, or the *Dominus vobiscum*.

### 362

The elevation of the sacrament was taken out of the Old Testament; the Jews observed two forms, the one called *Thruma*, the other *Trumpha*; *Thruma* was when they took an offering out of a basket, and lifted it up above them (like as they now lift up the oblate), and showed the same to our Lord God, after which they either burned or ate it: *Trumpha*, was an offering which they lifted not up above them, but showed it towards the four corners of the world, as the papists, in the mass, make crosses, and other apish toys, towards the four corners of the world.

When I first began to celebrate mass in Popedom, and to make such crossings with marvellous twistings of the fingers, and could not rightly hit the way, I said: 'Mary, God's mother, how am I plagued with the mass, and especially with the crossings.' Ah, Lord God! we were in those times poor plagued people, and yet it was nothing but mere idolatry. They terrified some in such sort with the words of consecration, especially good and godly men who meant seriously, that they trembled and quaked at the pronouncing of these words: *Hoc est corpus meum,* for they were to pronounce them, *sine ulla hesitatione;* he that stammered, or left out but one word, committed a great sin. Moreover, the words were to be spoken, without any abstraction of thought, in such a way, that only he must hear them that spake them, and none of the people standing by. Such an honest friar was I fifteen years together; the Lord of his mercy forgive me. The elevation is utterly to be rejected by reason of the adoring thereof. Some churches, seeing we have put down the elevation, have followed us therein, which gives me great satisfaction.

### 363

The operative cause of the sacrament is the word and institution of Christ, who ordained it. The substance is bread and wine, prefiguring the true body and blood of Christ, which is spiritually received by faith. The final cause of instituting the same, is the benefit and the fruit, the strengthening of our faith, not doubting that Christ's body and blood were given and shed for us, and that our sins by Christ's death certainly are forgiven.

### 364

Question was made touching the words 'given for you', whether they were to be understood of the present administering, when the sacrament is distributed, or of when it was offered and accomplished on the cross? I said:

I like it best when they are understood of the present administering, although they may be understood as fulfilled on the cross; it matters not that Christ says: 'Which is given for you', instead of: 'Which shall be given for you': for Christ is *Hodie et Heri,* today and yesterday. I am, says Christ, he that doeth it. Therefore, I approve that *Datur* be understood in such manner, that it show the use of the work. It was likewise asked, whether honour and reverence were to be shown to the sacrament? I said: When I am at the altar, and receive the sacrament, I bow my knees in honour thereof; but in bed I receive it lying.

### 365

They that do not hold the sacrament as Christ instituted it, have no sacrament. All papists do not, therefore they have no sacrament; for they receive not the sacrament, but offer it. Moreover, they administer but one kind, contrary to Christ's institution and command. The sacrament is God's work and ordinance, and not man's. The papists err in attributing to the sacrament, that it justifies, *ex opere operato,* when the work is fulfilled.

### 366

These words, 'Drink ye all of it' concern, say the papists, only the priests. Then these words must also concern only the priests, where Christ says: 'Ye are clean, but not all' that is, all the priests.

# Of the Church

### 367

The true church is an assembly or congregation depending on that which does not appear, nor may be comprehended in the mind, namely, God's Word; what that says, they believe without addition, giving God the honour.

### 368

We tell our Lord God plainly, that if he will have his church, he must maintain and defend it; for we can neither uphold nor protect it; if we could, indeed, we should become the proudest asses under heaven. But God says: I say it, I do it: it is God only that speaks and does what he pleases; he does nothing according to the fancies of the ungodly, or which they hold for upright and good.

### 369

The great and worldly-wise people take offence at the poor and mean form of our church, which is subject to many infirmities, transgressions, and sects, wherewith she is plagued; for they say the church should be altogether pure, holy, blameless, God's dove, etc. And the church, in the eyes and sight of God, has such an esteem; but in the eyes and sight of the world, she is like unto her bridegroom, Christ Jesus, torn, spit on, derided, and crucified.

The similitude of the upright and true church and of Christ, is a poor silly sheep; but the similitude of the false and hypocritical church, is a serpent, an adder.

### 370

Where God's word is purely taught, there is also the upright and true church; for the true church is supported by the Holy Ghost, not by succession of inheritance. It does not follow, though St. Peter had been bishop at Rome, and at the, same time Christian communion had been at Rome, that, therefore, the pope and the Romish church are true; for if that should be of value or conclusive, then they must needs confess that Caiaphas, Annas, and the Sadducees were also the true church; for they boasted that they were descended from Aaron.

### 371

It is impossible for the Christian and true church to subsist without the shedding of blood, for her adversary, the devil, is a liar and a murderer. The church grows and increases through blood; she is sprinkled with blood; she is spoiled and bereaved of her blood; when human creatures will reform the church, then it costs blood.

### 372

The form and aspect of the world is like a paradise; but the true Christian church, in the eye of the world, is foul, deformed, and offensive; yet, nevertheless, in the sight of God, she is precious, beloved, and highly esteemed. Aaron, the high-priest, appeared gloriously in the temple, with his ornaments and rich attire, with odoriferous and sweet-smelling perfumes; but Christ appeared most mean and lowly.

Wherefore I am not troubled that the world esteems the church so meanly; what care I that the usurers, the nobility, gentry, citizens, country-people, covetous men, and drunkards, contemn and esteem me as dirt? In due time, I will esteem them as little. We must not suffer ourselves to be deceived or troubled as to what the world thinks of us. To please the good is our virtue.

### 373

The church is misery on earth, first, that we may keep in mind we are banished servants, and exiled out of Paradise for Adam's sake. Secondly, that we may always remember the misery of the Son of God, who, for our sake, was made man, walked in this vale of misery, suffered for us, died, and rose again from the dead, and so brought us again to our paternal home, whence we were driven. Thirdly, that we may remember our habitation is not of this world, but that we are here only as strangers and pilgrims; and that there is another and everlasting life prepared for us.

### 374

The very name, the church, is the highest argument and proof of all hypocrites. The pharisees, the scribes, yea, the whole senate of Jerusalem, cried out against Stephen, and said: 'This man ceaseth not to speak blasphemous words against this holy place and the law.' Cain, Ishmael, Saul, the Turks and Jews, bore and do bear the name and title of the church. But Moses finely solves this argument: 'They have moved me to jealousy with that which is not God, they have provoked me to anger with their vanities: and I will move them to jealousy with those which are not a people: I will provoke them to anger with a foolish nation.' Here was *quid pro quo;* as if God should say: 'Could ye find in your hearts to forsake me? so can I again forsake you'; for God and nation, the Word and the church, are *correlativa;* the one cannot be without the other.

### 375

Like as a child in the mother's womb is compassed about with a thin and tender caul, which the Greeks name *chorion* (the afterbirth), and needs no more sustenance than so much as the *cotylidones,* from which the fruit receives nourishment, bring with them; nor does the after-birth break, except the fruit be ripe, and about to be timely brought to the light of this world; even so the church also is inclosed in the Word and bound therein, and seeks none other doctrine concerning God's will than that which is revealed in the same; therewith she is content, and thereupon she remains and depends by faith, until she shall behold God's presence, and shall hear God himself preach of the mysteries and hidden things which on earth we see by faith.

But in case some vain-glorious professors, by untimely motion, force and break the after-birth, as the papists and other seducers do in contemning the office of preaching, and expect visions and revelations from heaven, this must be compared with untimely births, still-born children, and abortions.

### 376

The amaranth is a flower that grows in August: it is more a stalk than a flower, is easily broken off, and grows in joyful and pleasant sort; when all other flowers are gone and decayed, then this, being sprinkled with water, becomes fair and green again; so that in winter they used to make garlands thereof. It is called amaranth from this, that it neither withers nor decays.

I know nothing more like unto the church than this flower, amaranth. For although the church bathes her garment in the blood of the Lamb, and is coloured over with red, yet she is more fair, comely, and beautiful than any state and assembly upon the face of the earth. She alone is embraced and beloved of the Son of God, as his sweet and amiable spouse, in whom only he takes joy and delight, and whereon his heart alone depends; he utterly rejects and loathes others, that contemn or falsify his gospel.

Moreover, the church willingly suffers herself to be plucked and broken off, that is, she is loving, patient, and obedient to Christ her bridegroom in the cross; she grows and increases again, fair, joyful, and pleasant, that is, she gains the greatest fruit and profit thereby; she learns to know God aright, to call upon him freely and undauntedly, to confess his word and doctrine, and produces many fair and glorious virtues.

At last, the body and stalk remain whole and sound, and cannot be rooted out, although raging and swelling be made against some of the members, and these be torn away. For like as the amaranth never withers or decays, even so, the church can never be destroyed or rooted out. But what is most wonderful, the amaranth has this quality, that when it is sprinkled with water, and dipped therein, it becomes fresh and green again, as if it were raised and wakened from the dead. Even so likewise the church will by God be raised and wakened out of the grave, and become living again; will everlastingly praise, extol, and laud the Father of our Lord and Saviour Jesus Christ, his Son and our Redeemer, together with the Holy Ghost. For though temporal empires, kingdoms, and principalities have their changings, and like flowers soon fall and fade away, this kingdom, which is so deep rooted, by no power can be destroyed or wasted, but remains eternally.

### 377

An olive tree will live and bear fruit two hundred years; 'tis an image of the church; oil symbolizes the gentle love of the gospel, as wine emblems the doctrine of the law. There is such a natural unity and affinity between the vine and the olive tree, that when the branch of a vine is grafted upon an olive tree, it bears both grapes and olives. In like manner, when the church, which is God's Word, is planted in people's hearts, then it teaches both the law and the gospel, using both doctrines, and from both bringing fruit. The chesnut tree, in that it produces all the better fruit when it is soundly beaten, shadows forth man submissive to the law, whose actions are not agreeable to God, until he has been tried by tribulation. The lemon tree, with its fruit, figures Christ; the lemon tree has the property of bearing fruit at all seasons; when its fruits are ripe, they drop off, and are succeeded by a fresh growth; and this fruit is a sure remedy against poison. Jesus Christ, when his ministers and champions depart from earth, replaces them by others; his produce is ever growing, and it is a sure remedy against the poison of the devil.

### 378

I much marvel that the pope extols his church at Rome as, the chief; whereas the church at Jerusalem is the mother for there the doctrine was first revealed, and set forth by Christ, the Son of God himself, and by his apostles. Next was the church at Antioch, whence the Christians have their name. Thirdly, was the church at Alexandria; and still before the Romish, were the churches of the Galatians, of the Corinthians, Ephesians, of the Philippians, etc. Is it so great a matter that St. Peter was at Rome? which, however, has never yet been, nor ever will be proved, whereas our blessed Saviour Christ himself was at Jerusalem, where all the articles of our Christian faith were made; where St. James received his orders, and was bishop, and where the pillars of the church had their seat.

### 379

The papist rely upon this: the church cannot err; we are the church, *ergo,* we cannot err. To the *major*, I make this answer: true, the church cannot err in doctrine, but in works and actions she may easily err, yea, and often does err; and therefore she prays: 'Forgive us our trespasses', etc. The *minor* I utterly deny. Therefore when they argue and say: What the church teaches uprightly and pure, is true, this we admit; but when they argue and say: what the church does is upright and true, this we deny.

### 380

Many boast of their title to the church, whereas they know not the true church; the holy prophets much opposed the false church. The prophet Isaiah, in the beginning of his first chapter, describes two sorts of churches. The upright and true church is a very small heap and number, of little or no esteem, and lying under the cross. But the false church is pompous, boasting, and presuming; she flourishes, and is held in high repute, like Sodom, of which St. Paul complains (Rom. 8 and 9). The true church consists in God's election and calling; she is powerful and strong in weakness.

## 381

One of the jugglings of the sophists, wherewith the ungodly wretches deceive simple people, is this: a kingdom, say they, which is plagued and tormented, is a temporal kingdom. The Christian church is plagued and tormented: *ergo*, Christ's kingdom is a temporal kingdom. But I answer them: No, not so; the kingdom of Christ is not plagued, but our bodies, by reason of our sins, are plagued and tormented. As St. Paul says: 'We must through much tribulation enter into the kingdom of God.' He says not that the kingdom of God suffers externally. It is equally false when they say, God is love, God justifies, therefore love justifies.

Such, and the like fallacies, may sometimes puzzle even understanding minds, well exercised and practised; therefore we must take time to answer them, for every one cannot so suddenly detect them.

# Of Excommunication

## 382

THE ungodly have great power, riches, and respect; on the contrary, we, the true and upright Christians, have but only one poor, silly, and contemned Christ. Temporal things, money, wealth, reputation, and power they have already; they care nothing for Christ. We say to them: Ye are great lords on earth, we, lords in heaven; ye have the power and riches on earth, we, heavenly treasure, namely, God's Word and command; we have baptism, and the sacrament of the Lord's Supper, which is an office celestial. If any man among us, with the name of a Christian, will exercise unjust power, insolence, and wickedness, wilfully, then we excommunicate such a person, so that he shall not be present at the baptizing of children, nor shall be partaker of the holy communion, nor have conversation with other Christians.

But if he abandon and forsake the name of a Christian, and give up his profession, then we are willing with patience to suffer his tyranny, insolence, and usurped power; we are content to let him go like the heathen, or Jews, or Turks, and so commit our cause to God.

## 383

Our dealing and proceeding against the pope is altogether excommunication, which is simply the public declaration that a person is disobedient to Christ's word. Now we affirm in public, that the pope and his retinue believe not;

therefore we conclude that he shall not be saved, but be damned. What is this, but to excommunicate him? Briefly, to put Christ's word in execution, and to accomplish and execute his command, this is excommunication.

### 384

I will proceed with excommunication after this manner: first, when I myself have admonished an obstinate sinner then I will send unto him two persons, as two chaplains, or two of the aldermen of the town, two churchwardens, or two honest men of the assembly; if then he will not be reformed, but still runs on in stubbornness, and persists in his sinful life, I will declare him openly to the church in this manner: Loving friends, I declare unto you, that N. N. has been admonished, first by myself in private; afterwards also by two chaplains; thirdly, by two aldermen, or two churchwardens, as it may be, yet he will not desist from his sinful kind of life; wherefore, I earnestly desire you to assist, and advise you to kneel down with me, and let us pray against him, and deliver him over to the devil, etc.

Hereby we should doubtless prevail so far, that people would not live in such public sin and shame; for this would be a strict excommunication, not like the pope's money-bulls, profitable to the church. When the person were reformed and converted, we might receive him into the church again.

### 385

Christ will have that a sinner be first warned and admonished, not only once or twice by private and single persons not in office, but also by them that are in office of public preaching, before the severe sentence of excommunication be published and declared. But while the ministry of the Word calls to the Lord's Supper all such of the faithful as repent of their sins, and admits them to the bosom of Christ's church, it must justly reject the hardened impenitent, and abandon them to the judgment of God, excluding them here from the society of the faithful, and, should they die in their sins, from Christian burial.

### 386

Nothing would more hinder excommunication than for men to do what pertains to a Christian. Thou hast a neighbour whose life and conversation is well known unto thee, but unknown to thy preacher or minister: When thou seest this neighbour growing rich by unlawful dealing, living lasciviously, in adultery, etc.; that he governs his house and family negligently, etc.; then thou oughtest, Christian-like, to warn and earnestly admonish him to desist from his sinful courses, to have a care of his salvation, and to abstain from giving offence. Oh, how holy a work wouldst then thou perform, didst thou in this way win thy neighbour? But I pray, who does this? for, first, truth is a hateful thing; he that, in these times, speaks the truth, procures hatred. Therefore, thou wilt rather keep thy neighbour's friendship and good-will, especially when he is rich and powerful, by holding thy peace and keeping silence, and conniving, than incur his displeasure and make him thy adversary.

Again, we have less excommunication now, forasmuch as in some sort we are all subject to blaspheming alike, and therewith are stained; so that we are afraid to pull out the mote we see in our neighbour's eye, lest we be hit in the teeth with the beam that appears in our own.

But the chief cause why excommunication is fallen, is that the number of upright and true Christians in every place is very small; for, if from our hearts we loved and practised true and upright godliness and God's Word, as we all ought, then we should regard the command of Christ our blessed Saviour far above all the wealth, welfare, or favour of this temporal life. For this command of Christ, touching the admonishing and warning a sinning brother, is even as necessary as this: 'Thou shalt do no murder, thou shalt not commit adultery, not steal,' etc., seeing that when, either out of fear or for some other worldly respect, thou omittest this admonition, there depends thereon, not thy neighbour's body and goods, but the salvation of his soul.

### 387

Take heed, I say, that in any case thou contemn not the excommunication of the true church; a contempt certainly involving the displeasure of God; for Christ says: 'Verily I say unto you, what ye bind on earth, shall be also bound in heaven,' etc. The pope, however, in his tyranny, abuses the power of excommunication. If a poor man, at a certain appointed day, cannot make payment of the taxation the pope imposes upon him, he is excommunicated; and in the same way he thunders his bulls and his excommunications against us, because we avow the all-saving doctrine of the gospel; yet our Saviour Christ comforts us, saying: 'Happy are ye when men revile and persecute you for my sake, and speak all manner of evil against you,' etc. And again: 'They will excommunicate you, or put you out of the synagogue.'

Most assuredly the pope's bull is not Christ's excommunication, by reason it is not done or taken in hand according to Christ's institution; it is of no value in heaven, but to him, who thus abuses it against Christ's command, it brings most sure and certain destruction, for it is a sin wherewith God's name is blasphemed.

### 388

Like as this external and visible excommunication is used against those only that live in public sins, even so the hidden and invisible excommunication, which is not of men, or done by men visibly, but is of God himself, and done by him only, often excludes from the kingdom of Christ, invisibly, persons whom we take to be fair, upright, good, and honest Christians. For God judges not according to outward works or kind of life, as men do, but views the heart; he judges hypocrites whom the church can neither judge nor punish; the church judges not what is hidden and invisible.

All are not stained so grossly with open offences, that we can tax them in public, as were fitting, with any one particular sin and transgression. For although many covetous persons, adulterers, etc., are among us, yet they proceed so craftily, and in such sort act their sins, that we cannot detect them. Yet although such be with us in the church, among the Christian assembly, hear sermons and God's Word, and, with upright and godly Christians, receive the holy sacrament, yet, *de facto*, they are excommunicated by God, by reason they live in sin against their own consciences, and amend not their lives. Such sinners may deceive men, but they cannot deceive God; he at the day of judgment will cause his angels to gather all offenders together, and will cast them into unquenchable fire.

### 389

Christ says: 'Receive ye the Holy Ghost, whosoever sins ye remit, they are remitted unto them; and whosoever sins ye retain, they are retained.' And 'If thy brother shall trespass against thee, go and tell him his fault between thee, and him alone; if he shall hear thee, thou hast gained thy brother. But if he will not hear thee, then take with thee one or two more,' etc.; and 'If he shall neglect to hear them, tell it unto the church. But if he neglect to hear the church, let him be unto thee as an heathen man, and a publican.' And St. Paul: 'If any man that is called a brother be a fornicator, or covetous, or an idolater, or a railer, or a drunkard, or an extortioner, with such an one, eat not, etc.; put away from you that wicked person.' Also: 'If there come any to you, and bring not this doctrine, receive him not unto your house, neither bid him God speed; for he that biddeth him God speed, is partaker of his evil deeds.'

These, and such like sentences, are the unchangeable will, decrees, and ordinances of the high Majesty of God; we have no power to alter or omit them, much less to abolish them; but, on the contrary, have earnest command, with true diligence to hold thereunto, disregarding the power or reputation of any person whatsoever. And although excommunication in Popedom has been and is shamefully abused, and made a mere torment, yet we must not suffer it to fall, but make right use of it, as Christ has commanded, to the raising of the church, not to exercise tyranny, as the pope has done.

# OF PREACHERS AND PREACHING

---

### 390

Some there are that rail at the servants of God, and say: What though the Word and sacraments be upright and the truth, as indeed they be, when God speaks of them; 'tis not therefore God's Word when a man talks thereof.

### 391

Divinity consists in use and practice, not in speculation and meditation. Every one that deals in speculations, either in household affairs or temporal government, without practice, is lost and nothing worth. When a tradesman makes his account, how much profit he shall reap in the year, but puts nothing in practice, he trades in vain speculations, and finds afterwards that his reckoning comes far too short. And thus it goes also with speculating divines, as is seen to this day, and as I know by experience.

### 392

No man should undertake anything, except he be called thereunto. Calling is two-fold; either divine, which is done by the highest power, which is of faith; or else it is a calling of love, which is done by one's equal, as when one is desired by one's friend to preach a sermon. Both vocations are necessary to secure the conscience.

### 393

Young people must be brought up to learn the Holy Scriptures; when such of them as know they are designed for the ministry present themselves and offer their service, upon a parish falling void, they do not intrude themselves, but are as a maid who, being arrived at woman's estate, when one makes suit to marry her, may do it, with a good and safe conscience towards God and the world. To thrust out another is to intrude; but when in the church a place is void, and thou sayest: I will willingly supply it, if ye please to make use of me; then thou art received, it is a true vocation and calling. Such was the manner of Isaiah, who said: 'Here I am; send me.' He came of himself when he heard they stood in need of a preacher; and so it ought to be; we must look whether people have need of us or no, and then whether we be desired or called.

### 394

To the poor is the gospel declared, for the rich regard it not. If the pope maintained us not with that he has got, though much against his will, we might even starve for want of food. The pope has swallowed stolen goods, and must spew them all up again, as Job says: he must give them to those to whom he wishes evil. Scarce the fiftieth part is applied to the profit of the church; the rest he throws away; we obtain but the fragments under the table. But we are assured of better wages after this life; and, truly, if our hope were not fixed there, we were of all people the most miserable.

### 395

I would not have preachers torment their hearers, and detain them with long and tedious preaching, for the delight of hearing vanishes therewith, and the preachers hurt themselves.

### 396

God was at Moses several times before he could get him forward; at last, after many excuses, he went, but unwillingly. If I had been Moses, I would, with the aid of some lawyer, have framed a bill of complaint against our Lord God, for breaking his promise; for he said to Moses: 'I will be with thee', but he performed not what he promised. In like manner God comforts and encourages with similar promises in the gospel, saying: 'And ye shall find rest for your souls.' But, alas! we see and find the contrary, by John the Baptist, by his dearest Son, our blessed Saviour Christ Jesus, by all the saints and holy martyrs, and by all true Christians; so that, according to the lawyers, our Lord God has lost the cause. Christ spake unto me as he spake to St. Paul: 'Arise and preach, and I will be with thee.' I have read that as an example. It is, indeed, an office exceeding dangerous to preach Christ; had I known as much before as I know now, I should never have been drawn thereunto, but, with Moses, would have said: 'Send whom thou wilt send.'

## 397

One asked me: Which is greater and better – to strive against adversaries, or to admonish and lift up the weak? I answered: Both are very good and necessary; but the latter is somewhat preferable; the weak, by striving against the adversaries, are also edified and bettered – both are God's gifts. He that teaches, attend his teaching; he that admonishes, attend his admonishing.

## 398

Dr. Forsteim asked Luther whence the art proceeded of speaking so powerfully, that both God-fearing and ungodly people were moved? He answered: it proceeds from the first commandment of God: 'I am the Lord thy God'; i.e., against the ungodly I am a strong and jealous God, towards the good and godly, a merciful God; I do well and show mercy to them, etc. For he will have us preach hell-fire to the proud and haughty, and paradise to the godly, reprove the wicked, and comfort the good, etc. The instruments and worktools of God are different, even as one knife cuts better than another. The sermons of Dr. Cordatus and Dr. Cruciger are taken more to heart than the preaching of many others.

## 399

The world can well endure all sorts of preachers except us, whom they will not hear; in former times they were forced, under Popedom, to hear the ungodly tyrants, and to carry those on their shoulders that plagued them in body and soul, in wealth and honour. But us, who by God's command reprove them, they will not hear: therefore the world must go to rack. We must vanish by reason of poverty, but the papists, by reason of punishment; their goods are not of proof, and are rejected of God.

## 400

A good preacher should have these properties and virtues: first, to teach systematically; secondly, he should have a ready wit; thirdly, he should be eloquent; fourthly, he should have a good voice; fifthly, a good memory; sixthly, he should know when to make an end; seventhly, he should be sure of his doctrine; eighthly, he should venture and engage body and blood, wealth and honour, in the word; ninthly, he should suffer himself to be mocked and jeered of every one.

### 401

The defects in a preacher are soon spied; let a preacher be endued with ten virtues, and but one fault, yet this one fault will eclipse and darken all his virtues and gifts, so evil is the world in these times. Dr. Justus Jonas has all the good virtues and qualities a man may have; yet merely because he hums and spits, the people cannot bear that good and honest man.

### 402

Luther's wife said to him: Sir, I heard your cousin, John Palmer, preach this afternoon in the parish church, whom I understood better than Dr. Pomer, though the Doctor is held to be a very excellent preacher. Luther answered: John Palmer preaches as ye women use to talk; for what comes into your minds, ye speak. A preacher ought to remain by the text, and deliver that which he has before him, to the end people may well understand it. But a preacher that will speak everything that comes in his mind, is like a maid that goes to market, and meeting another maid, makes a stand, and they hold together a goose-market.

### 403

An upright shepherd and minister must improve his flock by edification, and also resist and defend it; otherwise, if resisting be absent, the wolf devours the sheep, and the rather, where they be fat and well fed. Therefore St. Paul presses it home upon Titus, that a bishop by sound doctrine should be able both to exhort and to convince gainsayers; that is, to resist false doctrine. A preacher must be both soldier and shepherd. He must nourish, defend, and teach; he must have teeth in his mouth, and be able to bite and to fight.

There are many talking preachers, but there is nothing in them save only words; they can talk much, but teach nothing uprightly. The world has always had such Thrasos, such boasting throat-criers.

### 404

I know of no greater gift than that we have, namely, harmony in doctrine, so that throughout the principalities and imperial cities of Germany, they teach in conformity with us. Though I had the gift to raise the dead, what were it, if all other preachers taught against me? I would not exchange this concord for the Turkish empire.

### 405

God often lays upon the necks of haughty divines all manner of crosses and plagues to humble them; and therein they are well and rightly served; for they will have honour, whereas this only belongs to our Lord God. When we are found true in our vocations and calling, then we have reaped honour sufficient, though not in this life, yet in that to come; there we shall be crowned with the unchangeable crown of honour, 'which is laid up for us'. Here on earth we must seek for no honour, for it is written: Woe unto you when men shall bless you. We belong not to this life, but to another far better. The world loves that which is its own; we must content ourselves with that which it bestows upon us, scoffing, flouting, and contempt. I am sometimes glad that my scholars and friends are pleased to give me such wages; I desire neither honour nor crown here on earth, but I will have compensation from God, the just judge in heaven.

From the year of our Lord 1518, to the present time, every Maundy Thursday, at Rome, I have been by the pope excommunicated and cast into hell; yet I still live. For every year, on Maundy Thursday, all heretics are excommunicated at Rome, among whom I am always put first and chief. This do they on that blessed, sanctified day, whereas they ought rather to render thanks to God for the great benefit of his holy supper, and for his bitter death and passion. This is the honour and crown we must expect and have in this world. God sometimes can endure honour in lawyers and physicians; but in divines he will no way suffer it; for a boasting and an ambitious preacher soon contemns Christ, who with his blood has redeemed poor sinners.

### 406

A preacher should needs know how to make a right difference between sinners, between the impenitent and confident, and the sorrowful and penitent; otherwise the whole Scripture is locked up. When Amsdorf began to preach before the princes at Schmalcalden, with great earnestness he said: The gospel belongs to the poor and sorrowful, and not to you princes, great persons and courtiers that live in continual joy and delight, in secureness, void of all tribulation.

**407**

A continual hatred is between the clergy and laity, and not without cause; for the unbridled people, citizens, gentry, nobility, yea, and great princes also, refuse to be reproved. But the office of a preacher is to reprove such sinners as lie in open sin, and offend against both the first and second table of God's commandments; yet reproof is grievous for them to hear, wherefore they look upon the preachers with sharp eyes.

**408**

To speak deliberately and slowly best becomes a preacher; for thereby he may the more effectually and impressively deliver his sermon. Seneca writes of Cicero, that he spake deliberately from the heart.

**409**

God in the Old Testament made the priests rich; Anna, and Caiaphas had great revenues. But the ministers of the Word, in which is offered everlasting life and salvation by grace, are suffered to die of hunger and poverty, yea, are driven and hunted away.

**410**

We ought to direct ourselves in preaching according to the condition of the hearers, but most preachers commonly fail herein; they preach that which little edifies the poor simple people. To preach plain and simply is a great art: Christ himself talks of tilling ground, of mustard-seed, etc.; he used altogether homely and simple similitudes.

**411**

When a man first comes into the pulpit, he is much perplexed to see so many heads before him. When I stand there I look upon none, but imagine they are all blocks that are before me.

**412**

I would not have preachers in their sermons use Hebrew, Greek, or foreign languages, for in the church we ought to speak as we used to do at home, the plain mother tongue, which every one is acquainted with. It may be allowed in courtiers, lawyers, advocates, etc., to use quaint, curious words. Doctor Staupitz is a very learned man, yet he is a very irksome preacher; and the people had rather hear a plain brother preach, that delivers his words simply to their understanding, than he. In churches no praising or extolling should be sought after. St. Paul never used such high and stately words as Demosthenes and Cicero did, but he spake, properly and plainly, words which signified and showed high and stately matters, and he did well.

### 413

If I should write of the heavy burthen of a godly preacher, which he must carry and endure, as I know by mine own experience, I should scare every man from the office of preaching. But I assure myself that Christ at the last day will speak friendly unto me, though he speaks very unkindly now. I bear upon me the malice of the whole world, the hatred of the emperor, of the pope, and of all their retinue. Well, on in God's name; seeing I am come into the lists, I will fight it out. I know my quarrel and cause are upright and just.

### 414

It is a great thing to be an upright minister and preacher; if our Lord God himself drove it not forward, there would but little good ensue. Preachers must be endued with a great spirit, to serve people in body and soul, in wealth and honour, and yet, nevertheless, suffer and endure the greatest danger and unthankfulness. Hence Christ said to Peter thrice: 'Peter, lovest thou me?' Afterwards he said: 'Feed my sheep'; as if to say: Peter, if thou wilt be an upright shepherd, and careful of souls, then thou must love me; otherwise, it is impossible for thee to be an upright and a careful shepherd; thy love to me must do the deed.

### 415

Our manner of life is as evil as is that of the papists. Wycliffe and Huss assailed the immoral conduct of papists; but I chiefly oppose and resist their doctrine; I affirm roundly and plainly, that they preach not the truth. To this am I called; I take the goose by the neck, and set the knife to its throat. When I can show that the papist's doctrine is false, which I have shown, then I can easily prove that their manner of life is evil. For when the word remains pure, the manner of life, though something therein be amiss, will be pure also. The pope has taken away the pure word and doctrine, and brought in another word and doctrine, which he has hanged upon the church. I shook all Popedom with this one point, that I teach uprightly, and mix up nothing else. We must press the doctrine onwards, for that breaks the neck of the pope. Therefore the prophet Daniel rightly pictured the pope, that he would be a king that would do according to his own will, that is, would regard neither spirituality nor temporality, but say roundly: Thus and thus will I have it. For the pope derives his institution neither from divine nor from human right; but is a self-chosen human creature and intruder. Therefore the pope must needs confess, that he governs neither by divine nor human command. Daniel calls him a god, *Maosim*; he had almost spoken it plainly out, and said *Mass*, which word is written (Deut. 26), St. Paul read Daniel thoroughly, and uses nearly his words, where he says: The son of perdition will exalt himself above all that is called God, or that is worshipped, etc. (2 Thess. 2).

### 416

The humility of hypocrites is, of all pride, the greatest and most haughty, as that of the Pharisee who humbled himself and gave God thanks, but soon spoiled all again, when he said: 'I am not like others, etc., nor as this publican.' There are people who flatter themselves, and think they only are wise; they contemn and deride the opinions of all others; they will allow of nothing but only what pleases them.

### 417

Ambition is the rankest poison to the church, when it possesses preachers. It is a consuming fire. The Holy Scripture is given to destroy the desires of the flesh; therefore we must not therein seek after temporal honour. I much marvel for what cause people are proud and haughty; we are born in sin, and every moment in danger of death. Are we proud of our scabs and scalds? we, who are altogether an unclean thing.

### 418

Honour might be sought for in Homer, Virgil, and in Terence, and not in the Holy Scripture; for Christ says: 'Hallowed be thy name – not ours, but thine be the glory.' Christ charges us to preach God's Word. We preachers should of the world be held and esteemed as *injusti stulti,* to the end God be *justus, sapiens, et misericors;* that is his title, which he will leave to none other. When we leave to God his name, his kingdom, and will, then will he also give unto us our daily bread, remit our sins, and deliver us from the devil and all evil. Only his honour he will have to himself.

### 419

It were but reasonable I should in my old age have some rest and peace, but now those that should be with and for me, fall upon me. I have plague enough with my adversaries, therefore my brethren should not vex me. But who is able to resist? They are fresh, lusty, young people, and have lived in idleness; I am now aged, and have had much labour and pains. Nothing causes Osiander's pride more than his idle life; for he preaches but twice a week, yet has a yearly stipend of four hundred guilders.

### 420

God in wonderful wise led us out of the darkness of the sophists, and cast me into the game, now more than twenty years since. It went weakly forward at the first, when I began to write against the gross error of indulgences. At that time Doctor Jerome withstood me, and said: What will you do, they will not endure it? but, said I, what if they must endure it?

Soon after him came Silvester Prierio into the list; he thundered and lightned against me with his syllogisms, saying: Whosoever makes doubt of any one sentence or act of the Romish church, is a heretic: Martin Luther doubts thereof; *ergo*, he is a heretic. Then it went on, for the pope makes a three-fold distinction of the church. First, a substantial, i.e., the body of the church. Secondly, a significant church, i.e., the cardinals. Thirdly, an operative and powerful church; i.e., the pope himself. No mention is made of a council, for the pope will be the powerful church above the Holy Scripture and councils.

### 421

Our auditors, for the most part, are epicurean; they measure our preaching as they think good, and will have easy days.

The Pharisees and Sadducees were Christ's enemies, yet they heard him willingly; the Pharisees, to the end they might lay hold on him; the Sadducees, that they might flout and deride him. The Pharisees are our friars; the Sadducees, our gentry, citizens, and country folk: our gentlemen give us the hearing, and believe us, yet will do what seems good to them; that is, they remain epicureans.

### 422

A preacher should be a logician and a rhetorician, that is, he must be able to teach, and to admonish; when he preaches touching an article, he must, first, distinguish it. Secondly, he must define, describe, and show what it is. Thirdly, he must produce sentences out of the Scriptures, therewith to prove and strengthen it. Fourthly, he must, with examples, explain and declare it. Fifthly, he must adorn it with similitudes; and, lastly, he must admonish and rouse up the lazy, earnestly reprove all the disobedient, all false doctrine, and the authors thereof; yet, not out of malice and envy, but only to God's honour, and the profit and saving health of the people.

### 423

'Their priests do teach for hire.' Some there be who abuse this sentence, wresting it against good and godly teachers and preachers, as if it were not right for them to take the wages ordained for the ministers of the church, on which they must live. They produce the sentence where Christ says: 'Freely ye have received, freely give'; they allege also the example of St. Paul, who maintained himself by the work of his hands, to the end he might not be burthensome to the church.

These accusations proceed out of hatred to the function of preaching, to which Satan is a deadly enemy. These ungodly people, by filling the ears of the simple with such speeches, not only occasion the preachers to be condemned, but also the function of preaching to be suspected; whereas they ought, with all diligence, to endeavour that the ministers, for the Word's sake, might again be restored to their honest dignity.

It is true, as Christ says: 'Freely ye have received, freely give'; for he will have the chief end of preaching to be directed to God's honour only, and the people's salvation; but it follows not that it is against God for the church to maintain her ministers, who truly serve her in the Word, though it were against God and all Christianity, if the ministers of the church should omit the final cause, for which the office of preaching is instituted, and should look and have regard only to their wages, or aim at lucre and gain, and not uprightly, purely, and truly proceed in the office of teaching.

Like as the ministers of the church, by God's command, are a in duty bound to seek and promote God's Honour, and the saving health and salvation of the people, with true and upright doctrine, even so the church and congregation have command from God to maintain their ministers, and honourably nourish and cherish them; for Christ says: 'Every labourer is worthy of his hire.' Now, if he be worthy, then no man ought to cast it in his teeth that he takes wages. St. Paul more clearly expresses himself: 'The Lord hath also commanded, that they which preach the gospel, should live off the gospel.' He puts on the office of the law, and says: 'Do ye not know, that they which do minister about holy things, live off the things of the temple? And they which wait at the altar, are partakers with the altar.' Moreover, he makes use of very fine similitude, saying: 'Who goeth at warfare at anytime at his own charges? Who planteth a vineyard, and eateth not of the fruit thereof?' But especially mark the comparison which he gives in his Epistle to the Corinthians: 'If we have sown unto you spiritual things, is it a great matter if we shall reap your carnal things?' Indeed, every Christian, but especially the officers of the church, ministers, and preachers, should so carry themselves that they fall not into suspicion of being greedy and covetous; yet they must not so conceive it, as if it were wrong to receive of the church and assembly, that which is needful for the maintenance of the body.

Therefore no man should take umbrage that godly rulers provide for the churches, by honestly maintaining her true ministers; nay, we should bewail that the majority of princes and rulers neglect the true and pure religion, and provide not for our children and posterity, so that, through such meanness, there will be either none, or most unlearned ministers.

### 424

Scripture requires humble hearts, that hold God's Word in honour, love, and worth, and that pray continually: 'Lord, teach me thy ways and statutes.' But the Holy Ghost resists the proud, and will not dwell with them. And although some for a time diligently study in Holy Scripture and teach and preach Christ uprightly, yet, as soon as they become proud, God excludes them out of the church. Therefore, every proud spirit is a heretic, not in act and deed, yet before God.

But it is a hard matter for one who has some particular gift and quality above another, not to be haughty, proud, and presumptuous, and not to contemn others; therefore God suffers them that have great gifts to fall many times into heavy tribulations, to the end they may learn, when God draws away his hand, that then, they are of no value. St. Paul was constrained to bear on his body the sting or thorn of the flesh, to preserve him from haughtiness. And if Philip Melancthon were not now and then plagued in such sort as he is, he would have strange conceits.

### 425

I learn by preaching to know what the world, the flesh, the malice and wickedness of the devil is, all which could not be known before the gospel was revealed and preached, for up to that time I thought there were no sins but incontinence and lechery.

### 426

At court these rules ought to be observed: we must cry aloud, and accuse; for neither the gospel nor modesty belong to the court; we must be harsh, and set our faces as flints; we must, instead of Christ, who is mild and friendly, place Moses with his horns in the court. Therefore I advise my chaplains and ministers to complain at court of their wants, miseries, poverty, and necessities; for I myself preached concerning the same before the prince elector, who is both good and godly, but his courtiers do what they please. Philip Melancthon and Justus Jonas were lately called in question at court, for the world's sake; but they made this answer: Luther is old enough, and knows how and what to preach.

### 427

Cursed are all preachers that in the church aim at high and hard things, and, neglecting the saving health of the poor unlearned people, seek their own honour and praise, and therewith to please one or two ambitious persons.

When I preach, I sink myself deep down. I regard neither Doctors nor Magistrates, of whom are here in this church above forty; but I have an eye to the multitude of young people, children, and servants, of whom are more than two thousand. I preach to those, directing myself to them that have need thereof. Will not the rest hear me? The door stands open unto them; they may be gone. I see that the ambition of preachers grows and increases; this will do the utmost mischief in the church, and produce great disquietness and discord; for they will needs teach high things touching matters of state, thereby aiming at praise and honour; they will please the worldly wise, and meantime neglect the simple and common multitude.

An upright, godly, and true preacher should direct his preaching to the poor, simple sort of people, like a mother that stills her child, dandles and plays with it, presenting it with milk from her own breast, and needing neither malmsey nor muscadine for it. In such sort should also preachers carry themselves, teaching and preaching plainly, that the simple and unlearned may conceive and comprehend, and retain what they say. When they come to me, to Melancthon, to Dr. Pomer, etc., let them show their cunning, how learned they be; they shall be well put to their trumps. But to sprinkle out Hebrew, Greek, and Latin in their public sermons, savours merely of show, according with neither time nor place.

**428**

In the Psalm it is said: Their voice went out into the whole world. But St. Paul to the Romans gives it thus: 'Their sound went out into all the earth,' which is all one. Many sentences are in the Bible, wherein St. Paul observed the translation of the Seventy Interpreters, for he contemned them not; and whereas he was preacher to the Greeks, therefore he was constrained to preach as they understood.

In such sort did he use that sentence, 1 Corinthians 15: 'Death is swallowed up in victory,' whereas in the Hebrew, it is 'in the end'; yet 'tis all one. St. Paul was very rich and flowing in words; one of his words contains three of Cicero's orations, or the whole of Isaiah and Jeremiah. O! he was an excellent preacher; he is not in vain named *vas electum*. Our Lord God said: I will give a preacher to the world that shall be precious. There was never any that understood the Old Testament so well as St. Paul, except John the Baptist, and John the Divine. St. Peter excels also. St. Matthew and the rest well describe the histories, which are very necessary; but as to the things and words of the Old Testament, they never mention what is couched therein.

St. Paul translated much out of Hebrew into Greek, which none besides were able to do; in handling one chapter, he often expounds four, five, or six. Oh, he dearly loved Moses and Isaiah, for they, together with king David, were the chief prophets. The words and things of St. Paul are taken out of Moses and the Prophets.

Young divines ought to study Hebrew, to the end they may be able to compare Greek and Hebrew words together, and discern their properties, natures, and strength.

# Of Antichrist

⟐

## 429

Antichrist is the pope and the Turk together; a beast full of life must have a body and soul; the spirit or soul of antichrist, is the pope, his flesh or body the Turk. The latter writes and assails and persecutes God's church corporally; the former spiritually and corporally too, with hanging, burning, murdering, etc. But, as in the apostle's time, the church had the victory over the Jews and Romans, so now will she keep the field firm and solid against the hypocrisy and idolatry of the pope, and the tyranny and devastations of the Turk and her other enemies.

## 430

'And the king shall do according his will, and he shall exalt himself, and magnify himself above every god, and shall speak marvellous things against the God of gods, and shall prosper until the indignation be accomplished: for that that is determined shall be done. Neither shall he regard the God of his fathers, nor the desire of women, nor regard any god, for he shall magnify himself above all.'

This prophecy, as all the teachers agree, points directly at the antichrist, under the name of Antiochus; for antichrist will regard neither God nor the love of women – that is, the state of matrimony. These two, antichrist contemns on earth – God, that is religion, and mankind. He will not regard women, that is, he will contemn temporal and house-government, laws, jurisdiction, emperors and kings: for through women children are born, and brought up, to the perpetuation of mankind and replenishing of the world; where women are not regarded, of necessity temporal and house government is also contemned, and laws, and ordinances, and rulers.

Daniel was an exceeding high and excellent prophet, whom Christ loved, and touching whom he said: Whoso readeth, let him understand. He spoke of that antichrist persecutor as clearly as if he had been an eye-witness thereof. Read the 11th chapter throughout. It applies to the time when the emperor Caligula and other tyrants ruled; it distinctly says: 'He shall plant the tabernacles of his palace between the seas, in the glorious holy mountain'; that is, at Rome, in Italy. The Turk rules also between two seas, at Constantinople, but that is not the holy mountain. He does not honour or advance the worship of *Maosim*, nor does he prohibit matrimony. Therefore Daniel points directly at the pope, who does both, with great fierceness. The prophet says further: 'He shall also be forsaken of his king.' It is come to that pass already, for we see kings and princes leave him. As to the forms of religion under the pope and Turk, there is no difference, but in a few ceremonies; the Turk observes the Mosaical, the pope the Christian ceremonies – both sophisticate and falsify them; for, as the Turk corrupts the Mosaic bathings and washings, so the pope corrupts the sacrament of baptism and of the Lord's supper.

The kingdom of antichrist is described also in the revelation of John, where it is said: 'And it was given unto him to make war with the saints and to overcome them.' This might seem prophesied of the Turk and not of the pope, but we must, on investigation, understand it of the pope's abominations and tyranny in temporal respects. It is further said in the Apocalypse: 'It shall be for a time, and times, and half a time.' Here is the question; what is a time? If time be understood a year, the passage signifies three years and a half, and hits Antiochus, who for such a period persecuted the people of Israel, but at length died in his own filth and corruption. In like manner will the pope also be destroyed; for he began his kingdom, not through power of the divine authority, but through superstition and a forced interpretation of some passages of Scripture. Popedom is built on a foundation which will bring about its fall. Daniel prophesies thus: 'And through his policy he shall cause craft to prosper in his hand; but he shall be broken without hand.' This refers specially to the pope, for all other tyrants and monarchs fall by temporal power and strength. However, it may hit both pope and Turk. Both began to reign almost at one time, under the emperor Phocas, who murdered his own master, the emperor Maurice, with his empress and young princes, well nigh nine hundred years since. The pope began to govern the church spiritually at the same time that Mohammed founded his power; the pope's temporal kingdom stood scarce three hundred years, for he plagued and harassed kings and emperors. I cannot well define or comprehend this prophecy: 'A time, and times, and half a time.' I do not know whether it refers to the Turk, who began to rule when Constantinople was taken, in the year 1453, eighty-five years ago. If I calculate a time to be the age of Christ (thirty years) this expression would mean one hundred and five years, and the Turk would still have twenty years swing to come. Well, God knows how it stands, and how he will deliver those that are his. Let us not vex ourselves with seeking over-knowledge. Let us repent and pray.

Seeing the pope is antichrist,[1] I believe him to be a devil incarnate. Like as Christ is true and natural God and man, so is antichrist a living devil. It is true, too, what they say of the pope, that he is a terrestrial god, – for he is neither a real god nor a real man, but of the two natures mingled together.

He names himself an earthly god, as though the only true and Almighty God were not God on earth! Truly, the pope's kingdom is a horrible outrage against the power of God and against mankind; an abomination of desolation, which stands in the holy place. 'Tis a monstrous blasphemy for a human creature to presume, now Christ is come, to exalt himself in the church above God. If it had been done amongst the Gentiles, before the coming of Christ, it would not have been so great a wonder. But though Daniel, Christ himself, and his apostles, Paul and Peter, have given us warning of that poisoned beast and pestilence, yet we Christians have been, and still are, so doltish and mad, as to adore and worship all his idols, and to believe that he is lord over the universal world, as heir to St. Peter; whereas neither Christ nor St. Peter left any succession upon earth.

The pope is the last blaze in the lamp, which will go out, and ere long be extinguished, the last instrument of the devil, that thunders and lightens with sword and bull, making war through the power and strength of others, as Daniel says: 'He is powerful, but not by his own strength.' It has been affirmed that the pope has more power in one finger, than all the princes in Germany; but the spirit of God's mouth has seized upon that shameless strumpet, and startled many hearts, so that they regard him no more; a thing

---

1. The identity of antichrist with the pope had already been asserted by John Huss, in his *De Anatontia Antichristi*.)

no emperor, with sword and power, had been able to accomplish; the devil scorns these weapons: but when he is struck with God's Word, then the pope is turned to a poppy and a frothy flower.

### 431

The word Papa, Pope, comes, as I think, of the word Abba, repeated twice, meaning father of fathers. Of old, the bishops were called *Papa*; Jerome, writing to Augustine, who was bishop of Hippo, calls him *Holy Pope*: and in the legend of St. Cyprian, martyr, we read that the judge asked him: Art thou the Cyprian whom the Christians call their pope? It seems to me to have been a term applied to all the bishops. Children call their fathers *papa*; the bishops were the spiritual *papas* of the people.

Who, thirty years ago, would have dared to say of the pope what we now say of him? None then ventured to express himself respecting him in other terms than those of veneration and supplication.

### 432

Whence comes it that the popes pretend 'tis they who form the church, when, all the while, they are bitter enemies of the church, and have no knowledge, certainly no comprehension, of the holy gospel? Pope, cardinals, bishops, not a soul of them has read the Bible; 'tis a book unknown to them. They are a pack of guzzling, stuffing wretches, rich, wallowing in wealth and laziness, resting secure in their power, and never, for a moment, thinking of accomplishing God's will. The Sadducees were infinitely more pious than the papists, from whose holiness God preserve us. May he preserve us, too, from security, which engenders ingratitude, contempt of God, blasphemy, and the persecution of divine things.

### 433

Some one, speaking of the signs and marvels which are to herald the coming of antichrist, when he shall present himself previous to the last judgment, said he was to be armed with a breath of fire, which would overthrow all who might seek to oppose him. Dr. Luther observed: These are parables, but they agree in a measure with the prophecies of Daniel; for the throne of the pope is a throne of flame, and fire is his arm, as the scimitar is the Turk's. Antichrist attacks with fire, and shall be punished with fire. The villain is now full of fear, crouching behind his mountains, and submitting to things against which heretofore he would have hurled his lightning and his thunder.

## 434

On the 8th August, came a letter from Bucer, relating that the council of Vienne was over, that the cardinals had returned home, and that the gospel had been eagerly received at Piacenza and Bologna. The pope, enraged at this result, had sent for a German, named Corfentius, to whom he transmitted a safe conduct; but, despite this, when Corfentius reached Rome, he was seized and thrown into the Tiber. Dr. Luther observed: Such is the good faith of the Italian papists! Happy the man who puts no trust in them. If the men of God, who preach the gospel in Italy, remain firm, there will be much bloodshed. See what snares are laid for us here in Germany; there's not a single hour wherein we can regard ourselves as safe. Had not God watched over us, we must long since have succumbed.

## 435

Some one asked how happened it St. James had been at Compostella. Dr. Martin replied: Just as it happens, that the papists reckon up sixteen apostles, while Jesus Christ had but twelve. In many places, the papists boast of having some of the milk of the Virgin Mary, and of the hay in which Christ lay in the cradle. A Franciscan boasted he had some of this hay in a wallet he carried with him. A roguish fellow took out the hay, and put some charcoal in its place. When the monk came to show the people his hay, he found only the wood. However, he was at no loss: 'My brethren,' said he, 'I brought out the wrong wallet with me, and so cannot show you the hay; but here is some of the wood that St. Lawrence was grilled upon.'

## 436

Kings and princes coin money only out of metals, but the pope coins money out of everything – indulgences, ceremonies, dispensations, pardons; 'tis all fish comes to his net. 'Tis only baptism escapes him, for children came into the world without clothes to be stolen, or teeth to be drawn.

## 437

In Italy, the monasteries are very wealthy. There are but three or four monks to each; the surplus of their revenues goes to the pope and his cardinals.

## 438

A gentleman being at the point of death, a monk from the next convent came to see what he could pick up, and said to the gentleman: Sir, will you give so and so to our monastery? The dying man, unable to speak, replied by a nod of the head, whereupon the monk, turning to the gentleman's son, said: You see, your father makes us this bequest. The son said to the father: Sir, is it your pleasure that I kick this monk down stairs? The dying man nodded as before, and the son forthwith drove the monk out of doors.

### 439

A professor at Wittenberg, named Vitus Ammerbach, having advanced the proposition that, some head or other being necessary for the church, the pope might as well be that head as another, Luther said: Greece was never under the authority of the pope, nor Judea, nor Scythia, yet in all these countries were Christians of great piety. 'Tis great presumption in Ammerbach to propound these fallacies.

### 440

Some one observed: The papists flatter themselves our doctrines will not last long, but will come to nothing, like those of Arius, which, say they, endured but for forty years. Dr. Luther replied: The sect of Arius maintained itself for nearly sixty years; but as it was based on heretical principles, it ended in confusion and destruction, whereas our opponents are compelled, despite themselves, to admit that we have right on our side. Our light so shines in the eyes of all men, that none can deny it.

### 441

They once showed here, at Wittenberg, the drawers of St. Joseph and the breeches of St. Francis. The bishop of Mayence boasted he had a gleam of the flame of Moses' bush. At Compostella they exhibit the standard of the victory that Jesus Christ gained over death and the devil. The crown of thorns is shown in several places.

### 442

When Wolsey, who was the son of a butcher, was made cardinal, a merry fellow said: 'Please God he come to be pope, for then we shall have meat on fast days. St. Peter, because he was a fisherman, prohibited meat, in order to raise the price of fish; this butcher's son will do the same for fish.'

### 443

The cuckoo takes the eggs out of the linnet's nest, and puts her own in their place. When the young cuckoos grow big, they eat the linnet. The cuckoo, too, has a great antipathy towards the nightingale. The pope is a cuckoo; he robs the church of her true eggs, and substitutes in their place his greedy cardinals, who devour the mother that has nourished them. The pope, too, cannot abide that nightingale, the preaching and singing of the true doctrine.

### 444

They show, at Rome, the head of St. John the Baptist, though 'tis well known that the Saracens opened his tomb, and burned his remains to ashes. These impostures of the papists cannot be too seriously reprehended.

### 445

The papists, for the most part, are mere gross blockheads. One of their priests I knew, baptized with this form of words: Ego te baptiste in nomine Christe. Another, in singing, used to say, *elema,* instead of *clama,* and when corrected, only bawled all the louder, *elema, elema.* Another said, *elicere,* instead of *dicere.* At Bamberg, they exhibit, once a year, a book, which they say contains the history of the emperor Henry and his wife Cunegonde, who made, on their marriage-day, a vow of virginity. Birkheimer, when he passed through Bamberg, asked to see this book, and when it was brought to him, found it was only a copy of Cicero's *Topics.* In one convent, the brethren read *munsimus,* instead of *sumpsimus.* A young brother, just fresh from study, correcting this error, the rest said to him: 'Mind thy own business; we have always read *munsimus,* and we are not going to change our reading for thee.'

### 446

Two jesters held a disputation before the pope, who was at dinner, the one maintaining, the other denying, the immortality of the soul. The pope said, that he who advocated the immortality of the soul adduced excellent reasons, but that, for his own part, he should side with the man who denied its immortality, seeing that it was a convenient doctrine, holding out a very desirable prospect, and 'tis to such wretches as these the government of the church is to be confided.

### 447

Albert, bishop of Mayence, had a physician attached to his person, who, being a protestant, did not enjoy the prelate's favour. The man seeing this, and being an avaricious, ambitious, world-seeker, denied his God, and turned back to popery, saying to his associates: I'll put Jesus Christ by for awhile, till I've made my fortune, and then bring him out again. This horrible blasphemy met with its just reward; for next day the miserable hypocrite was found dead in his bed, his tongue hanging from his mouth, his face as black as a coal, and his neck twisted half round. I was myself an ocular witness of this merited chastisement of impiety.

## 448

Philip Melancthon, on the authority of a person who had filled an important post at the court of Clement VII, mentioned that every day, after the pope had dined or supped, his cup-bearer and cooks were imprisoned for two hours, and then, if no symptoms of poison manifested themselves in their master, were released. 'What a miserable life' observed Luther; ''tis exactly what Moses has described in Deuteronomy: "And thy life shall hang in doubt before thee, and thou shalt fear, day and night, and shall have none assurance of thy life. In the morning, thou shalt say: would God it were even! and at even, thou shalt say: would God it were morning!"'

## 449

Mary, the humble virgin of Nazareth, strikes these potentates and popes fiercely, when she sings: 'I will put down the mighty from their seats.' Doubtless she had a sweet sounding voice.

The pope and his crew are mere worshippers of idols, and servants of the devil, with all their doings and living; for he regards not at all God's Word, nay, condemns and persecutes it, and directs all his juggling to the drawing us away from the true faith in Christ. He pretends great holiness, under colour of the outward service of God, for he has instituted orders with hoods, with shavings, fasting, eating of fish, saying mass, and such like: but in the groundwork, 'tis altogether the doctrine of the devil; and the cause why the pope so stiffly holds such devilish doctrine is that which the gospel relates (Matt. 4). The devil has shown him the kingdoms of the world, and made promise to him as he did to Christ. This makes him contemn and scorn our sermons and God's service, by which we are beggars, and endure much, while for his doctrine he gets money and wealth, honour and power, and is so great a monarch, that he can bring emperors under his girdle.

## 450

I cannot imagine how there should be peace between us and the papists, for neither will yield to the other; 'tis an everlasting war, like that between the woman's seed and the old serpent. When temporal kings are weary of warring, they make a truce, more or less enduring, but in our case, there can be no such cessations; for we cannot depart from the gospel, nor will they desist from their idolatry and blaspheming; the devil will not suffer his feet to be chopped off, nor will Christ have the preaching of his Word hindered; therefore I cannot see how any peace or truce may be between Christ and Belial.

### 451

After the persecution of the church ceased, the popes aimed at the government, out of covetousness and ambition. The first was Hildebrand, or rather Hell-brand; they affrighted the people with their excommunication, which was so fearful a thing, that it descended upon the children, nay, fell upon servants. On the other hand, the pope seeking the goodwill of the people, granted and sold the remission of sins, were they never so heavy. Had one ravished the Virgin Mary, or crucified Christ anew, the pope would, for money, have pardoned him. This power and domination of the pope's, God has brought to confusion and destruction by my pen: for God, out of nothing, can make all things, and of the least means produce the greatest results.

### 452

Popedom must needs be brought to the stake, and pay for all. The pope shall be devoured by the friars, his creatures. The great and innumerable multitude of monks and friars, said cardinal Campeggio, produces great evil; for they shake that fair monarchy of popedom, so carefully erected; and he said right; the Rat King is being paid home by his rats. By divinity he cannot be defended, for 'tis no argument of his canonists and shaven crew, that his rule has long been a custom. How should the pope be able to judge, who has no skill or experience in matters of temporal government. How foolishly decides he touching matrimonial causes. He has forbidden his greased retinue to enter into the state of matrimony, though he commands it to be held and observed as a sacrament. If matrimony be a sacrament, it cannot be for the heathen; for the unbelieving Gentiles have nothing to do with them.

### 453

'Tis a mere fable to say that Constantine the Emperor gave to the pope so much property and people as he boasts of. This I read, that Constantine gave much alms to the poor, commanding the bishops to distribute them, by which means they grew to be great lords. But he gave them neither countries nor cities; wherefore the world wonders whence the popes derived such dominions. In former times the popes were not lords over emperors and kings, but were instituted or ordained by the emperors.

## 454

The world remains the world it was thousands of years ago; that is, the spouse of the devil. The world says now, as the Pharisees said to their servants, whom they had sent to take Christ prisoner: 'Are ye also deceived? have any of the rulers or Pharisees believed in him? This people that knoweth not the law are accursed.' Even so says the world now: Do the great ones and bishops believe in the Lutheran doctrine?

## 455

The pope denies not the sacrament, but he has stolen from the laity the one part or kind thereof; neither does he teach the true use of it. The pope rejects not the Bible, but he persecutes and kills upright, good, and godly teachers, as the Jews persecuted and slew the prophets that truly expounded and taught the Scriptures. The pope will permit the substance and essence of the sacrament and Bible to remain; but he will compel and force us to use them according to his will and pleasure, and will constrain us to believe the fictitious transubstantiation, and the real presence, *corporaliter*. The pope does nothing else than pervert and abuse all that God has ordained and commanded.

## 456

The chief cause that I fell out with the pope was this: the pope boasted that he was the head of the church, and condemned all that would not be under his power and authority: for he said, although Christ be the head of the church, yet, notwithstanding, there must be a corporal head of the church upon earth. With this I could have been content, had he but taught the gospel pure and clear, and not introduced human inventions and lies in its stead. Further, he took upon him power, rule, and authority over the Christian church, and over the Holy Scriptures, the Word of God; no man must presume to expound the Scriptures, but only he, and according to his ridiculous conceits; so that he made himself lord over the church, proclaiming her at the same time a powerful mother, and empress over the Scriptures, to which we must yield and be obedient; this was not to be endured. They who, against God's word, boast of the church's authority, are mere idiots. The pope attributes more power to the church, which is begotten and born, than to the Word, which has begotten, conceived, and born the church.

We, through God's grace, are not heretics, but schismatics, causing, indeed, separation and division, wherein we are not to blame, but our adversaries, who gave occasion thereto, because they remain not by God's word alone, which we have, hear, and follow.

## 457

When our Lord God intends to plague and punish one, he leaves him in blindness, so that he regards not God's word, but condemns the same, as the papists now do. They know that our doctrine is God's word, but they will not allow of this syllogism and conclusion: When God speaks, we must hear him; now God speaks through the doctrine of the gospel; therefore we must hear him. But the papists, against their own consciences, say, No; we must hear the church.

It is very strange: they admit both propositions, but will not allow of the consequences, or permit the conclusions to be right. They urge some decree or other of the Council of Constance, and say, though Christ speak, who is the truth itself, yet an ancient custom must be preferred, and observed for law. Thus do they answer, when they seek to wrest and pervert the truth.

If this sin of antichrist be not a sin against the Holy Ghost, then I do not know how to define and distinguish sins. They sin herein wilfully against the revealed truth of God's word, in a most stubborn and stiff: necked manner. I pray, who would not, in this case, resist these devilish and shameless lying lips? I marvel not John Huss died so joyfully, seeing be heard of such abominable impieties and wickednesses of the papists. I pray, how holds the pope concerning the church? He preserves her, but only in an external lustre, pomp, and succession. But we judge her according to her essence, as she is in herself, in her own substance, that is, according to God's word and sacraments. The pope is reserved for God's judgment, therefore only by God's judgment he shall be destroyed. Henry VIII, king of England, is now also an enemy to the pope's person, but not to his essence and substance; he would only kill the body of the pope, but suffer his soul, that is, his false doctrine, to live; the pope can well endure such an enemy; he hopes within the space of twenty years to recover his rule and government again. But I fall upon the pope's soul, his doctrine, with God's word, not regarding his body, that is, his wicked person and life. I not only pluck out his feathers, as the king of England and prince George of Saxony do, but I set the knife to his throat, and cut his windpipe asunder. We put the goose on the spit; did we but pluck her, the feathers would soon grow again. Therefore is Satan so bitter an enemy unto us, because we cut the pope's throat, as does also the king of Denmark, who aims at the essence of popery.

## 458

'Tis wonderful how, in this our time, the majesty of the pope is fallen. Heretofore, all monarchs, emperors, kings, and princes feared the pope's power, who held them all at his nod; none durst so much as mutter a word against him. This great god is now fallen; his own creatures, the friars and monks, are his enemies, who, if they still continue with him, do so for the sake of gain; otherwise they would oppose him more fiercely than we do.

## 459

The pope's crown is named *regnum mundi,* the kingdom of the world. I have heard it credibly reported at Rome, that this crown is worth more than all the princedoms of Germany. God placed Popedom in Italy not without cause, for the Italians can make out many things to be real and true which in truth are not so: they have crafty and subtle brains.

## 460

If the pope were the head of the Christian church, then the church were a monster with two heads, seeing that St. Paul says that Christ is her head. The pope may well be, and is, the head of the false church.

## 461

Where the linnet is, there is also the cuckoo, for he thinks his song a thousand times better than the linnet's. Even thus, the pope places himself in the church, and so that his song may be heard, overcrows the church. The cuckoo is good for something, in that its appearance gives tidings that summer is at hand; so the pope serves to show us that the last day of judgment approaches.

## 462

There are many that think I am too fierce against Popedom; on the contrary, I complain that I am, alas! too mild; I wish I could breathe out lightning against pope and Popedom, and that every word were a thunderbolt.

## 463

'Tis all idle dream the papists entertain of antichrist; they suppose he should be a single person, that should govern, scatter money amongst them, do miracles, carry a fiery oven about him, and kill the saints.

## 464

In Popedom they make priests not to preach and teach God's Word, but only to celebrate mass, and to gad about with the sacrament. For, when a bishop ordains a man, he says: Take unto thee power to celebrate mass, and to offer for the living and the dead. But we ordain priests according to the command of Christ and St. Paul, namely, to preach the pure gospel and God's Word. The papists in their ordinations make no mention of preaching and teaching God's Word, therefore their consecrating and ordaining is false and unright, for all worshipping which is not ordained of God or erected by God's Word and command, is nothing worth, yea, mere idolatry.

## 465

Next unto my just cause the small repute and mean aspect of my person gave the blow to the pope. For when I began to preach and write, the pope scorned and contemned me; he thought: 'Tis but one poor friar; what can he do against me? I have maintained and defended this doctrine in Popedom, against many emperors, kings, and princes, what then shall this one man do? If he had condescended to regard me, he might easily have suppressed me in the beginning.

## 466

A German, making his confession to a priest at Rome, promised, on oath, to keep secret whatsoever the priest should impart unto him, until he reached home; whereupon the priest gave him a leg of the ass on which Christ rode into Jerusalem, very neatly bound up in silk, and said: This is the holy relic on which the Lord Christ corporally did sit, with his sacred legs touching this ass's leg. Then was the German wondrous glad, and carried the said holy relic with him into Germany. When he got to the borders, he bragged of his holy relic in the presence of four others, his comrades, when, lo! it turned out that each of them had likewise received from the same priest a leg, after promising the same secrecy. Thereupon, all exclaimed, with great wonder: Lord! had that ass five legs?

## 467

A picture being brought to Luther, in which the pope, with Judas the traitor, were represented hanging on the purse and keys, he said: 'Twill vex the pope horribly, that he, whom emperors and kings have worshipped, should now be figured hanging on his false pick-locks. It will also grieve the papists, for their consciences will be touched. The purse accords well with the cardinal's hats and their incomes, for the pope's covetousness has been so gross, that in all kingdoms he has not only raked to himself Annates, Palliummoney, etc., but has also sold for money the holy sacrament, indulgences, fraternities, Christ's blood, matrimony, etc. Therefore his purse is filled with robberies, upon which justly ought to be exclaimed, as in the Revelations; 'Recompense them as they have done to you, and make it double unto them, according to their works.' Therefore, seeing the pope has damned me and given me over to the devil, so will I, in requital, hang him on his own keys.

### 468

It is abominable that in so many of the pope's decrees, there is not one single sentence of Holy Scripture, or one article of the Catechism mentioned. The pope intending to conduct the government of his church in an external way, his teachings were blasphemous; such as that a stinking friar's hood, put upon a dead body, procured remission of sins, and was of equal value with the merits of our blessed Saviour Christ Jesus.

### 469

It is no marvel that the papists hate me so vehemently, for I have well deserved it at their hands. Christ more mildly reproved the Jews than I the papists, yet they killed him. These, therefore, think they justly persecute me, but, according to God's laws and will, they shall find their mistake. In the day of the last judgment I will denounce the pope and his tyrants, who scorn and assail the Word of God, and his sacraments. The pope destroys poor married priests, that receive and observe God's Word and statutes, whereas by all their laws they are only to be displaced from their office. So Prince George has banished and driven away from Oschitz ten citizens and householders, with twenty-seven children, martyrs to the Word. Their sighs will rise up to heaven against him.

### 470

The pope and his crew can in nowise endure the idea of reformation; the mere word creates more alarm at Rome, than thunderbolts from heaven, or the day of judgment. A cardinal said, the other day: Let them eat, and drink, and do what they will; but as to reforming us, we think that is a vain idea; we will not endure it. Neither will we protestants be satisfied, though they administer the sacrament in both kinds, and permit priests to marry; we will also have the doctrine of the faith pure and unfalsified, and the righteousness that justifies and saves before God, and which expels and drives away all idolatry and false-worshipping; these gone and banished, the foundation on which Popedom is built falls also.

### 471

We will have the holy sacrament administered in both kinds, that it shall be free for priests to marry, or to forbear, and we will in no way suffer ourselves to be bereaved of the article of justification: 'That by faith only in Jesus Christ we are justified and saved before God; without any works, merits and deserts, merely by grace and mercy.' This we must keep and preserve, pure and unfalsified, if we intend to be saved. As to private mass, we cannot hinder it, but must leave it to God, to be acted by those over whom we have neither power nor command; yet, nevertheless, we will openly teach and preach against it, and show that it is abominable blasphemy and idolatry. Either we must go together by the ears, or else they, in our countries, must yield unto us in this particular; if it come to pass that herein they yield unto us, then must we be contented; for, like as the Christians dealt with the Arians, and as St. Paul was constrained to carry himself towards the Jews, even so must we also leave the papists to their own consciences, and seeing they will not follow us, so we neither can nor will force them, but must let them go and commit it to God's judgment; and truly, sincerely, and diligently hold unto and maintain our doctrine, let the same vex, anger, and displease whom it will.

### 472

The papists see they have an ill cause, and, therefore, labour to maintain it with very poor arguments, that cannot endure the proof, and may be easily confuted.

They say: 'The praising of anything is an invocation; the saints are to be praised, therefore they are to be invoked.' I answer: No, in nowise; for every praising is not invoking: married people are to be praised, but not to be invoked; for invocation belongs only to God, and not to any creature, either in heaven or on earth; no, not to any angel. They say: 'The doctrine of the remission of sins is necessary: indulgences, pardons, and graces are remissions of sins; therefore they are necessary.' No: the pope's pardons are not remissions of sins, but satisfactions for remitting the punishments: mere fables and fictions.

### 473

When I was in Rome, a disputation was openly held, at which were present thirty learned doctors besides myself, against the pope's power; he boasting, that with his right hand he commands the angels in heaven, and with his left draws souls out of purgatory, and that his person is mingled with the godhead. Calixtus disputed against these assertions, and showed that it was only on earth that power was given to the pope to bind and to loose. The other doctors hereupon assailed him with exceeding vehemence, and Calixtus discontinued his arguments, saying, he had only spoken by way of disputation, and that his real opinions were far other wise.

### 474

For the space of many hundred years there has not been a single bishop that has shown any zeal on the subject of schools, baptism, and preaching; 'twould have been too great trouble for them, such enemies were they to God. I have heard divers worthy doctors affirm, that the church has long since stood in need of reformation; but no man was so bold as to assail Popedom; for the pope had on his banner, *Noli me tangere;* therefore every man was silent. Dr. Staupitz said once to me: 'If you meddle with Popedom, you will have the whole world against you;' and he added – 'yet the church is built on blood, and with blood must be sprinkled.'

### 475

I would have all those who intend to preach the gospel, diligently read the popish abominations, their decrees and books; and, above all things, thoroughly, consider the horrors of the mass – on account of which idol God might justly have drowned and destroyed the whole world – to the end their consciences may be armed and confirmed against their adversaries.

### 476

That Italian monk's book, the *Conformities,* wherein a comparison is drawn between Christ and St. Francis, is a tissue of such horrible lies, that he who wrote it must have been possessed of a devil, not only spiritually but corporally. Christ, he says, is a figure or emblem of St. Francis; and he affirms that Christ gave to St. Francis the power of saving or condemning whom he pleased.

## 477

In a monastery at Luneburg, there stands to this day a great altar, whereon are represented the life and miracles of Christ; his birth, his entry into Jerusalem, his passion, death, descent into hell, resurrection, and ascension. Just by is set forth, in like manner, the birth of St. Francis, his miracles, sufferings, death, and ascent into heaven, so that they esteemed the works of St. Francis of equal value with those of our blessed Saviour Christ Jesus; a great and abominable blasphemy.

## 478

The pope's decretals are naught; he that drew them up was an ass. They are a book put together like a beggar's coat, patched up with all sorts of rags. There is nothing in them about the church; they all aim at temporal matters. Yet the pope says, these decretals are to have equal authority with the gospel and the writings of the apostles.

## 479

In the pope's decretals are many horrible and diabolical canons; they are a great plague and evil for the church. The shameless pope presumes to say: 'Whoso believes and observes not my decrees, it were in vain for him to believe in Christ, or give credit to the four Evangelists.' Is not this the language of the very devil, infusing deadly poison into the church? Again, he says in one of his decretals: That though he led people into hell, they ought to follow him; whereas, on the contrary, the office of a true bishop is to comfort the broken and sorrowful in heart, and to lead them to Christ. Fie upon this reprobate villain! must he teach consciences to despair in this sort? Whoever reads the decretals, will often find fair sentences of Scripture monstrously lugged in as confirmation; and, in other cases, when the Scripture is dead against them, that it is roundly said: the Romish church has otherwise decided. Thus, like an infernal dog, the pope dares to subject God's Word to human creatures. 'Tis just the same with Thomas Aquinas, who, in his books, argues, *pro et contra,* and when he cites a passage in Scripture, he goes on: Aristotle maintains the contrary; so that the Holy Scripture must give place to Aristotle, a heathen. The world heeds not this abominable darkness, but contemns the truth, and falls into horrible errors. Therefore, let us make good use of our time, for things will not always remain as now.

### 480

In the decretals, the pope domineers and triumphs like a victor; there he is on his dunghill, in possession, thundering and lightening with these words: 'We have cognizance and authority, and by divine command we judge; all others ought to be obedient unto us.' No human creature may criticise the pope; he only and alone has power to judge and criticise the whole universal world. I am persuaded, that in the pope's spiritual laws it is written above one thousand times, that the pope's actions may not be criticised by any man whatsoever.

### 481

The spiritual law of the pope is a filthy book, stinking of money. Take out of it covetousness and ambition, there remains nothing of its own proper substance, yet it has a great lustre, for all unhappiness must begin *in nomine Domini*. Like as all righteousness and saving health is only 'in the name of the Lord', so, under the colour and cover of God's name, all idolatry and superstition come. Therefore the commandment fitly says: 'Thou shalt not take the name of the Lord thy God in vain.'

### 482

Gratian, the lawyer, who collected the decretals together, endeavoured with diligence to arrange them congruously, and to separate the good from the evil. The good man meant well, but the result was naught; for he proceeded thus; he rejected that which was good, to justify that which was evil, and thus undertaking the impossible, became amazed and affrighted.

### 483

The fasting of the friars is more easy to them than our eating to us. For one day of fasting there are three of feasting. Every friar for his supper has two quarts of beer, a quart of wine, and spice-cakes, or bread prepared with spice and salt, the better to relish their drink. Thus go on these poor fasting brethren; getting so pale and wan, they are like the fiery angels.

### 484

If the emperor would merit immortal praise, he would utterly root out the order of the Capuchins, and, for an everlasting remembrance of their abominations, cause their books to remain in safe custody. 'Tis the worst and most poisonous sect. The Augustine and Bernardine friars are no way comparable with these confounded lice.

### 485

Francis was an Italian, born in the city of Assisi, doubtless an honest and just man. He little thought that such superstition and unbelief would proceed out of his life. There have been so many of those grey friars, that they offered to send forty thousand of their number against the Turks, and yet leave their monasteries sufficiently provided for.

The Franciscan and grey friars came up under the emperor Frederick II, at the time St. Elizabeth was canonized, in the year 1207. Francis worked his game eighteen years; two years under the emperor Philip, four years under the emperor Otho, and twelve years under the emperor Frederick II. They feign, that after his death he appeared to the pope in a dream, held a cup in his hand, and filled the same with blood that ran out of his side. Is not this, think ye, a fine and proper piece of government, that began with dreams and with lies? The pope is not God's image but his ape. He will be both God and emperor; as pope Innocent III said: I will either take the crown from the emperor Philip, or he shall take mine from me. Oh, such histories ought diligently to be written, to the end posterity may know upon what grounds Popedom was erected and founded; namely, upon mere lies and fables. If I were younger, I would write a chronicle of the popes.

### 486

If the pope should seek to suppress the mendicant friars, he would find fine sport; he has made them fat, and cherished them in his bosom, and assigned them the greatest and most powerful princes for protectors. If he should attempt to abolish them, they would all combine and instigate the princes against him, for many kings and princes, and the emperor himself, have friars for confessors. The friars were the pope's columns, they carried him as the rats carry their king; I was our Lord God's quicksilver, which he threw into the fishpond; that is, which he cast among the friars.

A friar is evil every way, whether in the monastery or out of it. For as Aristotle gives an example touching fire, that burns whether it be in Ethiopia or in Germany, even so is it likewise with the friars. Nature is not changed by any circumstances of time or place.

### 487

In Italy was a particular order of friars, called *Fratres Ignorantiae*, that is, Brethren of Ignorance, who took a solemn oath, that they would neither know, learn, nor understand anything at all, but answer all questions with

*Nescio.* Truly, all friars are well worthy of this title, for they only read and babble out the words, but regard not their meaning. The pope and cardinals think: should these brethren study and be learned, they would master us. Therefore, *saccum per neccum,* that is, hang a bag about their necks, and send them a-begging through cities, towns, and countries:

### 488

An honest matron here in Wittenberg, widow of the consul Horndorff, complained of the covetousness of the Capuchins, one of whom pressed her father, upon his deathbed, to bequeath something to their monastery, and got from him four hundred florins, for the use of the monastery, the friar constraining herself to make a vow, that she would mention the matter to no person. The man kept the money, which course he usually took, to the great hurt of all the children and orphans in that city. At last, by command of the magistrate, she told how the friar had acted. Many such examples have been, yet no creature dared complain. There was no end of the robbing, filching, and stealing, of those insatiable, money-diseased wretches.

### 489

When I was in the monastery at Erfurt, a preaching friar and a barefoot friar wandered together into the country to beg for the brethren, and to gather alms. These two played upon each other in their sermons. The bare-foot friar preaching first, said: 'Loving country people, and good friends! take heed of that bird the swallow, for it is white within, but upon the back it is black; it is an evil bird, always chirping, but profitable for nothing; and when angered, is altogether mad,' hereby describing the preaching friars, who wear on the outside black coats, and inside white linen. Now, in the afternoon, the preaching friar came into the pulpit, and played upon the bare-foot friar: Indeed, loving friends, I neither may nor can well defend the swallow; but the grey sparrow is far a worse and more hurtful bird than the swallow; for it bites the kine, and when it fouls into people's eyes, makes them blind, as ye may see in the book of Tobit. He robs, steals, and devours all he can get, as oats, barley, wheat, rye, apples, pears, peas, cherries, etc. Moreover, he is a lascivious bird: his greatest art is to cry: 'Scrip, scrip,' etc. The bare-foot friar might in better colours have painted the preaching friars, for they are proud buzzards and right epicureans; while the bare-foot friars, under colour of sanctity and humility, are more proud and haughty than kings or princes, and, most of all, have imagined and devised monstrous lies.

## 490

St. Bernard was the best monk that ever was, whom I love beyond all the rest put together; yet he dared to say, it were a sign of damnation if a man quitted his monastery. He had under him three thousand monks, not one of whom was damned, if his opinion be true, *sed vix credo*. St. Bernard lived in dangerous times, under the emperors Henry IV and V, Conrad, and Lothaire. He was a learned and able monk, but he gave evil example. The friars, especially the Alinorites and Franciscans, had easy days by their hypocrisy; they touched no money, yet they were vastly rich, and lived in luxury. The evil friars' life began betimes, when people, under colour of piety, abandoned temporal matters. The vocation and condition of a true Christian, such as God ordained and founded it, consists in three hierarchies – domestic, temporal, and church government.

## 491

The state of celibacy is great hypocrisy and wickedness. Augustine, though he lived in a good and acceptable time, was deceived through the exaltation of nuns. And although he gave them leave to marry, yet he said they did wrong to marry, and sinned against God. Afterwards, when the time of wrath and blindness came, and the truth was hunted away, and lying got the upper hand, the generation of poor women was contemned, under the colour of great holiness, but which, in truth, was mere hypocrisy. Christ with one sentence confutes all their arguments: God created them male and female.

## 492

The covetousness of the popes has exceeded all others, for the devil made choice of Rome as his peculiar habitation. The ancients said: Rome is a den of covetousness, a root of all wickedness. I have also read in a very old book, this verse following:

'Versus Amor, mundi caput est, et bestia terra.'

That is, when the word Amor is turned and read backward, *Roma*, Rome, the head of the world, a beast that devours all lands. At Rome, all is raked to their hands without preaching or church service, by superstition, idolatry, and selling their good works to the poor ignorant laity for money. St. Peter describes such covetousness with express and clear words, when he says: 'They have a heart exercised with covetous practices.' I am persuaded a man cannot know the disease of covetousness, unless he know Rome; for the deceits and jugglings in other parts are nothing in comparison with those at Rome.

### 493

The proverb says: Priests' livings are catching livings; priests' goods never prosper; and this we know to be true by experience, for such as have taken spiritual livings unto them are grown poor thereby and become beggars.

### 494

A reformation being lately made at Wurtzburg among the prebends, they were constrained to put away their woman cooks; this continued for a fortnight, when, as they could be without them no longer, they had leave to take them again. But the cooks refused to live with the prebends, unless they would take them as their wives, whereupon they received them on that condition, and were fain to apparel them anew, to the end they might not be known. I have heard a locksmith say, that for the space of a fortnight, day and night, he had work enough to do in making keys; for every one of those women would have a key to her prebend's chamber.

Such wicked wretches must the church have to be her rulers and governors. In the council of Basle it was decreed, that priests should wear long gowns down to the feet, high shoes, broad hats, and neither red nor green apparel, and that no man should dispute whether the soul was mortal or immortal. The pope is a king without God and matrimony, for he has abolished that which is divine and godly, and altered that which God instituted and ordained in the world.

### 495

Saint Augustine and others distinguish thus between heretics, schismatic, and bad Christians: A schismatic is one that raises divisions and dissensions, professing the true faith of the Christian church, but not at union with her as to certain ceremonies and customs; an evil Christian is he that agrees with the church both in doctrine of faith and ceremonies, but therewithal leads an evil life, and is of wicked conversation. But an heretic is one that introduces false opinions and doctrines against the articles of the Christian faith, contrary to the true meaning of Holy Scripture, and stubbornly maintains and defends them. The papists do not call me a heretic, but a schismatic; one that prepares discords and strifes. But I say, the pope is an arch heretic, for he is an adversary to my blessed Saviour Christ; and so am I to the pope, because he makes new laws and ordinances according to his own will and pleasure, and so directly denies the everlasting priesthood of Christ.

Let us but mark the two points in his decrees, where, with exceeding pompous majesty, he exalts himself above the Holy Scriptures. He is content to leave the expounding thereof to the Fathers, but the decision of their truth he reserves for the chair of Rome. Therefore he discharges against me his lightenings and thunderings, yea, also against his own decrees; for the pope himself says: Justice must give place and yield to the truth. For that purpose he produces the example of king Hezekiah, who brake in pieces the brazen serpent, which God had commanded to be erected. But the pope deals quite contrary to his own laws and decrees; for now he will have that truth must and shall give place to his innumerable and apparent errors. And indeed it is a grievous case, that youth have not seen such errors, or comprehended them; they think that the gospel has always been the same as now it is. If we had held God's Word in due honour and reverence, then such abominable errors and idolatries would never have risen or crept in among us.

### 496

Through concord small things and wealth increase, as the heathen said; but dissension is dangerous and hurtful, especially in schools, professions, high arts, and their professors, wherein the one ought to reach the hand to the other, kissing and embracing. But when we bite one another, then let us take heed lest we be swallowed up together. Therefore let us pray and strive; for the word of faith, and the prayers of the just, are the most powerful weapons; moreover, God himself sends his holy angels around them that fear him. We ought valiantly to fight, for we are under a Lord of hosts, and a prince of war; therefore with one hand we must build, and in the other hand take the sword – that is, we must both teach and resist.

It is now time to watch, for we are the mark they shoot at; our adversaries intend to make a confederacy with the Turk; they aim at us, but we must venture it, for antichrist will war and get the victory against the saints of God. We stand outwardly in the greatest danger, by reason of treachery and treason; the papists endeavour with money to corrupt our captains and officers. An ass laden with money may do anything, as Tacitus writes of us Germans; they have been taught to take money; there is neither fidelity nor truth on earth.

### 497

The papists have a fair and glittering external worship; they boast much of God's Word, of faith, of Christ, of the sacraments, of love, of hope, etc., but they utterly deny the power and virtue of all these; nay, teach that which is quite contrary thereunto. Therefore St. Paul very well says: 'They deny the power of godliness.' He does not say they deny godliness, but they deny the power, strength, and virtue thereof, by false and superstitious doctrine.

### 498

Luther, coming from Rome, showed the prince elector of Saxony a picture he had brought with him, whereon was painted how the pope had fooled the whole world with his superstitions and idolatries. There was the little ship of the church, as they term it, almost filled with friars, monks, and priests, casting lines out of the ship to those that were in the sea; the pope, with the cardinals and bishops, sat behind, in the end of the ship, overshadowed and covered by the Holy Ghost, who was looking up towards heaven, and through whom those swimming in the sea, in great danger of their lives, were hoisted up into the ship and saved.

These and like fooleries we then believed as articles of faith. The papists blind people by pretending that they go through much tribulation in this world; whereas they wallow in all the glory, pleasures, and delights of the earth. But let them be assured, that ere many years the power of their abominable blasphemies, idolatries, and damnable religion, will be broken, if not destroyed.

And on the contrary, we, who for the sake of confessing God's holy Word in truth, are terrified, banished, imprisoned, and slain here on earth by that man of sin, and God's enemy, the antichrist pope of Rome, at the last day, with unspeakable comfort, shall take possession of the fruits of our assured hopes – namely, everlasting consolation, joy, and salvation.

### 499

The pope places his cardinals in all kingdoms – peevish milk-sops, effeminate and unlearned blockheads, who lie lolling in king's courts, among the ladies and women. The pope has invaded all countries with these and his bishops. Germany is taken captive by popish bishops, for I can count above forty bishoprics, besides abbeys and cathedrals, which are richer than the bishoprics. Now, there are in Germany but eight and twenty principalities, so that the popish bishops are far more rich and powerful than the princes of the empire.

## 500

The devil begat darkness; darkness begat ignorance; ignorance begat error and his brethren; error begat free-will and presumption; free-will begat merit; merit begat forgetfulness of God; forgetfulness begat transgression; transgression begat superstition; superstition begat satisfaction; satisfaction begat the mass-offering; the mass-offering begat the priest; the priest begat unbelief; unbelief begat king hypocrisy; hypocrisy begat traffic in offerings for gain; traffic in offerings for gain begat purgatory; purgatory begat the annual solemn vigils; the annual vigils begat church-livings; church-livings begat avarice; avarice begat swelling superfluity; swelling superfluity begat fulness; fulness begat rage; rage begat licence; licence begat empire and domination; domination begat pomp; pomp begat ambition; ambition begat simony; simony begat the pope and his brethren, about the time of the Babylonish captivity.

After the Babylonish captivity, the pope begat the mystery of iniquity; the mystery of iniquity begat sophistical theology; sophistical theology begat rejecting of the Holy Scripture; rejecting of the Holy Scripture begat tyranny; tyranny begat slaughtering of the saints; slaughtering of the saints begat contemning of God; contemning of God begat dispensation; dispensation begat wilful sin; wilful sin begat abomination; abomination begat desolation; desolation begat doubt; doubt begat searching out the grounds of truth, and out of this, the desolator, pope, or antichrist, is revealed.

St. Paul complained and said: 'The time will come when they will not endure sound doctrine'; and elsewhere: 'This know also, that in the last days perilous times shall come: for men shall be lovers of themselves,' etc.

When first I read these sentences, I did not look towards Rome, but thought they had been spoken of the Jews and Turks.

## 501

In the Old Testament, the year Jubilee was observed every fiftieth year; the pope imitated this with the golden gate; which brought gain and money to the popes; so they afterwards changed the fiftieth year into the five and twentieth, then to the fifteenth, and then to the seventh year, so they might frequently get money.

## 502

If I had not been a doctor, Satan had made me work enough to do. It was no slight and easy matter for one to alter the whole religion of Popedom, so deeply rooted. But I promised and swore in baptism, that I would hold by Christ and his word, that I would steadfastly believe in him, and utterly renounce the devil and all his lies. And, indeed, the oath I took in baptism is renewed in all my tribulations; without this I could not have subsisted or resisted my troubles, but they had overwhelmed and made an end of me. I would willingly have shown obedience to the pope and bishops in any reasonable particular; but they would have, short and round, that I should deny Christ, and make God a liar, and say: the gospel is heresy.

### 503

In the New Testament, and in the Christian church, God's worship consists in the plain simple truth; no superstitions or worshipping of idols are there to be found; hence St. John, in his Epistle, writes: There are three that bear witness in earth:

1. The spirit; that is, the function of preaching.
2. Water; that is, baptism.
3. Blood; that is, the supper of the Lord.

But the pope and his seducing spirits contemn these witnesses, and have invented innumerable worshippings, ceremonies, and offerings; and instituted them of their own election, without God's Words, so that through errors the church is excluded from her bridegroom's ordinances.

### 504

Ceremonies are only middle things, instituted for the end of policy; namely to observe rules, and that everything in the church may proceed decently and in order, as the law of nature also teaches, and as we behold in the creating of all creatures.

### 505

It is of the devil himself that the papists hold the final cause of instituting human traditions to be, that thereby God is truly worshipped and served, and that, therefore, they are necessary to salvation. 'Tis most monstrous; for though such human traditions were the best and most esteemed works of Christianity, which they are not, yet to say they are necessary to salvation, or give God satisfaction for our sins, and so purchase grace, spoils all, and makes the best of works to be utterly rejected of God.

The like superstition and abomination lay in those works which they call *opera supererogationis,* that is, works which they had in overplus, and more than they, the friars, priests, and nuns themselves had need of, so sold them to the laity.

## 506

If we could but preserve the catechism, and set up schools for posterity, we had lived well; as for ceremonies, they might go whither they would, for they are the touch-powder, giving occasion to superstition; people thinking they are necessary to salvation and that their being omitted is sin.

## 507

The popish fasting is right murder, whereby many people have been destroyed, observing the fasts strictly, and, chiefly, by eating one sort of food, so that nature's strength thereby is wholly weakened.

For this cause Gerson was constrained at Paris to write a book of 'Comfort for troubled and perplexed Consciences', to the end they might neither be discouraged nor despair. For those that fast, spoil themselves and weaken their strength. Such darkness has been in Popedom, where they neither taught, nor intended to teach, the ten commandments, the creed, and the Lord's prayer.

## 508

There are two sorts of holiness, substantial and accidental; St. Francis was once substantially holy by his faith in Jesus Christ, but afterwards he became infatuated with the accidental holiness of the hood, an accessory wholly foreign to holiness. Ah, God! 'tis not the putting on this or that article of dress, that will give us a pass to heaven!

## 509

Luther received tidings from Denmark, that the king and the duke of Holstein had ordered a fast, to be observed three days, — as an admonition to the people to prayer and peace; whereupon he said: it is a very upright and good course; I wish all other kings and princes did the like; 'tis the most external humiliation, and when we add thereunto the inward humility of the heart, 'tis exceeding good.

### 510

Popedom stands upon the mass two manner of ways; first, spiritually, holding that the mass is a worshipping of God; secondly, corporally, being maintained and preserved, not by divine power, but by human and temporal princes.

The mass is the papist's rock, both spiritually and carnally; and now it is fallen in the spirit, and in due time God will also destroy it in the flesh.

### 511

The private mass, since the time of Gregory, now above eight hundred years, has deceived many saints. John Huss was taken captive by that deceitful painted stuff. I much wonder how God drew me out of this idolatry. Three years since there was here a man who certified me that in Asia no private mass was celebrated. I am assured that in Armenia, Ethiopia, India, and in the countries towards the east, there are many Christians to this day, who never heard mass.

The mass in France was not so highly esteemed as it has been in Germany; for when in the morning one had heard mass, he cared for no more, how many soever were held, but passed by them without showing any particular regard. When the French king heard mass, he always gave a French crown to the priest, which he laid upon a book that was brought and held before him.

### 512

The canon of the mass is pieced and patched up out of many lies. The Greeks have it not. When I was in Italy, I saw that they at Milan had no such canon, and when I offered to celebrate mass there, they said to me: *Nos sumus Ambrosiani.* They told me that in former time they had been at debate among themselves, whether they should receive into their church the book of Ambrose, or that of Gregory, and to that end prayed God by some miracle to decide for them. At night, they laid both the books in the church; in the morning, they found the book of Ambrose altogether whole and unmoved, upon the high altar, but the book of Gregory was torn all in pieces, scattered up and down the church. The same they construed thus: Ambrose should remain at Milan upon the alter, Gregory be scattered through the whole world.

### 513

The ornaments and gay apparel used in Popedom, in celebrating mass, and other ceremonies, were partly taken out from Moses, and partly from the heathen. For as the priests saw that the public shows and plays, held in the market places, drew away the people, who took delight therein, they were moved to institute shows and plays in the churches, so as to draw children and unlearned people to church. Such are the toys they exhibit on Easter-eve, very pleasing and acceptable, not for devotion's sake, but to delight the foolish fancy.

### 514

When I was a young friar at Erfurt, and had to go out into the villages for puddings and cheeses, I once came to a little town where I held mass. Now, when I had put on my vestments and trimmings, and approached the altar, the clerk or sexton of the church began merrily to strike upon the lute the *Kirie eleison,* whereat I, who scarcely could forbear laughing, was constrained to direct and tune my *Gloria in excelsis,* according to his *Kirie eleison.*

### 515

The Jews held their offerings *ex opere operato;* when a work was accomplished only externally, they thought that thereby sins were reconciled and satisfied, whereas all their offerings and sacrifices ought to have been signs of thanksgiving.

Even so is it likewise with the papists' error of the mass, whereby the mass-priest, an unlearned ass, affects to give full satisfaction for sins.

### 516

The mass ought to be abolished, chiefly for two reasons. First, because natural understanding judges that it is a dishonest kind of trading and gain to celebrate mass for twopence, or to sell it for three-half-pence. Secondly, because, according to the spirit, it is judged to be an abominable idolatry, making Christ to have died in vain, seeing they pretend thereby to make full satisfaction for sins with mere works. These two abuses are altogether inexcusable, yet all universities have conspired and vowed to maintain the mass. We can never agree with the papists as to this point. For if they should suffer the mass to be abolished, they must make full restitution of that which, with their lies and deceit, they have got and stolen from emperors, kings, princes, nobility, and other people.

### 517

Many Italians are well inclined to the Protestant religion, and would have been well satisfied therewith had I not touched the mass, to reject which they hold to be an abominable heresy. They depend thereon so surely, that they think he who has heard mass is free from all danger, and cannot sin, whatsoever he take in hand, and that no evil can befall him; hence it comes to pass, that after hearing mass, many sins and murders are committed. When I was at Rome, there was one who had sought his enemy two whole years, to be revenged upon him, but had not been able to find him out; at last, he spied him in the church, where he himself had heard mass, having just risen from before the altar; he forthwith stepped to him, stabbed him to death, and fled. My book on the abolition of the mass is written with much vehemence against the blasphemers, but it is not for those who are not entering upon the true path, who have just become born to the new life; nor should these be offended thereat; if, twenty years ago, any one had presumed to take from me the mass, he must have tugged hard, before he got it from me; for my heart hung thereon, and I adored it; now, God be praised, I am of another mind, and am fully assured, that the foundation and ground of the mass, and of Popedom, is nothing but imposture, extortion, and idolatry.

## 518

*Missa,* the mass, comes of the Hebrew word *Maosim,* that is, a collecting of alms, a stipend, or a tax for the sake of priests, or other people. The mass has devoured infinite sums of money.

# Of Purgatory

—※—

### 519

AUGUSTINE, Ambrose, and Jerome held nothing at all of purgatory. Gregory, being in the night-time deceived by vision, taught something of purgatory, whereas God openly commanded that we should search out and inquire nothing of spirits, but of Moses and the prophets.

Therefore we must not admit Gregory's opinion on this point; the day of the Lord will show and declare the same when it will be revealed by fire.

This sentence, 'And their works do follow them,' must not be understood of purgatory, but of the doctrine of good works, or of godly and true Christians, and of heretics. Arius the heretic, has had his judgment; the fire of faith has declared it. For the last day will discover and declare all things.

God has, in his word, laid before us two ways; one which by faith leads to salvation, – the other, by unbelief, to damnation.

As for purgatory, no place in Scripture makes mention thereof, neither must we any way allow it; for it darkens and undervalues the grace, benefits, and merits of our blessed, sweet Saviour Christ Jesus.

The bounds of purgatory extend not beyond this world; for here in this life the upright, good, and godly Christians are well and soundly scoured and purged.

# Of Councils

‒‒‒≈‒‒‒

### 520

THE pope styles himself a bishop of the catholic church, which title he never dared to take upon him before; for at the time when the council of Nicea was held, then there was no pope at all. The church at that time was divided into three parts; first, of Ethiopia; second, of Syria, to which Antioch belonged; third, of Rome, with her appertaining sects. In this manner they swarmed soon after the apostles' time, and instituted three sorts of councils; first, a general; second, a provincial; third, an episcopal, a council being to be held in every bishopric.

### 521

Since the time of the apostles, threescore general and provincial councils have been held, among which only four are especially worthy of praise; two, those of Nicea and Constantinople, maintained and defended the Trinity and the godhead of Christ; the other two, those of Ephesus and Chalcedon, maintained Christ's humanity. In the council of Nicea nothing is written or mentioned of any pope or bishop of Rome, as being there; only one bishop from the west, Ozius, bishop of Cordova, was present. The other bishops came from the churches in the east, Greece, Asia Minor, Egypt, Africa, etc.

Ah, Lord God! what are councils and conventions, but grasping and vanity, wherein men dispute about titles, honours, precedence, and other fopperies?

Let us consider what has been done by these councils in three hundred years; nothing but what concerns externals and ceremonies; nothing at all touching true divine doctrine, the upright worshipping of God, or faith.

### 522

In January, 1539, a book was sent to Luther, intituled, *Liber Conciliorum,* a large and carefully arranged collection. After reading it he said: this book will maintain and defend the pope, whereas in his own decrees, innumerable canons are against him and this book. And besides, councils have no power to make and ordain laws and ordinances in the church, what is to be taught and to be believed, or concerning good works; for all this has been already taught and confirmed. Councils have power to make ordinances only concerning external things, customs, and ceremonies; and this no further than as concerns persons, places, and times. When these cease, such ordinances also cease.

The Romish laws are now dead and gone, by reason Rome is dead and gone: it is now another place. In like manner; the decrees and ordinances of councils are now no longer valid, because their days have gone by. As St. Paul says: 'Why, as though living in the world, are ye subject to ordinances? (touch not, taste not, handle not, which all are to perish with the using) after the commandments of men? which things have indeed a show of wisdom in will-worship and humility, and neglecting of the body, not in any honour to the satisfying of the flesh.'

Did not decrees and statutes, like persons, times, and places, change and cease, the doctrine would of a mortal creature make an immortal; and, indeed, they name the pope an earthly god, fitly enough, for all his laws, decrees, and ordinances, savour of terrestrial, not of celestial things.

### 523

When God's Word is by the Fathers expounded, construed, and glossed, then, in my judgment, it is even as when one strains milk through a coal-sack, which must needs spoil and make the milk black; God's Word of itself is pure, clean, bright, and clear; but, through the doctrines, books, and writings of the Fathers, it is darkened, falsified, and spoiled.

### 524

The council of Nicea, held after the apostles' time, was the very best and purest; but, by and by, in the time of the emperor Constantine, it was weakened by the Arians; for at that time, out of dissembling hearts, they craftily subscribed that they concurred in one opinion with the true and upright catholic teachers, which in truth was not so; whereof ensued a great dissension.

### 525

The papists go craftily about endeavouring to suppress us; they intend such a reformation should be made, as will in no way suit us to adopt; if, for the sake of outward peace, we enter into accord with the papists, we should make the pure doctrine of our church suspected. Oh no; no such agreements for me. If the emperor Charles would appoint a national council, then there were some hope; but he will not go on: the papists will not yield, but will sit alone therein, and have full power to determine and conclude. By my advice, if it so fall out, we will all arise and leave them sitting alone; for the pope shall have no authority or power over us and our doctrine. We need no council for the sake of God's Word, for that is sure enough. We can well appoint and order fastings and such like things without a council, and without ensnaring the consciences, which shall be at liberty, and not troubled or tied therewith. Christ did not institute and command fastings with laws, but says: 'When the bridegroom shall be taken from them, then they shall fast.' Also he says: 'Go, sell all that thou hast.' Fasting will follow thereupon.

The Italians are so stiff-necked and proud, they will not be reformed by the Germans, no, not though they be convinced with the clear truth of God's Word. I have often thought with myself; how we might by a council, in some measure, come to an agreement between us, but I see no means can be found. For if the pope should acknowledge he had failed but in the least article, and should admit, in a council, his gross errors, then he would lose his authority and power; for he brags that he is the church's head, to whom all the members must yield obedience; hence the complaint in the council at Constance, and hence that council's setting itself over and above the pope, and deposing him. If the papists should give place to us, and yield in the least article, then the hoops in the garland were quite broken asunder, and all the world would cry out: Has it not been constantly affirmed that the pope is the head of the church and cannot err? How then comes he now to acknowledge his errors?

### 526

In a council ought to be two manner of voices; the first, the *vox consultiva vel deliberativa,* that is, when they consult and discourse concerning affairs open to kings, princes, and doctors, for each one to deliver his opinion. The second they call *decisiva vox,* a deciding voice, when they conclude what is to be believed and done; which voice the pope and his cardinals have usurped; for they decide and conclude what they will and please.

## 527

A council should be a purgatory, to purge, cleanse, and reform the church; and when new errors and heresies break and press in, to confirm, strengthen, and preserve pure doctrine, and resist, hinder, and quench new fires, and condemn false doctrine. But the pope would have a council to be one assembly, wherein he daily might make new decrees, orders and statutes, touching good works.

## 528

The imperial diet held at Augsburg, 1530, is worthy of all praise; for then and thence came the gospel among the people in other countries, contrary to the will and expectation both of emperor and pope. God appointed the imperial diet at Augsburg, to the end the gospel should be spread further abroad and planted. They overclimbed themselves at Augsburg, for the papists openly approved there of our doctrine. Before that diet was held, the papists had made the emperor believe, that our doctrine was altogether frivolous; and that when he came to the diet, he should see them put us all to silence, so that none of us should be able to speak a word in the defence of our religion; but it fell out far otherwise; for we openly and freely confessed the gospel before the emperor and the whole empire, and confounded our adversaries in the highest degree. The emperor discriminated understandingly and discreetly, and carried himself princely in this cause of religion; he found us far otherwise than the papists had informed him; and that we were not ungodly people, leading most wicked and detestable lives, and teaching against the first and second tables of the ten commandments of God. For this cause the emperor sent our confession and apology to all the universities; his council also delivered their opinions, and said: 'If the doctrines of these men be against the holy Christian faith, then his imperial majesty should suppress it with all his power. But if it be only against ceremonies and abuses, as it appears to be, then it should be referred to the consideration and judgment of learned people, or good and wise counsel.'

O! God's word is powerful; the more it is persecuted, the more and further it spreads itself abroad. I would fain the papist confutation might appear to the world; for I would set upon that old torn and tattered skin, and so baste it, that the stitches thereof should fly about; but they shun the light.

This time twelvemonth no man would have given a farthing for the protestants, so sure the ungodly papists were of us. For when my most gracious lord and master, the prince elector of Saxony, came before other princes to the diet, the papists marvelled much thereat, for they verily believed be would not have appeared, because, as they imagined, his cause was too bad and foul to be brought before the light. But what fell out? even this, that in their greatest security they were overwhelmed with the utmost fear and affright, because the prince elector, like an upright prince, appeared so early at Augsburg. The popish princes swiftly posted away to Innsbruck, where they held serious council with prince George, and the marquis of Baden, all of them wondering what the prince elector's so early approach to the diet should mean, and the emperor himself was astonished, and doubted whether he could come and go in safety; whereupon the princes were constrained to promise that they would stand, body, goods, and blood by the emperor, one offering to maintain 6000 horse, another so many thousands of foot soldiers, etc., to the end his majesty might be the better secured. Then was a wonder among wonders to be seen, in that God struck with fear and cowardliness the enemies of the truth. And although at that time the prince elector of Saxony was alone, and but only the hundredth sheep, the others being ninety and nine, yet it so fell out, that they all trembled and were afraid. When they came to the point, and began to take the business in hand, there appeared but a very small heap that stood by God's Word. But, that small heap, brought with us a strong and mighty King, a King above all emperors and kings, namely, Christ Jesus, the powerful Word of God. Then all the papists cried out, and said: Oh, it is insufferable, that so small and mean a heap should set themselves against the imperial power. But the Lord of Hosts frustrates the councils of princes. Pilate had power to put our blessed Saviour to death, but willingly he would not. Annas and Caiaphas willingly would have done it, but could not.

The emperor, for his own part, is good and honest; but the popish bishops and cardinals are undoubted knaves. And forasmuch as the emperor now refuses to bathe his hands in innocent blood, the frantic princes bestir themselves, and scorn and contemn the good emperor in the highest degree. The pope also for anger is ready to burst in pieces, because the diet should be dissolved without shedding of blood; therefore he sends the sword to the duke of Bavaria, intending to take the crown from the emperor's head, and set it upon the head of Bavaria; but he shall not accomplish it. In this manner ordered God the business, that kings, princes, yea, and the pope himself, fell from the emperor, and we joined him, which was a great wonder of God's providence, in that he whom the devil intended to use against us, God takes, and uses for us. O wonder above all wonders!

# OF THE FATHERS OF THE CHURCH

---

### 529

I WILL not presume to criticise too closely the writings of the Fathers, seeing they are received of the church, and have great applause, for then I should be held an apostate; but whoso reads Chrysostom, will find he digresses from the chief points, and proceeds to other matters, saying nothing, or very little, of that which pertains to the business. When I was expounding the Epistle to the Hebrews, and turned to what Chrysostom had written thereupon, I found nothing to the purpose; yet I believe that he at that time, as being the chief rhetorician, had many hearers, though he taught without profit; for the chief office of a preacher is to teach uprightly, and diligently to look to the chief points and grounds whereon he stands, and so instruct and teach the hearers, that they understand aright, and may be able to say: this is well taught. When this is done, he may avail himself of rhetoric to adorn his subject and admonish the people.

### 530

Behold what great darkness is in the books of the Fathers concerning faith; yet if the article of justification be darkened, it is impossible to smother the grossest errors of mankind. St. Jerome, indeed, wrote upon Matthew, upon the Epistles to Galatians and Titus; but, alas! very coldly. Ambrose wrote six books upon the first book of Moses, but they are very poor. Augustine wrote nothing to the purpose concerning faith; for he was first roused up and made a man by the Pelagians, in striving against them. I can find no exposition upon the Epistles to the Romans and Galatians, wherein anything is taught pure and aright. O what a happy time have we now, in regard to the purity of the doctrine; but alas! we little esteem it. After the Fathers came the pope, and with his mischievous traditions and human ordinances, like a breaking water-cloud and deluge, overflowed the church, snared consciences, touching eating of meat, friars' hoods, masses, etc., so that daily he brought abominable errors into the church of Christ; and to serve his own turn, took hold on St. Augustine's sentence, where he says, *Evangelio non crederem,* etc. The asses could not see what occasioned Augustine to utter that sentence, whereas he spoke it against the Manicheans, as much as to say: I believe you not, for ye are damned heretics, but I believe and hold with the church, the spouse of Christ, which cannot err.

### 531

Epiphanius compiled a history of the church long before Jerome; his writings are good and profitable, and, if separated from dissentious argument, worth printing.

### 532

I much like the hymns and spiritual songs of Prudentius; he was the best of the Christian poets; if he had lived in the time of Virgil, he would have been extolled above Horace. I wish the verses of Prudentius were read in schools, but schools are now become heathenish, and the Holy Scripture is banished from them, and sophisticated through philosophy.

### 533

We must read the Fathers cautiously, and lay them in the gold balance, for they often stumbled and went astray, and mingled in their books many monkish things. Augustine had more work and labour to wind himself out of the Fathers' writings, than he had with the heretics. Gregory expounds the five pounds mentioned in the gospel, which the husbandman gave to his servants to put to use, to be the five senses, which the beasts also possess. The two pounds, he construes to be the reason and understanding.

### 534

The more I read the books of the Fathers, the more I find myself offended; for they were but men, and, to speak the truth, with all their repute and authority, undervalued the books and writings of the sacred apostles of Christ. The papists were not ashamed to say, What is the Scripture? We must read the holy fathers and teachers, for they drew and sucked the honey out of the Scripture. As if God's Word were to be understood and conceived by none but by themselves, whereas the heavenly Father says: 'Him shall ye hear,' who in the gospel taught most plainly in parables and similitudes.

### 535

Augustine was the ablest and purest of all the doctors, but he could not of himself bring back things to their original condition, and he often complains that the bishops, with their traditions and ordinances, troubled the church more than did the Jews with their laws.

### 536

Faithful Christians should heed only the embassy of our blessed Saviour Christ, and what he says. All they who alter and construe the gospel through human authority, power, and repute, act very unchristianlike and against God. No temporal potentate allows his ambassador to exceed his instructions, not in one word; yet we, in this celestial and divine embassage and legation, will be so presumptuous as to add and diminish to and from our heavenly instructions, according to our own vain conceits and self-will.

### 537

I am persuaded that if at this time, St. Peter, in person, should preach all the articles of Holy Scripture, and only deny the pope's authority, power, and primacy, and say, that the pope is not the head of all Christendom, they would cause him to be hanged. Yea, if Christ himself were again on earth, and should preach, without all doubt the pope would crucify him again. Therefore let us expect the same treatment; but better is it to build upon Christ, than upon the pope. If, from my heart, I did not believe that after this life there were another, then I would sing another song, and lay the burthen on another's neck.

### 538

Lyra's Commentaries upon the Bible are worthy of all praise. I will order them diligently to be read, for they are exceeding good, especially on the historical part of the Old Testament. Lyra is very profitable to him that is well versed in the New Testament. The commentaries of Paulus, and Simigerus are very cold; they may well be omitted and left out, if Lyra should be reprinted.

### 539

Jerome should not be numbered among the teachers of the church, for he was a heretic; yet I believe that he is saved through faith in Christ. He speaks not of Christ, but merely carries his name in his mouth.

### 540

The Terminists, among whom I was, are sectaries in the high schools; they oppose the Thomists, the Scotists, and the Albertists; they are also called Occamists, from Occam, their founder. They are of the newest sect, and are now strongest in Paris.

The question with them was, whether the word *humanitas* means a general humanity, residing in every human creature, as Thomas and others hold. The Occamists and Terminists say: It is not in general; but it is spoken in particular of every human creature; as a picture of a human creature signifies every human creature.

They are called Terminists, because they speak of a thing in its own proper words, and do not apply them after a strange sort. With a carpenter we must speak in his terms, and with such words as are used in his craft, as a chisel, an axe. Even so we must let the words of Christ remain, and speak of the sacraments in *suis terminis,* with such words as Christ used and spake; as 'Do this,' must not be turned into 'Offer this', and the word *corpus* must not signify both kinds, as the papists tear and torment the words, and wilfully wrest them against the clear text.

### 541

His master of sentences, Peter Lombard, was a very diligent man, and of a high understanding; he wrote many excellent things. If he had wholly given himself to the Holy Scriptures, he had been indeed a great and a leading doctor of the church: but he introduced into his books unprofitable questions, sophisticating and mingling all together. The school divines were fine and delicate wits, but they lived not in such times as we. They got so far that they taught mankind were not complete, pure, or sound, but wounded in part, yet they said people by their own power, without grace, could fulfil the law; though when they had obtained grace, they were able more easily to accomplish the law, of their own proper power.

Such and the like horrible things they taught; but they neither saw nor felt Adam's fall, nor that the law of God is a spiritual law, requiring a complete and full obedience inwardly and outwardly, both in body and soul.

### 542

Gabriel Biel wrote a book upon the canon in the mass, which at that time I held for the best; my heart bled when I read it. I still keep those books which tormented me. Scotus wrote very well upon the *Magister sententiarum,* and diligently essayed to teach upon those matters. Occam was an able and sensible man.

# Of the Patriarchs and Prophets

⟡

## 543

DAVID's fall was very offensive, for the holy man fell into adultery, murder, and despising of God. He was afterwards visited and punished by God in such sort, that the whole nation forsook him. His counsellors — yea, his best beloved son, conspired and made a league against him, who before had such high fortune, and was held in such esteem.

On account of these offences, the ungodly, doubtless, boasted, and said: 'Where is the king now? where is now his God? what has become of his good fortune and prosperity?' For no doubt there were many kings more powerful than David; as the king of the Moabites, whom Isaiah calls a three-yeared cow; that is, strong, powerful, and fat.

It has always been so in the world — that it has gone evil with the godly, and well with the ungodly; of this complaint is made in many Psalms. We see at this day, that the popish bishops and ungodly princes live in great honour, wealth, and power, while good and God-fearing people are in poverty, disgrace, and trouble.

The Greek tragedies are not to be compared with the history of David.

## 544

All kings, princes, rulers, and ministers sin of necessity, and therefore have special need of the remission of sins. I am persuaded that Ahab was saved, inasmuch as God said to the prophet: 'Seest thou not how Ahab boweth himself before me?' For to whom God affords speech, that is, his word and promise, with him it stands well. Therefore, doubtless, he was saved, notwithstanding the Scriptures witness against him, even to his death. He believed the promise of the Messiah, and so at his death got hold of the forgiveness of sins. In like manner I am persuaded also of all those of whom the Scripture says: 'And he slept with his fathers,' that they are all in heaven. For this word, slept, shows some good in the Scriptures. But of whom it is written: They were made away and slain by the enemies or were devoured and torn in pieces by wild beasts, I am persuaded they are lost and damned.

### 545

Although God charged David to build the temple, he could not perform it, because he had shed much blood, and had carried the sword; not that he did wrong therein, but that he could not be the figure or type of Christ, who must have a peaceable kingdom, without shedding of blood. But Solomon was to accomplish it, who is called peaceable, through which Christ's kingdom was signified.

### 546

It is with us, as it was in the time of Judas Maccabæus, who defended his people, and yet was not able to suppress the enemies who possessed the government; while his own people were unthankful, and wrought him great mischief; these two oppressions make one weary.

The legends of the patriarchs far excelled the holiness of all the saints; for they went on in simple obedience towards God, in the works of their vocation. They performed such things as came to their hand, according to God's command, without respect; therefore Sara, Abraham's wife, excels all other women.

### 547

Philip Melancthon demanded of Luther: how it was, that though David was instituted and ordained a king immediately of God, yet he had many tribulations and plagues, as his psalms show? Luther said: David was not acquainted with many good days: he was plagued by the ungodly and false teachers, he saw that his people banded against him, he endured and suffered many insurrections and tumults, which taught him his lesson to pray. When he was without tribulation, he grew giddy-headed and secure, as we see in his adultery, and his murder of Uriah.

Ah, Lord God! how is it thou sufferest such great people to fall? This David had six wives, who doubtless were wise and understanding women; as was the wise Abigail; if they were all such, he was furnished with surpassing wives. Moreover, he had ten concubines; yet, notwithstanding, he was an adulterer.

### 548

Job had many tribulations; he was also plagued of his own friends, who fiercely assaulted him. The text says, that his friends fell upon him, and were full of wrath against him; they tormented him thoroughly, but he held his peace, suffered them to talk their talk, as if he should say, you know not what you prate about. Job is an example of God's goodness and mercy; for how upright and holy soever he was, yet he sorely fell into temptation; but he was not forsaken, he was again delivered and redeemed through God's grace and mercy.

### 549

Melancthon discoursing with Luther touching the prophets, who continually boast thus: 'Thus saith the Lord,' asked whether God in person spoke with them or no. Luther replied: They were very holy, spiritual people, who seriously contemplated upon holy and divine things; therefore God spake with them in their consciences, which the prophets held as sure and certain revelations.

We read in the books of the Jews that Isaiah was slain by king Ahaz, because be said: 'I saw the Lord sitting upon a throne,' etc. Doubtless, Ahaz said unto him: Thou wretch! how darest thou presume to say, 'Thou hast seen the Lord?' whereas God said to Moses, 'Shall a man see me, and live?' Thou art an insane heretic; thou blasphemest God; thou art worthy of death; take him away. And many think it quite just that Isaiah was slain for this, not enduring that any man should say he had done or seen greater things than Moses.

### 550

The history of Elijah is awful, and almost incredible. It was a fierce anger indeed, that so holy a man should pray it might not rain; but he saw that the teachers were slain, and that good and God-fearing people were hunted down, and persecuted. Therefore he prayed against those upon whom, with words and preaching, he could not prevail.

## 551

The majesty of the prophet Jonah is surpassing. He has but four chapters, and yet he moved therewith the whole kingdom, so that in his weakness, he was justly a figure and a sign of the Lord Christ. Indeed, it is surprising, that Christ should recur to this but in four words. Moses likewise, in few words describes the creation, the history of Abraham, and other great mysteries; but he spends much time in describing the tent, the external sacrifices, the kidneys and so on; the reason is, he saw that the world greatly esteemed outward things, which they beheld with their carnal eyes, but that which was spiritual, they soon forgot.

The history of the prophet Jonah is almost incredible, sounding more strange than any poet's fable; if it were not in the Bible, I should take it for a lie; for consider, how for the space of three days he was in the great belly of the whale, whereas in three hours he might have been digested and changed into the nature, flesh and blood of that monster; may not this be said to live in the midst of death? In comparison of this miracle, the wonderful passage through the Red Sea was nothing.

But what appears more strange is, that after he was delivered, he began to be angry, and to expostulate with the gracious God, touching a small matter not worth a straw. It is a great mystery. I am ashamed of my exposition upon this prophet, in that I so weakly touch the main point of this wonderful miracle.

## 552

The harsh arid sharp words of the prophets go to the heart, yet when they say: 'Jerusalem shall fall, and be destroyed,' the Jews held such preaching merely heretical, and would not endure it.

Even so say I: the Romish church shall fall, and be destroyed; but the papists will neither believe nor endure it; it is impossible, say they, for it is written in the article: 'I believe in the holy Christian church.' Many kings were destroyed before Jerusalem, as Sennacherib, etc.; when the prophet Jeremiah said: 'Jerusalem shall be destroyed,' which he spake through the Holy Ghost, so it fell out.

If the pope could bring against me only one such argument as the Jews had against Jeremiah and other prophets, it were not possible for me to subsist. But the pope disputes with me, not according to justice and equity, but with the sword and his power. He uses no written law, but club law. If I had no other argument against the pope than *de facto,* I would instantly hang myself; but my dispute is *jus.*

### 553

An upright Christian is like unto Jonah, who was cast into the sea, that is, into hell. He beheld the mouth of the monster gaping to devour him, and lay three days in its dark belly, without consuming. This history should be unto us one of the greatest comforts, and a manifest sign of the resurrection from the dead.

In such sort does God humble those that are his. But afterwards, Jonah went too far; he presumed to command God Almighty, and became a great man-slayer and a murderer, for he desired that a great city and many people should be utterly destroyed, though God chose to spare them. This was a strange saint.

### 554

To translate the prophets well from the Hebrew tongue, is a precious, great, and glorious work; no man before me well attained thereunto, and to me it is a hard task; let me be once clear from it, it shall rest.

### 555

It is easy to be conceived, that David dealt uprightly, and repentingly, in not rejecting Bathsheba, Uriah's wife, but marrying her. Forasmuch as he had shamed her, it was fitting for him to restore her to honour. God was also pleased with that conjunction; yet, for a punishment of the adultery, God caused the son, begotten in it, soon to die.

### 556

No man, since the apostles' time, has rightly understood the legend of Abraham. The apostles themselves did not sufficiently extol or explain Abraham's faith, according to its worth and greatness. I much marvel that Moses so slightly remembers him.

### 557

Job at one time lost ten children and all his cattle; he was punished in body and in goods, yet it was nothing in comparison of David's troubles, for though David had the promise which could neither fail nor deceive – namely, where God says: 'Thou shalt be king,' God thoroughly powdered and peppered his kingdom for his tooth; no miserable man ever surpassed David.

### 558

Adam had more children than the three that are mentioned in the Bible. The reason why particular mention is made of Seth, is the genealogy of our Lord

Christ, who was descended from that patriarch. Adam, doubtless, had many sons and daughters, full two hundred, I am persuaded, for he lived to a great, great age, nine hundred and thirty years. It is likely that Cain was born thirty years after the fall of his parents, as they were then comforted again. I believe they were often comforted by the angels, otherwise it had been impossible for them to enjoy each other's society, by reason they were filled with great sorrows and fears. At the last day, it will be known that Eve exceeded all women in sorrow and misery. Never came into the world a more miserable woman than Eve; she saw that for her sake we were all to die. Some affirm that Cain was conceived before the promise of the seed that should crush the serpent's head. But I am persuaded that the promise was made not half a day after the fall; for they entered into the garden about noon, and having appetites to eat, she took the apple; then, about two of the clock, according to our account, was the fall.

### 559

The reason that Abraham gave to Hagar, his concubine, and Ishmael, his son, only one flagon of wine, was that she might know she had no right to demand anything of the inheritance, but that what was given her proceeded out of good will, not of any obligation or reason of law, yet that, nevertheless, she might repair again to Abraham, and fetch more.

The text in Genesis says: 'Isaac and Ishmael buried Abraham'; hence it appears that Ishmael was not always with his father, but was nurtured out of the father's goodness and bounty, which was done to this end, that Abraham, intending to lead Christ through the right line, therefore Ishmael was separated like Esau.

### 560

I hold that Jacob was a poor, perplexed man; I would willingly, if I could, frame a Laban out of the rich glutton in the gospel of Luke, and a Jacob out of Lazarus who lay before the gate. I am glad that Rachael sat upon the idols, thereby to spite her father Laban.

### 561

Neither Cicero, nor Virgil, nor Demosthenes, are to be compared with David, in point of eloquence, as we see in the 119th Psalm, which he divides into two and twenty parts, each composed of eight verses, and yet all having but one thought – thy law is good. He had great gifts, and was highly favoured of God. I hold that God suffered him to fall so horribly, lest he should become too haughty and proud.

### 562

Some are of opinion that David acted not well in that, upon his death-bed, he commanded Solomon his son to punish Shimei, who had cursed and thrown dirt at him, in his flight before Absalom. But I say he did well, for the office of a magistrate is to punish the guilty, and wicked malefactors. He had made a vow, indeed, not to punish him, but that was to hold only so long as he lived.

In so strange and confused a government, where no man knew who was cook or who butler, as we used to say, David was often constrained to look through the fingers at many abuses and wrongs. But afterwards, when in Solomon's time, there was peace, then through Solomon he punished. In tumultuous governments, a ruler dares not proceed as in time of peace, yet, at last, it is fitting that evil be punished; and as David says: *Maledixit mihi maledictionem malam.*

### 563

Hezekiah was a very good, and pious king, full of faith, yet he fell. God cannot endure that a human creature should trust and depend upon his own works. No man can enter into heaven, without the remission of sins.

### 564

Elisha dealt uprightly, in permitting the children to be torn in pieces by two bears, for calling him bald-pate, since they mocked not him, but his God. And so as to the jeering and mocking of Elijah: 'Thou man of God,' etc., 'twas just that fire came down from heaven and devoured the mockers.

### 565

Many strange things, according to human sense and reason, are written in the books of the kings; they seem to be slight and simple books, but in the spirit they are of great weight. David endured much; Saul persecuted and plagued him ten whole years; yet David remained constant in faith, and believed that the kingdom pertained unto him. I should have gone my way, and said: Lord! thou hast deceived me; wilt thou make me a king, and sufferest me in this sort to be tormented, persecuted and plagued? But David was like a strong wall. He was also a good and a godly man; he refused to lay hands on the king when he had fit opportunity, for he had God's word, and that made him remain so steadfast; he was sure that God's word and promise never would or could fail him.

Surely Jonathan was an honest man, whom David loved entirely; he marked well that the kingdom belonged to David, therefore he intreated David not to root out him and his. Jonathan also wrought wonders, when he, alone with his armour-bearer, went over the mountain, and slew and destroyed the Philistines; for, doubtless, he said in himself, the Lord that overcomes with many, is able also to overcome with few. His death was a great grief to David. So it often happens, that the good are punished for the sake of the wicked and ungodly. The Son of God himself was not spared.

# Of the Apostles and
# Disciples of Christ

⁓≈⁓

## 566

THE reason why the disciples were afraid when Christ came unto them, the doors being shut, was, that they saw how it lately went with their Lord and Master, and feared it might go even so with them; especially considering that at the same time the Jews intended to act with violence against them. For as yet they scarcely believed that Christ was risen again from the dead, as may be gathered from the two disciples going to Emmaus, who said: We hoped he should have redeemed Israel; as much as to say: Now all our hope is at an end.

## 567

The reason why the papists boast more of St. Peter than of St. Paul is this: St. Paul had the sword, St. Peter the keys, and they esteem more of the keys, to open the coffers, to filch and steal, and to fill their thievish purse, than of the sword. That Caiaphas, Pilate, and St. Peter came to Rome, and appeared before the emperor, is mere fable; the histories touching that point do not accord. Christ died in the reign of Tiberius Caesar, who governed five years after his death. All histories unanimously agree, that St. Peter and St. Paul died under the emperor Nero, whose last year was the five and twentieth year after the death of Christ. But St. Peter was eighteen years at Jerusalem after Christ's death, as the Epistle to the Galatians witnesses; and after that, he was seven years at Antioch. Then, as they fable, he ruled afterwards five-and-twenty years at Rome.

No pope among them all yet ruled five-and-twenty years; and, according to this reckoning, St. Peter was not crucified under Nero. Saint Luke writes, that St. Paul was two whole years at liberty in Rome, and went abroad; he mentions nothing at all of St. Peter. It is a thing not to be believed that St. Peter ever was at Rome.

### 568

Saint John the Evangelist wrote, at first, touching the true nature of faith – that our salvation depends only upon Christ the Son of God and Mary, who purchased it with his bitter passion and death, and through the word is received into the heart by faith, out of his mere mercy and grace. At last he was constrained to write in his epistle also of works, by reason of the wickedness of those that, void of all shame, abused the gospel through indulging the flesh.

# Of Angels

⟆⟆

### 569

AN angel is a spiritual creature created by God without a body, for the service of Christendom and of the church.

### 570

The acknowledgment of angels is needful in the church. Therefore godly preachers should teach them logically. First, they should show what angels are, namely, spiritual creatures without bodies. Secondly, what manner of spirit they are, namely, good spirits and not evil; and here evil spirits must also be spoken of, not created evil by God, but made so by their rebellion against God, and their consequent fall; this hatred began in Paradise, and will continue and remain against Christ and his church to the world's end. Thirdly, they must speak touching their function, which, as the epistle to the Hebrews (1:14) shows, is to present a mirror of humility to godly Christians, in that such pure and perfect creatures as the angels do minister unto us, poor and wretched people, in household and temporal policy, and in religion. They are our true and trusty servants, performing offices and works that one poor miserable mendicant would be ashamed to do for another. In this sort ought we to teach with care, method, and attention, touching the sweet and loving angels. Whoso speaks of them not in the order prescribed by logic, may speak of many irrelevant things, but little or nothing to edification.

### 571

The angels are near to us, to those creatures whom by God's command they are to preserve, to the end we receive no hurt of the devil, though, withal, they behold God's face, and stand before him. Therefore when the devil intends to hurt us, then the loving holy angels resist and drive him away; for the angels have long arms, and although they stand before the face and in the presence of God and his son Christ, yet they are hard by and about us in those affairs, which by God we are commanded to take in hand. The devil is also near and about us, incessantly tracking our steps, in order to deprive us of our lives, our saving health, and salvation. But the holy angels defend us from him, insomuch that he is not able to work us such mischief as willingly he would.

### 572

It were not good for us to know how earnestly the holy angels strive for us against the devil, or how hard a combat it is. If we could see for how many angels one devil makes work, we should be in despair. Therefore the Holy Scriptures refer to them in few words: 'He hath given his angels charge over thee', etc. Also: 'The angel of the Lord encampeth round about those that fear him,' etc. Now, whosoever thou art, that fearest the Lord, be of good courage, take thou no care, neither be faint-hearted, nor make any doubt of the angels' watching and protection; for most certainly they are about thee, and carry thee upon their hands. How or in what manner it is done, take thou no heed. God says it, therefore it is most sure and certain.

### 573

I believe that the angels are all up in arms, are putting on their harness, and girding their swords about them. For the last judgment draws nigh, and the angels prepare themselves for the combat, and to strike down Turk and pope into the bottomless pit.

# Of the Devil and his Works

---

### 574

THE greatest punishment God can inflict on the wicked, is when the church, to chastise them, delivers them over to Satan, who, with God's permission, kills them, or makes them undergo great calamities. Many devils are in woods,, in waters, in wildernesses, and in dark pooly places, ready to hurt and prejudice people; some are also in the thick black clouds, which cause hail, lightnings, and thunderings, and poison the air, the pastures and grounds. When these things happen, then the philosophers and physicians say, it is natural, ascribing it to the planets, and showing I know not what reasons for such misfortunes and plagues as ensue.

### 575

Whoso would see the true picture, shape, or image of the devil, and know how he is qualified and disposed, let him mark well all the commandments of God, one after another, and then let him place before his eyes an offensive, shameless, lying, despairing, ungodly, insolent, and blasphemous man or woman, whose mind and conceptions are directed in every way against God, and who takes delight in doing people hurt and mischief, there thou seest the right devil, carnal and corporal. First, in such a person there is no fear, no love, no faith or confidence in God, but altogether contempt, hatred, unbelief, despair, and blaspheming of God. There thou seest the devil's head, directly opposing the first commandment. Secondly, a believing Christian takes God's name not in vain, but spreads abroad God's Word, calls upon Him from his heart, thanks Him for his benefits, confesses Him. But this picture and child of the devil does quite the contrary; he holds God's Word for a fable, fearfully abuses God's name, blasphemes God, and withal swears and rages abominably, calls upon the evil one and yields unto him. There thou seest the mouth and the tongue of the devil, directed against the second commandment. Thirdly, a true Christian esteems worthily of the office of preaching; he hears and learns God's Word with true earnestness and diligence, according to Christ's institution and command, not only to the amendment and comfort of himself, but also for good example to others; he honours and defends good and godly servants of the Word, permits them not to suffer want, etc. But this image and child of the devil regards no preaching, hears not God's Word, or very negligently, speaks evil thereof, perverts it, and makes scoff thereat; yea, hates the servants thereof, who, for ought he cares, may famish for want of food. There thou seest the ears of the devil, his throat and neck of steel, directly against the third commandment. Further, desirest thou to know how the body of the devil is shaped and fashioned, then hearken to the following commandments of the second table, and take good heed thereunto. For first, a good Christian honours his parents, and hearkens unto them, to the magistrates, and to the shepherds of souls, according as God has commanded. But this child of the devil hearkens not to his parents, serves and helps them not; nay, dishonours, contemns, and vexes them, forsakes them in their need, is ashamed of them when they are poor, and scorns them in their old age; he is disobedient to magistrates, and shows unto them no reverence, but speaks evil of them; he regards no admonition, reproof, civility, or honesty. There thou seest the breast of the devil. Secondly, an upright and true Christian envies not his neighbour, he bears no ill-will towards him, he desires not to be revenged of him, though he have cause, yea, he condoles with his neighbour, when hurt and grief assault him, helps, and to his power defends him against those who seek his life. But this child of the devil, although he cannot hurt his neighbour in body and life, or murder him with his fist, yet he hates and envies him, he is angry with him, and is his enemy in his heart, wishes his death, and when it goes evil with him, is glad and laughs in his sleeve, etc. There thou seest the devil's wrathful and murdering heart. Thirdly, a God-fearing Christian lives modestly and honestly, shuns all manner of wrongful dealing, stands in fear of God's wrath and everlasting punishment.

But the child of the devil does quite the contrary, is void of all shame and chastity, in words, behaviour and act. There thou seest the belly of the devil. Fourthly, a godly Christian lives by his labour, by his trade, with a good conscience; he deceives no man of that which is his, nay, lends, helps, and gives to the needy according to his ability. But this devilish child helps none, no, not in the least, but he trades in usury, covets, robs, and steals as he may, by power and deceit; he takes all manner of advantage to cheat and cozen his neighbour, by false wares, measures, weights, etc. There thou seest the hands and sharp-pointed claws of the devil. Fifthly, a godly creature speaks evil of no man, belies not his neighbour, nor bears false witness against him; yea, though he knows his neighbour faulty, yet out of love he covers his infirmities and sins, except by the magistrate he be called to confess the truth. But this child of the devil does quite the contrary; he slanders and backbites, betrays, and falsely accuses his neighbour, and perverts that which he has rightly spoken. There thou seest the devil's evil and wicked will. Sixth, and lastly, a true Christian covets not his neighbour's house, inheritance, or wealth, misleads not his wife or his daughter, entices not away his servants, covets nothing that is his, yea, according to his power, he helps to keep and preserve that which belongs to him. But this child of the devil imagines, endeavours, and, day and night, seeks opportunity to defraud his neighbour of his house, his grounds, lands, and people, to draw and entice his wife away unto himself, to flatter away his servants, to instigate his neighbour's tenants against him, to get his cattle from him, etc. There thou seest the devil's lust. Through lies, under the colour of the truth, he seduces and deceives godly people, like as he did Adam and Eve in Paradise; therefore the more holy the people be, the greater is the danger they stand in. For this cause, we ought to beware of the devil, and to take our refuge in Christ, who crushed his head, and delivered us from his lies.

### 576

Dr. Luther was asked, whether the Samuel who appeared to king Saul, upon the invocation of the pythoness, as is related in the first Book of Kings, was really the prophet Samuel. The doctor answered: 'No, 'twas a spectre, an evil spirit, assuming his form. What proves this is, that God, by the laws of Moses, had forbidden man to question the dead; consequently, it must have been a demon which presented itself under the form of the man of God. In like manner, an abbot of Spanheim, a sorcerer, exhibited to the emperor Maximilian all the emperors his predecessors, and all the most celebrated heroes of past times, who defiled before him each in the costume of his time. Among them were Alexander the Great and Julius Caesar. There was also the emperor's betrothed, whom Charles of France stole from him. But these apparitions were all the work of the demon.'

### 577

No malady comes upon us from God, who is good, and wishes us well; they all emanate from the devil, who is the cause and author of plagues, fevers, etc. When he is at work with jurisconsults, he engenders all sorts of dissensions and machinations, turning justice into injustice. Approaches he great lords, princes, kings, he gives birth to wars and massacres. Gains he access to divines, be produces the worst mischief of all: false doctrines, which seduce and ruin men's souls. God alone can check so many calamities.

### 578

The devil vexes and harasses the workmen in the mines. He makes them think they have found fine new veins of silver, which, when they have laboured and laboured, turn out to be mere illusions. Even in open day, on the surface of the earth, he causes people to think they see a treasure before them, which vanishes when they would pick it up. At times, treasure is really found, but this is by the special grace of God. I never had any success in the mines, but such was God's will, and I am content.

### 579

The emperor Frederic, father of Maximilian, invited a necromancer to dine with him, and, by his knowledge of magic, turned his guest's hands into *griffins' claws*. He then wanted him to eat, but the man, ashamed, hid his claws under the table.

He took his revenge, however, for the jest played upon him. He caused it to seem that a loud altercation was going on in the courtyard, and when the emperor put his head out of window to see what was the matter, he, by his art, clapped on him a pair of huge stag's horns, so that the emperor could not get his head into the room again until he had cured the necromancer of his disfigurement. I am delighted, said Luther, when one devil plagues another. They are not all, however, of equal power.

### 580

There was at Nieuburg a magician named Wildferer, who, one day, swallowed a countryman, with his horse and cart. A few hours afterwards, man, horse, and cart, were all found in a slough, some miles off. I have heard, too, of a seeming monk, who asked a wagoner, that was taking some hay to market, how much he would charge to let him eat his fill of hay? The man said, a kreutzer, whereupon the monk set to work, and had nearly devoured the whole load, when the wagoner drove him off.

## 581

August 25, 1538, the conversation fell upon witches who spoil milk, eggs, and butter in farm-yards. Dr. Luther said: 'I should have no compassion on these witches; I would burn all of them. We read in the old law, that the priests threw the first stone at such malefactors. 'Tis said this stolen butter turns rancid, and falls to the ground when any one goes to eat it.' He who attempts to counteract and chastise these witches, is himself corporeally plagued and tormented by their master, the devil. Sundry schoolmasters and ministers have often experienced this. Our ordinary sins offend and anger God. What, then, must be his wrath against witchcraft, which we may justly designate high treason against divine majesty, a revolt against the infinite power of God. The jurisconsults who have so learnedly and pertinently treated of rebellion, affirm that the subject who rebels against his sovereign, is worthy of death. Does not witchcraft, then, merit death, which is a revolt of the creature against the Creator, a denial to God of the authority it accords to the demon?

## 582

Dr. Luther discoursed at length concerning witchcraft and charms. He said, that his mother had had to undergo infinite annoyance from one of her neighbours, who was a witch, and whom she was fain to conciliate with all sorts of attentions; for this witch could throw a charm upon children, which made them cry themselves to death. A pastor having punished her for some knavery, she cast a spell upon him by means of some earth upon which he had walked, and which she bewitched. The poor man hereupon fell sick of a malady which no remedy could remove, and shortly after died.

## 583

It was asked: Can good Christians and God-fearing people also undergo witchcraft? Luther replied: Yes; for our bodies are always exposed to the attacks of Satan. The maladies I suffer are not natural, but devil's spells.

### 584

When I was young, some one told me this story: Satan had, in vain, set all his craft and subtlety at work to separate a married pair that lived together in perfect harmony and love. At last, having concealed a razor under each of their pillows, he visited the husband, disguised as an old woman, and told him that his wife had formed the project of killing him; he next told the same thing to the wife. The husband, finding the razor under his wife's pillow, became furious with anger at her supposed wickedness, and cut her throat, So powerful is Satan in his malice.

### 585

Luther, taking up a caterpillar, said: 'Tis an emblem of the devil in its crawling-walk, and bears his colours in its changing hue.

### 586

Dr. Luther said he had heard from the elector of Saxony, John Frederic, that a powerful family in Germany was descended from the devil, the founder having been born of a succubus. He added this story: A gentleman had a young and beautiful wife, who, dying, was buried. Shortly afterwards, this gentleman and one of his servants sleeping in the same chamber, the wife, who was dead, came at night, bent over the bed of the gentleman, as though she were conversing with him, and, after awhile, went away again. The servant, having twice observed this circumstance, asked his master whether he knew that, every night, a woman, clothed in white, stood by his bed-side. The master replied, that he had slept soundly, and had observed nothing of the sort. The next, night, he took care to remain awake. The woman came, and he asked her who she was, and what she wanted. She answered, that she was his wife. He returned: my wife is dead and buried. She answered, she had died by reason of his sins, but that if he would receive her again, she would return to him in life. He said, if it were possible, he should be well content. She told him he must undertake not to swear, as he was wont to do; for that if he ever did so, she should once more die, and permanently quit him. He promised this, and the dead woman, returning to seeming life, dwelt with him, ate, drank, and slept with him, and had children by him. One day that he had guests, his wife went to fetch some cakes from an adjoining apartment, and remained a long time absent. The gentleman grew impatient, and broke out into his old oaths. The wife not returning, the gentleman, with his friends, went to seek her, but, she had disappeared; only, the clothes she had worn lay on the floor. She was never again seen.

### 587

The devil seduces us at first by all the allurements of sin, in order thereafter to plunge us into despair: he pampers up the flesh, that he may, by and by, prostrate the spirit. We feel no pain in the act of sin, but the soul after it is sad, and the conscience disturbed.

### 588

He who will have, for his master and king, Jesus Christ, the son of the Virgin, who took upon himself our flesh and our blood, will have the devil for his enemy.

### 589

It is very certain that, as to all persons who have hanged themselves, or killed themselves in any other way, 'tis the devil who has put the cord round their necks, or the knife to their throats.

### 590

A man had a habit, whenever he fell, of saying: 'Devil take me.' He was advised to discontinue this evil custom, lest some day the devil should take him at his word. He promised to vent his impatience by some other phrase; but, one day, having stumbled, he called upon the devil, in the way I have mentioned, and was killed upon the spot, falling on a sharp-pointed piece of wood.

### 591

A pastor, near Torgau, came to Luther, and complained that the devil tormented him without intermission. The Doctor replied: He plagues and harasses me too, but I resist him with the arms of faith. I know of one person at Magdeburg, who put Satan to the rout, by spitting at him; but this example is not to be lightly followed; for the devil is a presumptuous spirit, and not disposed to yield. We run great risk when, with him, we attempt more than we can do. One man, who relied implicitly on his baptism, when the devil presented himself to him, his head furnished with horns, tore off one of the horns; but another man, of less faith, who attempted the same thing, was killed by the devil.

### 592

Henning, the Bohemian, asked Dr. Luther why the devil bore so furious -a hatred to the human race? The Doctor replied: 'That ought not to surprise you; see what a hate prince George bears me, so that, day and night, he is ever meditating how he shall injure me. Nothing would delight him more, than to see me undergo a thousand tortures. If such be the hatred of man, what must the hatred of the devil be?'

### 593

The devil cannot but be our enemy, since we are against him with God's Word, wherewith we destroy his kingdom. He is a prince and god of the world, and has a greater power than all the kings, potentates, and princes upon earth; wherefore he would be revenged of us, and assaults us without ceasing, as we both see and feel. We have against the devil a great advantage; powerful, wicked, and cunning as he is, he cannot hurt us, since 'tis not against him we have sinned, but against God. Therefore we have nothing to do with that arch-enemy; but we confess, and say: 'Against thee Lord, have we sinned,' etc. We know, through God's grace, that we have a gracious God, and a merciful Father in heaven, whose wrath against us, Christ Jesus, our only Lord and Saviour, has appeased with his precious blood. Now, forasmuch as through Christ we have remission of sins and peace with God, so must the envious devil be content to let us alone, in peace, so that henceforward he can neither upbraid nor hit us in the teeth concerning our sins against God's laws, for Christ has cancelled and torn in pieces the handwriting of our consciences, which was a witness against us, and nailed the same to his cross; to God be everlasting honour, praise, and glory in Christ Jesus, for the same. Amen.

### 594

The devil knows the thoughts of the ungodly, for he inspires them therewith. He sees and rules the hearts of all such people as are not kept safe and preserved by God's Word; yea, holds them captive in his snares, so that they must think, do, and speak according to his will. And St. Paul says: 'The god of this world blindeth the minds of them that believe not, lest the light of the glorious gospel of Christ, who is the image of God, should shine unto them,' etc. And Christ gives a reason how it comes to pass, that many hear the Word, yet neither understand nor keep the same, where he says: 'The devil cometh, and taketh the Word out of their hearts, lest they should believe, and be saved:' Therefore it is no marvel that the devil, through his Prophets, declares what shall happen and come to pass.

**595**

The Scripture clearly shows that the devil gives unto mankind evil thoughs, and suggests evil projects to the ungodly; as of Judas is written that the devil put it into his heart to betray Christ. And he not only instigated Cain to hate his brother Abel, but, moreover, to murder him. But the devil knows not the thoughts of the righteous, until they utter them. He knew not the thoughts of Christ's heart, nor knows he the thoughts of the godly, in whose heart Christ dwells. 'Tis a powerful, crafty and subtle spirit. Christ names him the Prince of the World; he goes about shooting all thoughts, his fiery darts, into the hearts even of the godly, as discord, hatred to God, despair, blaspheming, etc. St. Paul well understood all these assaults, and bitterly complains of them.

**596**

The apostle gives this title to the devil: 'That he hath the power of death.' And Christ calls him a murderer. He is so skilled, that he is able to cause death even with the leaf of a tree; he has more boxes and pots full of poisons, wherewith he destroys men, than all the apothecaries in the world have of healing medicine; if one poison will not dispatch, another will. In a word, the power of the devil is greater than we can imagine; 'tis only God's finger can resist him.

**597**

I maintain that Satan produces all the maladies which afflict mankind, for he is the prince of death. St. Peter speaks of Christ as healing all that are oppressed of the devil. He not only cured those who were possessed, but he restored sight to the blind, hearing to the deaf, speech to the dumb, strength to the paralytic; therefore I think all grave infirmities are blows and strokes of the devil, which he employs as an assassin uses the sword or other weapon. So God employs natural means to maintain the health and life of man, such as sleep, meat, drink, etc. The devil has other means of injury; he poisons the air, etc.

A physician repairs the work of God when damaged corporally; we, divines, spiritually; we mend the soul that the devil has spoiled. The devil gives poison to kill men; a physician gives theriacum, or some other drug, to save them; so the creature, through creatures, helping creatures. Physic has not its descent and origin out of books, God revealed it; or, as Syrach says: 'It cometh from the Most Highest; the Lord hath created medicines out of the earth.' Therefore we may justly use corporal physic, as God's creature. Our burgomaster here at Wittenberg lately asked me, if it were against God's will to use physic? for, said he, Doctor Carlstad has preached, that whoso falls sick, shall use no physic, but commit his case to God, praying that His will be done. I asked him: did he eat when he was hungry? He answered, yes. Then, said I, even so you may use physic, which is God's creature, as well as meat and drink, or whatever else we use for the preservation of life.

### 598

Satan plagues and torments people all manner of ways. Some he affrights in their sleep, with heavy dreams and visions, so that the whole body sweats in anguish of heart. Some he leads, sleeping, out of their beds and chambers up into high dangerous places, so that if, by the loving angels who are about them, they were not preserved, he would throw them down, and cause their death. The superstitious papists say, that these sleep-walkers are persons who have never been baptized; or, if they have been, that the priest was drunk when he administered the sacrament.

### 599

No creature can prevail against the devil, but only Christ; and he made trial of his art even upon him, as when he said unto him: 'If thou wilt fall down and worship me, I will give thee all the kingdoms of the whole world.'

No man can rightly comprehend this temptation; I would willingly die, on condition I could fundamentally preach thereof. Doubtless, the devil moved Christ much when he said: 'All this is mine, and I give it to whom I will'; for they are words of Divine Majesty, and belong only to God. True, the devil gives, but let us make a strong distinction between the real giver, who gives all that we have and are, and the dissembling murderer, who gives to those that serve and worship him for a short time, yet so that they must everlastingly perish. Christ contradicts him not, that he is a lord and a prince of the world; but he will not therefore worship him, but says: Avoid, Satan. Even so ought we to do. He must be, indeed, a most wicked, poisoned, and thirsty spirit, that he durst presume to tempt the Son of God to fall down and worship him. The arch villain, doubtless, in the twinkling of an eye, laid before the Lord a delusion of all the kingdoms of the world, and their glory, as Luke writes, thereby to move and allure him, to the end he should think: such honour might one receive, and yet nevertheless be the child of God.

## 600

When that envious, poisoned spirit, the devil, plagues and torments us, as is his custom, by reason of our sins, intending thereby to lead us into despair, we must meet him in this manner: 'thou deceitful and wicked spirit? how darest thou presume to persuade me to such things? Knowest thou not that Christ Jesus, my Lord and Saviour, who crushed thy head, has forbidden me to believe thee, yea, even when thou speakest the truth, in that he names thee a murderer, a liar, and the father of lies. I do not admit to thee, that I, as thy captive, shall be condemned to everlasting death and hellish torments, by reason of my sins, as thou falsely suggestest; but thou thyself, on the contrary, long since, by Christ my Lord and Saviour, wert stripped, judged, and with everlasting bonds and chains of darkness, art bound, cast down, and delivered to hell, reserved to the judgment of the great day, and finally, with all the ungodly, shalt be thrown into the bottomless pit of hell. Further, I demand of thee, by what authority thou presumest to exercise such power and right against me? whereas thou hast given me neither life, wife, nor child; no, not the least thing that I have; neither art thou my lord, much less the creator of my body and soul; neither hast thou made the members wherewith I have sinned. How, then, thou wicked and false spirit, art thou so insolent as to domineer over that which is mine, as if thou wert God himself.'

## 601

The people who in Popedom, are possessed of the devil, get not rid of him by such arts, words, or gestures as their charmers use; the devil suffers not himself to be driven out with mere phrases, as: 'Come out, thou unclean spirit,' for these charmers mean it not earnestly. The power of God must effect it.

The devil may be driven out, either by the prayers of the whole church, when all Christians join their supplications together in a prayer so powerful, that it pierces the clouds, or the person that would drive out the wicked enemy by himself, must be of highly enlightened mind, and of strong and steadfast courage, certain of his cause; as Elijah, Elisha, Peter, Paul, etc.

## 602

The cause that so many poor people in the time of Christ were possessed, was, that the true doctrine was almost sunk and quenched by the people of Israel, a few excepted, – as Zacharias, Elizabeth, Simeon, Anna, etc. And I believe if the Pharisees had continued to rule, and that Christ had not come,

Judaism would have been turned into Paganism, – as, before the shining of the gospel, was seen in Popedom, where the people understood as little of Christ and his Word, as the Turks and heathens.

### 603

The devil well knew the Scripture, where it is said: 'Behold, a virgin shall conceive and bear a child.' Also: 'Unto us a child is born.' But because Christ has carried himself humbly and lowly, went about with public sinners, and by reason thereof was held in no esteem, – therefore the devil looked another way over Christ, and knew him not; for the devil looks a-squint upwards, after that which is high and pompous, not downwards, nor on that which is humble and lowly. But the everlasting, merciful God does quite the contrary; he beholds that which is lowly, as the 113th Psalm shows: 'Our God hath his dwelling on high, and yet humbleth to behold what is in heaven and on earth.' And Isaiah: 'I will look to him that is poor, and of a contrite spirit, and trembleth at my word.' God cares not for that which is high; yea, it is an abomination before him. St. Luke says: 'That which is highly esteemed among men, is abomination in the sight of God.' Therefore he that intends to climb high, let him beware of the devil, lest he throw him down; for the nature and manner of the devil is, first to hoist up into heaven, and afterwards to cast down into hell.

### 604

In cases of melancholy and sickness, I conclude it is merely the work of the devil. For God makes us not melancholy, nor affrights nor kills us, for he is a God of the living. Hence the Scripture: 'Rejoice, and be of good comfort.' God's Word and prayer is physic against spiritual tribulations.

### 605

I would rather die through the devil, than through the emperor or pope; for then I should die through a great and mighty prince of the world. But if he eat a bit of me 'twill be his bane; he shall spew me out again; and, at the day of judgment, I in requital will devour him.

### 606

The devil needs not to tell me I am not good or upright; neither would I wish to be so, that is, to be without feeling of my sins, or to think I need no remission of them; for, if that were the case, all the treasure of Christ were lost on me, seeing he says himself: 'He came not for the sake of the just, but to call sinners to repentance.'

### 607

I hold that a devil, once overcome with God's Word and Spirit, must be gone, and dare not return again with the same temptation; Christ says: 'Avoid, Satan.' And in another place: 'Come out, thou unclean spirit.' Then say the devils: 'Suffer us to enter into the herd of swine.' Origen says: 'I believe that the saints strangle and slay many devils in combating' – that is, break their power.

### 608

Witchcraft is the devil's own proper work, wherewith, when God permits, he not only hurts people, but often makes away with them; for in this world we are as guests and strangers, body and soul cast under the devil; he is god of this world, and all things are under his power, whereby we are preserved in temporal life, – as meat, drink, air, etc.

The devil is so crafty a spirit, that he can ape and deceive our senses. He can cause one to think he sees something, which he sees not, that he hears thunder, or a trumpet, which he hears not. Like as the soldiers of Julius Caesar thought they heard the sound of a trumpet, as Suetonius writes, and yet there was no such thing. Oh, Satan is a master in aping and deceiving people, and every human sense.

And especially, is he artful when he deceives people spiritually, bewitching and deceiving the hearts and consciences, in such sort that they hold and receive erroneous and ungodly doctrine and opinion, for the upright and divine truth.

We see at this day how easy a matter it is for him so to do, by the sectaries and seducers; for he has so bewitched and deceived their hearts, that they hold that for the clear truth, which is altogether lies, errors, and abominable darkness. They hold themselves wise and learned in divine matters; other people they regard as geese, which neither see nor understand anything.

### 609

The poisonous serpent takes such delight in doing mischief, that he not only deceives secure and proud spirits with his delusions, but also undertakes, through his deceptions, to bring into error those who are well instructed and grounded in God's Word. He vexes me often so powerfully, and assaults me so fiercely with heavy and melancholy thoughts, that I forget my loving Lord and Saviour Christ Jesus, or at least behold him far otherwise than he is to be beheld. There is none of us so free, but that often he is thus deceived and bewitched with false opinions. Therefore we should learn how to know this conjuror, to the end he may not come behind us, being sleepy and secure, and so delude us with his witchcraft. And truly, if he find us not sober and watching, and not armed with spiritual weapons, that is, with God's Word and with faith, then most surely he will overcome us.

## 610

When I could not be rid of the devil with sentences out of the Holy Scripture, I made him often fly with jeering words; sometimes I said unto him: Saint Satan! if Christ's blood, which was shed for my sins, be not sufficient, then I desire that thou wouldst pray to God for me. When he finds me idle, with nothing in hand, he is very busy, and before I am aware, he wrings from me a bitter sweat: but when I offer him the pointed spear, God's Word, he flies; yet, before he goes, makes a grievous hurricane. When I began to write against the pope, and the gospel was going on, the devil set himself strongly to work, rumbling and raging about, for he would willingly have preserved purgatory at Magdeburg. There was a citizen, whose child died, for whom he refused to have vigils and masses sung. The devil played his freaks, came every night, about twelve o'clock, into the chamber where the boy died, and made a whining like a young child. The good citizen being therewith full of sorrow, knew not what course to take. The popish priests said: O, now you see how it goes when vigils are not solemnized. Whereupon the citizen sent to me, desiring my advice, (for the sermon I had lately preached on this text: 'They have Moses and the prophets,' had been printed, and been read by him); and I wrote to him from Wittenberg, and advised him not to suffer any vigils at all to be held, for he might be fully assured that these were merely pranks of the devil; whereupon, the children and servants in the house jeered the devil, and said: What doest thou, Satan? Avoid, thou cursed spirit, get thee gone to the place where thou oughtest to be, to the pit of hell. When the devil marked their contempt, he left off his game, and came there no more. He is a proud spirit, and cannot endure scorn.

## 611

Though Satan ceases not to plague the Christians, and to shoot at us his fiery darts, 'tis very good and profitable for us, for thereby he makes us the more sure of the word and doctrine, so that faith increases, and is stronger in us. We are often shaken, and, indeed, now and then the devil drives out of us a sour and bitter sweat, but he cannot bring us to despair; for Christ always has kept the field, and through us he will keep it still. Through hope, in all manner of trials and temptations, we hold ourselves on Christ.

## 612

'Tis a fearful thing when Satan torments the sorrowful conscience with melancholy; then the wicked villain, masterlike, disguises himself in the person of Christ, so that it is impossible for a poor creature, whose conscience is troubled, to discover the knavery. Hence many of those, that neither know nor understand the same, run headlong into despair, and make away with themselves; for they are blinded and deceived so powerfully by him, that they are fully persuaded it is not the devil, but Christ himself, that thus vexes and torments them.

I am a doctor of Holy Scripture, and for many years have preached Christ; yet, to this day, I am not able to put Satan off, or to drive him away from me, as I would; neither am I able so to comprehend Christ and to take hold on him, as in Holy Scripture he is placed before me; but the devil continually seeks how to put another Christ into my mind. Yet; nevertheless, we ought to render humble thanks to Almighty God, who has hitherto preserved us by his holy Word; through faith and by prayer, so that we know how to walk before him in humility and fear, and not to depend or presume on our own wisdom, righteousness, strength, and power, but to cheer and comfort ourselves in Christ, who is always more than sufficiently strong and powerful; and, although we be weak and faint, yet we continually vanquish and overcome through his power and strength in us poor, weak, and feeble creatures. For this may his holy name be blessed and magnified for evermore. Amen.

## 613

The devil has two occupations, to which he applies himself incessantly, and which are the foundation stones of his kingdom – lying and murder. God says: 'Thou shalt do no murder.' Thou shalt have none other gods but me. Against these two commandments, the devil, with all his force, fights without intermission.

He now plays no more with people, as heretofore, by means of rumbling spirits, for he sees that the condition of the time is far otherwise than what it was twenty years past. He now begins at the right end, and uses great diligence.

The rumbling spirits are mute among us; but the spirits of sedition increase above measure, and get the upper hand: God resist them.

## 614

The power the devil exercises is not by God commanded, but God resists him not, suffering him to make tumults, yet no longer or further than he wills, for God has set him a mark, beyond which he neither can nor dare step.

When God said, concerning Job, to Satan: 'Behold, he is in thy hands, yet spare his life,' this power was by God permitted, as if God should say: I will so far permit and give thee leave, but touch not his life.

## 615

It is almost incredible how God enables us, weak flesh and blood, to enter combat with the devil, and to beat and overcome so powerful a spirit as he, and with no other weapon but only his Word, which by faith we take hold on. This must needs grieve and vex that great and powerful enemy.

## 616

The devil is like a fowler; of the birds he catches, he wrings most of their necks, but keeps a few alive, to allure other birds to his snare, by singing the song he will have in a cage. I hope he will not get me into his cage.

## 617

Let not man flatter himself that the devil is in hell, far from the ungodly, as the archbishop of Mayence thinks; the devil dwells in his hard heart, and impels him according to his will and pleasure. For if the devil had no power but to plague us in body and goods, and vexed and tormented us only with the cares and troubles of this life, he were no devil to make account of. But he has learned a higher art; he takes away and falsifies the article of justification, *privative et positive*, and either tears the same quite out of our hearts, as in Popedom, or defiles it through sects and heresies, which hang thereon a gloss about works, or what not, leaving the husks of the nuts to the hearers, but the kernels are gone.

## 618

The devil has two manner of shapes or forms, wherein he disguises himself; he either appears in the shape of a serpent, to affright and kill; or else in the form of a silly sheep, to lie and deceive; these are his two court colours. The devil is a foolish spirit, for he gives means and occasion to Christ to defend himself, in that he plagues the poor and wake Christians; for thereby he confirms the authority of Christ and his apostles; as when they make the sick whole and sound, the devil had rather he had left them at peace and quiet, but his wicked desire to do mischief drives him forward, to the end he may be brought to confusion.

### 619

Our songs and psalms sorely vex and grieve the devil, whereas our passions and impatiences, our complainings and cryings, our 'alas!' or 'woe is me!' please him well, so that he laughs in his fist. He takes delight in tormenting us, especially when we confess, praise, preach, and laud Christ. For seeing the devil is a prince of this world, and our utter enemy, we must be content to let him pass through his country; he will needs have imposts and customs of us, and strike our bodies with manifold plagues.

### 620

God gives to the devil and to witches power over human creatures in two ways; first, over the ungodly, when he will punish them by reason of their sins; secondly, over the just and godly, when he intends to try whether they will be constant in the faith, and remain in his obedience. Without God's will and our own consent, the devil cannot hurt us; for God says: 'Whoso touches you, toucheth the apple of mine eye.' And Christ: 'There cannot fall an hair from your head, without your heavenly Father's notice.'

### 621

The devil's power is not so well seen in the fall of carnal people, and of the wise of this world, who live like senseless creatures and heathen, as in the fall of the saints who were endued with the Holy Ghost; as Adam, David, Solomon, Peter, etc., who committed great sins, and fell by God's will, to the end they should not proudly exalt themselves by reason of God's gifts.

### 622

By good experience, I know the devil's craft and subtlety, that he not only blows the law into us, to terrify and affright us, and out of mole-hills to make mountains, – that is, to make a very hell of what is but a small and little sin, which as a wondrous juggler he can perform artfully; but also, can sometimes make such to be great and heavy sins which are no sins; for he brings one threatening sentence or other out of the Holy Scriptures, and before we are aware, gives so hard a blow to our hearts, in a moment, that we lose all light and sight, and take him to be the true Christ, whereas it is only the envious devil.

### 623

When tribulations approach, excommunicate them in the name of Christ Jesus, and say: God has forbidden me to receive that coin, because it is minted by the devil; we reject it as prohibited.

When heavy temptations come upon thee, expel them by what means thou best mayest; talk with good friends, of such things as thou takest delight in.

### 624

When I write against the pope, I am not melancholy, for then I labour with the brains and understanding, then I write with joy of heart; so that not long since Dr. Reisenpusch said to me: I much marvel you can be so merry; if the case were mine, it would go near to kill me. Whereupon I answered: Not the pope or all his shaven retinue can make me sad; for I know that they are Christ's enemies; therefore I fight against him with joyful courage.

### 625

The devil gives heaven to people before they sin, but after they sin, brings their consciences into despair. Christ deals quite contrary, for he gives heaven after sins committed, and makes consciences joyful.

Last night as I waked out of my sleep, the devil came and said: God is far from thee, and hears not thy prayers. Whereupon I said: Very well, I will call and cry the louder. I will place before my sight the world's unthankfulness, and the ungodly doings of kings, potentates, and princes; I will also think upon the raging heretics; all these will inflame my praying.

### 626

The hound of hell, in Greek, is called Cerberus; in Hebrew, Scorphur: he has three throats – sin, the law, and death.

### 627

In Job are two chapters (40 and 41) concerning Behemoth the whale, before whom no man is in safety. 'Wilt thou (saith the text) draw leviathan out with a hook? Will he make many supplications unto thee? will he speak soft words unto thee?' These are images and figures whereby the devil is signified.

## 628

At Mohlburg, in Thuringia, not far from Erfurt, there was a musician, who gained his living by playing at merrymakings. This man came to the minister of his parish, and complained that he was every day assailed by the devil, who threatened to carry him off, because he had played at an unlawful marriage. The minister consoled him, prayed for him, recited to him numerous passages of Scripture, directed against the devil; and, with some other pious men, watched over the unfortunate man, day and night, fastening the doors and windows, so that he might not be carried off. At length the musician said: 'I feel that Satan cannot harm my soul, but he will assuredly remove my body'; and that very night, at eight o'clock, though the watch was doubled, the devil came in the shape of a furious wind, broke the windows, and carried off the musician, whose body was found next morning, stiff and black, stuck on a nut-tree. 'Tis a most sure and certain story, added Luther.

## 629

We cannot expel demons with certain ceremonies and words, as Jesus Christ, the prophets, and the apostles did. All we can do, is in the name of Jesus Christ, to pray the Lord God, of his infinite mercy, to deliver the possessed persons. And if our prayer is offered up in full faith, we are assured by Christ himself (St. John 16:23), that it will be efficacious, and overcome all the devil's resistance. I might mention many instances of this. But we cannot of ourselves expel the evil spirits, nor must we even attempt it.

## 630

Men are possessed by the devil two ways; corporally and spiritually. Those whom he possesses corporally, as mad people, he has permission from God to vex and agitate, but he has no power over their souls. The impious, who persecute the divine doctrine, and treat the truth as a lie, and who, unhappily, are very numerous in our time, these the devil possesses spiritually. They cannot be delivered, but remain, horrible to relate, his prisoners, as in the time of Jesus Christ were Annas, Caiaphas, and all the other impious Jews whom Jesus himself could not deliver, and as, nowadays, are the pope, his cardinals, bishops, tyrants, and partisans.

### 631

When Satan says in thy heart: 'God will not pardon thy sins, nor be gracious unto thee,' I pray, how wilt thou then, as a poor sinner, raise up and comfort thyself, especially when other signs of God's wrath beat upon thee, as sickness, poverty, etc. And when thy heart begins to preach and say: behold, here thou liest in sickness; thou art poor and forsaken of every one: why, thou must turn thyself to the other side, and say: Well, let it outwardly seem as it will, yea, though mine own heart felt infinitely more sorrow, yet I know for certain, that I am united and made one with my Lord and Saviour Christ; I have his word to assure me of the same, which can neither fail nor deceive me, for God is true, and performs what he promises.

### 632

The devil often casts this into my breast: How if thy doctrine be false and erroneous, wherewith the pope, the mass, friars and nuns are thus dejected and startled? at which the sour sweat has drizzled from me. But at last, when I saw he would not leave, I gave him this answer: Avoid, Satan; address thyself to my God, and talk with him about it, for the doctrine is not mine, but his; he has commanded me to hearken unto this Christ.

# Of Temptation and Tribulation

*⚬⚬⚬*

## 633

Whoso, without the word of grace and prayer, disputes with the devil touching sin and the law, will lose; therefore let him leave off betimes. For the devil is armed against us with Goliath's sword, with his spear and weapons; that is, he has on his side, to assist him, the testimony of our own consciences, which witness against us in that we have transgressed all God's commandments; therefore the devil has a very great advantage against us.

The devil often assaults me, by objecting, that out of my doctrine great offences and much evil have proceeded, and with this he many a time vehemently perplexes me. And although I make him this answer: That much good is also raised thereby, which by God's grace is true, yet he is so nimble a spirit, and so crafty a rhetorician, that, master-like, he can pervert this into sin. He was never so fierce and full of rage as he is now. I feel him well.

But when I remember myself, and take hold on the gospel, and meet him therewith, then I overcome him and confute all his arguments; yet for a time I often fail. He says: The law is also God's Word; why, then, is the gospel always objected against me? I say: True: the law is also God's Word; but it is as far different from the gospel, as heaven is from earth; for in the gospel, God offers unto us his grace; he will be our God merely out of love, and he presents unto us his only begotten Son, who delivers us from, sin and death, and has purchased for us everlasting righteousness and life; thereon do I hold, and will not make God a liar. God indeed has also given the law, but, in every respect, for another use and purpose.

What I teach and preach, I teach openly, by clear daylight, not in a corner. I direct the same by the gospel, by baptism, and by the Lord's prayer. Here Christ stands, him I cannot deny; upon the gospel do I ground my cause, etc. Yet the devil, with his crafty disputing, brings it so near unto me, that the sweat of anguish drops from me.

Thus was St. Paul constrained to defend himself at Philippi, when both Jews and Gentiles hit him in the teeth, saying: 'That he troubled their city.' And, at Thessalonica, saying: 'These are they that turn the world upside down; they do contrary to the decrees of Caesar.' And at Caesarea, saying: 'This is a pestilent fellow, that hath moved sedition among all the Jews throughout the world.' So the devil stirred up the Jews against Christ, accusing him of rebellion, that he forbad to pay tribute unto Caesar, and that he blasphemed, in calling himself the Son of God. So I say to Satan: Like as thou camest to confusion by Christ and St. Paul, even so, Mr. Devil, shall it go with thee, if thou meddlest with me.

### 634

All heaviness of mind and melancholy come of the devil; especially these thoughts: that God is not gracious unto him, that God will have no mercy upon him, etc. Whosoever thou art, possessed with such heavy thoughts, know for certain, that they are a work of the devil. God sent his Son into the world, not to affright, but to comfort.

Therefore be of good courage, and think, that henceforward thou art not the child of a human creature, but of God, through faith in Christ, in whose name thou art baptized; therefore the spear of death cannot enter into thee; he has no right unto thee, much less can he hurt or prejudice thee, for he is everlastingly swallowed up through Christ.

### 635

It is better for a Christian to be sorrowful than secure, as the people of the world are. Well is it for him that stands always in fear, yet knows he has in heaven a gracious God, for Christ's sake; as the Psalm says: 'The Lord's delight is in them that fear him, and put their trust in his mercy.'

There are two sorts of tribulations; one, of the spirit; another, of the flesh. Satan torments the conscience with lies, perverting that which is done uprightly, and according to God's Word; but the body, or flesh, he plagues in another kind.

No man ought to lay a cross upon himself, or to adopt tribulation, as is done in Popedom; but if a cross or tribulation come upon him, then let him suffer it patiently, and know that it is good and profitable for him.

### 636

Luther being informed of one that was fiercely tempted and plagued in his conscience, because he found not in himself a complete righteousness, that he was not so righteous as God in the law required, and that, in praying, he always felt blaspheming against Christ, said: It is a good sign ; for blaspheming of God is two-fold; one *activa*, or operative, when one wilfully seeks occasion to blaspheme God; the other, a constrained blaspheming of God, *passiva*, when the devil, against our wills, possesses us with evil cogitations, which we desire to resist. With such, God will have us to be exercised, to the end we may not lie snoring in laziness, but strive and pray against them. By this means such things, in time, will vanish away and cease, especially at our last end; for then the Holy Ghost is present with his Christians, stands by them, drives away the devil, and makes a sweet, quiet, and peaceable conscience. Wherefore, for his spiritual disease, let him take this my physic; that he trouble not him self about anything, but be of good comfort, trust in God, and hold on to the Word – the devil, of his own accord, will soon cease from stirring up such temptation.

Concerning this tribulation, that he finds not a full and complete righteousness in himself, let him know, that no human creature finds it in this life; it is altogether angelical, which shall fall unto us in the life to come. Here we must content ourselves with Christ's righteousness; which he fully merited for us, with his innocent and spotless life.

### 637

Christ said to the adulteress: 'Neither do I condemn thee, go, and sin no more.' To the murderer, he said: 'This day shalt thou be with me in Paradise.' But to the Scribes and Pharisees, who set themselves against the righteousness of the gospel, Christ said: 'Woe be unto you.'

When one out of weakness denies God's Word, as many at this time do, under prince George, it is no sin against the Holy Ghost. Peter sinned in denying Christ, but not against the Holy Ghost. On the contrary, Judas persisted in sinning; he repented not aright, but remained hardened.

## 638

It is impossible for a human heart, without crosses and tribulations, to think upon God.

## 639

Not all can bear tribulations alike; some are better able to bear a blow of the devil; as we three, Philip Melancthon, John Calvin, and myself.

## 640

David, doubtless, had worse devils than we, for without great tribulations, he could not have had so great and glorious revelations. David made psalms: we also will make psalms, and sing as well as we can, to the honour of our Lord God, and to spite and mock the devil and his spouse.

## 641

When David sang his song: 'O my son Absalom, my son, my son Absalom, would God I had died for thee, O Absalom my son, my son,' etc. Ah! how sorrowful and perplexed a man was he. The very words denote that his grief of heart was excessive.

The good and holy king had vehement tribulations and crosses, which altogether eclipsed and darkened the promises made by God unto him. They were fearful and horrible examples. To hold fast and sure to the Word, in time or such trials and vexations, as David did, Oh! this is of inestimable value.

## 642

The upright and true Christian church has to strive not only with flesh and blood, but with spiritual wickedness in high places. The spiritual combat is most heavy and dangerous; flesh and blood take away but only body, wife and children, house, land, and what is temporal; but the spiritual evil takes away the soul, everlasting life and salvation.

## 643

The Lord our God is a God of humble and perplexed hearts, who are in need, tribulation, and danger. If we were strong, we should be proud and haughty. God shows his power in our weakness; he will not quench the glimmering flax, neither will he break in pieces the bruised reed.

## 644

Faith's tribulation is the greatest and sharpest torment, for faith must overcome all other tribulations; so that if faith be foiled, all other tribulations must needs fall upon human creatures; but if faith hold up her head, and be sound and in health, all other tribulations and vexations must grow sick, weak, and decrease. This tribulation of faith was that thorn which St. Paul felt, and which pierced through flesh and spirit, through soul and body. Such tribulations was David possessed with, when he made this psalm: 'Lord, rebuke me not in thy anger.' No doubt he would rather have been slain with a sword, than have suffered such wrath and indignation from God.

## 645

Heavy thoughts bring on physical maladies; when the soul is oppressed, so is the body. Augustine said well: Anima plus *est ubi amat, quam ubi animat*. When cares, heavy cogitations, sorrows, and passions superabound, they weaken the body, which, without the soul, is dead, or like a horse without a driver. But when the heart is at rest, and quiet, then it takes care of the body, and gives it what pertains thereunto. Therefore we ought to abandon and resist anxious thoughts, by all possible means.

## 646

The life of no human creature is without discontent; every one has his tribulations, and many a one, rather than be without them, will procure disquietness to himself. No man is content with that which God gives him.

## 647

Ah! how willingly would I now die, for I am faint and overwrought, and at this time I have a joyful and peaceable heart and conscience. I know full well, so soon as I shall be again in health, I neither shall have peace nor rest, but sorrow, weariness, and tribulations. But even that great man, St. Paul, could not be exempt from tribulations.

## 648

When spiritual tribulations approach, we say: cursed be the day wherein I was born; and we begin to sweat. In such tribulations was our blessed Saviour Christ, in the garden, when he said: 'Father, let this cup pass from me.' Here the will was against the will, yet he turned himself presently according to his Father's will, and was comforted by an angel. Christ, who in our flesh was plagued and tempted, is the best mediator and advocate with God, in our tribulation. He is president, when we are only respondents, if we will but suffer him to mediate. Seems it God is angry with us when we are in tribulation and temptation, yet when we repent and believe, we shall find, that under such anger God's grace and goodness towards us lie hid. Therefore, let us patiently attend God's leisure, and constantly remain in hope.

### 649

On the 8th of August, 1529, Luther, with his wife, lay sick of a fever. Overwhelmed with dysentery, sciatica, and a dozen other maladies, he said: God has touched me sorely, and I have been impatient: but God knows better than we whereto it serves. Our Lord God is like a printer, who sets the letters backwards, so that here we must so read them; when we are printed off, yonder, in the life to come, we shall read all clear and straightforward. Meantime we must have patience.

Tribulation is a right school and exercise of flesh and blood. The Psalms, almost in every verse, speak of nothing but tribulations, perplexities, sorrows, and troubles; they are a book of tribulations.

### 650

Christ received the thief on the cross, and Paul, after so many blasphemings and prosecutions, We, then, have no cause at all to doubt. And, indeed, we must all in that way attain to salvation. Yet, though we have no cause to fear God's wrath, for old Adam's sake we must stand in fear; for we cannot take such hold on the grace and mercy of God as we ought. He had but only the first six words in the creed: 'I believe in God the Father,' yet these were far above his natural wisdom, reason, and understanding.

### 651

The devil plagues and torments us in the place where we are most tender and weak. In Paradise, he fell not upon Adam, but upon Eve. It commonly rains where it was wet enough before.

When one is possessed with the doubt, that though be call upon the Lord he cannot be heard, and that God has turned his heart from him, and is angry, cogitations which we suffer, which are forced upon us, he must against them arm himself with God's Word, promising to hear him. As to the when and how God will hear him, this is stark naught; place, time, and person are accidental things; the substance and essence is the promise.

### 652

I have often need, in my tribulations, to talk even with a child, in order to expel such thoughts as the devil possesses me with; and this teaches me not to boast, as if of myself I were able to help myself, and to subsist without the strength of Christ. I need one, at times, to help me, who, in his whole body, has not so much divinity as I have in one finger.

### 653

In this life are many different degrees of tribulations, as there are different persons. Had another had the tribulations which I have suffered, he would long since have died; while I could not have endured the buffetings which St. Paul did, nor St. Paul the tribulations which Christ suffered. The greatest and heaviest grief is, when one dies in the twinkling of an eye. But hereof we ought not to dispute, but to refer the same to God's judgment.

### 654

When I am assailed with heavy tribulations, I rush out among my pigs, rather than remain alone by myself. The human heart is like a millstone in a mill; when you put wheat under it, it turns and grinds and bruises the wheat to flour; if you put no wheat, it still grinds on, but then 'tis itself it grinds and wears away. So the human heart, unless it be occupied with some employment, leaves space for the devil, who wriggles himself in, and brings with him a whole host of evil thoughts, temptations, and tribulations, which grind out the heart.

### 655

No papist among them will throw himself into the flames for his doctrine, whereas our people readily encounter fire and death, following therein the example of the holy martyrs, St. Agnes, St. Agatha, St. Vincent, St. Lawrence, etc. We are sheep for the slaughter. Only the other day, they burned, at Paris, two nobles and two magistrates, victims in the cause of the gospel, the king himself (Francis I), setting fire to the faggots.

### 656

My tribulations are more necessary for me than meat and drink; and all they that feel them ought to accustom themselves thereunto, and learn to bear them. If Satan had not so plagued and exercised me, I should not have been so great an enemy unto him, or have been able to do him such hurt. Tribulations keep us from pride, and therewith increase the acknowledgment of Christ and of God's gifts and benefits. For, from the time I began to be in tribulation, God gave me the victory of overcoming that confounded, cursed, and blasphemous life wherein I lived in Popedom. God did the business in such a way, that neither the emperor nor the pope was able to suppress me, but the devil must come and set upon me, to the end God's strength may be known in my weakness.

### 657

Our tribulations and doubts, wherewith the devil plagues us, can be driven away by no better means than by contemning him; as when one contemns a fierce cur, in passing quietly by him, the dog then not only desists from biting, but also from barking; but when one enrages him by timorously throwing something at him, then he falls upon and bites him. Even so, when the devil sees that we fear him, he ceases not to torment and plague us.

### 658

A woman at Eisenach lay very sick, having endured horrible paroxysms, which no physician was able to cure, for it was directly a work of the devil. She had had swoonings, and four paroxysms, each lasting three or four hours. Her hands and feet bent in the form of a horn; she was chill and cold; her tongue rough and dry; her body much swollen. She seeing Luther, who came to visit her, was much rejoiced thereat, raised herself up, and said: Ah! my loving father in Christ, I have a heavy burthen upon me, pray to God for me; and so fell down in her bed again. Whereupon Luther sighed, and said: 'God rebuke thee, Satan, and command thee that thou suffer this, his divine creature, to be at peace.' Then turning himself towards the standers by, he said: 'She is plagued of the devil in the body, but the soul is safe, and shall be preserved; therefore let us give thanks to God, and pray for her;' and so they all prayed aloud the Lord's prayer. After which, Luther concluded with these words: 'Lord God, heavenly Father! who hast commanded us to pray for the sick, we beseech thee, through Jesus Christ, thy only beloved Son, that thou wouldst deliver this thy servant from her sickness, and from the hands of the devil. Spare, O Lord, her soul, which, together with her body, thou hast purchased and redeemed from the power of sin, of death, and of the devil.' Whereupon the sick woman said: 'Amen.' The night following she took rest, and the next day was graciously delivered from her disease and sickness.

**659**

A letter, written by Luther to Doctor Benedict Paul, whose son had lately been killed by a fall from the top of a house: 'Although it be nowhere forbidden in Holy Scripture to mourn and grieve for the death of a godly child or friend – nay, we have many examples of the godly, who have bewailed the death of their children and friends – yet there ought to be a measure in sorrowing and mourning. Therefore, loving doctor, while you do well to mourn and lament the death of your son, let not your grief exceed the measure of a Christian, in refusing to be comforted. I would have you, first, consider 'twas God gave that son unto you, and took him from you again; secondly, I would wish you to follow the example of that just and godly man, Job, who, when he had lost all his children, all his wealth and substance, said: 'Have we received good at the hand of the Lord, and shall we not receive evil? The Lord gave, and the Lord hath taken away, blessed be the name of the Lord,' etc. He rightly considered that both good and evil come of the Lord; even so do you likewise; then you shall see that you have much greater gifts and benefits left of God to you than the evil you now feel. But you look now only upon the evil that your son is dead; and, meantime, you forget the glorious treasure God has given you, in the true knowledge of his word, a good and peaceable conscience, which alone should overweigh all evil which may happen unto you; why, then, do you plague and torment yourself with the death of your son? But, admit the loss a great and heavy one, 'tis no new thing; you are not alone therein, but have companions who have had like misfortunes. Abraham had much more sorrow of heart, concerning his son, while he was yet living, than if he had been dead. How think ye was it with him in his heart, when, with his naked sword, he was to strike off the head of his son? How was it also, think you, with Jacob, when he was informed that his loved son Joseph was torn in pieces by wild beasts? Or what father was ever perplexed and troubled in heart like David, when by his son Absalom he was persecuted and driven out of his kingdom, and when that son, in a state of rebellion, was slain and damned? Doubtless, David's heart at that time, with great grief, might have melted. Therefore, when you rightly behold and consider these and like examples of such high, enlightened people, you ought to feel that this your sorrow of heart is nothing comparable with theirs. Therefore know, loving brother, that God's mercy is greater than our tribulations. You have, indeed, cause to mourn, as you think, but it is nothing else than sugar mingled with vinegar; your son is very well provided for; he lives now with Christ; oh! would to God that I, too, had finished my course; I would not wish myself here again. Your suffering is only a corporal cross. You are a good logician and teach others that art; make use thereof yourself now; put it in practice; define, divide, conclude, distinguish that which is spiritual, and separate it from that which is corporal.'

### 660

When Satan will not leave off tempting thee, then bear with patience, hold on hand and foot, nor faint, as if there would be no end thereof, but stand courageously, and attend God's leisure, knowing that what the devil cannot accomplish by his sudden and powerful assaults, he thinks to gain by craft, by persevering to vex and tempt thee, thereby to make thee faint and weary, as in the Psalm is noted: 'Many a time have they afflicted me from my youth up; yet they have not prevailed against me,' etc. But be fully assured, that in this sport with the devil, God, with all his holy angels, takes delight and joy; and assure thyself, also, that the end thereof will be blessed and happy, which thou shalt certainly find to thy everlasting comfort.

### 661

Concerning predestination, it is best to begin below, at Christ, as then we both hear and find the Father; for all those that have begun at the top have broken their necks. I have been thoroughly plagued and tormented with such cogitations of predestination; I would needs know how God intended to deal with me, etc. But at last, God be praised! I clean left them; I took hold again on God's revealed word.; higher I was not able to bring it, for a human creature can never search out the celestial will of God; this God hides, for the sake of the devil, to the end the crafty spirit may be deceived and put to confusion. The revealed will of God the devil has learned from us, but God reserves his secret will to himself. It is sufficient for us to learn and know Christ in his humanity, in which the Father has revealed himself.

### 662

Christ, on the tenth day, came again into Jerusalem, and on the fourteenth day he was killed. His cogitations and tribulations then were concerning the sins of the whole world, concerning God's wrath and death, of which all ought to stand in fear. But before he was thus personally made sin for us, he was a man of sorrows, and acquainted with grief; his tribulations were concerning his labour and pains, which he knew would be spent in vain upon his own nation, the Jews, and over which he wept bitterly, because they knew not the time of their visitation.

### 663

More and greater sins are committed when people are alone than when they are in society. When Eve, in paradise, walked by herself, the devil deceived her. In solitary places are committed murders, robberies, adulteries, etc.; for in solitude the devil has place and occasion to mislead people. But whosoever is in honest company is ashamed to sin, or at least has no opportunity for it; and moreover, our Saviour Christ promised: 'Where two or three be gathered together in my name, there will I be in the midst of them.'

When king David was idle and alone, and went not out to the wars, then he fell into adultery and murder. I myself have found that I never fell into more sin than when I was alone. God has created mankind for fellowship, and not for solitariness, which is clearly proved by this strong argument: God, in the creation of the world, created man and woman, to the end that the man in the woman should have a fellow.

### 664

We find in no history any human creature oppressed with such sorrow as to sweat blood, therefore this history of Christ is wonderful; no man can understand or conceive what his bloody sweat is. And it is more wonderful, that the Lord of grace and of wrath, of life and of death, should be so weak, and made so sorrowful, as to be constrained to seek for solace and comfort of poor and miserable sinners, and to say: Ah, loving disciples! sleep not, wake yet a little, and talk one with another, that at least I may hear some people are about me. Here the Psalm was rightly applied, which says: 'Thou hast made him a little lower than the angels,' etc. Ah, that bloody sweat was pressed out of our blessed, sweet Saviour Christ Jesus, through the immeasurable heavy burden which lay on his innocent back; namely, the sins of the universal world, against which, doubtless, he prayed: 'O Lord, rebuke me not in thine anger, neither chasten me in thy hot displeasure.'

# Of Luther's Adversaries

---

### 665

SUCH fellows as Tetzel, Cochlaeus, Lemnius, I nothing regard. We should have no dealing with such backbiters and slanderers, they are most detestable; they appear not openly in the field, nor come right in our sight, but, in their poisoned hatred, scorn everything we do. They boast highly of the Fathers; let them: we have one Father, which is in heaven, who is above all fathers; their piece and patchwork is of no weight.

They write under the inspiration of a corrupt and vicious heart, and we all know that their works are mere impudent lies. The article of the Holy Trinity is nowhere written expressly in Holy Scripture, yet it is believed; therefore, they say, we ought also to believe traditions and ordinances of men without God's Word.

### 666

This Wetzell they have preferred at Leipzig, is a mischievous fellow. He was condemned to die, and would have been executed, but was saved at my intercession, and honourably entertained; now he requites me by his insolences. However, 'tis a wretch that has condemned himself; he is not worthy to be answered; he will have his judge. The papists will gain nothing by their railing. When they blaspheme, we should pray, and be silent, and not carry wood to the fire.

I am glad this fellow is at Leipzig; he is there like a mouse taken in a trap, for he is full of evil opinions; when they break out, he will get his payment. He got much poison from Campanus, who wrote a blasphemous book under this title: Against all that were and are in the world since the apostles' time. He has lost the general praise. He is reserved in his preachings; and cold, colder than ice. He dares not break out and say what he has in his heart; he goes like a shackled hare; he fears his hearers; his mouth is shut, his words captive, as in a dungeon. The words of an eloquent man should move others, and pierce the heart. But they that teach nothing uprightly or purely, are but half-learned; duncelike, bold, and presumptuous; as Carlstad is with his *Touto*, out of which he made *Autos*.

### 667

The emperor Sigismund was, as it were, made captive by the papists. They made him do what they pleased; to wear a deacon's coat, and, at Christmas, to read the gospel to the pope; so that every emperor is now said to be a deacon of the Romish church, the pope's mass-servant. The emperor, after he performed this ceremony, had never any success against the Turks or in Germany. The kingdom of Bohemia is fallen, which before was a very fair kingdom.

### 668

Latomus was the best among all my adversaries: his point was this: 'What is received of the church, ought not to be rejected.' As the Jews said: 'We are God's people;' so the papists cry: 'The church cannot err.' This was the argument against which the prophets and apostles fought; Moses says: 'They moved me to jealousy with that which was not God, and I will provoke them to anger with a foolish nation.' And St. Paul: 'That he is a Jew which is one inwardly;' and Isaiah: 'In him shall the Gentiles trust.'

'It is impossible,' say they, 'that God should forsake his church, for he declares, "I am with you always, unto the end of the world,"' etc. The question is, to whom do these words: with you, refer? which is the true church whereof Christ spake? The perplexed, broken and contrite in heart, or the Romish courtesans and knaves.

### 669

Philip Melancthon showing Luther a letter from Augsburg, wherein he was informed, that a very learned divine, a papist in that city, was converted, and had received the gospel, Luther said: I like those best that do not fall off suddenly, but ponder the case with considerate discretion, compare together the writings and arguments of both parties, and lay then on the gold balance, and in God's fear search after the upright truth; out of such, fit people are made, able to stand in controversy. Such a man was St. Paul, who at first was a strict Pharisee and man of works, who stiffly and earnestly held over and defended the law; but afterwards preached Christ in the best and purest manner against the whole nation of the Jews.

### 670

That impious knave, Martin Cellarius, thought to flatter me by saying: 'Thy calling is superior to that of the apostles;' but I at once checked him, replying sharply: 'By no means; I am in no degree comparable with the apostles.' He sent me four treatises he had written, about Moses' temple, and the allegories it involved; but I returned them at once, for they were full of the most arrogant self-glorification.

### 671

Erasmus of Rotterdam is the vilest miscreant that ever disgraced the earth. He made several attempts to draw me into his snares, and I should have been in danger, but that God lent me special aid. In 1525, he sent one of his doctors, with 200 Hungarian ducats, as a present to my wife; but I refused to accept them, and enjoined my wife to meddle not in these matters. He is a very Caiaphas.

'Qui Satanam non odit, amet tua carmina Erasme,
Atque idem jungat furias et mulgeat orcum.'

### 672

Erasmus is very pitiful with his prefaces, though he tries to smooth them over; he appears to see no difference between Jesus Christ our Saviour, and the wise pagan legislator Solon. He sneers at St. Paul and St. John; and ventures to say, that the Epistle to the Romans, whatever it might have been at a former period, is not applicable to the present state of things. Shame upon thee, accursed wretch! 'Tis a mere Momus, making his mows and mocks at everything and everybody, at God and man, at papist and Protestant, but all the while using such shuffling and double-meaning terms, that no one can lay hold of him to any effectual purpose. Whenever I pray, I pray for a curse upon Erasmus.

### 673

Carlstad opposed me merely out of ambition, for he flattered himself that on earth was not a more learned man than he. And although in his writings he imitated me, yet he played strange tricks with my manner. He wanted to be the great man, and truly I would willingly have left the honour to him, so far as it had not been against God. For, I praise my God, I was never so presumptuous as to think myself wiser than another man. When at first I wrote against indulgences, I designed simply to have opposed them, thinking that, afterwards, others would come and accomplish what I had begun.

### 674

We ought utterly to contemn and reject Campanus, and not to esteem him worthy of an answer, for thereby he becomes more audacious and insolent. Let us despise him, so will he soonest be smothered and suppressed.

### 675

Luther being informed that the preaching of James Schenck was everywhere extolled, said: O! how acceptable to me would these reports be, if with his preaching he brought not in such sweet-mouthed, smooth, and stately words, of which St. Paul complains to the Romans, whereby hearers are deceived. They are like the wind Cecias, which blows so mild and still, so soft and warm, that the blossoms of trees, and other herbs and flowers, are enticed to spring forth to their destruction. Even so the devil, when he preaches Christ in his ministers, intends to destroy Christ; and although he speak the truth, yet even therewith he lies. An honest man may well go up the stairs when a knave lies hid behind them; for the devil can well endure that Christ sit upon the tongue, meantime he himself lies hid under it, so that the people are tickled and inflamed with what they hear; but such smooth tattling lasts not long; for Satan, through the gospel, will pervert the gospel, because presumptuous and secure spirits acknowledge not their sins. And where there is no tinder to make it catch, there Christ has no room or place wherein he may work; for he is come only to them that are of perplexed, broken hearts and spirits. But these contemners of the law are haughty and proud spirits, just as the people in Popedom, under the tradition of the law, were far from observing the law, that being altogether strange to them. Therefore the preaching of the law is a preparation for the gospel, and gives matter for Christ to work upon, who is the only work-master of faith.

## 676

On the 15th of April, 1539, certain positions, printed at Leipzig, were sent to Luther, wherein John Hammer subtly maintained that the law concerned the Christians nothing at all; be also divided repentance into three parts, and said: The Jews had one kind of repentance, the Gentiles another kind, and the Christians a third. Whereupon Luther said: Who could have ever thought such extravagant spirits should come? 'Tis an utter and mischievous error, to distinguish repentance according to persons, whereas there is only one kind of repentance given to all mankind, seeing that all, one as well as another, have angered and offended one only God, whether Jews, Gentiles, or Christians. 'Tis as gross, abominable, and manifest error, as it were to say that men have another kind of repentance than women have; princes than subjects; masters than servants; rich than poor – making God to be a respecter of persons: as though the prophets had not taught uprightly of repentance, and as though the repentance of the Ninevites was not upright and true; whence, at last, would follow, that if we preached not repentance out of the law, Christ was not under the law, whereas he was, for our sakes, under the curse of the law.

## 677

On the 13th of September, 1538, a warm disputation was held, nearly five hours long, in which Luther powerfully inveighed against innovators, telling them that they would destroy the gospel, and abolish the law, and would bring to evil those minds which were too secure. He said he would resist them to his last breath, did it cost him his life. In the evening, he discoursed of the heresy of Arius; when that innovator began to preach his doctrine, Peter, patriarch of Alexandria, denounced it as erroneous, and against Christ's honour, seeing that he who denies the divinity of Christ, certainly deprives him of his honour. Arius began by denying that Christ was God, affirming that he was only a creature, though a perfect creature. But when the godly bishops resisted him, he said, secondly, that Christ, the most perfect of creatures, yea, above the angels, had made all other creatures. Thirdly, he alleged that Christ was God, emanating from God, as light from light; and he taught so subtly, that many people joined him, and shared his opinions. The pious bishop of Milan, Auxentius, against whom Hilary wrote an epistle, fell into his errors.

Arius finished by saying, that Christ was not born of the Father, equal to God, but was of one substance with the Father, and would not give up this assertion as to his creation. Then began the strife about the word Homousion, which was inserted in the Athanasian creed, but which is nowhere written in the Holy Scripture, that he was born of the Father, yet it was pertinent, and in respect to his human nature rightly spoken.

The heresies of Arius continued very long, above three hundred years. They were in highest flourish under Constantine; under Domitian they tyrannized; under Jovian, Valentinian, and Gratian, they somewhat decreased. They lasted the time of seven emperors, until the Goths came. The great Turk, to this day, is an Arian. We thus see that there is no heresy, no error, no idolatry, however gross, which does not obtain partisans and supporters. 'Tis manifest, in the present day, at Rome, where the pope is honoured as a God.

## 678

Philip Melancthon has a good conscience, and therefore takes matters to heart. Christ well and thoroughly exercised our forefathers; he who belongs to Christ must feel the serpent's sting in the heel. No doubt the mother of our Lord was a poor maid, for she was betrothed to a carpenter, also poor.

Let us then be merry and contented in poverty and trouble, and remember that we have a rich master, who will not leave us without help and comfort; in so doing, we shall have peaceful consciences, let it go with us as God please. The ungodly want this peace in their hearts; as Isaiah says: 'They are as the waves of the sea; neither have the covetous usurers any peace of conscience.'

## 679

Erasmus was poisoned at Rome and at Venice with epicurean doctrines. He extols the Arians more highly than the Papists; he ventured to say that Christ is named God but once in St. John, where Thomas says: 'My Lord and my God.' His chief doctrine is, we must carry ourselves according to the time, or, as the proverb goes, hang the cloak according to the wind; he only, looked to himself, to have good and easy days, and so died like an epicurean, without any one comfort of God.

## 680

This do I leave behind me as my will and testament, whereunto I make you witnesses. I hold Erasmus of Rotterdam to be Christ's most bitter enemy. In his catechism, of all his writings that which I can least endure, he teaches nothing decided; not one word says: Do this, or, do not this; he only therein throws error and despair into youthful consciences. He wrote a book against me, called *Hyperaspites*, wherein he proposed to defend his work on free-will, against which I wrote my *De servo Arbitrio*, which has never yet been confuted, nor will it ever be by Erasmus, for I am certain that what I wrote on the matter is the unchangeable truth of God. If God live in heaven, Erasmus will one day know and feel what he has done.

Erasmus is the enemy to true religion, the open adversary of Christ, the complete and faithful picture and image of Epicurus and of Lucian.

## 681

I care not at all for an open enemy of the church, such as the papists with their power and persecutions; I regard them not, for by them the true church cannot receive hurt, nor can they hinder God's Word; nay, the church, through their raging and persecution, rather increases. But it is the inward evil of false brethren that will do mischief to the church. Judas betrayed Christ; the false apostles confused and falsified the gospel. Such are the real fellows through whom the devil rages and spoils the church.

## 682

I know not well how to render the word *hypocrita*. Mere hypocrite, as we commonly accept it, is too mild and soft a name for a false brother; it should convey almost as much as *sycophanta*, a wicked villain, who for his own private gain does mischief to others. Such, hypocrites were the servants of king Saul, who, for the sake of their bellies, spake against righteous David, backbiting him in the king's presence, whereby the land was stained. *Hypocrita is* not only a hypocrite or a flatterer that pretends love towards one *and* speaks that which tickles the ears, but one that produces mischief under colour of holiness, as the examples in the twenty-third chapter of Matthew clearly show. St. Jerome says: Feigned holiness is a double evil.

## 683

The greatest and fiercest strife that Christians have, is with false brethren. If a false brother would openly say: I am a Pilate, a Herod, an Annas, that is, if he would put off the name of a believing Christian, and profess himself an open enemy to Christ, then we would patiently endure all the evil he could work upon us. But that such should bear the name of Christians, we cannot and will not endure; this rule and government over the conscience, we divines take properly unto us, and say: It is ours through the Word, we will not suffer ourselves to be bereaved of it, by any means.

### 684

We have hooted away the friars and priests, by the preaching of the gospel, and now the false brethren plague us. Truly 'tis a right sentence: 'He came unto his own, and his own received him not.'

### 685

I marvel that nothing is written of the villany Judas did to Christ. I am persuaded he did it for the most part with the tongue; for Christ, not in vain, complains of him in the 41st Psalm. Doubtless he went to the high priests and elders, and spake grievously against Christ, saying: I baptize also, but now I see, 'tis frivolous and nothing worth. Moreover, he was a thief; he thought to make great gain in betraying Christ (as Wetzell and others think by our means to be made great lords); he was a wicked, desperate villain, or Christ would have forgiven him, as he forgave Peter. But Peter fell out of weakness; Judas out of wickedness.

### 686

Judas was as necessary among the apostles as any three of them. For he confuted many arguments of the heretics, who alleged that no man can baptize, but he that has the Holy Ghost. What he did in his office was good and right, but when he played the thief, he did wrong and sinned. Therefore we must separate and distinguish his person from his office; for Christ commanded him not to steal, but to execute his office, to preach, to baptize, etc. Judas likewise confuted what some object to us, who say: There are among you protestants, many wicked wretches, false brethren, and unchristian-like offenders. Herein comes Judas and says: I was also an apostle, I behaved and carried myself, as an understanding worldly-wise companion and politician, much better than the others, my fellow apostles; no man thought that such mischief was hid in me. Judas at the Lord's Supper, was directly the pope, who also has got hold of the purse, is a covetous wretch, a thief, and belly-god, who will also speak in praise of Christ: in truth, 'tis a right Iscariot.

# Of Offences

## 687

When we read that Judas hanged himself, that his belly burst in pieces, and that his bowels fell out, we may take this as a sample how it will go with all Christ's enemies. The Jews ought to have made a mirror of Judas, and have seen therein how they in like manner should be destroyed. An allegory or mystery herein lies hid, for the belly signifies the whole kingdom of the Jews, which shall also fall away and be destroyed, so that nothing thereof shall remain. When we read that the bowels fell out, this shows that the posterity of the Jews, their whole generation, shall be spoiled and go to the ground.

## 688

I may compare the state of a Christian to a goose, tied up over a wolf's pit to catch wolves. About the pit stand many ravening wolves, that would willingly devour the goose, but she is preserved alive, while they, leaping at her, fall into the pit, are taken and destroyed. Even so, we that are Christians are preserved by the sweet loving angels, so that the devils, those ravening wolves, the tyrants and persecutors, cannot destroy us.

## 689

We little know how good and necessary it is for us to have adversaries, and for heretics to hold up their heads against us. For if Cerinthus had not been, then St. John the Evangelist had not written his gospel; but when Cerinthus opposed the godhead in our Lord Christ, John was constrained to write and say: In the beginning was the Word; making the distinction of the three persons so clear, that nothing could be clearer. So when I began to write against indulgences and against the pope, Dr. Eck set upon me, and aroused me out of my drowsiness. I wish from my heart this man might be turned the right way, and be converted; for that I would give one of my fingers; but if he will remain where he is, I wish he were made pope, for he has well deserved it, for hitherto he has had upon him the whole burthen of Popedom, in disputing and writing against me. Besides him, they have none that dare fall upon me; he raised my first cogitations against the pope, and brought me so far, or otherwise I never should have gone on.

### 690

A liar is far worse, and does greater mischief, than a murderer on the highway; for a liar and false teacher deceives people, seduces souls, and destroys them under the colour of God's Word; such a liar and murderer was Judas, like his father the devil. It was a marvel how Judas should sit at the table with Christ, and not blush for shame, when Christ said: 'One of you shall betray me,' etc. The other disciples had not the least thought that Judas would betray Christ; each was rather afraid of himself, thinking Christ meant him; for Christ trusted Judas with the purse, and the whole management of the house-keeping, whence he was held in great repute by the apostles.

### 691

A scorpion thinks when his head lies hid under a leaf, that he cannot be seen; even so the hypocrites and false saints think, when they have hoisted up one or two good works, that all their sins therewith are covered and hid.

### 692

False Christians that boast of the gospel, and yet bring no good fruits, are like the clouds without rain, wherewith the whole element is overshadowed, gloomy and dark, and yet no rain falls to fructify the ground: even so, many Christians affect great sanctity and holiness, but they have neither faith nor love towards God, nor love towards their neighbour.

### 693

Job says: 'The life of a human creature is a warfare upon earth.' A human creature, especially a Christian, must be a soldier, ever striving and fighting with the enemy. And St. Paul describes the armour of a Christian, Ephesians 6, thus:

First, the girdle of truth; that is, the confession of the pure doctrine of the gospel, an upright, not a hypocritical or feigned faith.

Secondly, the breast-plate of righteousness, by which is not meant the righteousness of a good conscience, although this be also needful: for it is written, 'Enter not into judgment with thy servant,' etc; and St. Paul: 'I know nothing of myself, yet I am not thereby justified,' but the righteousness of faith, and of the remission of sins, which Paul means in that place, touching which Moses spake, Genesis 15: 'Abraham believed God, and that was imputed unto him for righteousness.'

Thirdly, the shoes wherewith the feet are shod; viz. the works of the vocation, whereby we ought to remain, and not to go further, or to break out beyond the appointed mark.

Fourthly, the shield of faith; similar to this is the fable of Perseus with the head of Gorgon, upon which whoso looked died immediately; as Perseus held and threw Gorgon's head before his enemies, and thereby got the victory, even so a Christian must likewise hold and cast the Son of God, as Gorgon's head, before all the evil instigations and crafts of the devil, and then most certainly he shall prevail and get the victory.

Fifthly, the helmet of salvation; that is, the hope of everlasting life. The weapon wherewith a Christian fights, the enemy is: 'The sword of the spirit' (1 Thess. 5), that is, God's word and prayer; for as the lion is frightened at nothing more than at the crowing of a cock, so the devil can be overcome and vanquished with nothing else than with God's word and prayer; of this Christ himself has given us an example.

### 694

Our life is like the sailing of a ship; as the mariners in the ship have before them a haven towards which they direct their course, and where they will be secure from all danger, even so the promise of everlasting life is made unto us, that we therein, as in a safe haven, may rest calm and secure. But seeing our ship is weak, and the winds and waves beat upon us, as though they would overwhelm us, therefore we have need of a good and experienced pilot, who with his counsel and advice may rule and govern the vessel, that it run not on a rock, or utterly sink and go down. Such a pilot is our blessed Saviour Christ Jesus.

## 695

Ingratitude is a very irksome thing, which no human creature can tolerate; yet our Lord God can endure it. If I had had to do with the Jews, patience would have failed me; I had never been able so long to endure their stubbornness. The prophets were always poor, contemned people; plagued and persecuted not only by outward and open, but also by inward and secret enemies, for the most part of their own people. That which the pope does against us is nothing to compare with that which Jeckel and others do, to our sorrow of heart.

## 696

We ought diligently to be aware of sophistry, which not only consists in doubtful and uncertain words, that may be construed and turned as one pleases, but also, in each profession, in all high arts, as in religion, covers and cloaks itself with the fair name of Holy Scripture, alleging to be God's word, and spoken from heaven. Those are unworthy of praise who can pervert everything, screwing, contemning, and rejecting the meanings and opinions of others, and, like the philosopher Carneades, disputing *in utraque parte*, and yet conclude nothing certain. These are knavish tricks and sophistical inventions. But a fine understanding, honestly disposed, that seeks after truth, and loves that which is plain and upright, is worthy of all honour and praise.

## 697

Offences by Christians are far more abominable than those by the heathen. The prophet Jeremiah says: 'The punishment of the iniquity of the daughter of my people, is greater than the punishment of the sin of Sodom,' etc. And Ezekiel: 'Thou hast justified Sodom with thine abominations.' And Christ: 'It will be more tolerable for Sodom at the day of judgment, than with thee.' But so it must be: 'He came unto his own, and his own received him not.' Truly this makes the godly altogether faint and out of heart, so that they rather desire death, for, with sorrow of heart, we find that many of our people offend others. We ought diligently to pray to God against offences, to the end his name may be hallowed. St. Paul says: 'Also of our ownselves shall men arise, speaking perverse things, to draw away disciples after them.' Therefore the church has no external esteem or succession; it inherits not.

## 698

True, much offence proceeds out of my doctrine; but I comfort myself, as St. Paul did Titus: whereas this doctrine is revealed for the sake of the faith of

God's chosen, for whose sake we also preach, we mean it earnestly. For the sake of others I would not drop one word. I have cracked many hollow nuts, and yet I thought they had been good, but they fouled my mouth, and filled it with dust; Carlstad and Erasmus are mere hollow nuts, and foul the mouth.

### 699

It has been asked: Is an offence, committed in a moment of intoxication, therefore excusable? Most assuredly not; on the contrary, drunkenness aggravates the fault. Hidden sins unveil themselves when a man's self-possession goes from him; that which the sober man keeps in his breast, the drunken man lets out at the lips. Astute people, when they want to ascertain a man's true character, make him drunk. This same drunkenness is a grievous vice among us Germans, and should be heavily chastised by the temporal magistrate, since the fear of God will not suffice to keep the brawling guzzlers in check.

### 700

A rich Jew, on his death bed, ordered that his remains should be conveyed to Ratisbon. His friends, knowing that even the corpse of a Jew could not travel without paying heavy toll, devised the expedient of packing the carcass in a barrel of wine, which they then forwarded in the ordinary way. The wagoners, not knowing what lay within, tapped the barrel, and swilled away right joyously, till they found out they had been drinking Jew's pickle. How it fared with them you may imagine.

# OF A CHRISTIAN LIFE

⟨⟨⟩⟩

## 701

A CHRISTIAN'S worshipping is not the external, hypocritical mask that our spiritual friars wear, when they chastise their bodies, torment and make themselves faint, with ostentatious fasting, watching, singing, wearing hair shirts, scourging themselves, etc. Such worshipping God desires not.

## 702

'Tis a great blindness of people's hearts that they cannot accept of the treasure of grace presented unto them. Such people are we, that though we are baptised, have Christ, with all his precious gifts, faith, the sacraments, his Word, all which we confess to be holy, yet we can neither say nor think that we ourselves are holy; we deem it too much to say, we are holy; whereas the name Christian is far more glorious and greater than the name holy.

## 703

We can call consecrated robes, dead men's bones, and such trumpery, holy, but not a Christian; the reason is, we gaze upon the outward mask, we look after the seeming saint, who leads an austere life. Hence that vain opinion in Popedom, that they call the dead saints; an error strengthened by Zuinglius. Human wisdom gapes at holyworkers, thinking whoso does good works is just and righteous before God.

## 704

There's no better death than St. Stephen's, who said: 'Lord receive my spirit.' We should lay aside the register of our sins and deserts, and die in reliance only upon God's mere grace and mercy.

## 705

We ought to retain the feast of John the Baptist, with whom the New Testament began, for it is written: 'All the prophets and the law prophesied until John,' etc. We should observe it, too, for the sake of the fair song, which in Popedom we read, but understood not, of Zachariah, which, indeed, is a most excellent song; as is shown in St. Luke's preface, where he says: 'And Zachariah was full of the Holy Ghost,' etc.

## 706

A householder instructs his servants and family in this manner: Deal uprightly and honestly, be diligent in that which I command you, and ye may then eat, drink, and clothe yourselves as ye please. Even so, our Lord God regards not what we eat, drink, or how we clothe ourselves; all such matters, being ceremonies or middle things, he leaves freely to us, on the understanding, however, that we ground nothing thereon as being necessary to salvation.

## 707

'Twas a strange thing the world should have been offended at him who raised the dead, made the blind to see, and the deaf to hear, etc. They who deem such a man a devil, what manner of God would they have? But here it is. Christ would give to the world the kingdom of heaven, but they will have the kingdom of the earth, and here they part; for the highest wisdom and sanctity of the hypocrites sees nothing but temporal honour, carnal will, mundane life, good days, money and wealth, all which must vanish and cease.

## 708

The whole world takes offence at the plainness of the second table of God's ten commandments, because human sense and reason partly understand what is done contrary thereto. When God and his Word is contemned, the world is silent and regards it not; but when a monastery is taken, or flesh eaten on a Friday, or a friar marries, O, then the world cries out: Here are abominable offences!

## 709

The obedience towards God is the obedience of faith and good works; that is, he who believes in God, and does what God has commanded, is obedient unto him; but the obedience towards the devil is superstition and evil works; that is, who trusts not in God, but is unbelieving, and does evil, is obedient unto the devil.

## 710

In the Old Testament are two sorts of sacrifices: the first was called the early morning sacrifice; thereby is shown that we first should offer unto Christ, not oxen or cattle, but ourselves, acknowledging God's gifts, corporal and spiritual, temporal and eternal, and giving him thanks for them. Secondly, the evening sacrifice; whereby is signified that a Christian should offer a broken, humble, and a contrite heart, consider his necessities and dangers, both corporal and spiritual, and call upon God for help.

## 711

God wills, say some, that we should serve him freely and willingly, whereas he that serves God out of fear of punishment, of hell, or out of a hope and love of recompence, serves and honours God not uprightly or truly. This argument is of the stoics, who reject the affections of human nature. It is true we ought willingly to serve, love, and fear God, as the chief good. But God can well endure that we love him for his promise' sake, and pray unto him for corporal and spiritual benefits; he therefore has commanded us to pray. So God can also endure that we fear him for the punishment's sake, as the prophets remember. Indeed, it is somewhat, that a human creature can acknowledge God's everlasting punishment and rewards. And if one looks thereupon, as not being the chief end and cause, then it hurts him not, especially if he has regard to God himself, as the final cause, who gives everything for nothing, out of mere grace, without our deserts.

## 712

The word, to worship, means to stoop and bow down the body with external gestures; to serve in the work. But to worship God in spirit is the service and honour of the heart; it comprehends faith and fear in God. The worshipping of God is twofold, outward and inward – that is, to acknowledge God's benefits, and to be thankful unto him.

### 713

A certain prince of Germany, well known to me, went to Compostella in Spain, where they pretend St. James, brother of the Evangelist St. John, lies buried. This prince made his confession to a Franciscan, an honest man, who asked him if he were a German? The prince answered, yes. Then the friar said: 'O, loving child, why seekest thou so far away that which thou hast much better in Germany? I have seen and read the writings of an Augustine friar, touching indulgences and the pardons of sin, wherein he powerfully proves that the true remission of sins consists in the merits and sufferings of our Lord and Saviour Jesus Christ. O loving son, remain thereby, and permit not thyself to be otherwise persuaded. I purpose shortly, God willing, to leave this unchristian life, to repair into Germany, and to join the Augustine friar.'

### 714

Since the gospel has been preached, which is not above twenty years, such great wonders have been done as were not in many hundred years before. No man ever thought such alterations should happen; that so many monasteries should be made empty, that the private mass should be abolished in Germany, despite heretics, sectaries, and tyrants. Rome has twice been ravaged, and many great princes, who persecuted the gospel, have been thrown down to the ground and destroyed.

# Of Marriage and Celibacy

### 715

A PREACHER of the gospel, being regularly called, ought, above all things, first, to purify himself before he teaches others. Is he able, with a good conscience, to remain unmarried? let him so remain; but if he cannot abstain living chastely, then let him take a wife; God has made that plaster for that sore.

### 716

It is written in the first book of Moses, concerning matrimony: God created a man and a woman; and blessed them. Now, although this sentence was chiefly spoken of human creatures, yet we may apply it to all the creatures of the world – to the fowls of the air, the fish in the waters, and the beasts of the field, wherein we find a male and a female consorting together, engendering and increasing. In all these, God has placed before our eyes the state of matrimony. We have its image, also, even in the trees and earth.

### 717

Between husband and wife there should be no question as to *meum* and *tuum*. All things should be in common between them, without any distinction or means of distinguishing.

### 718

St. Augustine said, finely: A marriage without children is the world without the sun.

### 719

Maternity is a glorious thing, since all mankind have been conceived, born, and nourished of women. All human laws should encourage the multiplication of families.

### 720

The world regards not, nor comprehends the works of God. Who can sufficiently admire the state of conjugal union, which God has instituted and founded, and whence all human creatures, yea, all states proceed. Where were we, if it existed not? But neither God's ordinance, nor the gracious presence of children, the fruit of matrimony, moves the ungodly world, which beholds only the temporal difficulties and troubles of matrimony, but sees not the great treasure that is hid therein. We were all born of woman — emperors, kings, princes, yea, Christ himself, the Son of God, did not disdain to be born of a virgin. Let the contemners and rejecters of matrimony go hang, the Anabaptists and Adamites, who recognise not marriage, but live all together like animals, and the papists, who reject married life, and yet have strumpets; if they must needs contemn matrimony, let them be consistent and keep no concubines.

### 721

The state of matrimony is the chief in the world after religion; but people shun it because of its inconveniences, like one who, running out of the rain, falls into the river. We ought herein to have more regard to God's command and ordinance, for the sake of the generation, and the bringing up of children, than to our untoward humours and cogitations; and further, we should consider that it is a physic against sin and unchastity. None, indeed, should be compelled to marry; the matter should be left to each man's conscience, for bride-love may not be forced. God has said: 'It is not good that the man should be alone;' and St. Paul compares the church to a spouse, or bride and a bridegroom. But let us ever take heed that, in marrying, we esteem neither money nor wealth, great descent, nobility, nor lasciviousness.

### 722

He who intends to marry, should consider these points following: 1. God's command. 2. The Lord Christ's confirmation thereof. 3. The gift or present of Christ. 4. The first blessing. 5. The promise that is made thereunto. 6. The communion and fellowship. 7. The examples of the holy patriarchs. 8. The temporal laws and ordinances. 9. The precious benediction and blessing. 10. The examples of the wicked. 11. The threatening of St. Paul. 12. The natural rights. 13. The nature and kind of the creation. 14. The practice of faith and hope.

### 723

The Lord has never changed the rules he imposed on marriage, but in the case of the conception of his Son Jesus Christ. The Turks, however, are of opinion that 'tis no uncommon thing for a virgin to bear a child. I would by no means introduce this belief into my family.

### 724

Dr. Forsteimius asked, whether a man, whose wife, guilty of adultery, has run away from him, might marry another, while the former wife yet lived, without the offence of adultery? Luther answered: St. Paul says: 'If the unbelieving depart, let him depart; a brother or a sister is not under bondage in such cases, but God hath called us to peace.' Here St. Paul plainly permits the other marriage.

### 725

Men have broad and large chests, and small narrow hips, and more understanding than the women, who have but small and narrow breasts, and broad hips, to the end they should remain at home, sit still, keep house, and bear and bring up children.

### 726

Marrying cannot be without women, nor can the world subsist without them. To marry is physic against incontinence. A woman is, or at least should be, a friendly, courteous, and merry companion in life, whence they are named, by the Holy Ghost, house-honours, the honour and ornament of the house, and inclined to tenderness, for thereunto are they chiefly created, to bear children, and be the pleasure, joy, and solace of their husbands.

### 727

Dr. Luther said one day to his wife: You make me do what you will; you have full sovereignty here, and I award you, with all my heart, the command in all household matters, reserving my rights in other points. Never any good came out of female domination. God created Adam master and lord of living creatures, but Eve spoilt all, when she persuaded him to set himself above God's will. 'Tis you women, with your tricks and artifices, that lead men into error.

### 728

On what pretence can man have interdicted marriage, which is a law of nature? 'Tis as though we were forbidden to eat, to drink, to sleep. That which God has ordained and regulated, is no longer a matter of the human will, which we may adopt or reject with impunity. 'Tis the most certain sign of God's enmity to Popedom, that he has allowed it to assail the conjugal union of the sexes.

### 729

There is no greater plague in this life than a morose and unchaste wife. Solomon says, that to be married to a woman one dislikes, is the worst of calamities.

### 730

When I began to discern the impiety and tyranny of celibacy, distrusting my own judgment, I called upon Dr. Jerome Schurff, and asked him to point out to me, in the decretals, some assigned reasons for imposing this tyranny upon the consciences of priests. I had not then the same feeling with regard to monks, who had made a vow on the subject. The doctor gave me no distinct answer, vaguely saying, that the pope compelled no one to assume the priesthood, so he left me as much in doubt and difficulty as before.

### 731

It was mentioned at table that a book had just been published, setting forth the apology of bigamy: the doctor for awhile remained silent, and seemed plunged in grave reverie. At length he said: 'I have often wondered at the king of Arabia having seven hundred wives.' Some one observed: 'Sir doctor, what say you to Solomon, who had three hundred wives, or queens, and seven hundred concubines? The text, moreover, adding, that the number of young girls at his court had not been reckoned up.' The doctor replied: ''Tis to be kept in mind that the list of queens in Scripture comprehends the royal family of David, who were supported by his son. The elector of Saxony has a great number of ladies at his court, princesses, noble damsels, women of honour, maids of honour, women of the bedchamber, and what not; but it does not follow that these are all his wives. As to Solomon's having entertained all these women as his wives, 'tis out of the question, impracticable.' Some one asked, did Solomon perform penitence? Luther replied: 'No, but the Scripture tells us, "He slept with his fathers," wherefore I conclude he was admitted to beatitude, such being the meaning of that expression, which is not employed with reference to Absalom. Scotus has formally damned Solomon.'

### 732

'Tis a grand thing for a married pair to live in perfect union, but the devil rarely permits this. When they are apart, they cannot endure the separation, and when they are together, they cannot endure the always seeing one another. 'Tis as the poet says: *Nec tecum vivere possum, nec sine te.* Married people must assiduously pray against these assaults of the devil. I have seen marriages where, at first, husband and wife seemed as though they would eat one another up: in six months they have separated in mutual disgust. 'Tis the devil inspires this evanescent ardour, in order to divert the parties from prayer.

### 733

We must hold no relations with those who seek to set up houses of evil resort. We must resolutely repress the devil, instead of encouraging him. They who would restore the bagnios are not Christians, but pagans, knowing not God. The Lord has said he will punish debauchery, and assuredly he will also punish those who foster and authorize it. It may be said, if we have not public establishments of the kind, the result will be fearful disorder in families. I answer that God, of his grace, has instituted a remedy, marriage. I hold that the example of public licence in this respect is calculated to draw women and girls into vice. We must in no way tolerate, or even wink at, aught that is contrary to the will of God: *fiat justitia et pereat mundus.*

### 734

Both the Old and the New Testament attribute eminence and honour to the married state. Abraham had three wives; Jesus Christ was present at a marriage ceremony, and performed his first miracle there. St. Paul, himself a widower, enjoins bishops to marry, and predicts that the injunction of celibacy, will cause much evil; St. Peter was a son-in-law, and consequently must have been himself married; St. James, our Saviour's brother, and indeed all the apostles, except St. John, were married men; Spiridiron, bishop of Cyprus, was a married man, and so was bishop Hilary, of whom we have a letter, addressed to his daughter, telling her he knows a rich man, meaning Christ, who, if she remains pious and good, will give her a fine robe, adorned with gold.

### 735

There are two sorts of adultery; spiritual adultery, committed only in sight of God, when one desires the husband or wife of another; and bodily adultery, when the offence is actually committed, a crime most odious, but little regarded by the world, a crime at once against God, against society, and against one's family.

### 736

I am persuaded that if God had not ordained marriage, but had left men to associate with the first women they met, they themselves would very speedily have become tired of this disorderly course, and have prayed for marriage, since 'tis the very prohibition to do wrong which most excites to wrong. The ancients said: *Nitimur in vetitum, semper cupimusque negates. Quod licet ingratum est, quod non licet acrius urit.*

### 737

Dr. Luther said, in reference to those who write satirical attacks upon women, that such will not go unpunished. If the author be one of high rank, rest assured he is not really of noble origin, but a surreptitious intruder into the family. What defects women have, we must check them for in private, gently by word of mouth, for woman is a frail vessel. The doctor then turned round and said: let us talk of something else.

### 738

Mention was made of a young girl who, to avoid violence offered her by a nobleman, threw herself from the window, and was killed. It was asked, was she responsible for her death? Doctor Luther said: No: she felt that this step formed her only chance of safety, it being not her life she sought to save, but her chastity.

### 739

There was at Frankfort-on-the-Oder, a schoolmaster, a pious and learned man, whose heart was fervently inclined to theology, and who had preached several times with great applause. He was called to the dignity of deacon, but his wife, a violent, fierce woman, would not consent to his accepting the charge, saying, she would not be the wife of a minister.

It became a question, what was the poor man to do? which was he to renounce, his preachership, or his wife? Luther, at first, said jocosely: 'Oh, if he has married, as you tell me, a widow, he must needs obey her.' But, after awhile, he resumed, severely: 'The wife is bound to follow her husband, not the husband his wife. This must be an ill woman, nay, the devil incarnate, to be ashamed of a charge with which our Lord and his apostles were invested. If she were my wife, I should shortly say to her: "Wilt thou follow me, aye or no? Reply forthwith," and if she replied: No: I would leave her, and take another wife.'

### 740

He who has an old, spiteful, quarrelsome, sickly wife, may fairly reckon himself in purgatory.

### 741

It was asked, does he who, by his own consent, carries off a girl he loves, commit a sin or offence, since *volenti non fit injuria*. Dr. Luther replied: The injury is done, not to her who gives her consent, but to her parents, who, against their will, are deprived of their daughter. 'Tis therefore a robbery, and as such, justly visited of the imperial law with severe punishment. The Roman antichrist, however, in his decretals, excuses this crime.

### 742

The polygamy of the patriarchs, Gideon, David, Solomon, etc., was a matter of necessity, not of libertinism. The Jews were constrained to have several wives, from the necessity of the promise, and of consanguinity. Abraham, Isaac, and Jacob received from God the promise that he would multiply their seed as the stars of heaven, or the sands of the sea shore. The Jews, having their attention constantly directed to this promise, to accomplish it were fain to take several wives each. The necessity of consanguinity was this, that when a man was elected judge or king, all his poor female relations crowded about him, and he had to take them as wives or concubines. Concubinage was lawful among the Jews, and was, indeed, a mode of aiding distressed relatives, widows and orphans, to whom it secured food and raiment. It was a burdensome imposition rather than an agreeable relaxation. Solomon's wives, most of them, were probably no more to him than my nieces, Magdalen and Elizabeth, are to me, who have remained under my roof virgins, as when they came here.

### 743

When the emperor Sigismund convoked a council at Constance, the cardinal would not hear of any reform, and said: We will have no *Schismam*. The emperor rejoined: What, know ye not Priscian? You should say, *Schisma*, not *Schismam*. But the cardinals replied: We are above all rules and laws, and care not a rush for Priscian.

### 744

Jephtha made a foolish and a superstitious vow; so that after he had got the victory, he had to slay his own daughter. It had been well if, at that time, some godly man had been present, and had said unto him – Jephtha! thou shouldst not slay thy daughter, for the sake of thy rash and foolish vow; thou must understand the law of vows according to equity, and not so precisely according to the word, for thou didst not mean it so. Thus, the godly young man, Jonathan, was released from the vow he had made to his father, king Saul, and was delivered from death. The reason why Jephtha's daughter bewailed her virginity two months, was, that she died without children, which among the Jews was held a great calamity; as we see in Hannah, Samuel's mother. And, indeed, 'tis an irksome thing to honest married people, to be barren; children are the best pledges and bonds of matrimony. They are the best wool of the sheep.

### 745

The lawyers and canonists are of opinion, that the substance of matrimony is the consent of the bride and bridegroom, and that the privilege and power of the parents is but an accidental thing, without which matrimony may well be accomplished, and that we ought not to resist or hinder the substance, for the sake of the accidents. And 'tis quite true that consent is the substance and ground of matrimony, for where no love or consent is, there must needs be an unhappy marriage. And further, when such children are punished, thinking thereby to affright them, we shall nothing prevail, for youth in this matter will not desist through temporal punishment.

### 746

When one in Popedom is godfather or mother to another's child, this relationship bars marriage between those persons. Now, this is altogether ridiculous, or rather 'tis one of the Pope's money-nets. Marriages made for the sake of wealth, are commonly accursed; rich women, for the most part, are haughty, cross, and negligent, and waste more than they bring.

### 747

There are two causes of divorce: first, adultery; but first, Christians ought to labour and to use diligent persuasions to reconcile the married pair; sharply, withal, reproving the guilty person. The second cause is much like; when one runs away from the other, and after returning runs away again. Such have commonly their mates in other places, and richly deserve to be punished.

### 748

I advise in everything that ministers interfere not in matrimonial questions. First, because we have enough to do in our own office; secondly, because these affairs concern not the church, but are temporal things, pertaining to temporal magistrates; thirdly, because such cases are in a manner innumerable; they are very high, broad and deep, and produce many great offences, which may tend to the shame and dishonour of the gospel. Moreover, we are therein ill dealt with; they draw us into the business, and then, if the issue is evil, the blame is altogether laid upon us. Therefore, we will leave them to the lawyers and magistrates. Ministers ought only to advise and counsel the consciences, out of God's Word, when need requires.

### 749

In the synod of Leipzig, the lawyers concluded, that secret marriages should be punished with banishment, and the parties be disinherited. Whereupon I sent them word, I would not allow thereof; it were too gross. Yet I hold it fitting, that they who secretly contract themselves, ought sharply to be reproved; yea, also, in some measure punished.

### 750

Master John Holstein asked, when two contract themselves, *verbis de futuro*, as when I say, I will marry thee, is this to be understood of the time to come, or no? Luther said: those words ought to be understood of the present time; for this word (*Volo*) I will, signifies a present will. All bargains, contracts, and promises are to be understood as of the present time; as when a fellow says to a maid: When I come again, which will be, God willing, two years hence, I wilt marry thee. These words are to be understood of the present time, and when he comes again, he must marry her; and it is not in his power, in the interval, to alter his mind.

### 751

The hair is the finest ornament women have. Of old, virgins used to wear it loose, except when they were in mourning. I like women to let their hair fall down their back; 'tis a most agreeable sight.

### 752

The reproduction of mankind is a great marvel and mystery. Had God consulted me in the matter, I should have advised him to continue the generation of the species by fashioning them of clay, in the way Adam was fashioned; as I should have counselled him also, to let the sun remain always suspended over the earth, like a great lamp, maintaining perpetual light and heat.

### 753

The celibacy of spiritual persons began in the time of Cyprian, who lived two hundred and fifty years after the birth of Christ; so that this superstition has continued thirteen hundred years. St. Ambrose and others believed – not that they were human creatures, like other people.

### 754

St. Ulrich, bishop of Augsburg, related a fearful thing that befell at Rome. Pope Gregory, who confirmed celibacy, ordered a fish-pond at Rome, hard by a convent of nuns, to be cleared out. The water being let off, there were found, at the bottom, more than six thousand skulls of children, that had been cast into the pond and drowned. Such were the fruits of enforced celibacy. Hereupon Pope Gregory abolished celibacy, but the popes who succeeded him, re-established it.

In our own time, there was in Austria, at Nieuberg, a convent of nuns, who, by reason of their licentious doings, were removed from it, and placed elsewhere, and their convent filled with Franciscans. These monks, wishing to enlarge the building, foundations were dug, and in excavating there were found twelve great pots, in each of which was the carcass of an infant. How much better to let these people marry, than, by prohibition thereof, to cause the murder of so many innocent creatures.

# OF PRINCES AND POTENTATES

---

### 755

GOVERNMENT is a sign of the divine grace, of the mercy of God, who has no pleasure in murdering, killing, and strangling. If God left all things to go which way they would, as among the Turks and other nations, without good government, we should quickly despatch one another out of this world.

### 756

Parents keep their children with greater diligence and care than rulers and governors keep their subjects. Fathers and mothers are masters naturally and willingly; it is a self-grown dominion; but rulers and magistrates have a compulsory mastery; they act by force, with a prepared dominion; when father and mother can rule no more, the public police must take the matter in hand. Rulers and magistrates must watch over the sixth commandment.

### 757

The temporal magistrate is even like a fish-net, set before the fish in a pond or a lake, but God is the plunger, who drives the fish into it. For when a thief, robber, adulterer, murderer, is ripe, he hunts him into the net, that is, causes him to be taken by the magistrate, and punished; for it is written: 'God is judge upon earth.' Therefore, repent, or thou must be punished.

## 758

Princes and rulers should maintain the laws and statutes, or they will be contemned. They should, above all, hold the gospel in honour, and bear it ever in their hands, for it aids and preserves them, and enobles the state and office of magistracy, so that they know where their vocation and calling is, and that with good and safe conscience they may execute the works of their office. At Rome, the executioner always craved pardon of the condemned malefactor, when he was to execute his office, as though he were doing wrong, or sinning in executing the criminal; whereas 'tis his proper office, which God has set. St. Paul says: 'He beareth not the sword in vain;' he is God's minister, a revenger, to execute wrath upon him that does evil. When the magistrate punishes, God himself punishes.

## 759

It is impossible that where a prince or potentate is ungodly, his counsellors should not be ungodly. As is the master, such are also his servants. This follows necessarily and certainly. Solomon says: 'A master that hath pleasure in lying, his servants are ungodly;' it never fails.

## 760

The magistracy is a necessary state in the world, and to be held in honour; therefore we ought to pray for magistrates, who may easily be corrupted and spoiled. *Honores mutant mores, numquam in meliores* : Honours alter a man's manners, and seldom for the better. The prince who governs without laws, according to his own brain, is a monster, worse than a wild beast; but he who governs according to the prescribed laws and rights, is like unto God, who is an erecter and founder of laws and rights.

## 761

Governors should be wise, of a courageous spirit, and should know how to rule alone without their counsellors.

## 762

Temporal government is preserved not only by laws and rights, but by divine authority; 'tis God maintains governments, otherwise the greatest sins in the world would remain unpunished. Our Lord God, in the law, shows what his will is, and how the evil should be punished. And forasmuch as the law punishes not a potentate, prince, or ruler, therefore our Lord God, one day, will call him to an account and punish him. In this life, governors and rulers catch but only gnats and little flies with their laws, but the wasps and great humble bees tear through, as through a cobweb; that is, the small offences and offenders are punished, but the abominable extortioners and oppressors who grind the faces of the poor, the fatherless and widows, go scot-free, and are held in high honour.

### 763

To the business of government appertain, not common, illiterate people, or servants, but champions; understanding, wise, and courageous men, who are to be trusted, and who aim at the common good and prosperity, not seeking their own gain and profit, or following their own desires, pleasures, and delights; but how few governors and rulers think hereon? They make a trade and traffic of government; they cannot govern themselves: how, then, should they govern great territories and multitudes of people. Solomon says: 'A man that can rule and curb his mind, is better than he that assaulteth and overcometh cities,' etc.

I could well wish that Scipio, that much-honoured champion, were in heaven; he was able to govern and overcome himself, and to curb his mind, the highest and most laudable victory. Frederick, prince elector of Saxony, was another such prince; he could curb himself, though by nature of an angry mood. In the song of Solomon, it is said: 'My vineyard which is mine, is before me;' that is, God has taken the government to himself, to the end no man may brag and boast thereof. God will be king and ruler; he will be minister and pastor; he will be master in the house; he alone will be governor; *pastor, episcopus, Caesar, rex, vir et uxor errant, sed non Deus.*

### 764

Potentates and princes, now-a-days, when they take in hand an enterprise, do not pray before they begin, but set to work calculating: three times three make nine, twice seven are fourteen – so-and-so will do so-and-so – in this manner will the business surely take effect – but our Lord God says unto them: For whom, then, do ye hold me? for a cypher? Do I sit here above in vain, and to no purpose? You shall know, that I will twist your accounts about finely, and make them all false reckonings.

### 765

Pilate was a more honest and just man than any papist prince of the empire. I could name many of these, who are in no degree comparable with Pilate;

for he kept strictly to the Roman laws. He would not that the innocent should be executed and slain without hearing, and he availed himself of all just means whereby to release Christ; but when they threatened him with the emperor's disfavour, he was dazzled, and forsook the imperial laws, thinking, it is but the loss of one man, who is both poor and contemned; no man takes his part; what hurt can I receive by his death? Better it is that one man die, than that the whole nation be against me.

Dr. Mathesius and Pomer debated this question, why Pilate scourged Christ, and asked: What is truth? The former argued that Pilate did it out of compassion; but the other, that it was done out of tyranny and contempt. Whereupon Luther said: Pilate scourged Christ out of great compassion, to the end he might still, thereby, the insatiable wrath and raging of the Jews. And in that he said to Christ: What is truth? he meant: Why wilt thou dispute concerning truth in these wicked times ? Truth is here of no value. Thou must think of some other plan; adopt some lawyer's quiddity, and then, perchance, thou mayest be released.

### 766

Philip Melancthon and myself have justly deserved, at God's hands, as much riches in this world as any one cardinal possesses; for we have done more in his business than a hundred cardinals. But God says unto us: Be ye contented that ye have me. When we have him, then have we also the purse; for although we had the purse and had not God, so had we nothing.

God said to Ezekiel: 'Thou son of man, Nebuchadnezzar caused his army to serve a great service against Tyre, yet he had no wages; what shall I give him? I will give the land of Egypt to Nebuchadnezzar, that shall be his wages.' So plays God with great kingdoms, taking them from one, and giving them to another.

### 767

At the imperial diet, at Augsburg, certain princes there spoke in praise of the riches and advantages of their respective principalities. The prince elector of Saxony said he had, in his country, store of silver mines, which brought him great revenues. The prince elector palatine extolled his vineyards on the Rhine. When it became the turn of Eberhard, prince of Wirtemberg, he said: 'I am, indeed, but a poor prince, and not to be compared with either of you; yet, nevertheless, I have also in my country a rich and precious jewel; namely, that if at any time I should ride astray in my country, and were left all alone in the fields, yet I could safely and securely sleep in the bosom of any one of my subjects, who all, for my service, are ready to venture body, goods, and blood.' And, indeed, his people esteemed him as a *pater patriæ*. When the other two princes heard this, they confessed that, in truth, his was the most rich and precious jewel.

## 768

I invited to dinner, at my house at Wittenberg, prince Ernest of Luneberg, and prince William of Mecklenburg, who much complained of the immeasurable swilling and drinking kind of life at courts; and yet they will all be good Christians. I said: The potentates and princes ought to look into this. Then prince Ernest said: Ah! sir, we that are princes do even so ourselves, otherwise 'twould have gone down long since; confessing that the intemperance of princes caused the intemperance of the people. And truly, when the abbot throws the dice, the whole convent will play. The example of governors greatly influences the subjects.

## 769

Some one asked, whether sir Thomas More was executed for the gospel's sake or no? I answered: No, in no wise; he was a cruel tyrant; he was the king's chief counsellor; a very learned and wise man, doubtless, but he shed the blood of many innocent Christians that confessed the gospel; he tormented them with strange instruments, like a hangman; first, he personally examined them under a green tree, and then cruelly tortured them in prison. At last, he opposed the edict of the king and kingdom. He was disobedient, and was punished.

## 770

We have this advantage; no council has condemned us for heretics; the laws of the empire define a heretic to be one who obstinately maintains errors, which we have never done, but have shown and produced witnesses out of God's Word, and the Holy Scriptures; we willingly hear the opinions of others, but we will not endure the pope to be judge; we make him a party.

## 771

The emperor Maximilian in his campaigns was very superstitious. In times of danger, he would make a vow to offer up as sacrifice what first met him. One of his captains had taken captive a very fair virgin of an ancient family in

Germany, and of the protestant religion, whom he loved exceedingly; but he was forced by the emperor to kill her with his own hands. We Christians have a great advantage in war against our enemies, that of faith in prayer, whereas the infidels know nothing of faith or prayer.

## 772

Not long since king Ferdinand came into a monastery where I was, and going over it was attracted by these letters, written in large characters, on a wall:

'M.N.M.G.M.M.M.M.'

After reflecting for some time on their meaning, he turned to his secretary, and asked him what he thought they signified. The secretary replied: 'Your majesty will not be angry at my interpretation?' 'No, truly,' said the king. 'Well, then,' returned the secretary, 'I expound the letters thus: *M. N.* Mentitur Nausea (the archbishop of Vienna); *M. G.* Mentitur Gallus (the court preacher); *M. M. M. M.* Mentiuntur Majores (the Franciscans); Minores, (the Carmelites); Minotaurii (monks of the Alps); all are liars.' The king bit his lips, and passed on. 'Twas a very ingenious explanation of Mr. Secretary's.

## 773

Princes, now-a-days, have no order in the administration of their household. Four imperial towns spend more in luxuries and junkettings in one day, than Solomon spent, throughout all his kingdom, in a month. They are poor creatures, these princes, well entitled to our compassion.

## 774

God deals with great potentates, kings, and princes, even as children with playing cards. While they have good cards, they hold them in their hands; when they have bad, they get weary of them, and throw them under the chair; just so does God with great potentates: while they are governing well, he holds them for good; but so soon as they exceed, and govern ill, he throws them down from their seat, and there he lets them lie.

# OF DISCORD

---

## 775

THE 10th of February, 1546, John, prince elector of Saxony, said: A controversy were easily settled, if the parties would exhibit some concord. Luther said: We would willingly have concord, but no man seeks after the medium of concord, which is charity. We seek riches, but no man seeks after the right means how to be rich, namely, through God's blessing. We all desire to be saved, but the world refuses the means how to be saved – the Mediator Christ.

In former times potentates and princes referred their controversies to faithful people, and did not so readily thrust them into the lawyer's hands. When people desire to be reconciled and to come to an agreement, one party must yield, and give way to the other. If God and mankind should be reconciled and agreed, God must give over his right and justice, and must lay aside his wrath; and we, mankind, must also lay down our own righteousness, for we also would needs be gods in Paradise; we thought ourselves wise as God, through the serpent's seduction; then Christ was fain to make an agreement between us; he interposed in the cause, and would be a mediator between God and man; this Mediator for his pains got the portion of a peace-maker, namely, the cross; he that parts two fighters, commonly gets the hardest knocks for himself. Even so Christ suffered and presented us with his passion and death; he died for our sakes, and for the sake of our justification he arose again. Thus the generation of mankind became reconciled with God.

## 776

When two goats meet upon a narrow bridge over deep waters, how do they behave? neither of them can turn back again, neither can pass the other, because the bridge is too narrow; if they should thrust one another, they might both fall into the water and be drowned; nature, then, has taught them, that if the one lays himself down and permits the other to go over him, both remain without hurt. Even so people should rather endure to be trod upon, than to fall into debate and discord one with another.

## 777

A Christian, for the sake of his own person, neither curses nor revenges himself; but faith curses and revenges itself: To understand this rightly, we must distinguish God and man, the person and cause. In what concerns God and his cause, we must have no patience, nor bless; as for example, when the ungodly persecute the gospel, this touches God and his cause, and then we are not to bless or to wish good success, but rather to curse the persecutors and their proceedings. Such is called faith's cursing, which, rather than it would suffer God's Word to be suppressed and heresy maintained, would have all creatures go to wreck; for through heresy we lose God himself, Numbers 16. But individuals personally ought not to revenge themselves, but to suffer all things, and according to Christ's doctrine and the nature of love, to do good to their enemies.

# Of Sicknesses,
## and of the Causes Thereof

---

### 778

When young children cry lustily, they grow well and rapidly, for through crying, the members and veins are stretched out, which have no other exercise.

### 779

A question was put to Luther: How these two sentences in Scripture might be reconciled together; first, concerning the sick of the palsy, where Christ says: 'Son, be of good cheer, thy sins be forgiven thee.' Where Christ intimates that sin was the cause of the palsy, and of every sickness. Second, touching him that was born blind, where John says: 'That neither he nor his parents had sinned.' Luther answered: In these words Christ testifies that the blind had not sinned, and sin is not the cause of blindness, for only active sins, which one commits personally, are the cause of sicknesses and plagues, not original sin; therefore the sins which the sick of the palsy himself committed were the cause of his palsy, whereas original sin was not the cause of the blindness of him that was born blind, or all people must be born blind, or be sick of the palsy.

### 780

Experience has proved the toad to be endowed with valuable qualities. If you run a stick through three toads, and, after having dried them in the sun, apply them to any pestilent tumour, they draw out all the poison, and the malady will disappear.

## 781

The cramp is the lightest sickness, and I believe the falling sickness a piece of the cramp, the one in the head, the other in the feet and legs; when the person feeling either moves quickly, or runs, it vanishes.

## 782

Sleep is a most useful and most salutary operation of nature. Scarcely any minor annoyance angers me more than the being suddenly awakened out of a pleasant slumber. I understand, that in Italy they torture poor people by depriving them of sleep. 'Tis a torture that cannot long be endured.

## 783

The physicians in sickness consider only of what natural causes the malady proceeds, and this they cure, or not, with their physic. But they see not that often the devil casts a sickness upon one without any natural causes. A higher physic must be required to resist the devil's diseases; namely, faith and prayer, which physic may be fetched out of God's Word. The 31st Psalm is good thereunto, where David says: 'Into thine hand I commit my spirit.' This passage I learned, in my sickness, to correct; in the first translation, I applied it only to the hour of death: but it should be said My health, my happiness, my life, misfortune, sickness, death, etc.; stand all in thy hands. Experience testifies this; for when we think, now we will be joyful and merry, easy and healthy, God soon sends what makes us quite the contrary.

When I was ill at Schmalcalden, the physicians made me take as much medicine as though I had been a great bull. Alack for him that depends upon the aid of physic. I do not deny that medicine is a gift of God, nor do I refuse to acknowledge science in the skill of many physicians; but, take the best of them, how far are they from perfection? A sound regimen produces excellent effects. When I feel indisposed, by observing a strict diet and going to bed early, I generally manage to get round again, that is, if I can keep my mind tolerably at rest. I have no objection to the doctors acting upon certain theories, but, at the same time, they must not expect us to be the slaves of their fancies. We find Avicenna and Galen, living in other times and in other countries, prescribing wholly different remedies for the same disorders. I won't pin my faith to any of them, ancient or modern. On the other hand, nothing can well be more deplorable than the proceeding of those fellows, ignorant as they are complaisant, who let their patients follow exactly their own fancies; 'tis these wretches who more especially people the graveyards. Able, cautious, and experienced physicians, are gifts of God. They are the ministers of nature, to whom human life is confided; but a moment's negligence may ruin everything. No physician should take a single step, but in humility and the fear of God; they who are without the fear of God are mere homicides. I expect that exercise and change of air do more good than all their purgings and bleedings, but when we do employ medical remedies, we should be careful to do so under the advice of a judicious physician. See what happened to Peter Lupinus, who died from taking internally a mixture designed for external application. I remember hearing of a great law-suit, arising out of a dose of appium being given instead of a dose of opium.

### 784

'Tis a curious thing that certain remedies, which, applied by princes and great lords, are efficacious and curative, are wholly powerless when administered by a physician. I have heard that the electors of Saxony, John and Frederic, have a water, which cures diseases of the eye, when they them selves apply it, whether the disorder arise from heat or from cold; but 'tis quite useless when administered by a physician. So in spiritual matters, a preacher has more unction, and produces more effect upon the conscience than can a layman.

# OF DEATH

---

### 785

To die for the sake of Christ's word, is esteemed precious and glorious before God. We are mortal, and must die for the sake of our sins, but when we die for the sake of Christ and his word, and freely confess them, we die an honourable death; we are thereby made altogether holy relics, and have sold our hides dear enough. But when we Christians pray for peace and long life, 'tis not for our sake, to whom death is merely gain, but for the sake of the church, and of posterity.

The fear of death is merely death itself; he who abolishes that fear from the heart, neither tastes nor feels death. A human creature lying asleep is very like one that is dead; whence the ancients said, sleep is the brother of death. In like manner, life and death are pictured to us in the day and night, and in the change and alteration of the seasons.

The dream I had lately, will be made true; 'twas that I was dead, and stood by my grave, covered with rags. Thus am I long since condemned to die, and yet I live.

### 786

'Whoso keepeth my saying, shall never see death.' Luther expounded this passage of St. John thus: We must die and suffer death, but whoso holds on

God's Word, shall not feel death, but depart as in a sleep, and concerning him it shall not be said: 'I die, but I am forced to sleep.' On the other hand, whoso finds not himself furnished with God's Word, must die in anguish; therefore, when thou comest to die, make no dispute at all, but from thy heart say: I believe in Jesus Christ the Son of God; I ask no more.

## 787

One's thirty-eighth year is an evil and dangerous year, bringing many heavy and great sicknesses; naturally, by reason, perhaps, of the comets and conjunctions of Saturn and of Mars, but spiritually, by reason of the innumerable sins of the people.

## 788

Pliny, the heathen writer, says, book 20 cap. 1: The best physic for a human creature is, soon to die; Julius Caesar contemned death, and was careless of danger; he said: 'Tis better to die once than continually to be afraid of dying; this was well enough for a heathen, yet we ought not to tempt God, but to use the means which he gives, and then commit ourselves to his mercy.

It were a light and easy matter for a Christian to overcome death, if he knew it was not God's wrath; that quality makes death bitter to us. But a heathen dies securely; he neither sees nor feels that it is God's wrath, but thinks it is merely the end of nature. The epicurean says: 'Tis but to endure one evil hour.

## 789

When I hear that a good and godly man is dead, I am affrighted, and fear that God hates the world, and is taking away the upright and good, to the end be may fall upon and punish the wicked. Though I die, it makes no great matter; for I am in the pope's curse and excommunication; I am his devil, therefore he hates and persecutes me. At Coburg, I went about, and sought me out a place for my grave; I thought to have been laid in the chancel under the table, but now I am of another mind. I know I have not long to live, for my head is like a knife, from which the steel is wholly whetted away, and which is become mere iron; the iron will cut no more, even so it is with my head. Now, loving Lord God, I hope my time is not far hence; God help me, and give me a happy hour; I desire to live no longer.

### 790

We read of St. Vincent, that, about to die, and seeing death at his feet, he said: Death! what wilt thou? Thinkest thou to gain anything of a Christian? Knowest thou not that I am a Christian? Even so should we learn to contemn, scorn, and deride death. Likewise, it is written in the history of St. Martin, that being near his death, he saw the devil standing at his bed's feet, and boldly said: Why standest thou there, thou horrible beast? thou hast nothing to do with me. These were right words of faith. Such and the like ought we to cull out of the legends of the saints, wholly omitting the fooleries that the papists have stuffed therein.

### 791

Luther, at Wittenberg, seeing a very melancholy man, said to him: Ah! human creature, what dost thou? Hast thou nothing else in hand but to think of thy sins, on death, and damnation? Turn thine eyes quickly away, and look hither to this man Christ, of whom it is written: 'He was conceived by the Holy Ghost, born of the Virgin Mary, suffered, died, buried, descended into hell, the third day arose again from the dead, and ascended up into heaven,' etc. Dost think all this was done to no end? Comfort thyself against death and sin; be not afraid, nor faint, for thou hast no cause; Christ suffered death for thee, and prevailed for thy comfort and defence, and for that cause he sits at the right hand of God, his heavenly Father, to deliver thee.

### 792

So many members as we have, so many deaths have we. Death peeps out at every limb. The devil, a causer and lord of death, is our adversary, and hunts after our life; he has sworn our death, and we have deserved it; but the devil will not gain much by strangling the godly; he will crack a hollow nut. Let us die, that so the devil may be at rest. I have deserved death twofold; first, in that I have sinned against God, for which I am heartily sorry; secondly, I have deserved death at the devil's hands, whose kingdom of lying and murdering, through God's assistance, grace, and mercy, I have destroyed; therefore he justly wishes my death.

### 793

'There shall arise false prophets, insomuch that, if it were possible, they shall deceive the very elect.' This sentence was fulfilled, in the fathers; as in Jerome, Augustine, Gregory, Bernard, and others; they were seduced into errors, but remained not therein. St. Bernard wrote many evil and ungodly things, especially concerning the Virgin Mary; but when he was near his death, he said: 'I have lived wickedly. Thou, loving Lord Jesus Christ, hast a twofold right to the kingdom of heaven; first, it is thine inheritance, for thou art the only begotten Son of the Father; this affords me no comfort or hope of heaven. But, secondly, thou hast purchased the same with thy suffering and death; thou hast stilled the Father's wrath, hast unlocked heaven, and presented the same unto me as thy purchased good; of this have I joy and comfort.' Therefore he died well and happy. Likewise when St. Augustine was to die, he prayed the seven penitential psalms. When these fathers were in health, they thought not on this doctrine; but when they were upon their death-beds, they found in their hearts what they were to trust to; they felt it high time to abandon human fopperies, and to betake themselves only to Christ, and to rely upon his rich and precious merits.

### 794

Almighty, everlasting God, merciful heavenly Father, Father of our loving Lord Jesus Christ, I know assuredly, that everything which thou hast said, thou wilt and canst perform, for thou canst not lie; thy Word is upright and true. In the beginning, thou didst promise unto me thy loving and only begotten Son Jesus Christ; the same is come, and has delivered me from the devil, from death, hell, and sin. Out of his gracious will he has presented unto me the sacraments, which I have used in faith, and have depended on thy word; wherefore I make no doubt at all, but that I am well secured, and settled in peace; therefore if this be my hour, and thy divine will, so am I willing to depart hence with joy.

### 795

The school of faith is said to go about with death. Death is swallowed up in victory. If death, then sin. If death, then all diseases. If death, then all misery. If death, then all the power of the devil. If death, then all the fury of the world. But these things do not appear, but rather the contrary; therefore there is need of faith; for an open manifestation of things follows faith in due time, when the things, now invisible, will be seen.

### 796

When Adam lived, that is, when he sinned, death devoured life; when Christ died, that is, was justified, then life, which is Christ, swallowed up and devoured death; therefore God be praised, that Christ died, and has got the victory.

# Of the Resurrection

---

### 797

On Easter Sunday, 1544, Luther made an excellent sermon on the resurrection from the dead, out of the epistle appointed for that day, handling this sentence: 'Thou fool, that which thou sowest is not quickened except it die.' When Abraham intended to sacrifice his son, he believed that God out of the ashes would raise him again, and make him a father of children. The faith of Adam and of Eve preserved them, because they trusted and believed in the promised seed. For to him that believes everything is possible. The conception and birth of every human creature, proceeding out of a drop of blood, is no less a miracle and wonder-work of God, than that Adam was made out of a clod of earth, and Eve out of a fleshy rib. The world is full of such works of wonder, but we are blind, and cannot see them. The whole world is not able to create one member, no, not so much as a small leaf: The manner of the resurrection consists in these words: 'Arise, come, stand up, appear, rejoice ye which dwell in the dust of the earth.' I shall arise again, and shall speak with you; this finger wherewith I point must come to me again; everything must come again; for it is written: 'God will create a new heaven and a new earth, wherein righteousness shall dwell.' It will be no arid waste, but a beautiful new earth, where all the just will dwell together. There will be no carnivorous beasts, or venomous creatures, for all such, like ourselves, will be relieved from the curse of sin, and will be to us as friendly as they were to Adam in Paradise. There will be little dogs, with golden hair, shining like precious stones. The foliage of the trees, and the verdure of the grass, will have the brilliancy of emeralds; and we ourselves, delivered from our mundane subjection to gross appetites and necessities, shall have the same form as here, but infinitely more perfect. Our eyes will be radiant as the purest silver, and we shall be exempt from all sickness and tribulation. We shall behold the glorious Creator face to face; and then, what ineffable satisfaction will it be to find our relations and friends among the just! If we were all one here, we should have peace among ourselves but God orders it otherwise, to the end we may yearn and sigh after the future paternal home, and become weary of this troublesome life. Now, if there be joy in the chosen, so must the highest sorrow and despair be in the damned.

## 798

The 7th of August, 1538, Luther discoursed concerning the life to come, and said: In my late sickness I lay very weak, and committed myself to God, when many things fell into my mind, concerning the everlasting life, what it is, what joys we there shall have, and I was convinced that everything shall be revealed, which through Christ is presented unto us, and is already ours, seeing we believe it. Here on earth we cannot know what the creation of the new world shall be, for we are not able to comprehend or understand the creation of this temporal world, or of its creatures, which are visible and corporal. The joys that are everlasting are beyond the comprehension of any human creature. As Isaiah says: *'Ye shall be everlastingly joyful in glorious joy.'* But how comes it that we cannot believe God's Word, seeing that all things are accomplished which the Scripture speaks touching the resurrection of the dead? This proves original sin as the cause of it. The ungodly and damned at the last day shall be under the ground, but in some measure shall behold the great joys and glory of the chosen and saved, and thereby shall be so much the more pained and tormented.

Has our Lord God created this evanescent and temporal kingdom, the sky, and earth, and all that is therein, so fair; how much more fair and glorious will he, then, make yonder celestial everlasting kingdom.

## 799

When I lay sucking at my mother's breasts, I had no notion how I should afterwards eat, drink, or live. Even so we on earth have no idea what the life to come will be.

## 800

I hold the gnashing of teeth of the damned to be an external pain following upon an evil conscience, that is, despair, when men see themselves abandoned by God.

## 801

I wish from my heart Zuinglius could be saved, but I fear the contrary; for Christ has said, that those who deny him shall be damned. God's judgment is sure and certain, and we may safely pronounce it against all the ungodly, unless God reserve unto himself a peculiar privilege and dispensation. Even so, David from his heart wished that his son Absalom might be saved, when he said: 'Absalom my son, Absalom my son,' yet he certainly believed that he was damned, and bewailed him, not only in that he died corporally, but was also lost everlastingly; for he knew that he died in rebellion, in incest, and that he had hunted his father out of the kingdom.

## 802

The Fathers made four sorts of hell. 1. The fore-front, wherein, they say, the patriarchs were until Christ descended into hell. 2. The feeling of pain, yet only temporal, as purgatory. 3. Where unbaptized children are, but feel no pain. 4. Where the damned are, which feel everlasting pain. This is the right hell; the other three are only human imaginings. In Popedom they sang an evil song: 'Our sighs called upon thee, our pitiful lamentations sought thee,' etc. This was not Christianlike, for the gospel says: 'They are in Abraham's bosom.' Isaiah: 'They go into their chambers;' and Ecclesiasticus: 'The righteous is in the Lord's hand, let him die how he will, yea, although he be overtaken by death.' What hell is, we know not; only this we know, that there is such a sure and certain place, as is written of the rich glutton, when Abraham said unto him: 'There is a great space between you and us.'

## 803

Ah! loving God, defer not thy coming. I await impatiently the day when the spring shall return, when day and night shall be of equal length, and when Aurora shall be clear and bright. One day will come a thick black cloud, out of which will issue three flashes of lightning, and a clap of thunder will be heard, and, in a moment, heaven and earth will be covered with confusion. The Lord be praised, who has taught us to sigh and yearn after that day. In Popedom they are all afraid thereof, as is testified by their hymn, *Dies iræ dies illa*. I hope that day is not far off. Christ says: 'At that time, ye shall scarcely find faith on the earth.' If we make an account we shall find, that we have the gospel now only in a corner. Asia and Africa have it not, the gospel is not preached in Europe, in Greece, Italy, Hungary, Spain, France, England, or in Poland. And this little corner where it is, Saxony, will not hinder the coming of the last day of judgment. The predictions of the apocalypse are accomplished already, as far as the white horse. The world cannot stand long, perhaps a hundred years at the outside.

When the Turk begins to decline, then the last day will be at hand, for then the testimony of the Scripture must be verified. The loving Lord will come, as the Scripture says: 'For thus saith the Lord of Hosts, yet a little while and I will shake the heavens and the earth, and the sea and the dry land: and I will shake all nations, and the desire of all nations shall come.' At the last there will be great alteration and commotion; and already there are great commotions among men. Never had the men of law so much occupation as now. There are vehement dissensions in our families, and discord in the church.

## 804

About the time of Easter in April, when they least of all feared rain, Pharaoh was swallowed up in the Red Sea, and the nation of Israel delivered from Egypt. 'Twas at about the same time the world was created; at the same time the year is changed, and at the same time Christ arose again to renew the world. Perchance the last day will come about the same time. I am of opinion it will be about Easter, when the year is finest and fairest, and early in the morning, at sunrise, as at the destruction of Sodom and Gomorrah. The elements will be gloomy with earthquakes and thunderings about an hour or a little longer, and the secure people will say: 'Pish, thou fool, hast thou never heard it thunder?'

## 805

The science of alchemy I like very well, and, indeed, 'tis the philosophy of the ancients. I like it not only for the profits it brings in melting metals, in decocting, preparing, extracting, and distilling herbs, roots; I like it also for the sake of the allegory and secret signification, which is exceedingly fine, touching the resurrection of the dead at the last day. For, as in a furnace the fire extracts and separates from a substance the other portions, and carries upward the spirit, the life, the sap, the strength, while the unclean matter, the dregs, remain at the bottom, like a dead and worthless carcass; even so

God, at the day of judgment, will separate all things through fire, the righteous from the ungodly. The Christians and righteous shall ascend upwards into heaven, and there live everlastingly, but the wicked and the ungodly, as the dross and filth, shall remain in hell, and there be damned.

# Of Allegories

―――

## 806

ALLEGORIES and spiritual significations, when applied to faith, and that seldom, are laudable; but when they are drawn from the life and conversation, they are dangerous, and, when men make too many of them, pervert the doctrine of faith. Allegories are fine ornaments, but not of proof. We ought not lightly to make use of them, except the principal cause be first sufficiently proved, with strong grounds and arguments, as with St. Paul in the fourth chapter to Galatians. The body is the logic, but allegory the rhetoric; now rhetoric, which adorns and enlarges a thing with words, is of no value without logic, which roundly and briefly comprehends a matter. When with rhetoric men will make many words, without ground, it is but a trimmed thing, a carved idol.

## 807

An allegory is when a thing is signified and understood otherwise than as the words express. Of all languages, none is so rich in allegories as the Hebrew. The German tongue is full of metaphors, as when we say: He hangs the cloak according to the wind: Katherine von Borna is the morning star of Wittenberg, and so on. These are metaphors, that is, figurative words. Allegories are, as when Christ commands that one should wash another's feet, of baptizing, of the Sabbath, etc.

We must not hold and understand allegories as they sound; as what Daniel says, concerning the beast with ten horns; this we must understand to be spoken of the Roman empire. Even so, circumcision in the New Testament is an allegory, but in the Old Testament it is no allegory. The New Testament frames allegories out of the Old, as it makes two nations out of Abraham's sons.

### 808

The legend of St. George has a fine spiritual signification, concerning temporal government and policy. The virgin signifies the policy; she is vexed and persecuted by the dragon, the devil, who goes about to devour her; now he plagues her with hunger and dearth, then with pestilence, now with wars, till at length a good prince or potentate comes, who helps and delivers her, and restores her again to her right.

### 809

To play with allegories in Christian doctrine, is dangerous. The words, now and then, sound well and smoothly, but they are to no purpose. They serve well for such preachers as have not studied much, who know not rightly how to expound the histories and texts, whose leather is too short, and will not stretch. These resort to allegories, wherein nothing is taught certainly on which a man may build; therefore, we should accustom ourselves to remain by the clear and pure text. Philip Melancthon asked Luther what the allegory and hidden signification was, that the eagle, during the time he broods and sits upon the eggs, hunts not abroad; and that he keeps but one young, thrusting any others out of the nest. Likewise, why the ravens nourish not their young, but forsake them when they are yet bare, and without feathers? Luther answered: 'The eagle signifies a monarch, who alone will have the government, and suffer none besides himself to be his equal. The ravens are the harsh and hardhearted swine and belly-gods, the papists.

### 810

The allegory of a sophist is always screwed; it crouches and bows itself like a snake, which is never straight, whether she go, creep, or lie still; only when she is dead, she is straight enough.

### 811

When I was a monk, I was much versed in spiritual signification, and allegories. 'Twas all art with me; but afterwards, when through the epistle to the Romans,

I had come a little to the knowledge of Christ, I saw that all allegories were vain, except those of Christ. Before that time I turned everything into allegory, even the lowest wants of our nature. But afterwards I reflected upon historical facts. I saw how difficult a matter it was for Gideon to have fought the enemy, in the manner shown by the Scripture; there was no allegory there or spiritual signification; the Holy Ghost simply says, 'that Faith only, with three hundred men, beat so great a multitude of enemies.' St. Jerome and Origen, God forgive them, were the cause that allegories were held in such esteem. But Origen altogether is not worth one word of Christ. Now I have shaken off all these follies, and my best art is to deliver the Scripture in the simple sense; therein is life, strength, and doctrine; all other methods are nothing but foolishness, let them shine how they will. 'Twas thus Munzer troped with the third chapter of John: 'Unless one be born again of water,' and said: Water signifies tribulation; but St. Augustine gave us the true rule, that figures and allegories prove nothing.

### 812

Few of the legends are pure; the legends of the martyrs are least corrupted, who proved their faith by the testimony of their blood. The legends of the hermits, who dwell in solitudes, are abominable, full of lying miracles and fooleries, touching moderation, chastity, and nurture. I hold in consideration the saints whose lives were not marked by any particular circumstances, who, in fact, lived like other people, and did not seek to make themselves noted.

### 813

In the legend of the virgin Tecla, who, as they say, was baptized by St. Paul, 'tis said 'she awakened in him carnal desire'. Ah! loving Paul; thou hadst another manner of thorn in thy flesh than carnal. The friars, who live at their ease, and jollity, dream, according to their licentious cogitation, that St. Paul was plagued with the same tribulations as themselves.

### 814

The legend of St. Christopher is no history, but a fiction composed by the Greeks, a wise, learned, and imaginative people, in order to show what life that of a true Christian should be. They figure him a very great, tall and strong man, who bears the child Jesus upon his shoulders, as the name Christopher indicates; but the child was heavy, so that he who carries him is constrained to bend under the burden. He traverses a raging and boisterous sea, the world, whose waves beat upon him, namely, tyrants, and factions, and the devil, who would fain bereave him of soul and life; but he supports himself by a great tree, as upon a staff; that is, God's Word. On the other side of the sea stands an old man, with a lanthorn, in which burns a candle; this means the writings of the prophets. Christopher directs his steps thither, and arrives safely on shore, that is, at everlasting life. At his side is a basket, containing fish and bread; this signifies that God will here on earth nourish the bodies of his Christians, amid the persecutions, crosses, and misfortunes which they must endure, and will not suffer them to die of hunger, as the world would have them. 'Tis a fine Christian poem, and so is the legend of St. George; George, in the Greek, means a builder, that builds edifices justly and with regularity, and who resists and drives away the enemies that would assault and damage them.

### 815

'Tis one of the devil's proper plagues that we have no good legends of the saints, pure and true. Those we have are stuffed so full of lies, that, without heavy labour, they cannot be corrected. The legend of St. Catherine is contrary to all the Roman history; for Maxentius was drowned in the Tiber at Rome, and never came to Alexandria, but Maximian had been there, as we read in Eusebius, and after the time of Julius Caesar there had been no king in Egypt. He that disturbed Christians with such lies, was doubtless a desperate wretch, who surely has been plunged deep in hell. Such monstrosities did we believe in Popedom, but then we understood them not. Give God thanks, ye that are freed and delivered from them and from still more ungodly things.

# Of Spiritual and Church Livings

━━∅━━

## 816

My advice is that the sees of the protestant bishops be permitted to remain, for the profit and use of poor students and schools; and when a bishop, dean, or provost, cannot, or will not preach himself, then he shall, at his own charge, maintain other students and scholars, and permit them to study and preach. But when potentates and princes take spiritual livings to themselves, and will famish poor students and scholars, then the parishes of necessity must be wasted, as is the case already, for we can get neither ministers nor deacons. The pope, although he be our mortal enemy, must maintain us, yet against his will, and for which he has no thanks.

## 817

These times are evil, in that the church is so spoiled and robbed by the princes and potentates; they give nothing, but take and steal. In former times they gave liberally to her, now they rob her. The church is more torn and tattered than a beggar's cloak; nothing is added to the stipends of the poor servants of the church. They who bestow them to the right use are persecuted, it going with them as with St. Lawrence, who, against the emperor's command, divided the church livings among the poor.

## 818

The benefices under Popedom are unworthy that Christian use should be made of them, for they are the wages of strumpets, as the prophet says, and shall return to such again. The pope is fooled, in that he suffers the emperor and other princes to take possession of spiritual livings; he hopes thereby to preserve his authority and power. For this reason he wrote to Henry of England, that he might take possession of spiritual livings, provided he, the pope, were acknowledged, by the king, chief bishop. For the pope thinks: I must now, in these times of trouble and danger, court the beast; I must yield in some things. Ah! how I rejoice that I have lived to see the pope humbled; he is now constrained to suffer his patrons, his protectors, and defenders, to take possession of church livings to preserve his power, but he stands like a tottering wall, about to be overthrown. How will it be with the monasteries and churches that are fallen down and decayed? They shall never be raised up again, and the prophecy will be fulfilled. Popedom has been and will be a prey. Twelve years since, the pope suffered one prince to take possession of divers bishoprics; afterwards, at the imperial diet at Augsburg, the prince was compelled to restore them; now the pope gives him them again: this prince and his retinue may well forsake the gospel, seeing the pope yields so much to him. 'Tis a very strange time, and of which we little thought twenty years past, to see the pope, that grizly idol, of whom all people stood in fear, now permitting princes to contemn and scorn him, him whom the emperor dared not, thirty years past, have touched with but one word.

## 819

'Tis quite fitting a poor student should have a spiritual living to maintain his study, so that he bind not himself with ungodly and unchristianlike vows, nor consent to hold communion with the errors of the papists. Ah, that we might have but the seventh part of the treasure of the church, to maintain poor students in the church. I am sorry our princes have such desire for bishoprics; I fear they will be their bane, and that they will lose what is their own.

## 820

Cannons and fire-arms are cruel and damnable machines, I believe them to have been the direct suggestion of the devil. Against the flying ball no valour avails; the soldier is dead, ere he sees the means of his destruction. If Adam had seen in a vision the horrible instruments his children were to invent, he would have died of grief.

## 821

War is one of the greatest plagues that can afflict humanity; it destroys religion, it destroys states, it destroys families. Any scourge, in fact, is preferable to it. Famine and pestilence become as nothing in comparison with it. Pestilence is the least evil of the three, and 'twas therefore David chose it, willing rather to fall into the hands of God than into those of pitiless man.

## 822

Some one asked, what was the difference between Samson the strong man, and Julius Caesar, or any other celebrated general, endowed at once with vigour of body and vigour of mind? Luther answered: Samson's strength was an effect of the Holy Ghost animating him, for the Holy Ghost enables those who serve God with obedience to accomplish great things. The strength and the grandeur of soul of the heathen was also an inspiration and work of God, but not of the kind which sanctifies. I often reflect with admiration upon Samson; mere human strength could never have done what he did.

## 823

How many fine actions of the old time have remained unknown, for want of an historian to record them. The Greeks and Romans alone possessed historians. Even of Livy, we have but a portion left to us; the rest is lost, destroyed. Sabellicus proposed to imitate and continue Livy, but he accomplished nothing.

Victories and good fortune, and ability in war, are given by God, as we find in Hannibal, that famous captain, who hunted the Romans thoroughly, driving them out of Africa, Sicily, Spain, France, and almost out of Italy. I am persuaded he was a surpassing valiant man; if he had but had a scribe to have written the history of his wars, we should, doubtless have known many great and glorious actions of his.

## 824

Great people and champions are special gifts of God, whom he gives and preserves: they do their work, and achieve great actions, not with vain imaginations, or cold and sleepy cogitations, but by motion of God. Even so 'twas with the prophets, St. Paul, and other excelling people, who accomplished their work by God's special grace. The Book of Judges also shows how God wrought great matters through one single person.

## 825

Every great champion is not fitted to govern; he that is a soldier, looks only after victories, how he may prevail, and keep the field; not after policy, how people and countries may be well governed. Yet Scipio, Hannibal, Alexander, Julius and Augustus Caesars looked also after government, and how good rule might be observed.

## 826

A valiant and brave soldier seeks rather to preserve one citizen, than to destroy a thousand enemies, as Scipio the Roman said; therefore an upright soldier begins not a war lightly, or without urgent cause. True soldiers and captains make not many words, but when they speak, the deed is done.

## 827

They who take to force, give a great blow to the gospel, and offend many people; they fish before the net, etc. The prophet Isaiah, and St. Paul say: 'I will grind him (antichrist) to powder with the rod of my mouth, and will slay him with the spirit of my lips.' With such weapons we must beat the pope. Popedom can neither be destroyed nor preserved by force; for it is built upon lies; it must, therefore be turned upside down and destroyed with the word of truth. It is said: 'Preach thou, I will give strength.'

# Of Constrained Defence

—•—

**828**

THE question whether without offending God or our conscience, we may defend ourselves against the emperor, if he should seek to subjugate us, is rather one for lawyers, than for divines.

If the emperor proceed to war upon us, he intends either to destroy our preaching, and our religion, or to invade and confound public policy and economy, that is to say, the temporal government and administration. In either case, 'tis no longer as emperor of the Romans, legally elected, we are to regard him but as a tyrant; 'tis, therefore, futile to ask whether we may combat for the upright, pure doctrine, and for religion; 'tis for us a law and a duty to combat for wife, for children, servants, and subjects; we are bound to defend them against maleficent power.

If I live I will write an admonition to all the states of the Christian world, concerning our forced defence; and will show that every one is obliged to defend him and his against wrongful power. First, the emperor is the head of the body politic in the temporal kingdom, of which body, every subject and private person is a piece and member, to whom the right of enforced defence appertains, as to a temporal and civil person; for if he defend not himself, he is a slayer of his own body.

Secondly, the emperor is not the only monarch or lord in Germany; but the princes electors are, together with him, temporal members of the empire, each of whom is charged and bound to take care of it; the duty of every prince is to further the good thereof, and to resist such as would injure and prejudice it. This is especially the duty of the leading head, the emperor. 'Tis true, the princes electors, though of equal power with the emperor, are not of equal dignity and prerogative; but they and the other princes of the empire are bound to resist the emperor, in case he should undertake anything tending to the detriment of the empire, or which is against God and lawful right. Moreover, if the emperor should proceed to depose any one of the princes electors, then he deposes them all, which neither should, nor can be committed.

Wherefore, before we formally answer this question, whether the emperor may depose the princes electors, or whether they may depose the emperor; we must first clearly thus distinguish: a Christian is composed of two kinds of persons, namely, a believing or a spiritual person, and a civil or temporal person. The believing or spiritual person ought to endure and suffer all things; it neither eats, nor drinks, nor engenders children, nor has share or part in temporal doings and matters. But the temporal and civil person is subject to the temporal rights and laws, and tied to obedience; it must maintain and defend itself; and what belongs to it, as the laws command. For example, if, in my presence, some wretch should attempt to do violence to my wife or my daughter, then I should lay aside the spiritual person, and recur to the temporal; I should slay him on the spot, or call for help. For, in the absence of the magistrates, and when they cannot be had, the law of the nation is in force, and permits us to call upon our neighbour for help; Christ and the gospel do not abolish temporal rights and ordinances, but confirm them.

The emperor is not an absolute monarch, governing alone, and at his pleasure, but the princes electors are in equal power with him; he has, therefore, neither power nor authority alone to make laws and ordinances, much less has he power, right, or authority to draw the sword for the subjugation of the subjects and members of the empire, without the sanction of the law, or the knowledge and consent of the whole empire. Therefore, the emperor Otho did wisely in ordaining seven princes electors, who, with the emperor, should rule and govern the empire; but for this, it would not so long have stood and endured.

Lastly, we should know that when the emperor proposes to make war upon us, he does it not of and for himself; but for the interest of the pope, to whom he is liegeman, and whose tyranny and abominable idolatry he thus undertakes to maintain; for the pope regards the gospel not at all, and in raising war against the gospel, by means of the emperor, intends only to defend and preserve his authority, power, and tyranny. We must not, then, remain silent and inactive. But here one may object and say: Although David had been by God chosen king, and anointed by Samuel, yet he would not resist king Saul, or lay hands upon him; neither ought we to resist the emperor, etc. Answer: David, at that time, had but the promise of his kingdom; he had it not in possession; he was not yet settled in his government. In our case, we arm not against Saul, but against Absalom, against whom David made war, slaying the rebel by the hands of Joab.

I would willingly argue this matter at length, whether we may resist the emperor or no? though the jurisconsults, with their notions of temporal and natural rights, pronounce in the affirmative, for us divines 'tis a question of grave difficulty, having regard to these passages: 'Whosoever shall smite thee on thy right cheek, turn to him the other also.' And: 'Servants be subject to your masters with all fear, not only to the good and gentle, but also the froward.' We must beware how we act against God's Word, lest, afterwards, in our consciences, we be plagued and tormented. But still, we are certain of one thing, that these times are not the times of the martyrs, when Diocletian reigned and raged against the Christians; 'tis now another kind of kingdom and government. The emperor's authority and power, without the seven princes electors, is of no value. The lawyers write: the emperor has parted with the sword, and given it into our possession. He has over us but only *gladium petitorium*, he must seek it of us, when he proposes to punish, for of right he can do nothing alone. If his government were as that of Diocletian, we would readily yield unto him and suffer.

I hope the emperor will not make war upon us for the pope's sake; but should he play the part of an Arian, and openly fight against God's word, not as a Christian, but as a heathen, we are not bound to submit and suffer. 'Tis from the pope's side I take the sword, not from the emperor's; and the pope, 'tis evident, ought to be neither master nor tyrant.

To sum up:

*First*: the princes electors are not slaves.

*Secondly*: The emperor rules upon certain conditions.

*Thirdly*: He is sworn to the empire, to the princes electors, and other princes.

*Fourthly*: He has by oath bound himself unto them, to preserve the empire in its dignity, honour, royalty, and jurisdiction, and to defend every person in that which justly and rightly belongs to him; therefore, it is not to be tolerated that he should bring us into servitude and slavery.

*Fifthly*: We are entitled to the benefit of the laws.

*Sixthly* : He ought to yield to Christian laws and rights.

*Seventhly*: Our princes by oath are bound to the empire, truly to maintain privileges and jurisdictions in politic and temporal cases, and not to permit any of these to be taken away.

*Eighthly*: These cases are among equals, where one is neither more nor higher than another: therefore, if the emperor with tyranny deals contrary to equity and justice, he makes himself equal with others; for thereby he lays aside the person of a governor and loses his right over the subjects, by the nature of relatives; for princes and subjects are equally bound the one to the other, and a prince is clearly obliged to perform what he has sworn and promised, according to the proverb: Faithful master, faithful man.

*Ninthly*: The laws are above a prince and tyrant; for the laws and ordinances are not wavering, but always sure and constant, while a human creature is wavering and inconstant, for the most part following his lusts and pleasures, if by the laws he be not restrained.

If a robber on the highway should fall upon me, truly I would be judge and prince myself, and would use my sword, because nobody was with me, able to defend me; and I should think I had accomplished a good work; but if one fell upon me as a preacher for the gospel's sake, then with folded hands I would lift up mine eyes to heaven, and say: 'My Lord Christ! here I am; I have confessed and preached thee; is now my time expired? so I commit my spirit into thy hands,' and in that way would I die.

# Of Lawyers

---

### 829

Two doctors in the law came to Luther at Wittenberg, whom he received and saluted in this manner: O ye canonists! I could well endure you, if ye meddled only with imperial, and not with popish laws. But ye maintain the pope and his canons. I would give one of my hands, on condition all papists and canonists were compelled to keep the pope's laws and decrees; I would wish them no worse a devil.

The bishop of Mayence cannot boast, that with a good conscience he has three bishoprics; but ye maintain it to be lawful and right. Ye doctors who meddle with popish laws are nothing, for the popish laws are nothing; therefore a doctor in the popish laws is nothing; he is a chimera, a monster, a fable, nothing. A doctor in the imperial laws is half lame, he has had a stroke on the one side; the pope's laws and decrees altogether stink of ambition, of pride, of self-profit, covetousness, superstition, idolatry, tyranny, and such like blasphemies.

### 830

Ye that are studying under lawyers, follow not your preceptors in abuses or wrong cases, as if a man could not be a lawyer unless he practised such evil. God has not given laws to make out of right wrong, and out of wrong right, as the unchristianlike lawyers do, who study law only for the sake of gain and profit.

### 831

Every lawyer is sorely vexed at me because I preach so harshly against the craft; but I say I, as a preacher, must reprove what is wrong and evil. If I reproved them, as Martin Luther, they need not regard me, but forasmuch as I do it as a servant of Christ, and speak by God's command, they ought to hearken unto me; for if they repent not, they shall everlastingly be damned; but I, when I have declared their sins, shall be excused. If I were not constrained to give an account for their souls, I would leave them unreproved.

### 832

All they that serve the pope are damned; for, next the devil, no worse creature is than the pope, with his lying human traditions, aimed directly against Christ. The greatest part of the lawyers, especially the canonists, are the pope's servants, and although they will not have the name, yet they prove it in deed. They would willingly rule the church, and trample upon her true and faithful servants; therefore are they damned.

# Of Universities, Arts, etc

---

### 833

A lawyer is wise according to human wisdom, a divine according to God's wisdom.

### 834

Ah! how bitter an enemy is the devil to our church and school here at Wittenberg, which in particular he opposes more than the rest, so that tyranny and heresy increase and get the upper hand by force, in that all the members of the church are against one another; yea, also we, which are a piece of the heart, vex and plague one another among ourselves. I am verily persuaded that many wicked wretches and spies are here, who watch over us with an evil eye, and are glad when discord and offences arise among us; therefore we ought diligently to watch and pray; it is high time – pray, pray. This school is a foundation and ground of pure religion, therefore she ought justly to be preserved and maintained with lectures and with stipends against the raging and swelling of Satan.

### 835

Whoso after my death shall contemn the authority of this school here at Wittenberg, if it remain as it is now, church and school, is a heretic and a perverted creature; for in this school God first revealed and purified his word. This school and city, both in doctrine and manner of life, may justly be compared with all others; yet we are not altogether complete, but still faulty in our kind of living. The highest and chiefest divines in the whole empire hold and join with us – as Amsdorf, Brentius, and Rhegius – all desiring our friendship, and saluting us with loving and learned letters. A few years past, nothing was of any value but the pope, till the church mourned, cried, and sighed, and awakened our Lord God in heaven; as in the Psalm he says: 'For the trouble of the needy and the groans of the poor, I will now arise.'

### 836

Our nobility exhaust people with usury, insomuch that many poor people starve for want of food; the cry goes, I would willingly take a wife, if I knew how to maintain her, so that a forced celibacy will hence ensue. This is not good; such wicked courses will cause the poor to cry and sigh, will rouse up God and the heavenly host. Wherefore I say: Germany, take heed. I often make an account, and as I come nearer and nearer to forty years, I think with myself: now comes an alteration, for St. Paul preached not above forty years, nor St. Augustine; always, after forty years pure preaching of God's Word, it has ceased, and great calamities have ensued thereupon.

### 837

*Dialectica* speaks simply, straightforward, and plainly, as when I say: Give me something to drink. But *Rhetorica* adorns the matter, saying: Give me of the acceptable juice in the cellar, which finely froths and makes people merry. *Dialectica* declares a thing distinctly and significantly, in brief words. *Rhetorica* counsels and advises, persuades and dissuades; she has her place and fountain-head, whence a thing is taken; as, this is good, honest, profitable, easy, necessary, etc. These two arts St. Paul briefly taught, where he says: 'That he may be able by sound doctrine, both to exhort and to convince the gainsayers' (Titus 1.) Therefore, when I would teach a farmer concerning the tilling of his land, I define briefly and plainly, his kind of life; his house-keeping, fruits, profits, and all that belongs to the being of his life, *Dialectica*; but, if I would admonish him, according to *Rhetorica,* then I counsel and advise him, and praise his kind of life, in this manner, as: that it is the most quiet, the richest, securest, and most delightful kind of life, etc. Again, if I intend to chide or to find fault, then I must point out and blame his miscon-duct, evil impediments, failings, gross ignorance, and such like defects which are in the state of farmers. Philip Melancthon has illustrated and declared good arts: he teaches theirs in such sort, that the arts teach not him, but he the arts; I bring my arts into books, I take them not out of books. *Dialectica* is a profitable and necessary art, which justly ought to be studied and learned; it shows how we ought to speak orderly and uprightly, what we should acknowledge and judge to be right or wrong; 'tis not only necessary in schools, but also in consistories, in courts of justice, and in churches; in churches most especially.

### 838

I always loved music; whoso has skill in this art, is of a good temperament, fitted for all things. We must teach music in schools; a schoolmaster ought to have skill in music, or I would not regard him; neither should we ordain young men as preachers, unless they have been well exercised in music.

### 839

Singing has nothing to do with the affairs of this world, it is not for the law; singers are merry and free from sorrow and cares.

### 840

Music is one of the best arts; the notes give life to the text; it expels melancholy, as we see in king Saul. Kings and princes ought to maintain music, for great potentates and rulers should protect good and liberal arts and laws; though private people have desire thereunto and love it, yet their ability is not adequate. We read in the Bible, that the good and godly kings maintained and paid singers. Music is the best solace for a sad and sorrowful mind; by it the heart is refreshed and settled again in peace.

# Of $\mathcal{A}$stronomy and $\mathcal{A}$strology

---

### 841

Astronomy is the most ancient of all sciences, and has been the introducer of vast knowledge; it was familiarly known to the Hebrews, for they diligently noted the course of the heavens, as God said to Abraham: 'Behold the heavens; canst thou number the stars' etc. Heaven's motions are threefold; the first is, that the whole firmament moves swiftly round, every moment thousands of leagues, which, doubtless, is done by some angel. 'Tis wonderful so great a vault should go about in so short a time. If the sun and stars were composed of iron, steel, silver, or gold, they must needs suddenly melt in so swift a course, for one star is greater than the whole earth, and yet they are innumerable. The second motion is, of the planets, which have their particular and proper motions. The third is, a quaking or a trembling motion, lately discovered, but uncertain. I like astronomy and mathematics, which rely upon demonstrations and sure proofs. As to astrology, 'tis nothing.

### 842

Astronomy deals with the matter, and with what is general, not with the manner or form. God himself will be alone the Master and Creator, Lord and Governor, though he has ordained the stars for signs. And so long as astronomy remains in her circle, whereunto God has ordained her, so is she a fair gift of God; but when she will step out of her bounds-that is, when she will prophecy and speak of future things, how it will go with one, or what fortune or misfortune another shall have, then she is not to be justified. Chiromancy we should utterly reject. In the stars is neither strength nor operation; they are but signs, and have, therefore, just cause to complain of the astrologers, who attribute unto them what they have not. The astrologers commonly ascribe that to the stars, which they ought to attribute to the planets, that announce only evil events, except that star which appeared to the wise men in the east, and which showed that the revelation of the gospel was at the door.

In the year 1538, the Seigneur Von Minckwitz made a public oration in honour of astrology, wherein he sought to prove that the sentence in Jeremiah 10: 'Be not dismayed at the signs of heaven,' applied not to astrology, but to the images of the Gentiles. Luther said hereupon: These passages may be quibbled with, but not overthrown. Jeremiah speaks as Moses did of all the signs of heaven, earth, and sea; the heathen were not so silly as to be afraid of the sun or moon, but they feared and adored prodigies and miraculous signs. Astrology is no art; it has no principle, no demonstration, whereupon we may take sure footing; 'tis all haphazard work; Philip Melancthon, against his will, admits unto me, that though, as he says, the art is extant, there are none that understand it rightly. They set forth, in their almanacs, that we shall have no snow in summer time, nor thunder in winter; and this the country clowns know as well as the astrologers. Philip Melancthon says: That such people as are born *in ascendente Libra, in* the ascension of Liber towards the south, are unfortunate people. Whereupon I said: The astrologers are silly creatures, to dream that their crosses and mishaps proceed not from God, but from the stars; 'tis hence, they are not patient in their troubles and adversities. Astrology is uncertain; and as the *predicamenta* are feigned words in *Dialectica,* even so astronomy has feigned astrology; as the ancient and true divines knew nothing of the fantasies and divinity of the schoolteachers, so the ancient astronomers knew nothing of astrology. The nativities of Cicero and of others were shown me. I said: I hold nothing thereof, nor attribute anything unto them. I would gladly have the astrologers answer me this: Esau and Jacob were born together, of one father and one mother, at one time, and under equal planets, yet they were wholly of contrary natures, kinds, and minds. What is done by God, ought not to be ascribed to the stars. The upright and true Christian religion opposes and confutes all such fables. The way of casting nativities is like the proceedings in Popedom, whose outward ceremonies and pompous ordinances are pleasing to human wit and wisdom, as the consecrated water, torches, organs, cymbals, singing, ringing, but withal there's no certain knowledge. An astrologer, or horoscopemonger, is like one that sells dice, and bawls: Behold, here I have dice that always come up twelve. If once or twice their conjectures tell, they cannot sufficiently extol the art; but as to the infinite cases where they fail, they are altogether silent. Astronomy, on the contrary; I like; it pleases me by reason of her manifold benefits.

General prophecies and declarations, which declare generally what in future shall happen, accord not upon individuals and particular things.

When at one time many are slain together in a battle, no man can affirm they were all born under one planet, yet they die altogether in one hour, yea, in one moment.

## 843

God has appointed a certain and sure end for all things, otherwise Babylon might have said: I will remain and continue; and Rome: To me is the government and rule given without ceasing. To Alexander and others were given empires and kingdoms, yet astrology taught not that such great kingdoms were to be raised, nor how long they were to last.

Astrology is framed by the devil, to the end people may be scared from entering into the state of matrimony, and from every divine and human office and calling; for the starpeepers presage nothing that is good out of the planets; they affright people's consciences, in regard of misfortunes to come, which all stand in God's hand, and through such mischievous and unprofitable cogitations vex and torment the whole life.

Great wrong is done to God's creatures by the star-expounders. God has created and placed the stars in the firmament, to the end they might give light to the kingdoms of the earth, make people glad and joyful in the Lord, and be good signs of years and seasons. But the star-peepers feign that those creatures, of God created, darken and trouble the earth, and are hurtful; whereas all creatures of God are good, and by God created only for good, though mankind makes them evil, by abusing them. Eclipses, indeed, are monsters, and like to strange and untimely births. Lastly, to believe in the stars, or to trust thereon, or to be affrighted thereat, is idolatry, and against the first commandment.

# OF LEARNED MEN

---

### 844

LUTHER advised all who proposed to study, in what art soever, to read some sure and certain books over and over again; for to read many sorts of books produces rather confusion than any distinct result; just as those that dwell everywhere, and remain in no place, dwell nowhere, and have no home. As we use not daily the community of all our friends, but of a select few, even so we ought to accustom ourselves to the best books, and to make them familiar unto us, so as to have them, as we say, at our fingers' end. A fine talented student fell into a frenzy; the cause of his disease was, that he laid himself out too much upon books, and was in love with a girl. Luther dealt very mildly and friendly with him, expecting amendment, and said: Love is the cause of his sickness; study brought upon him but little of his disorder. In the beginning of the gospel it went so with myself.

### 845

Who could be so mad, in these evil times, as to write history and the truth? The brains of the Greeks were subtle and crafty; the Italians are ambitious and proud; the Germans rude and boisterous. Livy described the acts of the Romans, not of the Carthaginians. Blandus and Platina only flatter the popes.

## 846

Anno 1536, Luther wrote upon his tablets the following words: *Res et verba Philippus; verba sine re Erasmus; res sine verbis Lutherus; nec res, nec verba Carolostadius;* that is, what Philip Melancthon writes has hands and feet; the matter is good, and the words are good; Erasmus Roterodamus writes many words, but to no purpose; Luther has good matter, but the words are wanting; Carlstad has neither good words nor good matter. Philip Melancthon coming in at the moment, read these criticisms, and turning with a smile to Dr. Basil, said: Touching Erasmus and Carlstad, 'twas well said, but too much praise is accorded to me, while good words ought to be reckoned among the other merits of Luther, for he speaks exceeding well, and has substantial matter.

## 847

Luther, reproving Dr. Mayer, for that he was faint-hearted and depressed, by reason of his simple kind of preaching, in comparison with other divines, as he conceived, admonished him, and said: Loving brother, when you preach, regard not the doctors and learned men, but regard the common people, to teach and instruct them clearly. In the pulpit, we must feed the common people with milk, for each day a new church is growing up, which stands in need of plain and simple instruction. Keep to the catechism, the milk. High and subtle discourse, the strong wine, we will keep for the strong minded.

## 848

No theologian of our time handles and expounds the Holy Scripture so well as Brentius, so much so that I greatly admire his energy, and despair of equalling him. I verily believe none among us can compare with him in the exposition of St. John's gospel; though, now and then, he dwells somewhat too much upon his own opinions, yet he keeps to the true and just meaning, and does not set himself up against the plain simplicity of God's Word.

## 849

The discourse turning upon the great differences amongst the learned, Luther said: God has very finely distributed his gifts, so that the learned serve the unlearned, and the unlearned humble themselves before the learned, in what is needful for them. If all people were equal; the world could not go on; nobody would serve another, and there would be no peace. The peacock complained because he had not the nightingale's voice. God, with apparent inequality, has instituted the greatest equality; one man, who has greater gifts than another, is proud and haughty, and seeks to rule and domineer over others, and contemns them. God finely illustrates human society in the members of the body, and shows that one member must assist the other, and that none can be without the other.

## 850

Aristotle is altogether an epicurean; he holds that God heeds not human creatures, nor regards how we live, permitting us to do at our pleasure. According to him, God rules the world as a sleepy maid rocks a child. Cicero got much further. He collected together what he found good in the books of all the Greek writers. 'Tis a good argument, and has often moved me much, where he proves there is a God, in that living creatures, beasts, and mankind engender their own likeness. A cow always produces a cow; a horse, a horse, etc. Therefore it follows that some being exists which rules everything. In God we may acknowledge the unchangeable and certain motion of the stars of heaven; the sun each day rises and sets in his place; as certain as time, we have winter and summer, but as this is done regularly, we neither admire nor regard it.

# Of the Jews

—※—

### 851

THE Jews boast they are Abraham's children; and, indeed, 'twas a high honour for them, when the rich glutton in hell said, 'Father Abraham,' etc. But our Lord God can well distinguish these children; for to such as the glutton he gives their wages here in this life, but the rewards and wages for the others he reserves until the life to come.

### 852

The Jews are the most miserable people on earth. They are plagued everywhere, and scattered about all countries, having no certain resting-place. They sit as on a wheelbarrow, without a country, people, or government; yet they wait on with earnest confidence; they cheer up themselves and say: It will soon be better with us. Thus hardened are they; but let them know assuredly, that there is none other Lord or God, but only he that already sits at the right hand of God the Father. The Jews are not permitted to trade or to keep cattle, they are only usurers and brokers; they eat nothing the Christians kill or touch; they drink no wine; they have many superstitions; they wash the flesh most diligently, whereas they cannot be cleansed through the flesh. They drink not milk, because God said: 'Thou shalt not boil the young kid in his mother's milk.' Such superstitions proceed out of God's anger. They that are without faith, have laws without end, as we see in the papists and Turks; but they are rightly served, for seeing they refused to have Christ and his gospel, instead of freedom they must have servitude.

If I were a Jew, the pope should never persuade me to his doctrine; I would rather be ten times racked. Popedom, with its abominations and profanities, has given to the Jews infinite offence. I am persuaded if the Jews heard our preaching, and how we handle the Old Testament, many of them might be won, but, through disputing, they have become more and more stiff-necked, haughty, and presumptuous. Yet, if but a few of the rabbis fell off, we might see them come to us, one after another, for they are almost weary of waiting.

### 853

At Frankfort on the Maine there are very many Jews; they have a whole street to themselves, of which every house is filled with them. They are compelled to wear little yellow rings on their coats, thereby to be known; they have no houses or grounds of their own, only furniture; and, indeed, they can only lend money upon houses or grounds at great hazard.

### 854

I have studied the chief passages of Scripture, that constitute the grounds upon which the Jews argue against us; as where God said to Abraham: 'I will make my covenant between me and thee, and with thy seed after thee, in their generations, for an everlasting covenant,' etc. Here the Jews brag, as the papists do upon the passage: 'Thou art Peter.' I would willingly bereave the Jews of this bragging, by rejecting the Law of Moses, so that they should not be able to gainsay me. We have against them the prophet Jeremiah, where he says: 'Behold, the time cometh, saith the Lord, when I will make a new covenant with the house of Israel, and with the house of Judah, not as the covenant which I made with their fathers,' etc. 'But this shall be the covenant which I will make with the house of Israel; after this time, saith the Lord, I will give my laws into their hearts, and will write it in their minds,' etc.

Here, surely, the Jews must yield, and say: the law of Moses continued but for awhile, therefore it must be abolished. But the covenant of the circumcision, given before Moses' time, and made between God and Abraham, and his seed Isaac in his generation, they say, must and shall be an everlasting covenant, which they will not suffer to be taken from them.

And though Moses himself rejects their circumcising of the flesh, and presses upon the circumcising of the heart, yet, nevertheless, they boast of that everlasting covenant out of God's Word; and when they admit that the circumcision justifies not, yet, nevertheless, say they, it is an everlasting covenant, thinking it is a covenant of works, therefore we must leave unto them their circumcision.

I, for my part, with all God-fearing Christians, have this sure and strong comfort, that the circumcision was to continue but for awhile, until Messiah came; when he came, the commandment was at an end. Moses was wise; he kept himself within bounds, for in all his four books after Genesis, he wrote nothing of physical circumcision, but only of the circumcision of the heart. He dwells upon the Sacrifices, the Sabbath, and show-bread; but leaves this covenant of circumcision quite out, making no mention thereof; as much as to say: 'Tis little to be regarded. If it had been of such importance and weight as the Jews make it, he would doubtless have urged it accordingly. Again, in the Book of Joshua, mention is made of the circumcising of the heart. The papists, however, blind people, who know nothing at all of the Scriptures, are not able to confute one argument of the Jews; theirs is truly a fearful blindness.

### 855

The verse in the 115th Psalm is masterly: 'He shall bless them that fear the Lord, both small and great.' Here the Holy Spirit is a fierce thunder-clap against the proud, boasting Jews and papists, who brag that they alone are God's people, and will allow of none but of those that are of their church. But the Holy Ghost says: The poor contemned people are also God's people, for God saved many of the Gentiles without the law and circumcision, as without Popedom.

The Jews see not that Abraham was declared justified only through faith: Abraham believed God, and that was imputed unto him for righteousness. God with circumcision confirmed his covenant with this nation, but only for a certain time. True, the circumcision of the Jews, before Christ's coming, had great majesty; but that they should affirm that without it none are God's people, is utterly untenable. The Jews themselves, in their circumcision, were rejected of God.

### 856

Christ drove the buyers and sellers out of the Temple, not by any temporal authority, but by the jurisdiction and power of the church, which authority every High Priest in the Temple had. The glory of this Temple was great, that the whole world must worship there. But God, out of special wisdom, caused this Temple to be destroyed, to the end the Jews might be put to confusion, and no more brag and boast thereof.

### 857

There can be no doubt that of old time many Jews took refuge in Italy and Germany, and settled there.

Cicero, the eloquent Gentile, complains of the superstition of the Jews, and their multitude in Italy; we find their footsteps throughout Germany. Here, in Saxony, many names of places speak of them: Ziman, Damen, Resen, Sygretz, Schvitz, Pratha, Thablon. The Jews inhabited Ratisbon a long time before the birth of Christ. At Cremona there are but twenty-eight Christians. It was a mighty nation.

### 858

The Jews read our books, and thereout raise objections against us; 'tis a nation that scorns and blasphemes even as the lawyers, the papists, and adversaries do, taking out of our writings the knowledge of our cause, and using the same as weapons against us. But, God be praised, our cause haft a sure, good and steadfast ground, namely, God and his Word.

### 859

Two Jewish rabbis, named Schamaria and Jacob, came to me at Wittenberg, desiring of me letters of safe conduct, which I granted them, and they were well pleased; only they earnestly besought me to omit thence the word *Tola*, that is, Jesus crucified; for they must needs blaspheme the name Jesus. They said: 'Tis most wonderful that so many thousands of innocent people have been slaughtered, of whom no mention is made, while Jesus, the crucified, must always be remembered.

### 860

The Jews must be encountered with strong arguments, as where Jeremiah speaks touching Christ: 'Behold, the days come, saith the Lord, that I will raise unto David a righteous branch, and a king shall reign and prosper, and shall execute judgment and justice in the earth; in his days Judah shall be saved, and Israel shall dwell safely, and this is his name whereby he shall be called, THE LORD OUR RIGHTEOUSNESS.' This argument the Jews are not able to solve; yet if they deny that this sentence is spoken of Christ, they must show unto us another king, descended from David, who should govern so long as the sun and moon endure, as the promises of the prophets declare.

### 861

Either God must be unjust, or you, Jews, wicked and ungodly; for ye have been in misery and fearful exile, a far longer time than ye were in the land of Canaan. Ye had not the temple of Solomon more than three hundred years, while ye have been hunted up and down above fifteen hundred. At Babylon ye had more eminence than at Jerusalem, for Daniel was a greater and more powerful prince at Babylon than either David or Solomon at Jerusalem. The Babylonian captivity was unto you only a fatherly rod, but this last punishment was your utter extermination. You have been, above fifteen hundred years, a race rejected of God, without government, without laws, without prophets, without temple. This argument ye cannot solve; it strikes you to the ground like a thunder-clap; ye can show no other reason for your condition than your sins. The two rabbis, struck to the heart, silenced, and convinced, forsook their errors, became converts, and the day following, in the presence of the whole university at Wittenberg, were baptized Christians.

The Jews hope that we shall join them, because we teach and learn the Hebrew language, but their hope is futile. 'Tis they must accept of our religion, and of the crucified Christ, and overcome all their objections, especially that of the alteration of the Sabbath, which sorely annoys them, but 'twas ordered by the apostles, in honour of the Lord's resurrection.

### 862

There are sorcerers among the Jews, who delight in tormenting Christians, for they hold us as dogs. Duke Albert of Saxony well punished one of these wretches. A few offered to sell him a talisman, covered with strange characters, which he said effectually protected the wearer against any sword or dagger thrust. The duke replied: 'I will essay thy charm upon thyself, Jew,' and putting the talisman round the fellow's neck, he drew his sword and passed it through his body. 'Thou feelest, Jew!' said he, 'how 'twould have been with me, had I purchased thy talisman?'

### 863

The Jews have various stories about a king of Bastin, whom they call Og; they say he had lifted a great rock to throw at his enemies, but God made a hole in the middle, so that it slipped down upon the giant's neck, and he could never rid himself of it. 'Tis a fable, like the rest of the stories about him, but, perhaps, bears a hidden moral, as the fables of Æsop do, for the Jews had some very wise men among them.

## 864

The destruction of Jerusalem was a fearful thing; the fate of all other monarchies, of Sodom, of Pharaoh, the captivity of Babylon, were as nothing in comparison; for this city had been God's habitation, his garden and bed; as the Psalm says: 'Here will I dwell, for I have chosen her,' etc. There was the law, the priesthood, the temple; there had flourished David, Solomon, Isaiah, etc.; many prophets were there interred, so that the Jews had just cause to boast of their privileges. What are we poor miserable folk – what is Rome, compared with Jerusalem? But the Jews are so hardened that they listen to nothing; though overcome by testimonies, they yield not an inch. 'Tis a pernicious race, oppressing all men by their usury and rapine. If they give a prince or a magistrate a thousand florins, they extort twenty thousand from the subjects in payment. We must ever keep on our guard against them. They think to render homage to God by injuring the Christians, and yet we employ their physicians; 'tis a tempting of God. They have haughty prayers, wherein they praise and call upon God, as if they alone were his people, cursing and condemning all other nations, relying on the 23rd Psalm: 'The Lord is my shepherd, I shall lack nothing.' As if that psalm were written exclusively concerning them.

## 865

'Tis a vain boasting the Jews make of their privileges, after a lapse of above fifteen hundred years. During the seventy years, when they were captives at Babylon, they were so confused and mingled together, that even then they hardly knew out of what tribe each was descended. How should it be now, when they have been so long hunted and driven about by the Gentiles, whose soldiers spared neither their wives nor their daughters, so that now they are, as it were, all bastards, none of them knowing out of what tribe he is. In 1537, when I was at Frankfurt, a great rabbi said to me: My father had read very much, and waited for the coming of the Messiah, but at last he fainted, and out of hope said: As our Messiah has not come in fifteen hundred years, most certainly Christ Jesus must be he.

### 866

The Jews above all other nations had great privileges; they had the chief promises, the highest worship of God, and a worship more pleasing to human nature than God's service of faith in the New Testament. They agree better with the Turks than with the Christians; for both Jews and Turks concur in this, that there is but only one God; they cannot understand that three persons should be in one divine substance. They are also agreed as to bathings and washings, circumcision, and other external worshippings and ceremonies.

The Jews had excelling men among them, as Abraham, Isaac, Jacob, Moses, David, Daniel, Samuel, Paul, etc. Who can otherwise than grieve that so great and glorious a nation should so lamentably be destroyed? The Latin church had no excelling men and teachers, but Augustine; and the churches of the east none but Athanasius, and he was nothing particular; therefore, we are twigs grafted into the right tree. The prophets call the Jews, especially those of the line of Abraham, a fair switch, out of which Christ himself came.

### 867

In the porch of a church at Cologne there is a statue of a dean, who, in the one hand, holds a cat, and in the other a mouse. This dean had been a Jew, but was baptized, and became a Christian. He ordered this statue to be set up after his death, to show that a Jew and a Christian agree as little as a cat and a mouse. And truly, they hate us Christians as they do death: it galls them to see us. If I were master of the country, I would not allow them to practise usury.

### 868

The Jews knew well that Messiah was to come, and that they were to hear him, but they would not be persuaded that our Jesus was the Messiah. They thought that the Messiah would leave all things as he found them; but when they saw that Christ took a course contrary to their expectation, they crucified him: yet, they boast of themselves as being God's people.

### 869

A Jew came to me at Wittenberg, and said: He was desirous to be baptized, and made a Christian, but that he would first go to Rome to see the chief head of Christendom. From this intention, myself, Philip Melancthon, and other divines, laboured to dissuade him, fearing lest, when he witnessed the offences and knaveries at Rome, he might be scared from Christendom. But the Jew went to Rome, and when he had sufficiently seen the abominations acted there, he returned to us again, desiring to be baptized, and said: Now I will willingly worship the God of the Christians, for he is a patient God. If he can endure such wickedness and villany as is done at Rome, he can suffer and endure all the vices and knavaries of the world.

# Of the Turks

---

### 870

THE Turk is a crafty and subtle enemy, who wars not only with great power and boldness, but also with stratagem and deceit; he makes his enemies faint and weary, keeping them waking with frequent skirmishes, seldom fighting a complete battle, unless he have tolerable certainty of victory. Otherwise, when a battle is offered him, he trots away, depending upon his stratagems.

### 871

The power of the Turk is very great; he keeps in his pay, all the year through, hundreds of thousands of soldiers. He must have more than two millions of florins annual revenue. We are far less strong in our bodies, and are divided out among different masters, all opposed the one to the other, yet we might conquer these infidels with only the Lord's prayer, if our own people did not spill so much blood in religious quarrels, and in persecuting the truths contained in that prayer. God will punish us as he punished Sodom and Gomorrah, but I would fain 'twere by the hand of some pious potentate, and not by that of the accursed Turk.

### 872

They say, the famine in the Turkish camp, before Vienna, was so great that a loaf of bread fetched its weight in gold, whereas Vienna and the archduke's army had all things in abundance. This victory is evidently the work of God. The Turk had sworn to conquer Germany within the year, and had unfurled a consecrated standard, but he was put to the rout without accomplishing anything of importance.

### 873

On the last day of July, 1539, came news that the king of Persia had invaded the states of the Turk, and that the latter had been obliged to withdraw his forces from Wallachia. Dr. Luther said: I greatly admire the power of the king of Persia, who can measure his strength with an enemy so formidable as the Turk. Truly, these are two mighty empires. Yet Germany could well withstand the Turks if she would keep up a standing army of fifty thousand foot, and ten thousand horse, so that the losses by a defeat might at once be repaired. The Romans triumphed over all their enemies, by keeping constantly on foot forty-two legions of six thousand men each, disciplined troops, practised in war.

### 874

News came from Torgau that the Turks had led out into the great square at Constantinople twenty-three Christian prisoners, who, on their refusing to apostatize, were beheaded. Dr. Luther said: Their blood will cry up to heaven against the Turks, as that of John Huss did against the papists. 'Tis certain, tyranny and persecution will not avail to stifle the Word of Jesus Christ. It flourishes and grows in blood. Where one Christian is slaughtered, a host of others arise. 'Tis not on our walls or our arquebusses I rely for resisting the Turk, but upon the *Pater Noster.* 'Tis that will triumph. The Decalogue is not, of itself, sufficient. I said to the engineers at Wittenberg: Why strengthen your walls – they are trash; the walls with which a Christian should fortify himself are made, not of stone and mortar, but of prayer and faith.

### 875

The Turks are the people of the wrath of God. 'Tis horrible to see their contempt of marriage. 'Twas not so with the Romans.

### 876

Let us repent, pray, and await the Lord's will, for human defence and help is all too weak. Five years since, the emperor was well able to resist the Turks, when he had levied a great army of horse and foot, out of the whole empire,

Italians and Germans. But then he would not; therefore, meantime, many good people were butchered by the Turks. Ah, loving God, what is this life, but death! there is nothing but death, from the cradle unto old age. I fear all things go not right; the tyranny and pride of the Spaniards, doubtless, will give us over to the Turks, and make us subject to them. There is great treachery somewhere. I doubt the twenty thousand men, and the costly pieces of double cannon are wilfully betrayed to the Turk. It is not usual to carry such great pieces of ordnance into the field. The emperor Maximilian kept them safe at Vienna. It seems to me, as though he had said to the Turk: Take these pieces of ordnance as a present; slay and destroy all that cannot escape. This expedition has an aspect of treachery; for while our men slumber, the Turk constantly watches, attempting all he can, both with open power and with secret practices.

If the Turk were to cause proclamation to be made, that every man should be free from taxation and tribute for the space of three years, the common people would joyfully yield to him. But when he had got them into his claws, he would make use of his tyranny, as his custom is, for he takes the third son from every man; he is always father of the third child. Truly, it is a great tyranny, which chiefly concerns the princes of the empire themselves. I ever held the emperor in suspicion; yet he can deeply dissemble. I have almost despaired of him, since he opposed the known truth, which he heard at the Diet at Augsburg. The verse in the second Psalm holds ever good: 'Why do the heathen so furiously rage together, and why do the people imagine a vain thing? The kings of the earth stand up, and the rulers take counsel together, against the Lord, and against his anointed,' etc. David complained thereof, Christ felt it, the apostles lamented it; we feel it too. 'Twas therefore St. Paul said: 'Not many wise even after the flesh, not many mighty, not many noble are called,' etc. Let us call upon God the Father of our Lord Jesus Christ; let us pray, for it is high time.

### 877

The admirable great constancy of John, prince elector of Saxony, is worthy of everlasting memory and praise; who personally and steadfastly held over the pure doctrine of the gospel at the imperial diet at Augsburg, 1530. And, unhappily, Germany is a prey to discord all this time. See how furious a hate the papists bear to the partisans of the gospel. They have put their faith in the emperor against us, but they will come to confusion. A certain count had a great bonfire lighted in the night, when he learned the arrival of the emperor in Germany; and a popish priest, near Eisenach, said, he would bet all the cows he should have in the year, that Martin Luther and his adherents would be hanged before Michaelmas. These fellows thought it only needed for the emperor to march against the Lutherans, and they cherished horrible projects; but they were finely disappointed.

## 878

The emperor of the Turks maintains great pomp in his court. You have to traverse three vestibules before you reach the apartment wherein he sits. In the first vestibule are twelve chained lions; in the second, an equal number of panthers. He has under his rule very rich and populous countries; even within the last ten years, the number of his subjects has greatly increased.

The 21st of December, 1536, George, marquis of Brandenburg came to Wittenberg, and announced that the Turks had obtained a great victory over the Germans, whose fine army had been betrayed and massacred; he said that many princes and brave captains had perished, and that such Christians as remained prisoners, had been treated with extreme cruelty, their noses being slit, and themselves used most scornfully. Luther said: We, Germans, must consider hereupon that God's anger is at our gates, that we should hasten to repentance while there is yet time; by degrees, he subjugated the Saracens, who before were the lords of Syria, Asia, the Land of Promise, Assyria, Greece, and a portion of Spain. These Solyman utterly overthrew and well nigh annihilated. 'Tis thus God plays with kingdoms; as in Isaiah, it is threatened: 'I the Lord am a strong God over kingdoms; whoso sinneth I destroy.' The Venetians made no resistance. They are effeminate and pretend not to be warriors. 'Tis wonderful what progress the Turk has made in the last hundred years yet that is nothing in comparison with the progress the Roman empire made in fifty years, though, during twenty-three years of the fifty, it had to maintain a terrible war with Hannibal. Such was its aggrandizement, that Scipio declared it advisable that in the public prayers the petition for extended domination should be omitted, it being his opinion that now they had better see to the taking care of what they had got. Yet God overthrew this mighty empire by the hands of barbarians.

## 879

The elector of Saxony wrote to Dr. Luther that the Turks had gained a great victory. Cazianus, Ungnad, Schlick, had all been bribed by the enemy, and their names were now placarded all over Vienna, as condemned traitors.

These generals led the German army close to the Turkish camp; a Christian, who had made his escape from the infidels, came and warned them to be on their guard, but they treated his counsel with contumely. When the enemy approached, these traitors took to flight, with the cavalry, abandoning the infantry to slaughter. The Turks next feigned a retreat, whereupon the Christian generals ordered the cavalry, eleven hundred in number, to return to the charge, but the Turks surrounding them, cut them in pieces also. Cazianus had received eighteen thousand ducats from the Turks through a Jew, to betray the Christian army, and had promised to deliver the king himself into the enemies' hands. Luther, on hearing this news, said: *Auri sacra farces, quid non mortalia pectora cogis?* This traitor must everlastingly burn in hell. I would not betray a dog. I much fear it will go ill with Ferdinand, who has allowed so great an army to be thrust into the throat of the Turk, by the hands of a perjured Mameluke, who heretofore fell from the Turk to the Christians, and now has fallen again from the Christians to the Turk.

Our princes and rulers ought to march in person against the enemy, and not have him thus encountered; the Turk is not to be contemned. Truly, we Germans are jolly fellows; we eat, and drink, and game at our ease, wholly heedless of the Turk. Germany has been a fine and noble country, but 'twill be said of her, as of Troy, *fuit Ilium*. Let us pray to God, that, amidst such calamities, he will preserve our consciences. I dread lest the money and forces of Germany become exhausted, for then, perforce, we must yield to the Turk. They reproach me with all this, me, unhappy Martin Luther. They reproach me, too, with the revolt of the peasants, and with the sacramentarian sects, as though I had been their author. Often have I felt disposed to throw the keys before God's foot.

The Turks pretend, despite the Holy Scriptures, that they are the chosen people of God, as descendants of Ishmael. They say that Ishmael was the true son of the promise, for that when Isaac was about to be sacrificed, he fled from his father, and from the slaughter knife, and, meantime, Ishmael came and freely offered himself to be sacrificed, whence he became the child of the promise; as gross a lie as that of the papists concerning one kind in the sacrament. The Turks make a boast of being very religious, and treat all other nations as idolaters. They slanderously accuse the Christians of worshipping three gods. They swear by one only God, creator of heaven and earth, by his angels, by the four evangelists, and by the eighty heaven-descended prophets, of whom Mohammed is the greatest. They reject all images and pictures, and render homage to God alone. They pay the most honourable testimony to Jesus Christ, saying that he was a prophet of pre-eminent sanctity, born of the Virgin Mary, and an envoy from God, but that Mohammed succeeded him, and that while Mohammed sits, in heaven, on the right hand of the Father, Jesus Christ is seated on his left. The Turks have retained many features of the law of Moses, but, inflated with the insolence of victory, they, have adopted a new worship; for the glory of warlike triumphs is, in the opinion of the world, the greatest of all.

Luther complained of the emperor Charles's negligence, who, taken up with other wars, suffered the Turk to capture one place after another. 'Tis with the Turks as heretofore with the Romans, every subject is a soldier, as long as he is able to bear arms, so they have always a disciplined army ready for the field; whereas we gather together ephemeral bodies of vagabonds, untried wretches, upon whom is no dependence. My fear is, that the papists will unite with the Turks to exterminate us. Please God, my anticipation come not true, but certain it is, that the desperate creatures will do their best to deliver us over to the Turks.

### 880

Luther wrote a letter to the emperor's chief general in Hungary, admonishing him that he had against him four powerful enemies; he had not only to do with flesh and blood, but with the devil, with the Turk, with God's wrath, with our own sins; therefore he should remember to humble himself and to call upon God for help.

Luther heard that the emperor Charles had sent into Austria eighteen thousand Spaniards against the Turk. Whereupon he sighed, and said: 'Tis a sign of the last day when those cruel nations, the Spaniards and Turks, are to be our masters: I would rather have the Turks for enemies than the Spaniards for protectors; for, barbarous tyrants as they are, most of the Spaniards are half Moors, half Jews, fellows who believe nothing at all.

The great hope I have is, that the Turkish empire will be brought to an end by intestine dissensions, as it has been with all the kingdoms of the world, the Persian, the Chaldean, the Alexandrian, the Roman: I hope the four brothers, the sons of the great Turk, will dispute the sovereignty among themselves. Whoso climbs high, is in danger to fall; the best swimmer may be drowned. If it be the will of God, though the Turk has climbed high, he may fall to pieces in a moment.

### 881

The Turk will go to Rome, as Daniel's prophecy announces, and then the last day will not be very distant. Germany must be chastised by the Turks. I often reflect with sorrow, how utterly Germany neglects all good counsel. Victory, however, depends not on ourselves. There is a time for conquering the Turks, and a time for being conquered. The king of France long exalted himself in his pride, but in the end he was abused and made captive. The pope long despised God and man, but he too is fallen. They say the pope lately celebrated the circumcision of four of his sons, and invited the great khan, the king of Persia, and the chiefs of the Venetians, to the ceremony. He is extremely venerated by his subjects. He gives people a passport, called *vieh,* the bearer of which passes safely throughout the Turkish dominions, and is freely lodged wherever he goes.

# Of Countries and Cities

## 882

Our Lord God deals with countries and cities, as I do with an old hedge-stake, when it displeases me; I pluck it up and burn it, and stick another in its stead.

## 883

Tacitus describes Germany very well. He highly extols the Germans, by reason of their adherence to promises, especially in the state of matrimony, in which particular they excelled all other nations. In former times it stood well with Germany, but now the people are fallen from virtue, and become rude, proud, and insolent.

## 884

The best days were before the deluge, when the people lived long, were moderate in eating and drinking, beheld God's creatures with diligence, celestial and terrestrial, without wasting, warring, or debate; then a fresh, cool spring of water was more sweet, acceptable, and better relished, than costly wines.

## 885

Germany is like a brave and gallant horse, highly fed, but without a good rider; as the horse runs here and there, astray, unless he have a rider to rule him, so Germany is also a powerful, rich, and brave country, but needs a good head and governor.

## 886

This constant change in the fashion of dress will produce also an alteration of government and manners; we attend too much to these things. Emperor Charles frequently says: The Germans learn of the Spaniards to steal, and the Spaniards learn of the Germans to swill.

## 887

Venice is the richest of cities. She has two kingdoms, Cyprus and Candia. Candia once was full of robbers, for six hundred ruined merchants had fled thither. As the island is very hilly, they were not able, by force, to get rid of these robbers, so the Venetians made proclamation that they would receive all the robbers again to favour, upon condition that each should bring to them the head of a fellow-robber. By which means, one wretch being snapped by another, the island was cleared of those vipers. 'Twas a good and wise council. Venice respects neither decency nor honour; she seeks only her own profit, is always neutral, banging the cloak according to the wind. Now they hold with the Turk, ere long they will be for the emperor; what party has victory, has them.

## 888

Bembo, an exceeding learned man, who had thoroughly investigated Rome, said: Rome is a filthy, stinking puddle, full of the wickedest wretches in the world; and he wrote thus:

'Vivere qui sancte vultis, discedite Roma;
Omnia hie ecce licent, non licet esse probum.'

## 889

In the time of Leo X, there were in an Augustine convent at Rome, two monks, who revolted at the horrible wickedness of the papists, and, in their sermons, found fault with the pope. In the night, two assassins were introduced into their cells, and next morning they were found dead, their tongues cut out, and stuck on their backs. Whoso in Rome is heard to speak against the pope, either gets a sound strappado or has his throat cut; for the pope's name is *Noli me tangere*.

**890**

When I was at Rome, they showed me, for a precious holy relic, the halter wherewith Judas hanged himself. Let us bear this in mind, and consider in what ignorance our forefathers were.

# OF VOCATION AND CALLING

~~~

### 891

WHEN they who have the office of teaching; joy not therein, that is, have not regard to him that called and sent them; it is, for them, an irksome work. Truly, I would not take the wealth of the whole world, now to begin the work against the pope, which thus far I have wrought, by reason of the exceeding heavy care and anguish wherewith I have been burthened. Yet, when I look upon him that called me thereunto, I would not for the world's wealth, but that I had begun it.

It is much to be lamented, that no man is *content and* satisfied with that which God gives him in his vocation and calling. Other men's conditions please us more than our own; as the heathen said:

'Fertilior seges est alienis semper in agris,
Vicinumque pecus grandius uber habet.'

And another heathen:

'Optat ephippia bos piger, optat arare cabalius.'

The more we have the more we want. To serve God is for every one to remain in his vocation and calling, be it ever so mean and simple.

## 892

It is said, occasion has a forelock, but is bald behind. Our Lord has taught this by the course of nature. A farmer must sow his barley and oats about Easter; if he defer it to Michaelmas, it were too late. When apples are ripe they must be plucked from the tree, or they are spoiled. Procrastination is as bad as overhastiness. There is my servant Wolf: when four or five birds fall upon the bird-net, he will not draw it, but says: O, I will stay until more come, then they all fly away, and he gets none. Occasion is a great matter. Terence says well: I came in time, which is the chief thing of all. Julius Caesar understood occasion; Pompey and Hannibal did not. Boys at school understand it not, therefore they must have fathers and masters, with the rod to hold them thereto, that they neglect not time, and lose it. Many a young fellow has a school stipend for six or seven years, during which he ought diligently to study; he has his tutors, and other means, but he thinks: O, I have time enough yet. But I say: No, fellow. What little Jack learns not, great John learns not. Occasion salutes thee, and reaches out her forelock to thee, saying: 'Here I am, take hold of me;' thou thinkest she will come again. Then says she: Well, seeing thou wilt not take hold of my top, take hold of my tail; and therewith flings away.

Bonaventura was but a poor sophist, yet he could say: He that neglects occasion is of it neglected, and 'tis a saying with us: Take hold of time, while 'tis time, and now, while 'tis now. Our emperor Charles understood not occasion, when he took the French king prisoner before Pavia, in 1525; nor afterwards, when he got into his hands pope Clement, and had taken Rome in 1527; nor in 1529, when he almost got hold of the great Turk before Vienna. 'Twas monstrous negligence for a monarch to have in his hands his three great enemies, and yet let them go.

## 893

Germany would be much richer than she is, if such store of velvets and silks were not worn, nor so much spice used, or so much beer drunk. But young fellows without their liquor have no mirth at all; gaming makes not merry, nor lasciviousness, so they apply themselves to drinking. At the princely jollification lately held at Torgau, each man drank, at one draught, a whole bottle of wine; this they called a good drink. Tacitus wrote, that by the ancient Germans it was held no shame at all to drink and swill four-and-twenty hours together. A gentleman of the court asked: How long ago it was since Tacitus wrote this? He was answered, about fifteen hundred years. Whereupon the gentleman said: Forasmuch as drunkenness has been so ancient a custom, and of such long descent, let us not abolish it.

# Miscellaneous

## 894

Anno 1546, a case in law was related to Luther: A miller had an ass, which went into a fisherman's boat to drink; the boat, not being tied fast, floated away with the ass, so that the miller lost his ass, and the fisherman his boat. The miller complained that the fisher, neglecting to tie his boat fast, had lost him his ass; the fisher complained of the miller for not keeping his ass at home, and desired satisfaction for his boat. Query: What is the law? Took the ass the boat away, or the boat the ass? Luther said: Both were in error; the fisherman that he tied not fast his boat; the miller in not keeping his ass at home.

## 895

There was a miser, who, when he sent his man to the cellar for wine, made him fill his mouth with water, which he was to spit out on his return, to show he had drunk no wine. But the servant kept a pitcher of water in the cellar, wherewith, after taking his fill of the better drink, he managed to deceive his master.

## 896

A student of Erfurt, desiring to see Nuremberg, departed with a friend on a journey thither. Before they had walked half a mile, he asked his companion whether they should soon get to Nuremberg, and was answered: ''Tis scarce likely, since we have only just left Erfurt.' Having repeated the question, another half mile further on, and getting the same answer, he said: 'Let's give up the journey, and go back, since the world is so vast!'

### 897

Dr. Gomer related that a monk, who had introduced a girl into his cell, on quitting her in the morning for matins, rubbed his face with holy water. The girl, thinking to follow his example, daubed her face over with ink, which, in the obscurity, she mistook for the water. On his return, the monk, seeing her visage all black, thought 'twas the devil he had brought there, and, struck with fear, yelled out at the top of his voice, and with his cries collected the whole convent, so that his intrigue was discovered.

### 898

There are poets who affect to be carried away by their enthusiasm. There was Richius, for example; I remember his sitting with his legs out of window, pretending to be in a fit of poetic fury against the devil, whom he was abusing and vilifying with long, roundabout phrases. Stiegel, who chanced to pass under, for sport suddenly took hold of the brawling poet's leg, and frightened him horribly, the poor man thinking the devil had come to carry him off.

### 899

An idle priest, instead of reciting his breviary, used to run over the alphabet, and then say: 'O, my God, take this alphabet, and put it together how you will!'

### 900

A certain honest man, at Eisleben, complained to me of his great misery; he had bestowed on his children all his goods, and now in his old age they forsook and trod him under their feet. I said: Ecclesiasticus gives unto parents the best counsel, where he says: 'Give not all out of thy hands while thou livest,' etc., for the children keep not promises. One father, as the proverb says, can maintain ten children, but ten children cannot, or at least will not, maintain one father. There is a story of a certain father that, having made his last will, locked it up safe in a chest, and, together with a good strong cudgel, laid a note thereby, in these words: 'The father who gives his goods out of his hands to his children, deserves to have his brains beat out with cudgels.' Here is another story: A certain father, that was grown old, had given over all his goods to his children, on condition they should maintain him; but the children were unthankful, and being weary of him, kept him very hard and sparingly, and gave him not sufficient to eat. The father, being a wise man, more crafty than his children, locked himself secretly into a chamber, and made a great ringing and jingling with gold crowns, which, for that purpose, a rich neighbour had lent him, as though he had still much money in store. When his children heard this, they gave him ever afterwards good entertainment, in hopes he would leave them much wealth; but the father secretly restored the crowns again to his neighbour, and so rightly deceived his children.

## 901

As Luther's wife anointed his feet, by reason of some pain he felt, he said to her: Now thou anointest me, but in former times the wives were anointed by their husbands; for this word in Latin, *Uxor,* comes from *ungendo,* anointing; for as the heathen saw that many rubs and hindrances were in the state of matrimony, therefore, to prevent such misfortunes, they used to anoint both the legs of the new married women.

## 902

I have oftentimes noted, when women receive the doctrine of the gospel, they are far more fervent in faith, they hold to it more stiff and fast, than men do; as we see in the loving Magdalen, who was more hearty and bold than Peter.

## 903

There is no gown or garment that worse becomes a woman than when she will be wise.

## 904

I am a great enemy to flies: *Quia sunt imagines diaboli et hæreticorum.* When I have a good book, they flock upon it and parade up and down upon it, and soil it. 'Tis just the same with the devil; when our hearts are purest, he comes and soils them.

## 905

The stone of Thrace is found on the borders of the Euxine, and on a river in Scythia; it burns in the water, but is extinguished if oil be thrown on it. This property has not been given to it without reason; 'tis an image of the hypocrites, who burn with the ardour of an accumulation of good works, and flame all the more, the more they are sprinkled with the water of human traditions and ceremonial practices; but, on the contrary, when oil is poured over them, that is, the Word of God, lose their disorderly fury. Dioscorides and Nicander mention this stone.

**906**

The word *amianthus* comes from the Greek *a* and *mitho*, meaning, together, cleansing. 'Tis mentioned by Dioscorides, book v, cap. xciii. The amianthus (asbestos) is found in Cyprus, and is so soft that it can be woven into a tissue, which suffers no injury when thrown into the fire, but, on the contrary, derives additional beauty from the process. This stone is the image of the church, whereupon calamities and persecutions inflict no injury, but rather render her more brilliant and agreeable in God's eyes. The Ætita is a stone, found in eagles' nests, which has the property of aiding women in their labour, when tied to the left arm. This stone, further, has the property of detecting thieves.

**907**

The sparrow is a most voracious animal, and does great harm to the crops. The Hebrews call it *tschirp*. It should be destroyed wherever found.

**908**

Dr. Luther heard, one day, a nightingale singing very sweetly near a pond full of frogs, who, by their croaking, seemed as though they wanted to silence the melodious bird. The doctor said: Thus 'tis in the world; Jesus Christ is the nightingale, making the gospel to be heard; the heretics and false prophets, the frogs, trying to prevent his being heard.

**909**

Question was made why, in the Psalms and other portions of the Bible, there is repeated mention of ravens and sparrows, of all birds the least agreeable to the sight, and, in other respects, odious? Dr. Luther said: If the Holy Ghost could have named birds more objectionable than these, he would have done so, in order to show us that, as in their case, what we receive is not given to our merits.

## 910

Aristotle reckons swans among the birds which have strong web-feet, so as they may dwell about lakes and marshes. They are creatures that bring up a large family; they live to a great age, and their habits are worthy of close observation. They do not attack the eagle, but they successfully defend themselves against his aggressions. It is certain they sing very melodiously at the moment of their death, and some authors relate that they feed upon betony, in order to check the ardour of amorous passion, and to add strength to their wings. I don't know a more exact image of the church. The church rests upon strong feet, so that the power of hell may not overthrow her. She is surrounded by lakes and marshes, that is, she aspires not to earthly dominion. She checks impure tendencies, and prescribes chastity of life. She tenderly rears numerous children, who are the consolation of her old age. She attacks not tyrants, but she repels their assaults by means of her two powerful wings, the ministry of the Word and fervent prayer; 'twas with these weapons she overthrew Sennacherib, Julian, and other tyrants. Finally, the swan sings at the approach of death; so the church, when one of her members comes to his last moment, sings to him the glad notes of the Son of God.

## 911

The multitude of books is a great evil. There is no measure or limit to this fever for writing; every one must be an author; some out of vanity, to acquire celebrity and raise up a name; others for the sake of lucre and gain. The Bible is now buried under so many commentaries, that the text is nothing regarded. I could wish all my books were buried nine ells deep in the ground, by reason of the ill example they will give, every one seeking to imitate me in writing many books, with the hope of procuring fame. But Christ died not to favour our ambition and vain-glory, but that his name might be glorified.

The aggregation of large libraries tends to divert men's thoughts from the one great book, the Bible, which ought, day and night, to be in every one's hand. My object, my hope, in translating the Scriptures, was to check the so prevalent production of new works, and so to direct men's study and thoughts more closely to the divine Word. Never will the writings of mortal man in any respect equal the sentences inspired by God. We must yield the place of honour to the prophets and the apostles, keeping ourselves prostrate at their feet as we listen to their teaching. I would not have those who read my books, in these stormy times, devote one moment to them which they would otherwise have consecrated to the Bible.

## 912

I wrote this epitaph for my poor daughter Magdalen, who died when she was fourteen years old:

'Dormio eum sanctis hic Magdalena Lutheri.
Filia et hoc strato tecta quiesco meo.
Filia mortis eram peccati semine nata,
Sanguine sed O Christe redempta tuo.'

## 913

The voice of a faithful soul to Christ. 'Ego sum tuum peccatum, te mea justitia; triumpho igitur securus, quia nec as meum peccatum obruet tuam justitiam, nec tua justitia sinet me esse aut manere peccatorem. Benedicte Dominas Deus miserator meus et Redemtor in te solum confido.

## 914

*Luther's Prayer*

Sum tuus in vita, tua sunt mea funera Christe,
Da precor imperii sceptra tenere tut.
*Cur* etenim moriens tot vulnera saeva tulisti?
Si non sum regni portio parva tui.
Cur rigido latuit tua vita inclusa sepulcro,
Si non est mea mors, morte fugata tua?
Ergo mihi certam præstes O Christe salutem.

## 915

A certain English very learned gentleman, at Wittenberg, was much conversant with Luther at his table; but the gentleman had not the German tongue very familiarly, so gentleman said to him: I will give you my wife for a school mistress; she shall teach you German readily, for she therein far surpasses me. Yet, when women are ready in speaking, it is not to be commended; it becomes them much better when they keep silence and speak little.

## 916

On the 18th November, 1538, mention was made of the mundation of rivers arising from earthquakes. Dr. Luther observed: The Nile overflows its banks every year, but it deposits over the land of Egypt a fertilising slime. The Elbe overflows, also, but it only deposits sand, and carries away trees and houses. The name *Elbe* comes from *Elffe,* (eleven), because it is formed of the combined waters of eleven different streams. The dangers arising from water are manifold. We see strong men drowned in places where the depth of water is a mere nothing. 'Tis the work of the devil. The ships they build in some of the ports of the North Sea are of vast dimensions; one single vessel will cost 36,000 ducats. Noah's ark was a colossal structure; it was 300 cubits long, 50 wide, and 30 high; proportions quite incredible, if we were not assured of them in the Scripture.

## 917

A traveller who had fallen into the hands of some robbers, was murdered by them. In his last moments, seeing some ravens flying over his head, he exclaimed to them: I call upon you to avenge my death. Three days after, the robbers, going into the neighbouring town, saw some ravens on the roof of the inn where they were carousing. One of them said, sneeringly: I suppose those are the ravens come to avenge the death of the traveller we despatched the other day. The servant of the inn, overhearing these words, ran and repeated them to the magistrate, who had the robbers taken up, and, on inquiry being made, they were convicted of the murder and hanged.

## 918

Robbers are accursed of God; the blessing of the Lord is withdrawn from them, even in temporal matters, and when they think themselves at the summit of prosperity, they fall.

# RELATIVE DUTIES

## EXPRESSED IN SCRIPTURE WORDS BY LUTHER

### 1. *Clergy*

A BISHOP must be blameless, the husband of one wife, vigilant, sober, of good behaviour, given to hospitality, apt to teach, not given to wine, no striker, not greedy of filthy lucre, but patient, not a brawler, not covetous, one that rules well his own house, having his children in subjection with all gravity; not a novice; holding fast the faithful word, as he has been taught, that he may be able by sound doctrine both to exhort and convince the gainsayers (1 Tim. 3:2, 6; Titus 1:9).

### 2. *People*

The Lord has ordained, that they which preach the gospel should live of the gospel (1 Cor. 9:14, comp. Luke 10:7).

Let him that is taught in the word, communicate unto him that teaches, in all good things. Be not deceived, God is not mocked (Gal. 6:6, 7).

We beseech you, brethren, to know them which labour among you, and are over you in the Lord, and admonish you; and to esteem them very highly in love, for their work's sake; and be at peace among yourselves (1 Thess. 5:13, comp. 1 Tim. 5:17).

Obey them that have the rule over you, and submit yourselves, for they watch for your souls, as they that must give account, that they may do it with joy, and not with grief, for that is unprofitable for you (Heb. 13:17).

### 3. *Magistrates*

Let every soul be subject unto the higher powers; for there is no power but of God; the powers that be, are ordained of God. Whosoever therefore resists the power, resists the ordinance of God; and they that resist, shall receive to themselves damnation. For he bears not the sword in vain, for he is the minister of God, a revenger to execute wrath upon him that does evil (Rom. 13:1, 2, 4, comp. Ps. 82:3, 4; Ps. 101:6, 8).

### 4. *Subjects*

Render unto Caesar the things that are Ceasar's, and unto God the things that are God's (Matt. 22:21).

Wherefore ye must needs be subject, not only for wrath, but also for conscience sake. For, for this cause pay you tribute also: for they are God's ministers, attending continually upon this very thing. Render to all their dues; tribute to whom tribute is due, custom to whom custom, fear to whom fear, honour to whom honour (Rom. 13:5, 6, 7).

I exhort therefore, that, first of all, supplications, prayers, intercessions, and giving of thanks be made for all men; for kings, and for all that are in authority; that we may lead a quiet and peaceable life in all godliness and honesty, for this is good and acceptable in the sight of God our Saviour (1 Tim. 2:1, 2, 3).

Submit yourselves to every ordinance of man for the Lord's sake, whether it be to the king as supreme, or unto governors, as unto them that are sent by him for the punishment of evil doers, and for the praise of them that do well (1 Pet. 2:13, 14, comp. Titus 3:1).

### 5. *Husbands*

Husbands, dwell with your wives according to knowledge, giving honour unto the wife as unto the weaker vessel, and as being heirs together of the grace of life, that your prayers be not hindered (1 Pet. 3:7).

Husbands, love your wives, even as Christ also loved the church (Eph. 5:25). And be not bitter against them (Col. 3:19).

### 6. *Wives*

Wives, submit yourselves unto your own husbands, as unto the Lord (Eph. 5:22), even as Sarah obeyed Abraham, calling him Lord; whose daughters ye are as long as ye do well, and are not afraid with any amazement (1 Pet. 3:6).

### 7. *Parents*

Fathers, provoke not your children to anger, lest they be discouraged (Col. 3:21). But bring them up in the nurture and admonition of the Lord (Eph. 6:4).

### 8. *Children*

Children, obey your parents in the Lord; for this is right. Honour thy father and mother, which is the first commandment with promise; that it may be well with thee, and that thou mayest live long on the earth (Eph. 6:1, 3).

### 9. *Householders*

Masters, forbear threatening, knowing that your Master also is in heaven; neither is there respect of persons with him (Eph. 6:9, comp. Col. 4:1. Deut. 24:14).

### 10. *Man-servants, Maid-servants, and Work folks.*

Servants, be obedient to them that are your masters, according to the flesh, with fear and trembling, in singleness of your heart as unto Christ. Not with eye-service, as men-pleasers, but as the servants of Christ, doing the will of God from the heart; with good-will doing service as to the Lord, and not to men; knowing that whatsoever good thing any man doeth, the same shall he receive of the Lord, whether he be bond or free (Eph. 6:5, 8, comp. Titus 2:9, 10; 1 Tim. 6:2).

### 11. *Youth of both Sexes*

Younger, submit yourselves unto the elder; for God resisteth the proud, and giveth grace to the humble (1 Pet. 5:5, comp. Prov. 12:1; Eccles. 9:1; Prov. 24:14; Luke 2:52).

### 12. *Old Men*

Bid the aged men to be sober, grave, temperate, sound in faith, in charity, in patience (Titus 2:2).

### 13. *Old Women*

Bid the aged women that they be in behaviour as becometh holiness; not false accusers, not given to much wine; teachers of good things, that they may teach the young women to be sober, to love their husbands, to love their children, to be discreet, chaste, keepers at home, good, obedient to their own husbands, that the word of God be not blasphemed (Titus 2:3, 5).

14. *Widows*

She that is a widow indeed, and desolate, trusteth in God, and continueth in supplications and prayers night and day. But she that liveth in pleasure is dead while she liveth (1 Tim. 5:5).

15. *General Duties*

Thou shalt love thy neighbour as thyself. All the other commandments are briefly comprehended in this (Rom. 13:9). And continue instant in prayers for all men (1 Tim. 2:1, comp. Phil. 4:8, 9).

> Let each with diligence his duty know,
> And in that dwelling happiness shall flow.

# Christian Focus Publications

publishes books for all ages
Our mission statement –

## STAYING FAITHFUL

In dependence upon God we seek to help make His infallible word, the Bible, relevant. Our aim is to ensure that the Lord Jesus Christ is presented as the only hope to obtain forgiveness of sin, live a useful life and look forward to heaven with Him.

## REACHING OUT

Christ's last command requires us to reach out to our world with His gospel. We seek to help fulfill that by publishing books that point people towards Jesus and help them to develop a Christ-like maturity. We aim to equip all levels of readers for life, work, ministry and mission.

Books in our adult range are published in three imprints.

*Christian Focus* contains popular works including biographies, commentaries, basic doctrine, and Christian living. Our children's books are also published in this imprint.

*Mentor* focuses on books written at a level suitable for Bible College and seminary students, pastors, and other serious readers. The imprint includes commentaries, doctrinal studies, examination of current issues, and church history.

*Christian Heritage* contains classic writings from the past.

Christian Focus Publications Ltd
Geanies House, Fearn,
Ross-shire, IV20 1TW, Scotland, United Kingdom
info@christianfocus.com

For details of our titles visit us on our website
www.christianfocus.com